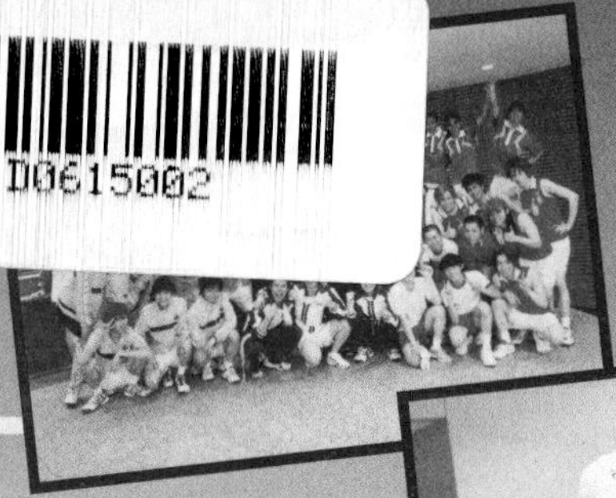

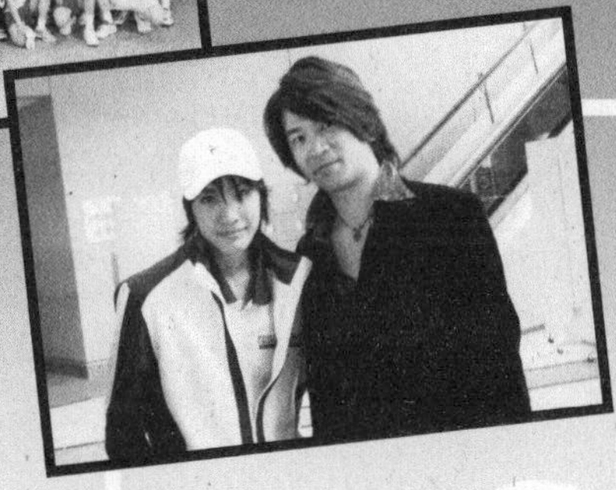

With the third Ryoma, Dori Sakurada.

I love the *Prince of Tennis* musical! I went to see the *Prince of Tennis* musical *Dream Live 4th*. It was so brilliantly done it actually seemed like the characters were right there in front of me. Consider the Prince of BBQ as the manga version of *Dream Live!*

— Takeshi Konomi, 2007

About Takeshi Konomi

Takeshi Konomi exploded onto the manga scene with the incredible **THE PRINCE OF TENNIS.** His refined art style and sleek character designs proved popular with **Weekly Shonen Jump** readers, and **THE PRINCE OF TENNIS** became the number one sports manga in Japan almost overnight. Its cast of fascinating male tennis players attracted legions of female readers even though it was originally intended to be a boys' comic. The manga continues to be a success in Japan and has inspired a hit anime series, as well as several video games and mountains of merchandise.

THE PRINCE OF TENNIS
VOL. 38
SHONEN JUMP Manga Edition

STORY AND ART BY
TAKESHI KONOMI

Translation/Joe Yamazaki
Touch-up Art & Lettering/Vanessa Satone, Eric Erbes
Design/Sam Elzway
Editor/Daniel Gillespie

VP, Production/Alvin Lu
VP, Sales & Product Marketing/Gonzalo Ferreyra
VP, Creative/Linda Espinosa
Publisher/Hyoe Narita

Printed in Canada

Published by VIZ Media, LLC
P.O. Box 77010
San Francisco, CA 94107

10 9 8 7 6 5 4 3 2 1
First printing, July 2010

PARENTAL ADVISORY
THE PRINCE OF TENNIS
is rated A and is suitable
for readers of all ages.
ratings.viz.com

THE WORLD'S
MOST POPULAR MANGA

www.viz.com

www.shonenjump.com

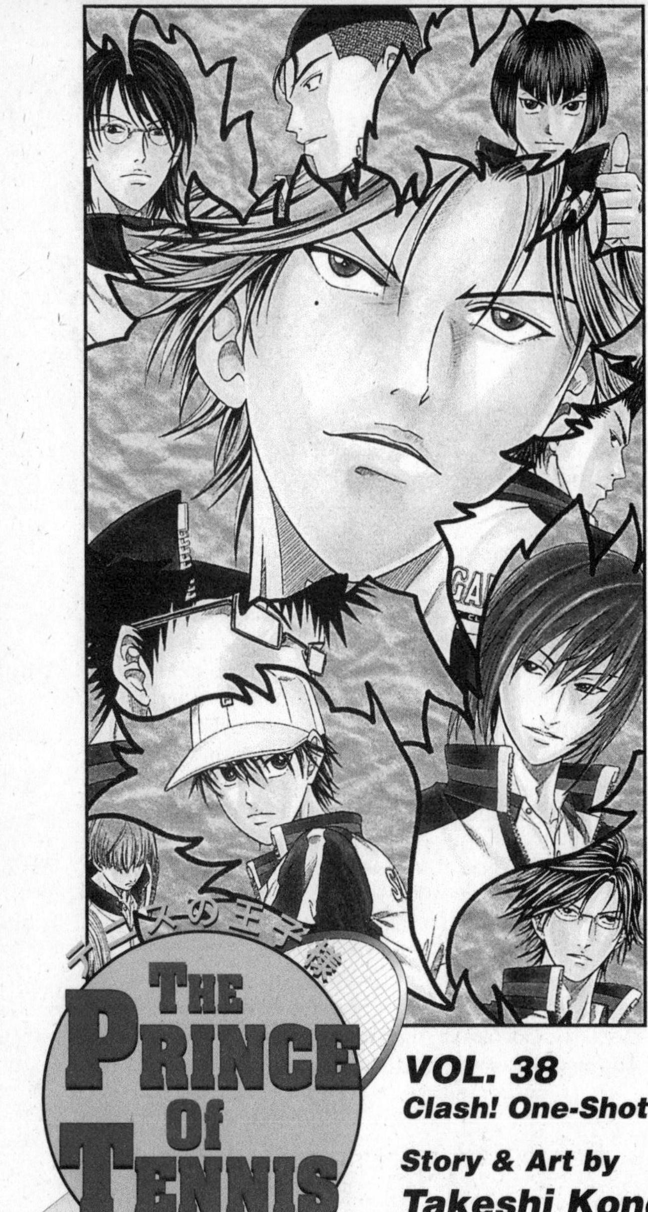
THE PRINCE OF TENNIS

VOL. 38

Clash! One-Shot Battle

Story & Art by

Takeshi Konomi

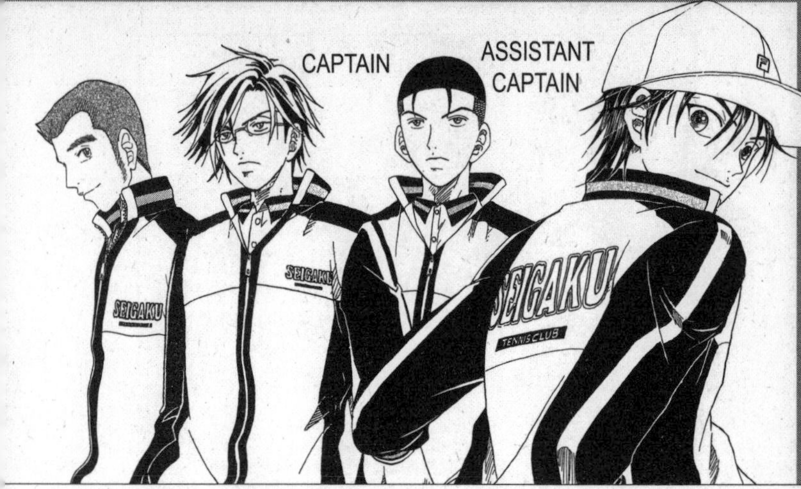
CAPTAIN
ASSISTANT CAPTAIN

• TAKASHI KAWAMURA • KUNIMITSU TEZUKA • SHUICHIRO OISHI • RYOMA ECHIZEN •

STORY & CHARACTERS

Seishun Academy student Ryoma Echizen is a tennis prodigy, with wins in four consecutive U.S. Junior Tennis Tournaments under his belt. He became a starter as a 7th grader and led his team to the District Preliminaries! Despite a few mishaps, Seishun won the Dirstrict Prelims and the City Tournament, and earned a ticket to the Kanto Tournament. The team came away victorious from its first-round matches, but Captain Kunimitsu injured his shoulder and went to Kyushu for treatment. Despite losing Kunimitsu and Assistant Captain Shuichiro to injury, Seishun pulled together as a team, winning the Kanto Tournament and earning a slot at the Nationals!

With Kunimitsu recovered and back on the team, Seishun enter the Nationals with their strongest line-up and defeat Okinawa's Higa Junior High in the opening round and Hyotei Academy in the quarterfinals. They advance to the semifinals against Osaka's Shitenhoji, last year's top-four team. Shusuke loses a close Singles 3 match to open the round. To avenge his loss, Momo and Kaoru come away victorious in Doubles 2! Taka battles his way to victory in the following Singles 2 match! And now, Seishun is just one step away from advancing to the finals!

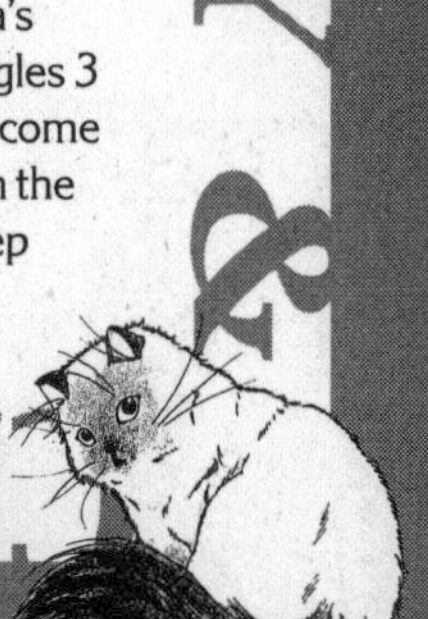

SEIGAKU I

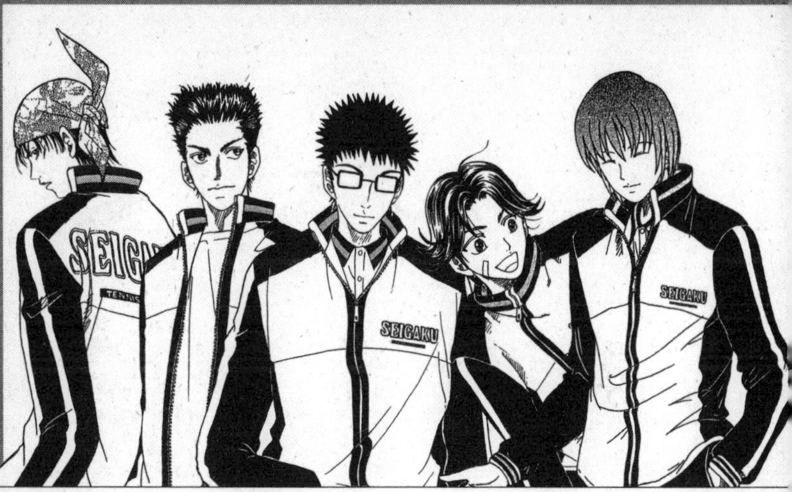
SEIGAKU
TENNIS
SEIGAKU
SEIGAKU

• KAORU KAIDO • TAKESHI MOMOSHIRO • SADAHARU INUI • EIJI KIKUMARU • SHUSUKE FUJI •

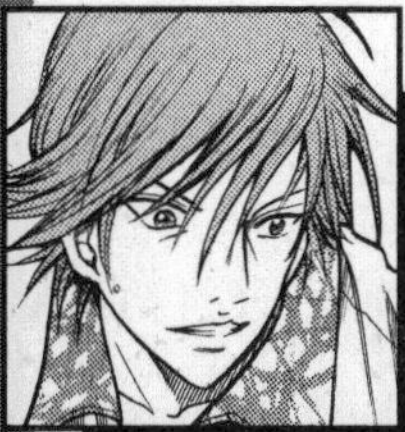
SHITENHOJI
KURANOSUKE SHIRAISHI

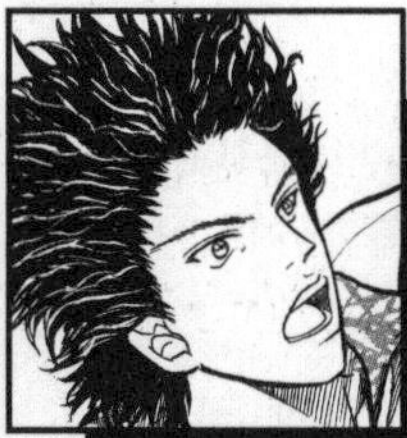
SHITENHOJI
SENRI CHITOSE

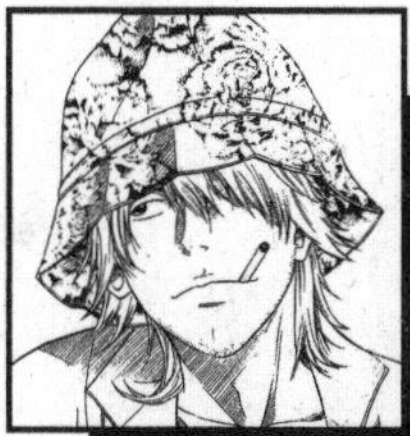
SHITENHOJI
OSAMU WATANABE

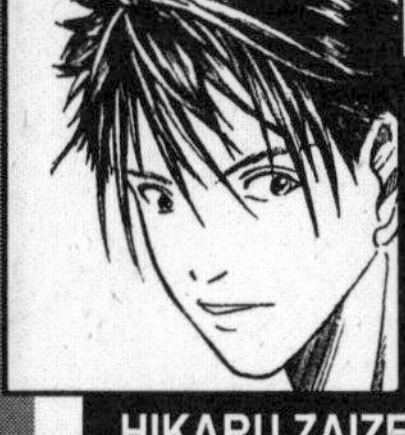
SHITENHOJI
HIKARU ZAIZEN

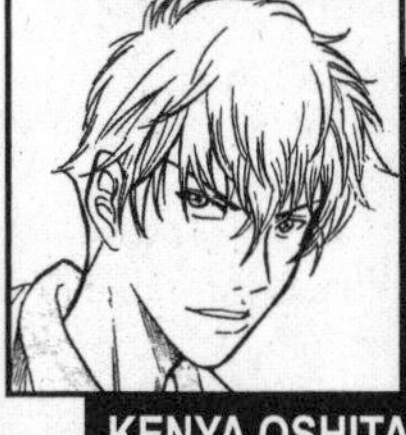
SHITENHOJI
KENYA OSHITARI

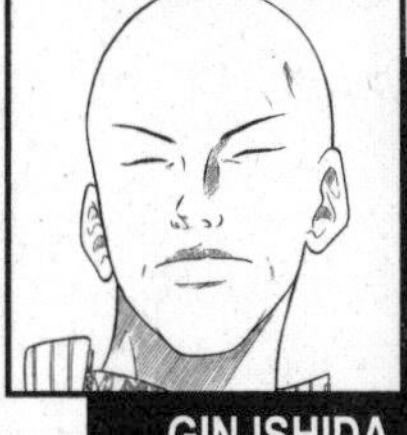
SHITENHOJI
GIN ISHIDA

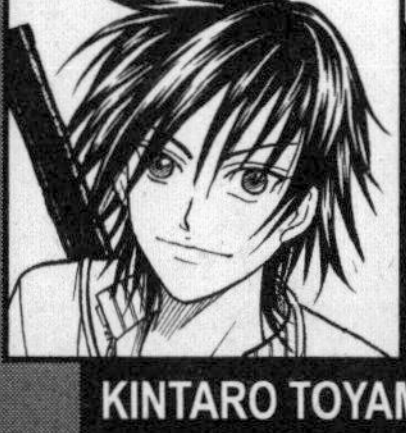
SHITENHOJI
KINTARO TOYAMA

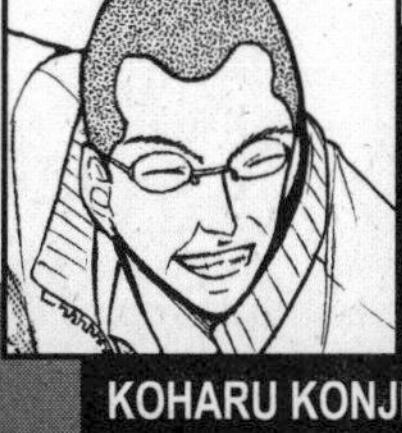
SHITENHOJI
KOHARU KONJIKI

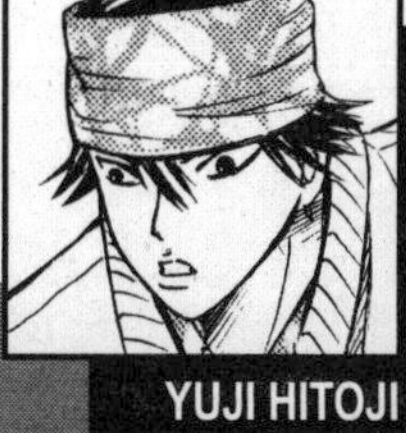
SHITENHOJI
YUJI HITOJI

CONTENTS

Vol. 38
Clash! One-Shot Battle

Genius 332: Setting the Stage   7

Genius 333: Pinnacle of Mastery vs. Pinnacle of Brilliance   25

Genius 334: Absolute Prediction   45

Genius 335: One's Limit   63

Genius 336: Final Round   81

Genius 337: Clash! One-Shot Battle   99
          Ryoma Echizen vs. Kintaro Toyama

Genius 338: Devil   117

Genius 339: The Upshot of the One-Shot Battle   135

Genius 340: To the Princes of Tennis   153

Genius 341: It's a Yakiniku Party Tonight!   171

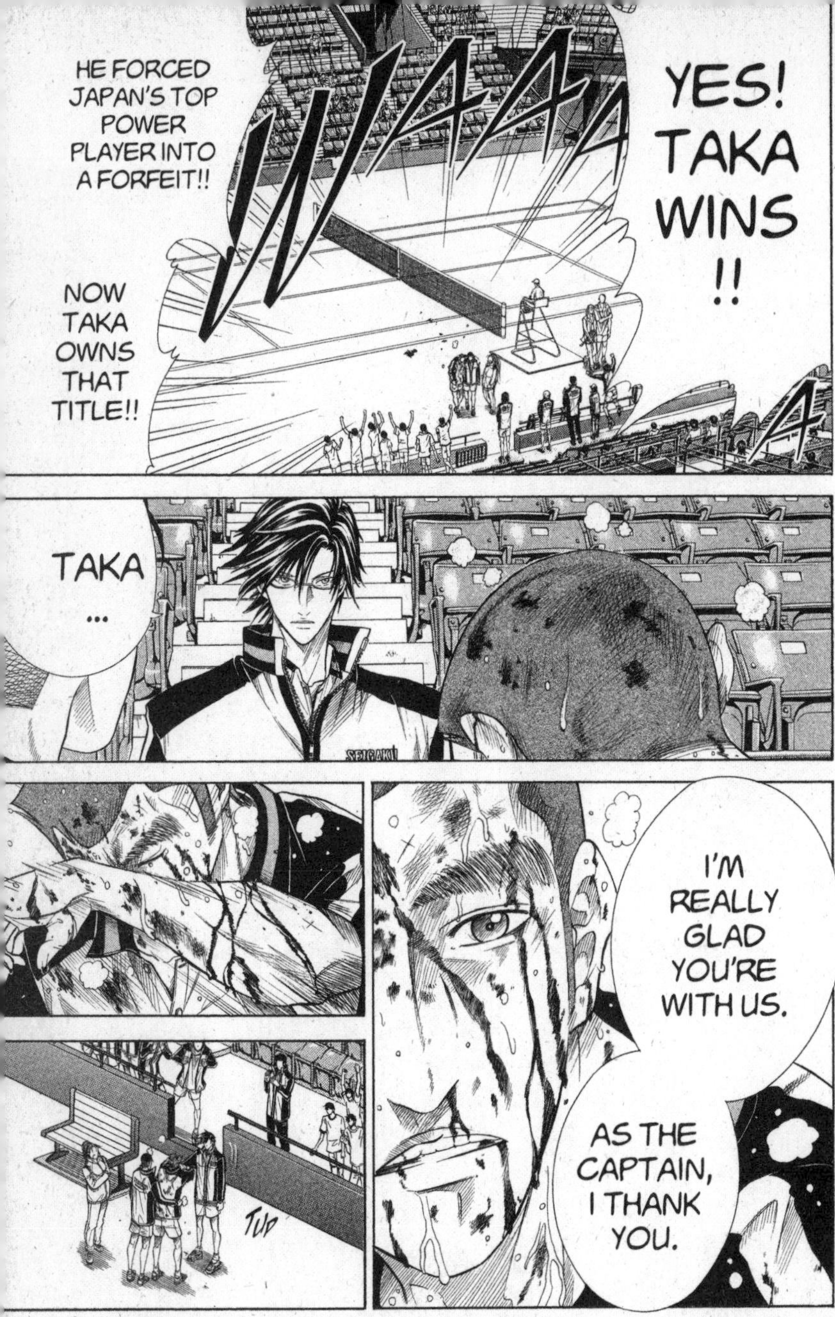
WAAAAA
YES! TAKA WINS!!
HE FORCED JAPAN'S TOP POWER PLAYER INTO A FORFEIT!!
NOW TAKA OWNS THAT TITLE!!
TAKA ...
I'M REALLY GLAD YOU'RE WITH US.
AS THE CAPTAIN, I THANK YOU.
TUP

GENIUS 332: SETTING THE STAGE

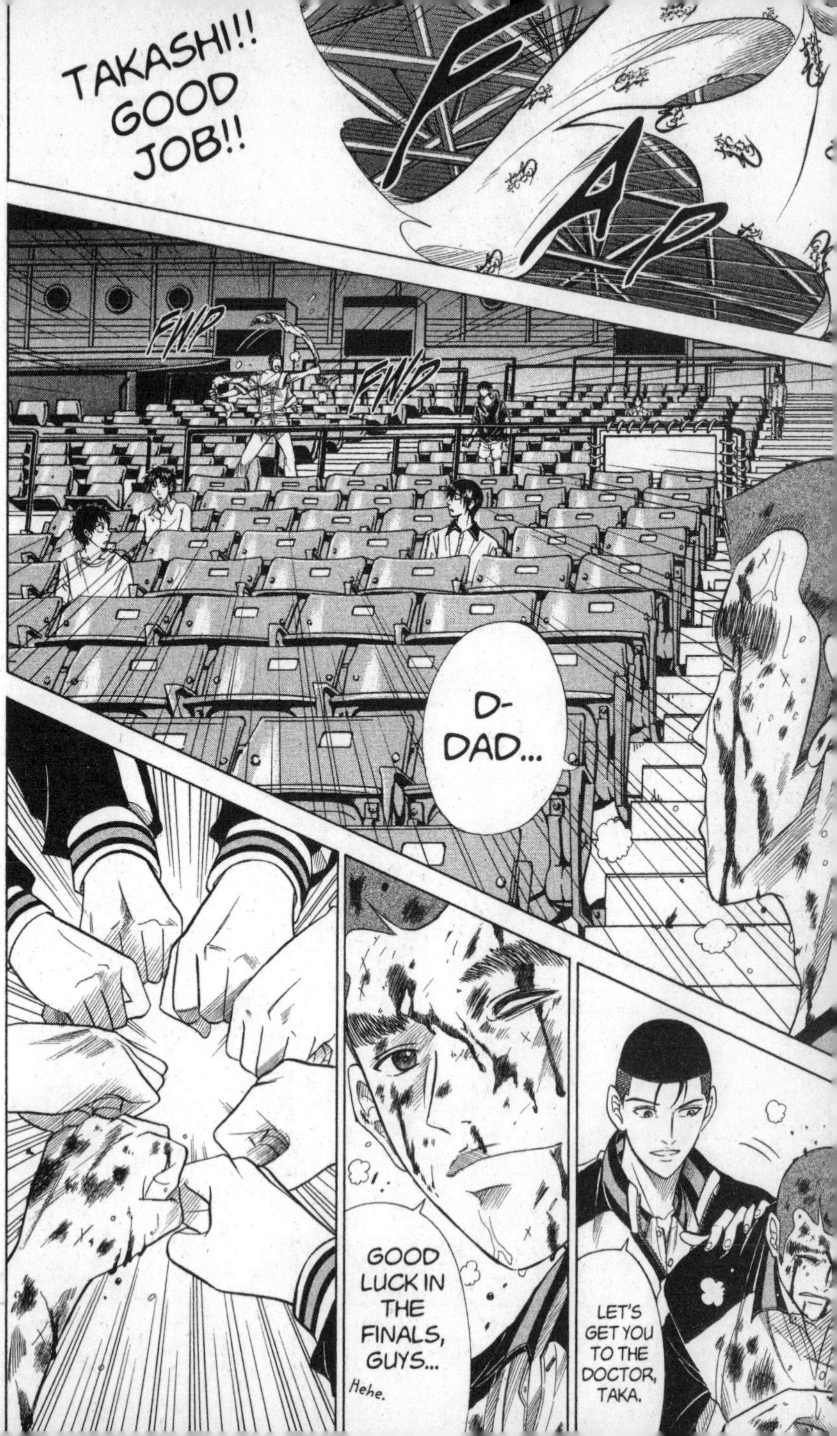
TAKASHI!! GOOD JOB!!
FAP
FWP
FWP
D-DAD...
LET'S GET YOU TO THE DOCTOR, TAKA.
GOOD LUCK IN THE FINALS, GUYS...
Hehe.

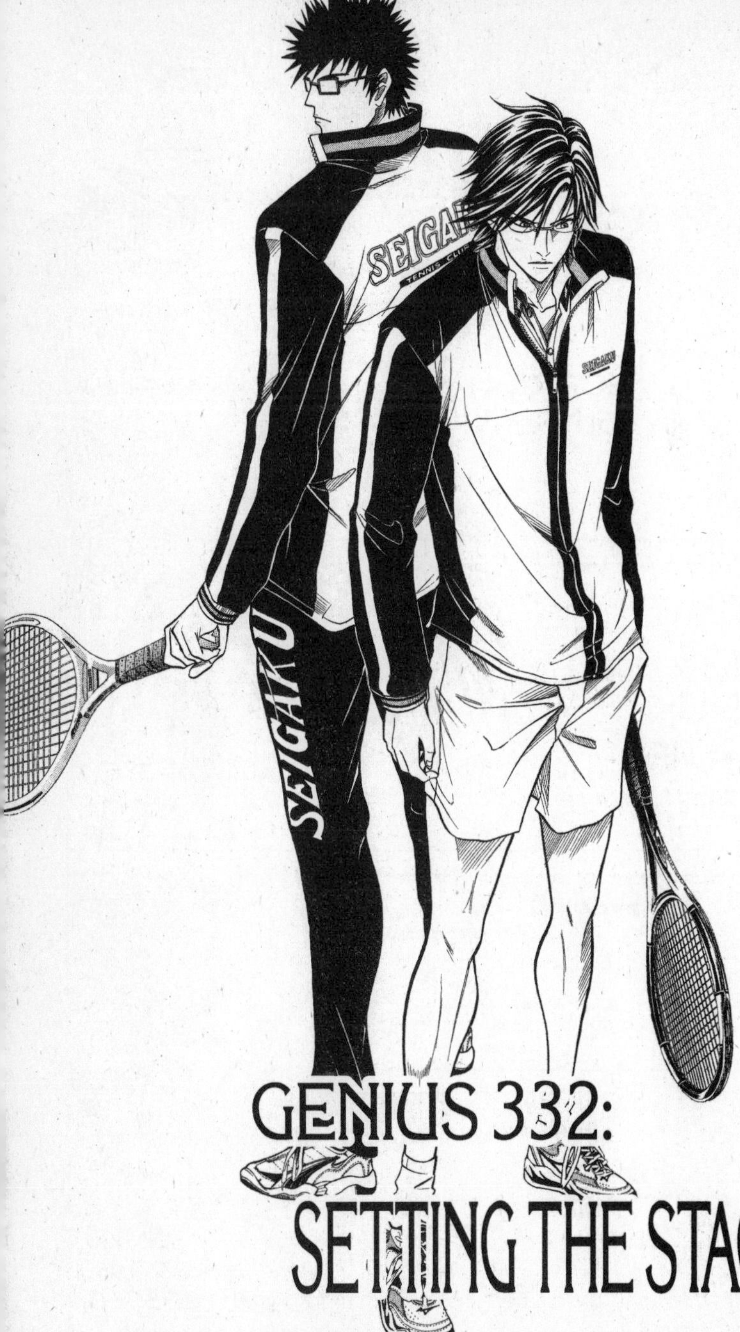
SEIGAKU
SEIGAKU
SEIGAKU

GENIUS 332: SETTING THE STAGE

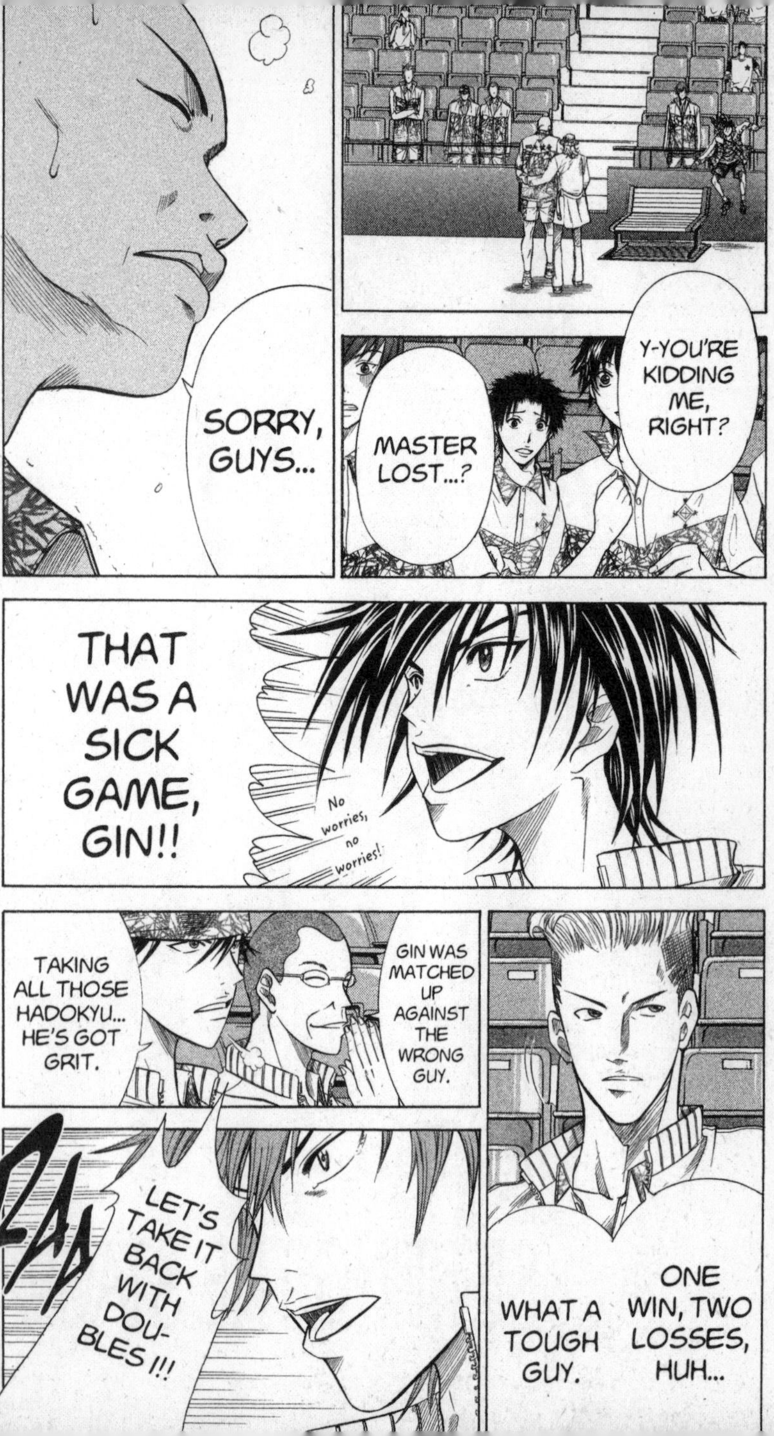
Y-YOU'RE KIDDING ME, RIGHT?
MASTER LOST...?
SORRY, GUYS...
THAT WAS A SICK GAME, GIN!!
No worries, no worries!
ONE WIN, TWO LOSSES, HUH...
WHAT A TOUGH GUY.
GIN WAS MATCHED UP AGAINST THE WRONG GUY.
TAKING ALL THOSE HADOKYU... HE'S GOT GRIT.
LET'S TAKE IT BACK WITH DOU-BLES!!!

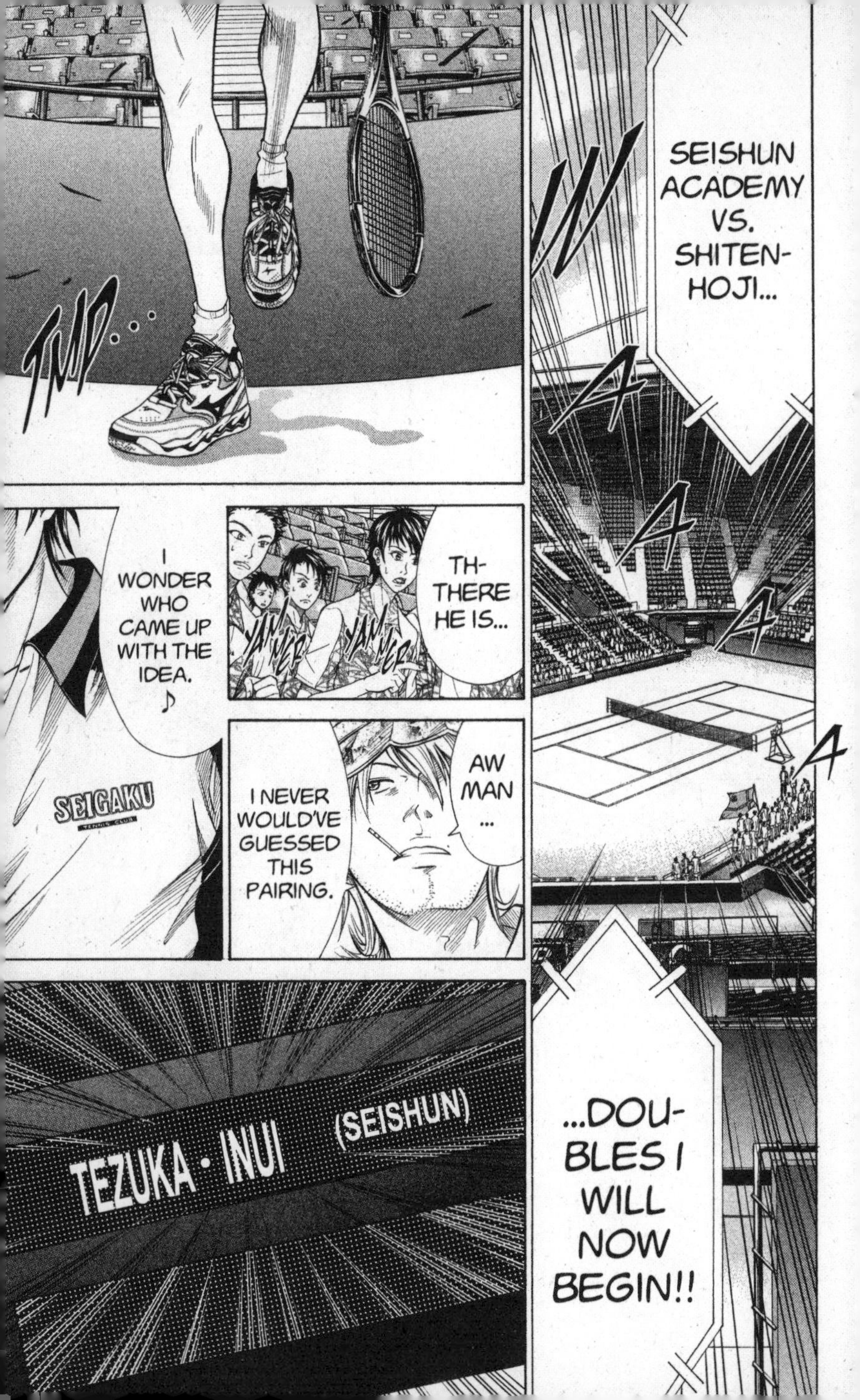
SEISHUN ACADEMY VS. SHITEN-HOJI...
WAAAAA
...DOUBLES I WILL NOW BEGIN!!
TMP...
YAMMER YAMMER
TH-THERE HE IS...
AW MAN ...
I NEVER WOULD'VE GUESSED THIS PAIRING.
I WONDER WHO CAME UP WITH THE IDEA. ♪
SEIGAKU
TENNIS CLUB
TEZUKA · INUI (SEISHUN)

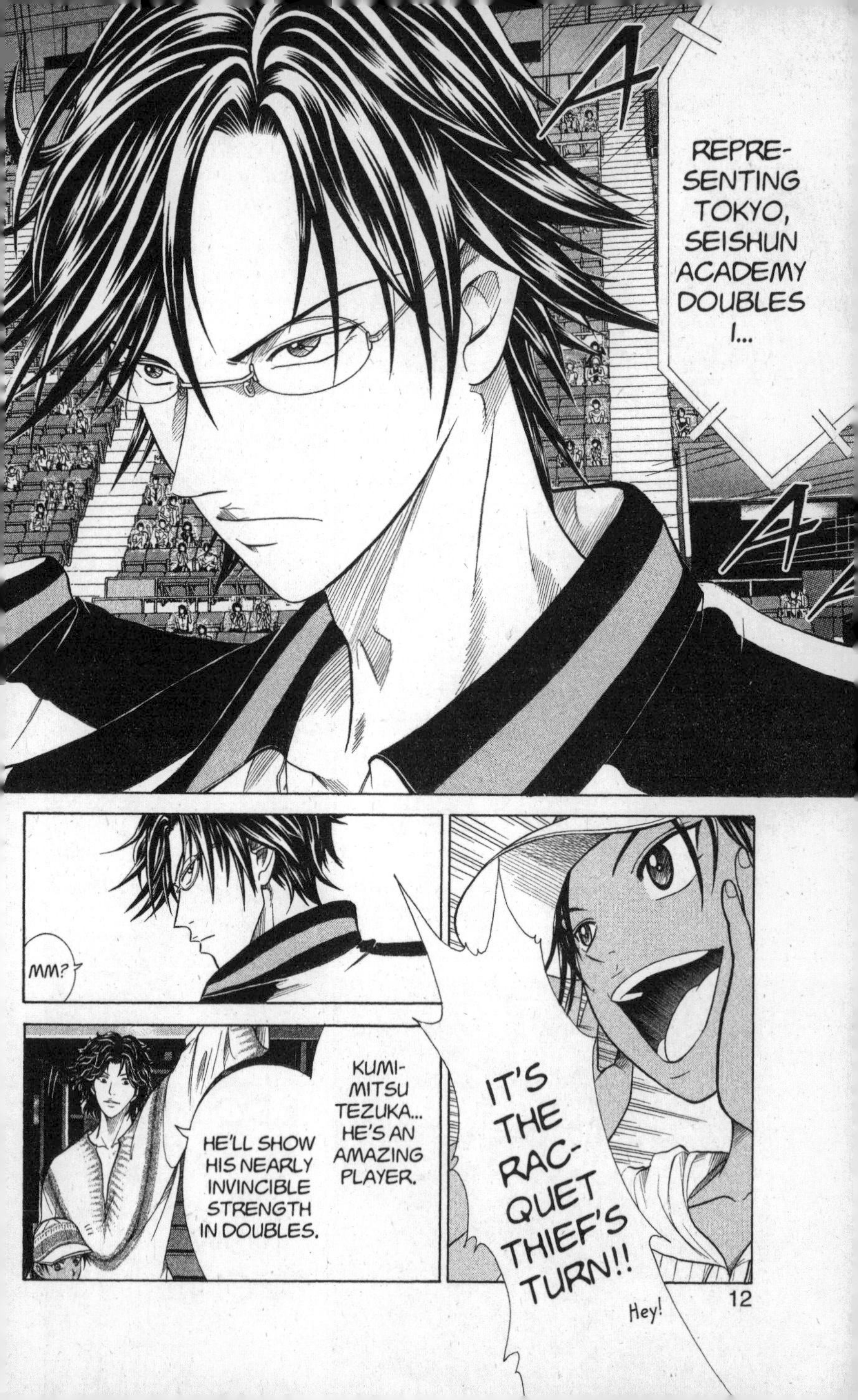
A
A
REPRESENTING TOKYO, SEISHUN ACADEMY DOUBLES I...
IT'S THE RACQUET THIEF'S TURN!!
Hey!
MM?
KUMIMITSU TEZUKA... HE'S AN AMAZING PLAYER.
HE'LL SHOW HIS NEARLY INVINCIBLE STRENGTH IN DOUBLES.

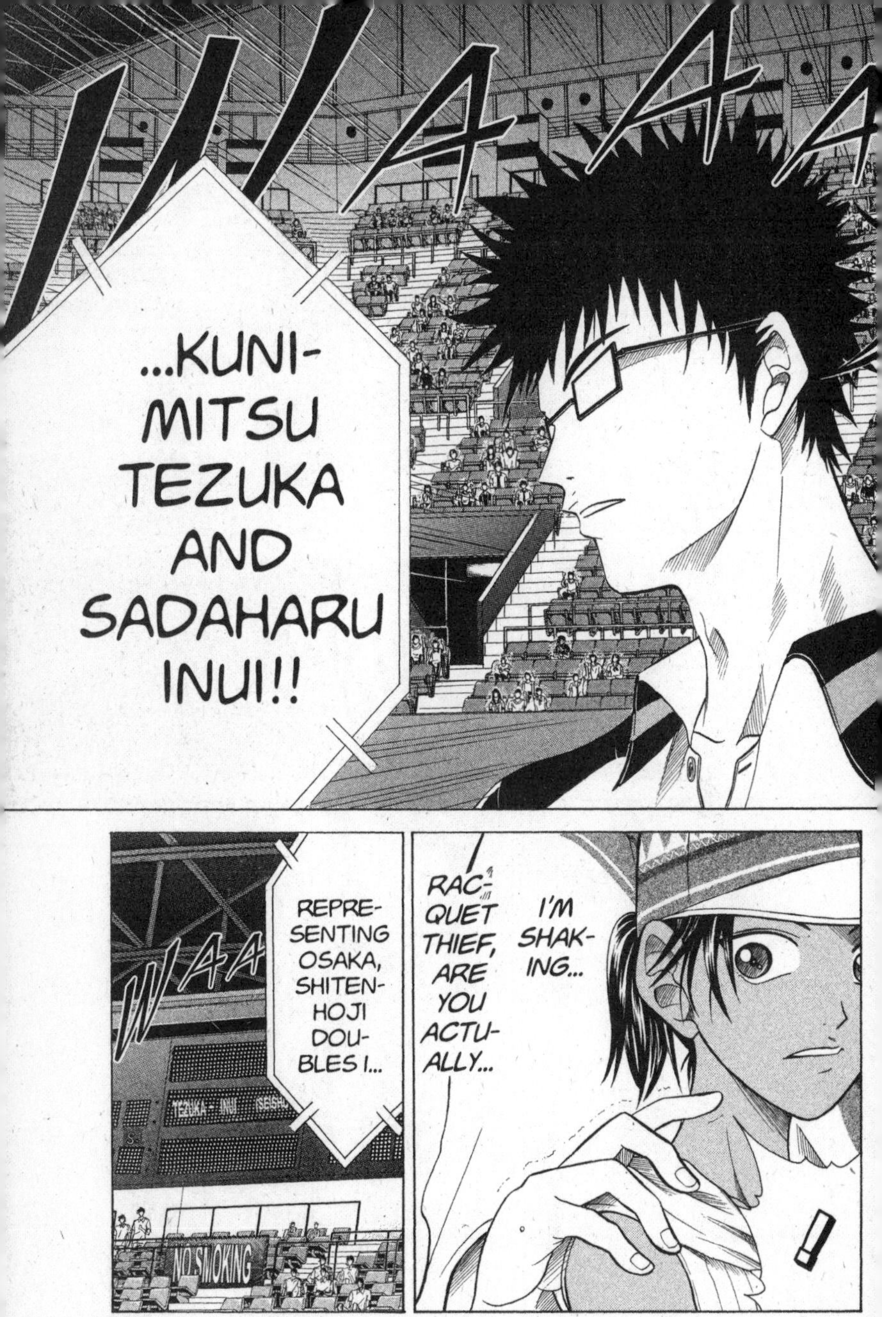
WAAAA
...KUNIMITSU TEZUKA AND SADAHARU INUI!!
I'M SHAKING...
RACQUET THIEF, ARE YOU ACTUALLY...
REPRESENTING OSAKA, SHITENHOJI DOUBLES I...
WAA
TEZUKA - INUI (SEISHU
NO SMOKING

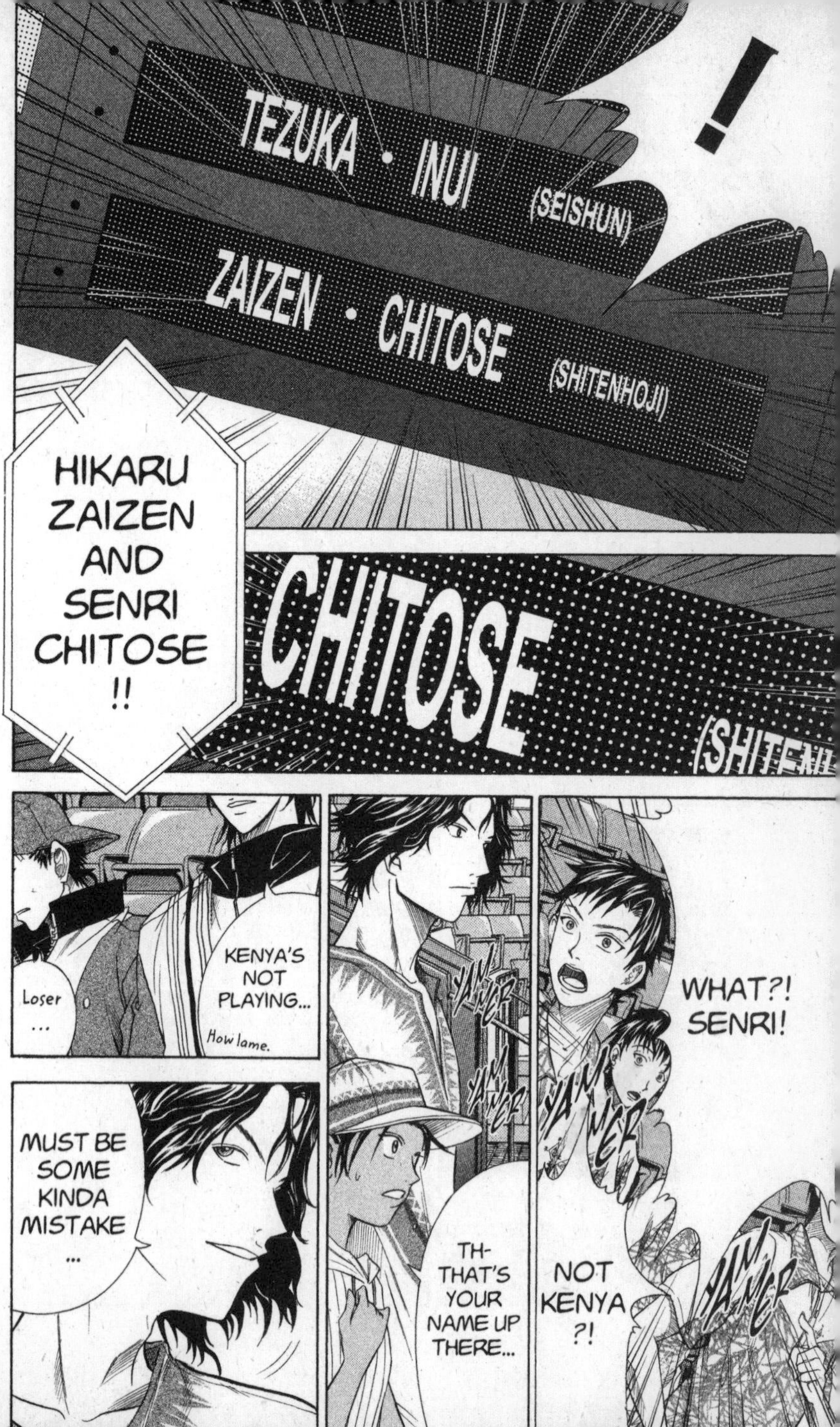
!
TEZUKA · INUI (SEISHUN)
ZAIZEN · CHITOSE (SHITENHOJI)
HIKARU ZAIZEN AND SENRI CHITOSE !!
CHITOSE
WHAT?! SENRI!
YAMMER
YAMMER
YAMMER
YAMMER
NOT KENYA ?!
TH- THAT'S YOUR NAME UP THERE...
KENYA'S NOT PLAYING...
How lame.
Loser ...
MUST BE SOME KINDA MISTAKE ...

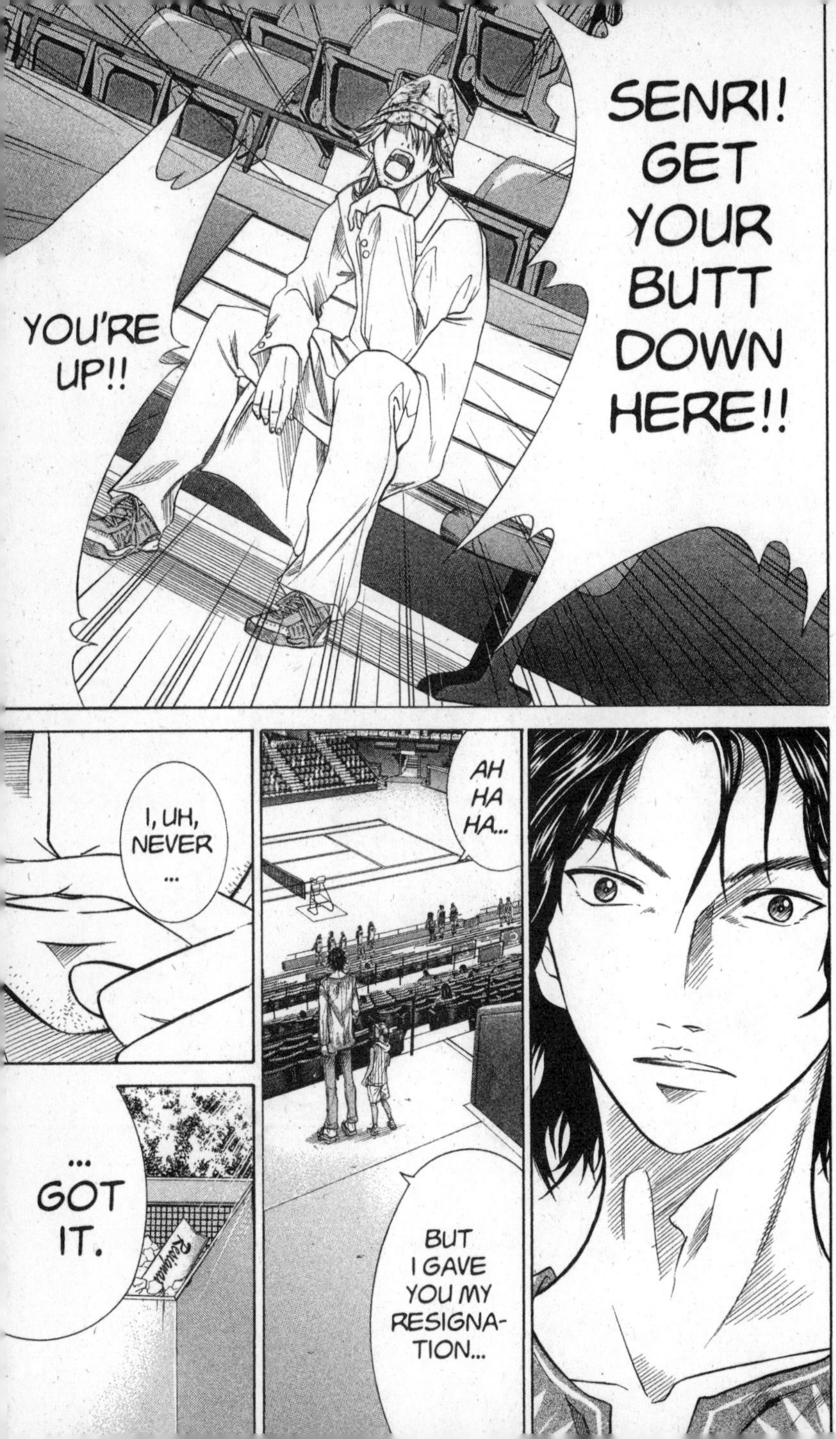
SENRI! GET YOUR BUTT DOWN HERE!!
YOU'RE UP!!
BUT I GAVE YOU MY RESIGNA-TION...
AH HA HA...
I, UH, NEVER ...
... GOT IT.

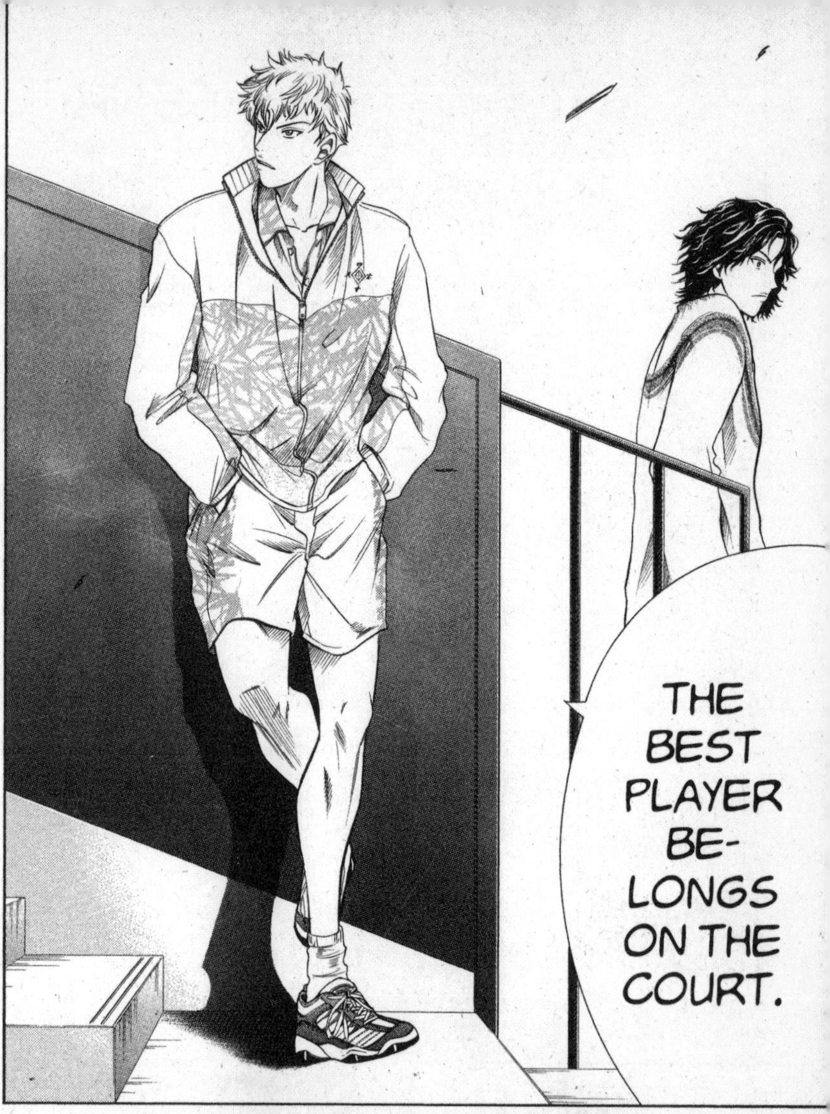
THE BEST PLAYER BE- LONGS ON THE COURT.
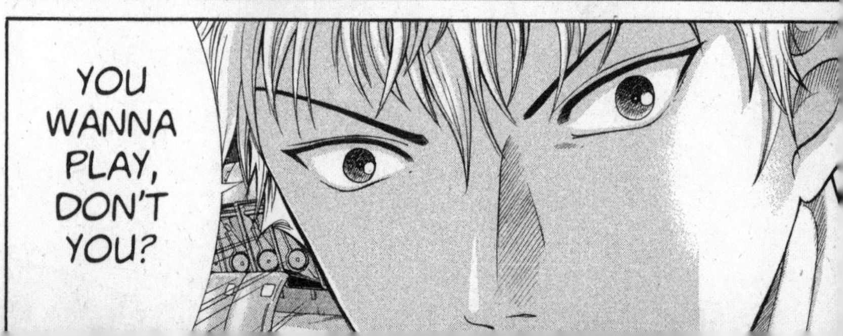
YOU WANNA PLAY, DON'T YOU?

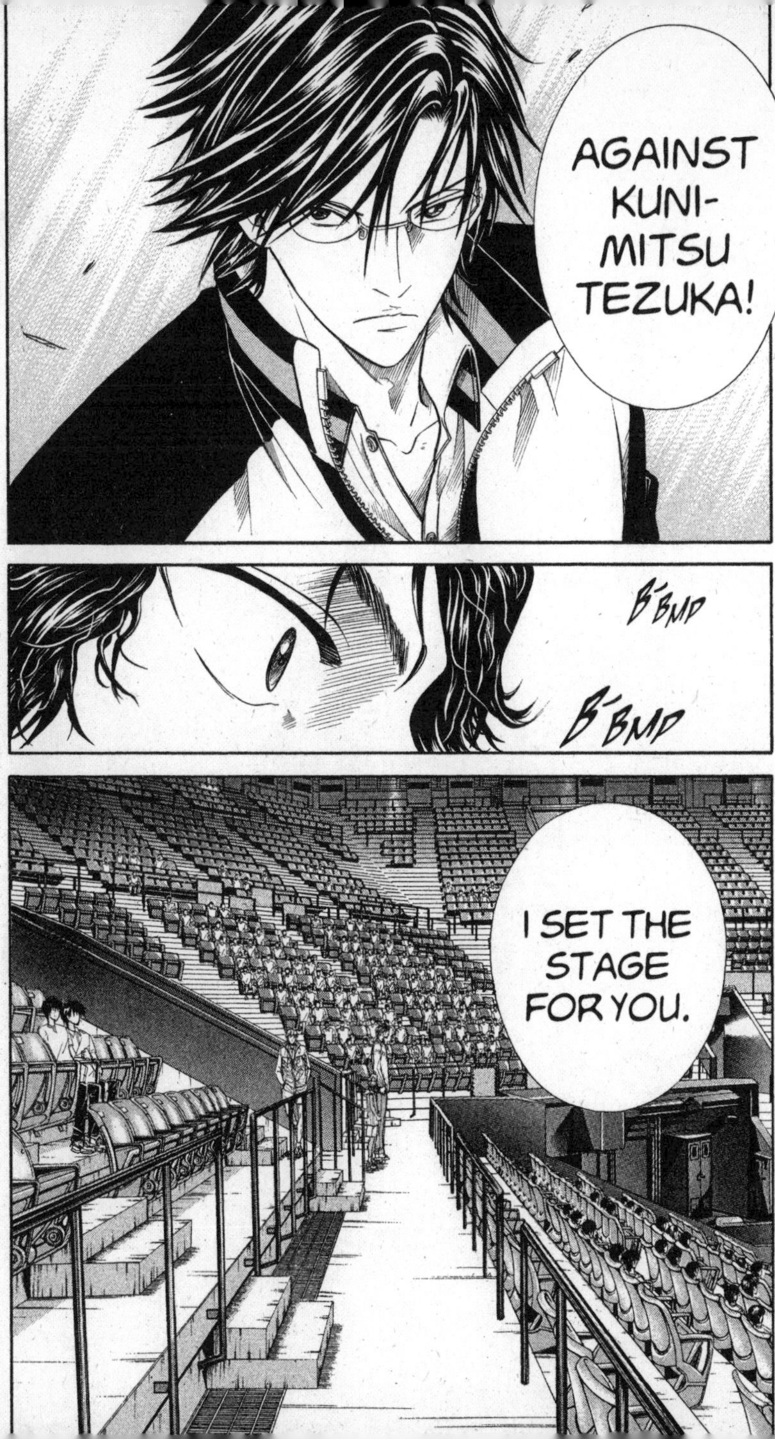
AGAINST KUNI-MITSU TEZUKA!
B-BMP
B-BMP
I SET THE STAGE FOR YOU.

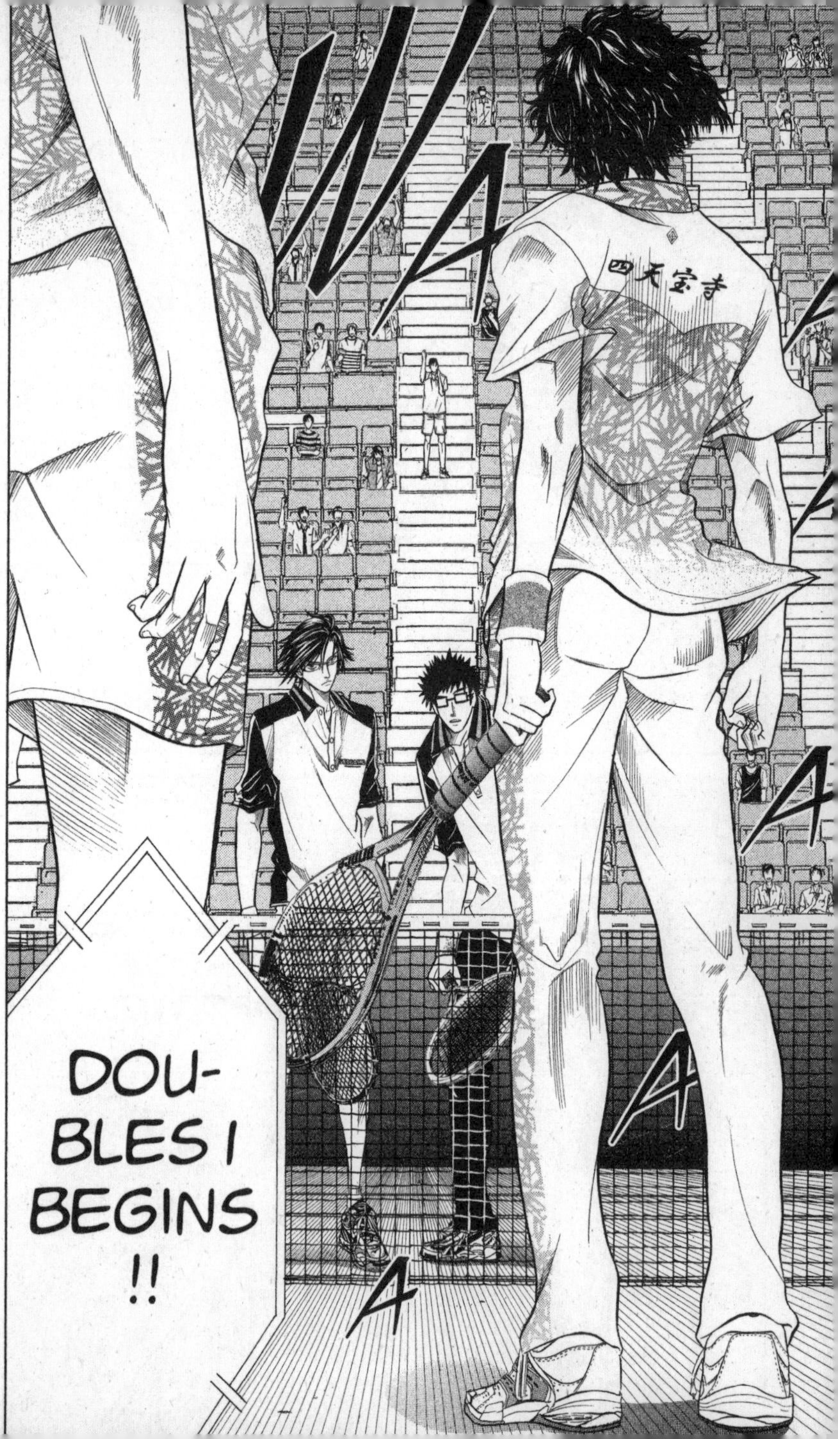
WAAAA
四天宝寺
DOU-
BLES 1
BEGINS
!!

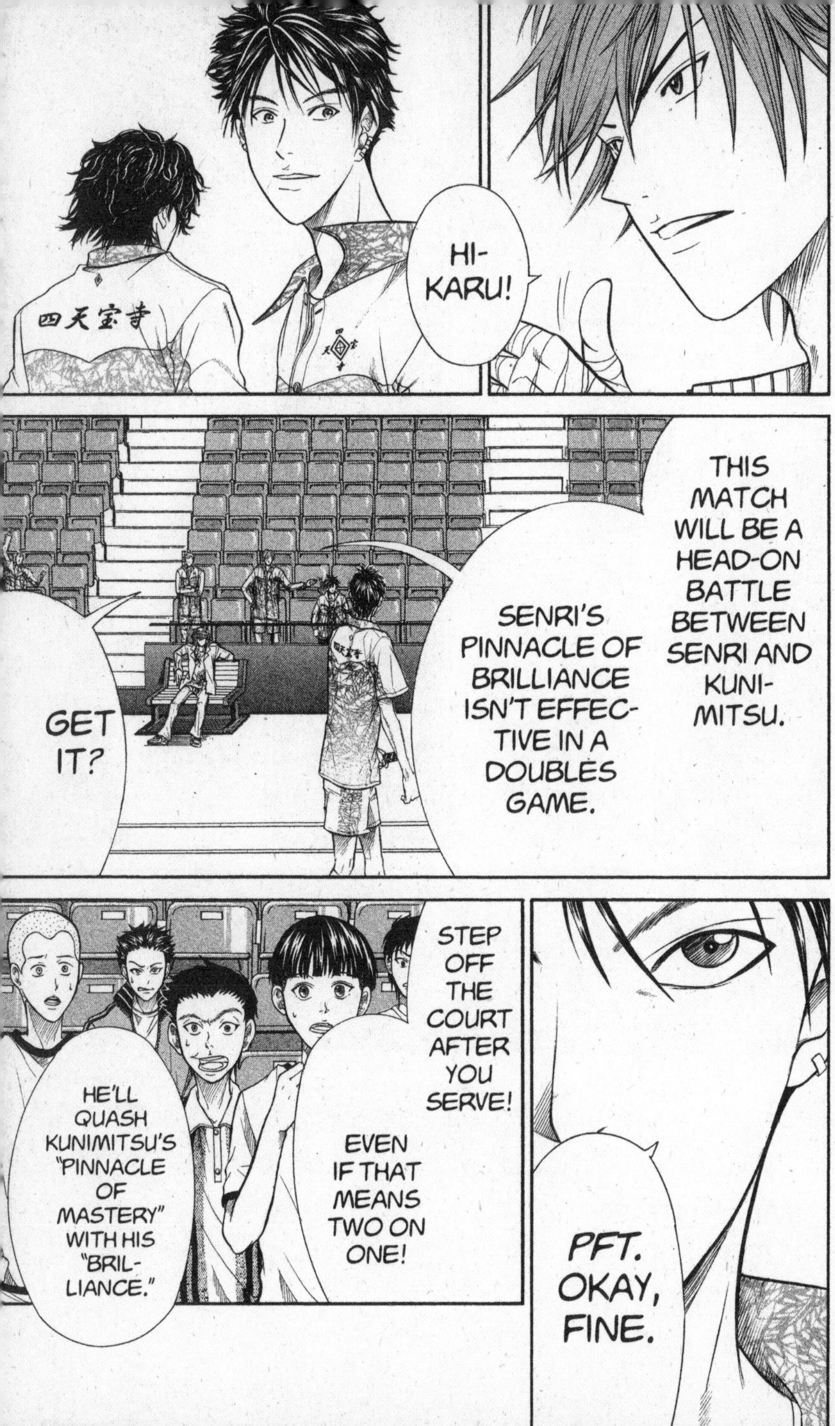
HI-KARU!
THIS MATCH WILL BE A HEAD-ON BATTLE BETWEEN SENRI AND KUNI-MITSU.
SENRI'S PINNACLE OF BRILLIANCE ISN'T EFFEC-TIVE IN A DOUBLES GAME.
GET IT?
STEP OFF THE COURT AFTER YOU SERVE!
PFT. OKAY, FINE.
EVEN IF THAT MEANS TWO ON ONE!
HE'LL QUASH KUNIMITSU'S "PINNACLE OF MASTERY" WITH HIS "BRIL-LIANCE."

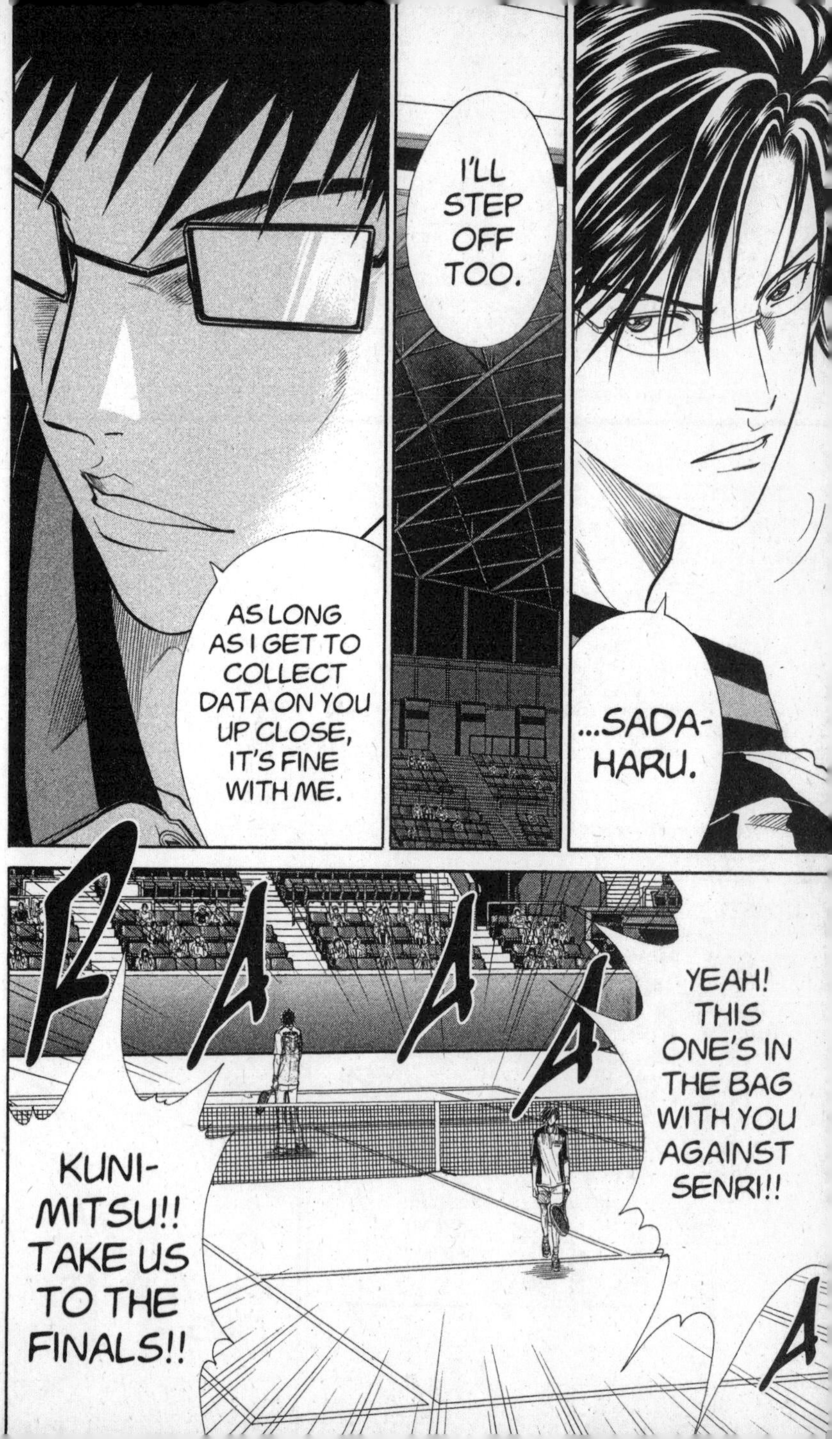
I'LL STEP OFF TOO.
...SADA-HARU.
AS LONG AS I GET TO COLLECT DATA ON YOU UP CLOSE, IT'S FINE WITH ME.
YEAH! THIS ONE'S IN THE BAG WITH YOU AGAINST SENRI!!
KUNI-MITSU!! TAKE US TO THE FINALS!!

READ THIS WAY

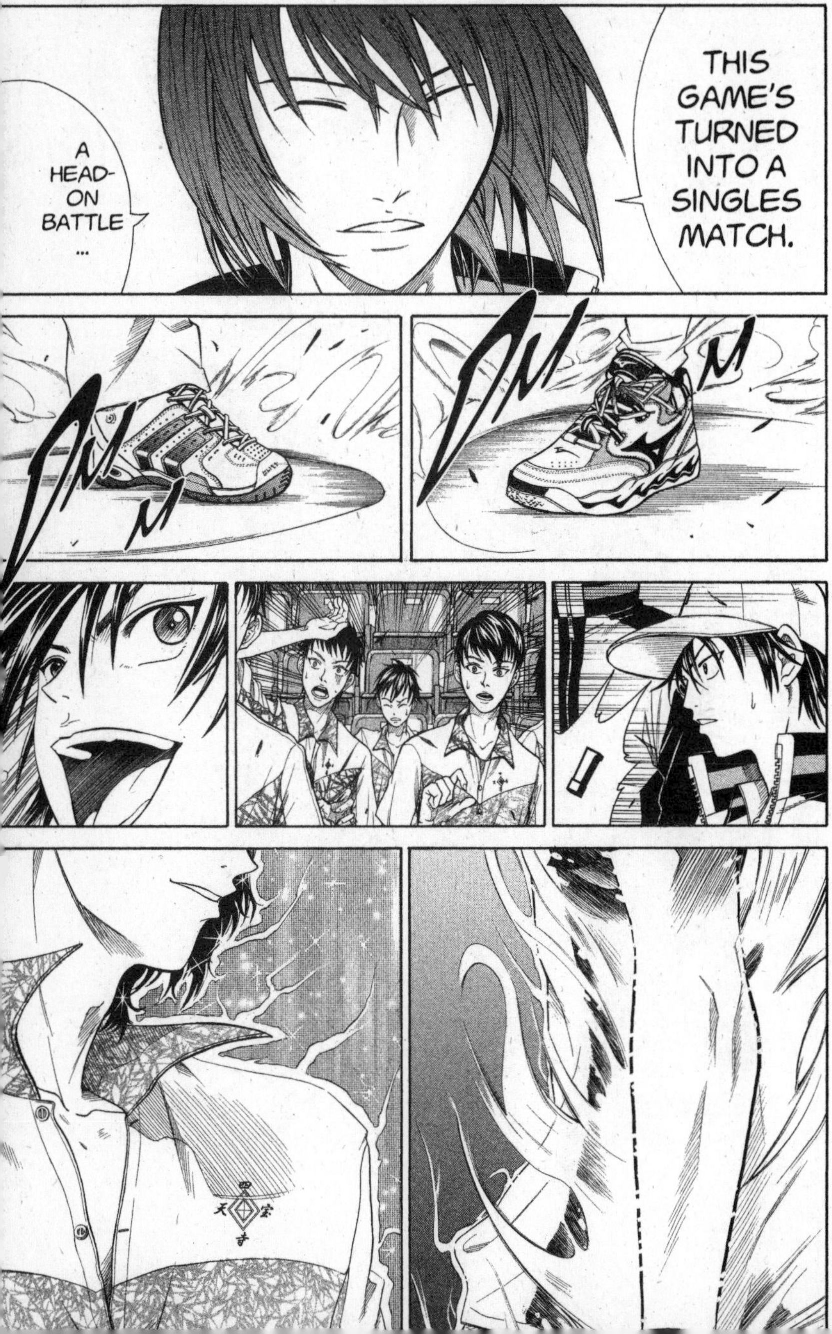
THIS GAME'S TURNED INTO A SINGLES MATCH.
A HEAD-ON BATTLE ...

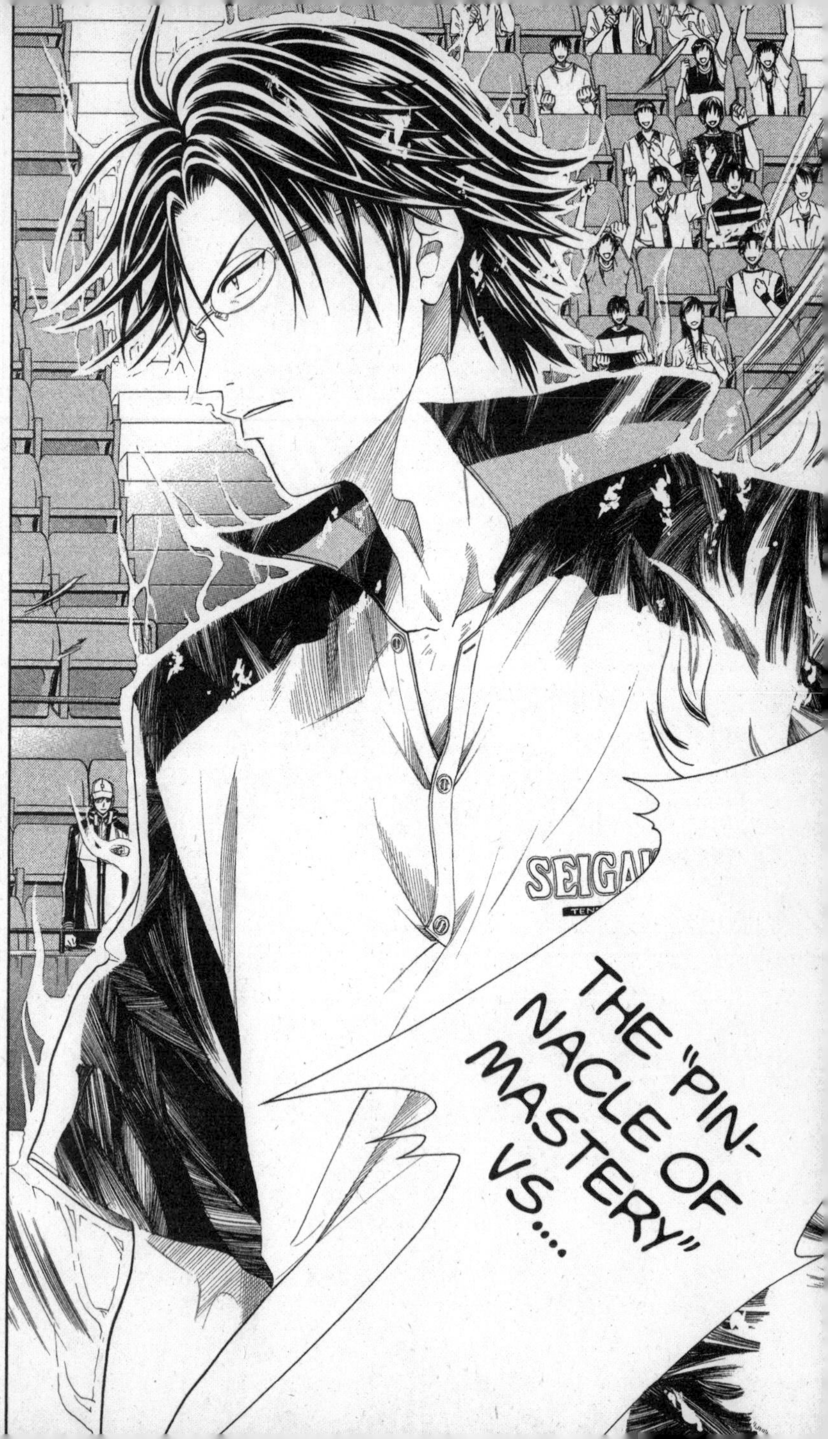
THE "PIN-NACLE OF MASTERY" VS....

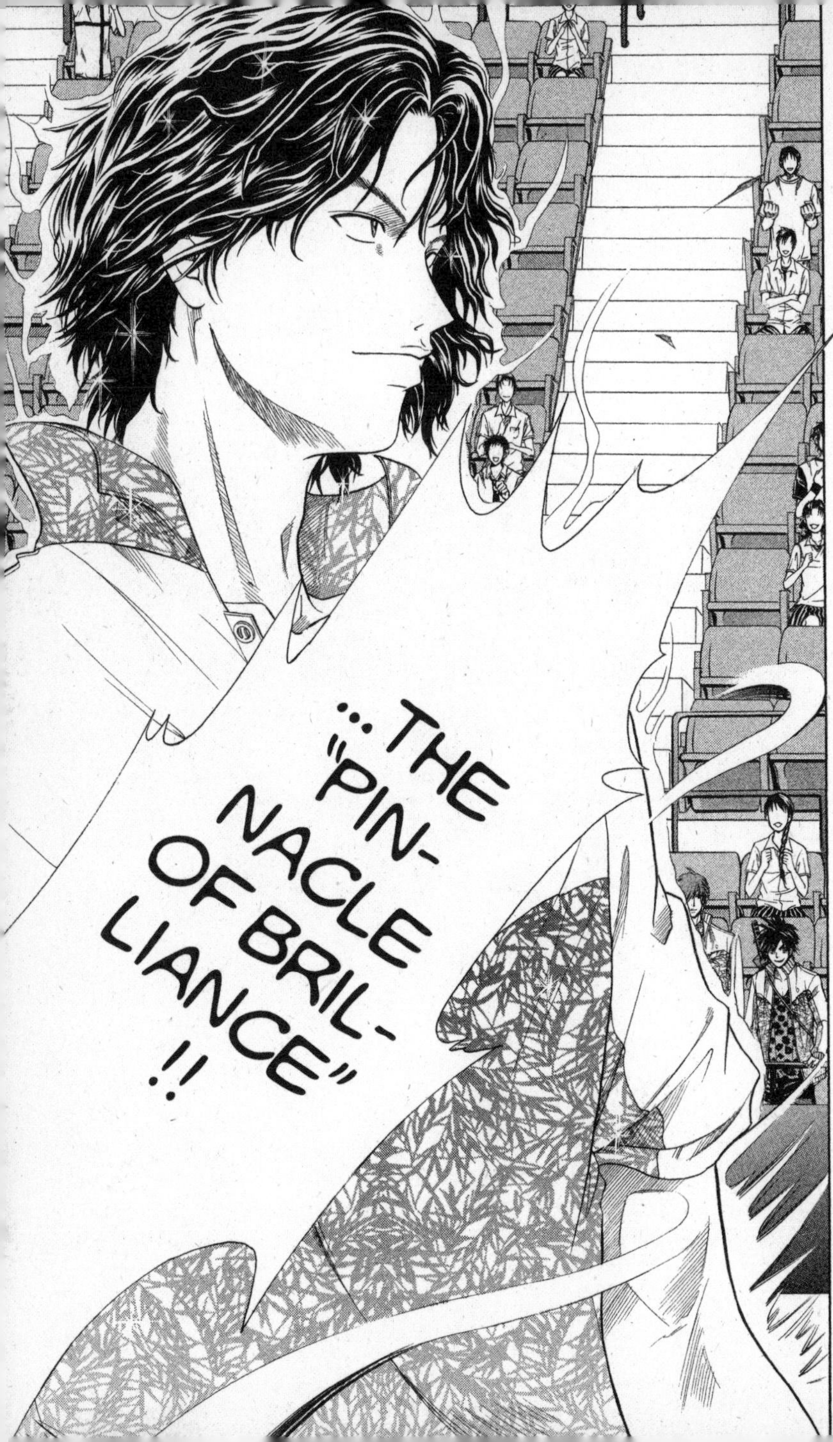
...THE "PIN-NACLE OF BRIL-LIANCE"!!

テニスの王子様

THE PRINCE OF TENNIS

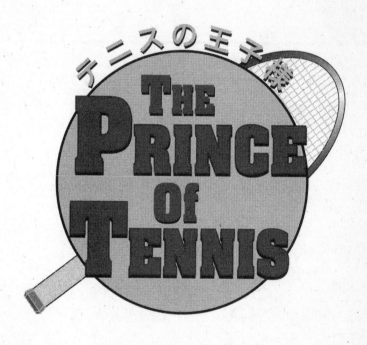

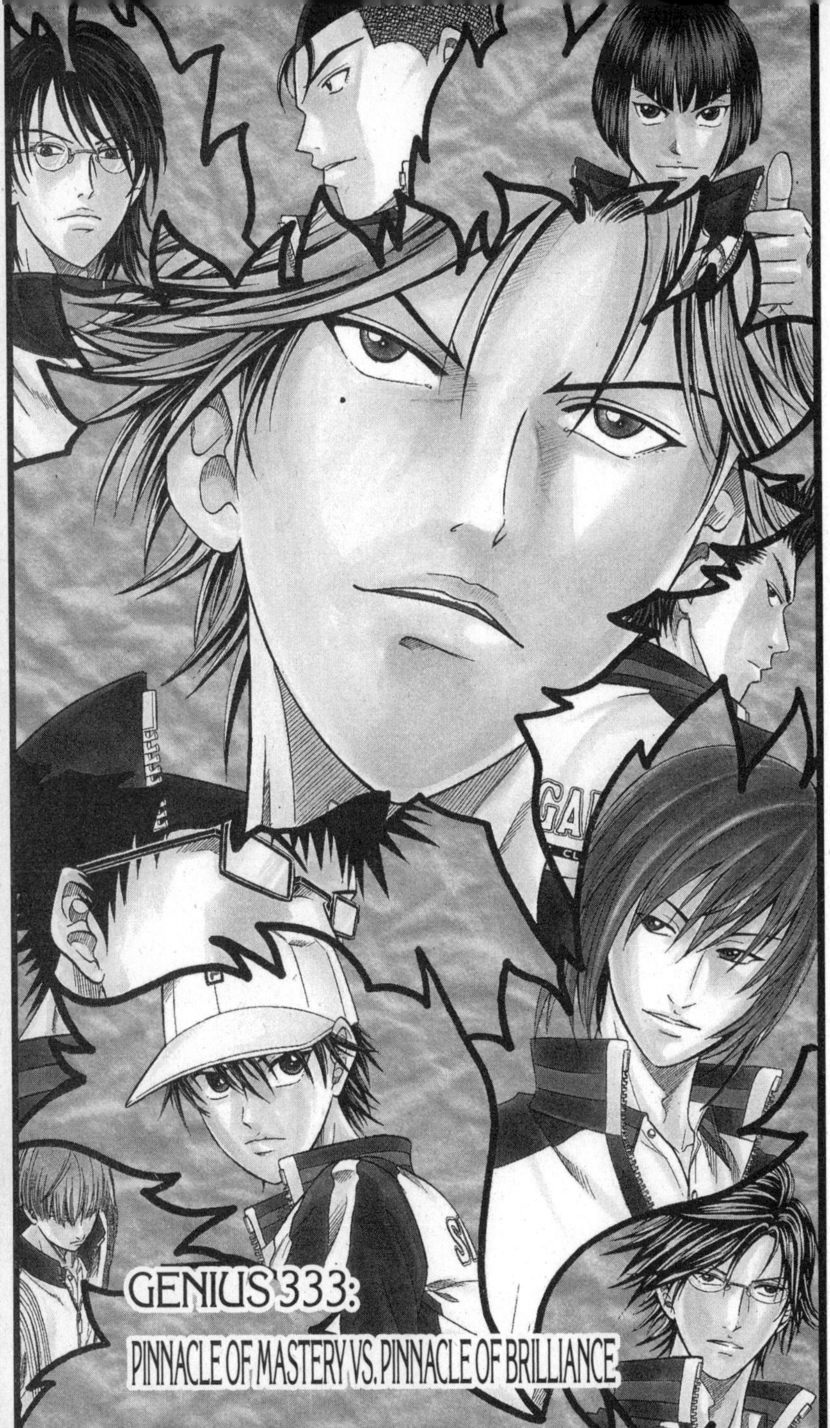

GENIUS 333: PINNACLE OF MASTERY VS. PINNACLE OF BRILLIANCE

テニスの王子様

THE PRINCE OF TENNIS

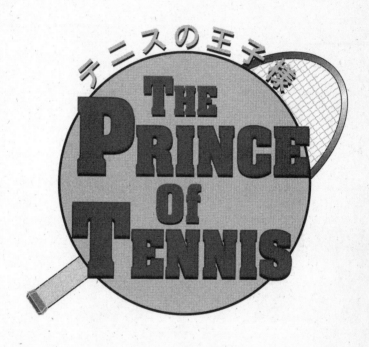

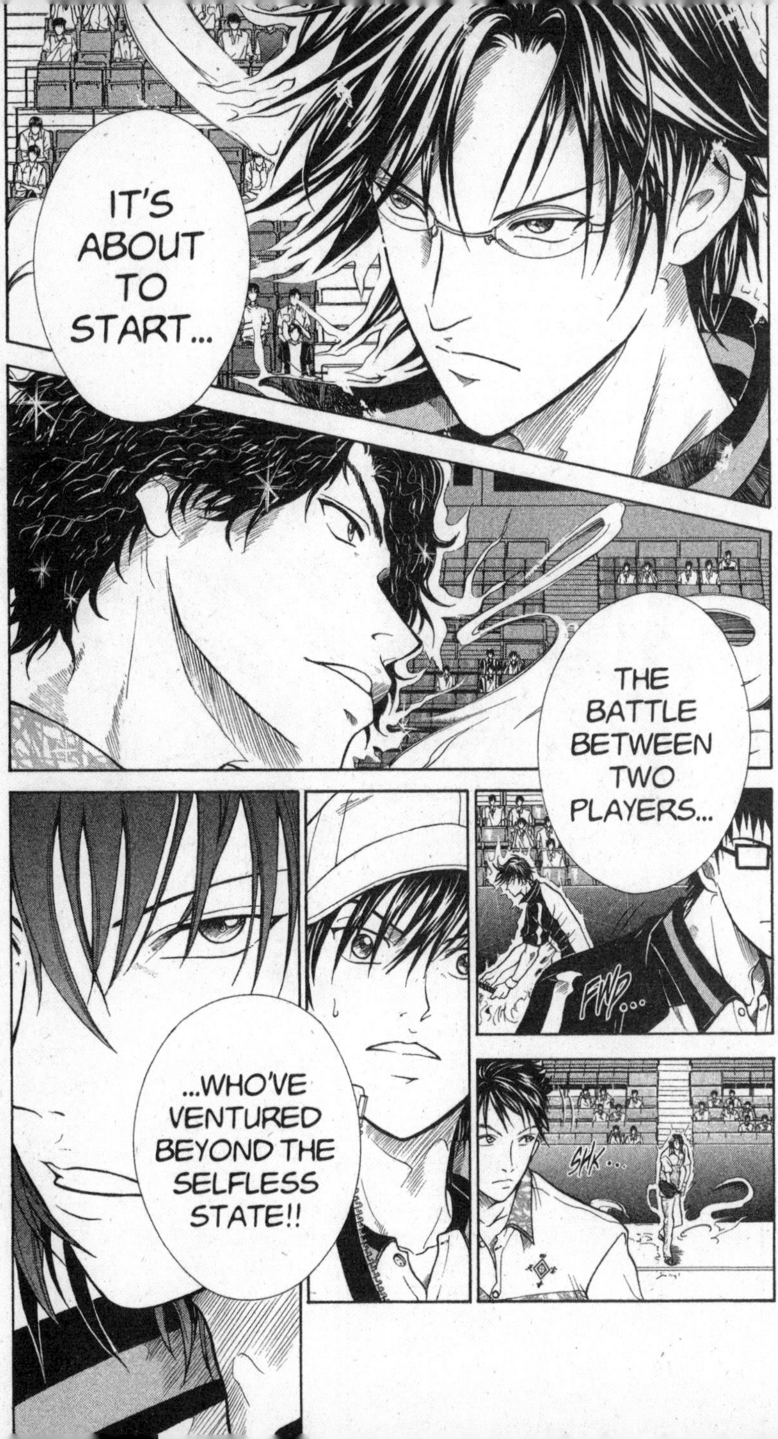
IT'S ABOUT TO START...
THE BATTLE BETWEEN TWO PLAYERS...
FWP...
SHK...
...WHO'VE VENTURED BEYOND THE SELFLESS STATE!!

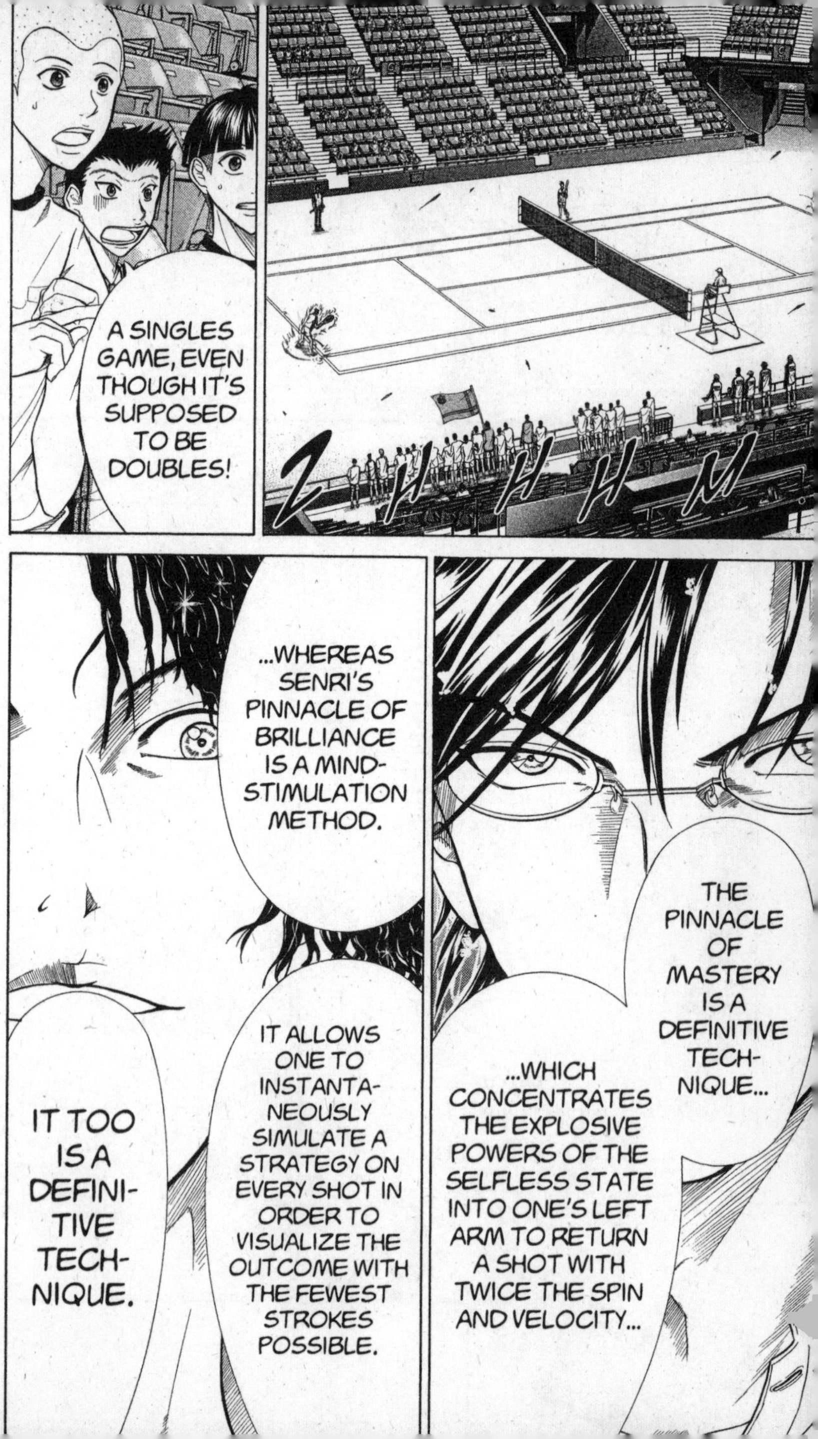
ZHHHM
A SINGLES GAME, EVEN THOUGH IT'S SUPPOSED TO BE DOUBLES!
THE PINNACLE OF MASTERY IS A DEFINITIVE TECH-NIQUE...
...WHICH CONCENTRATES THE EXPLOSIVE POWERS OF THE SELFLESS STATE INTO ONE'S LEFT ARM TO RETURN A SHOT WITH TWICE THE SPIN AND VELOCITY...
...WHEREAS SENRI'S PINNACLE OF BRILLIANCE IS A MIND-STIMULATION METHOD.
IT ALLOWS ONE TO INSTANTA-NEOUSLY SIMULATE A STRATEGY ON EVERY SHOT IN ORDER TO VISUALIZE THE OUTCOME WITH THE FEWEST STROKES POSSIBLE.
IT TOO IS A DEFINI-TIVE TECH-NIQUE.

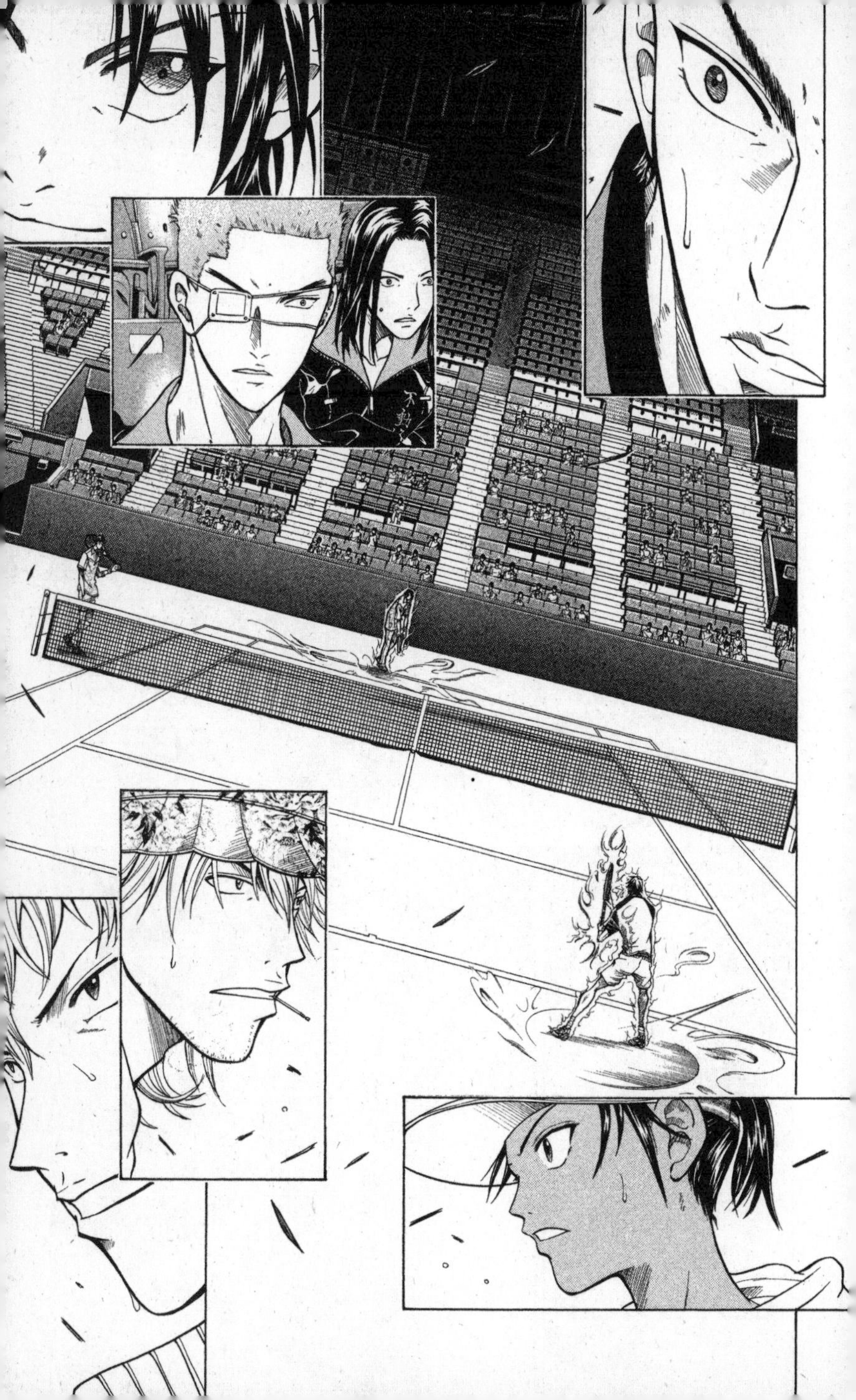

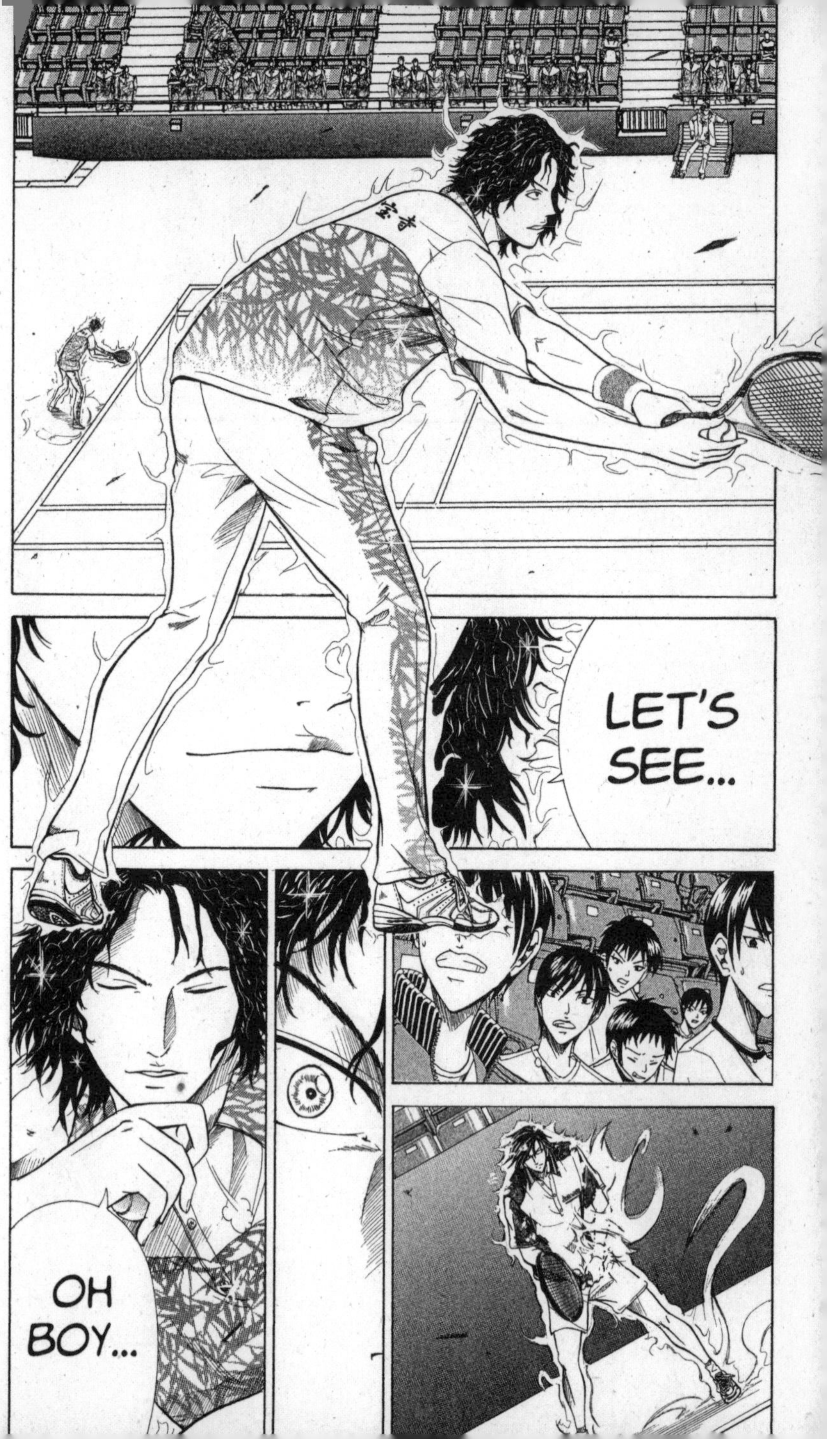
LET'S SEE...
OH BOY...

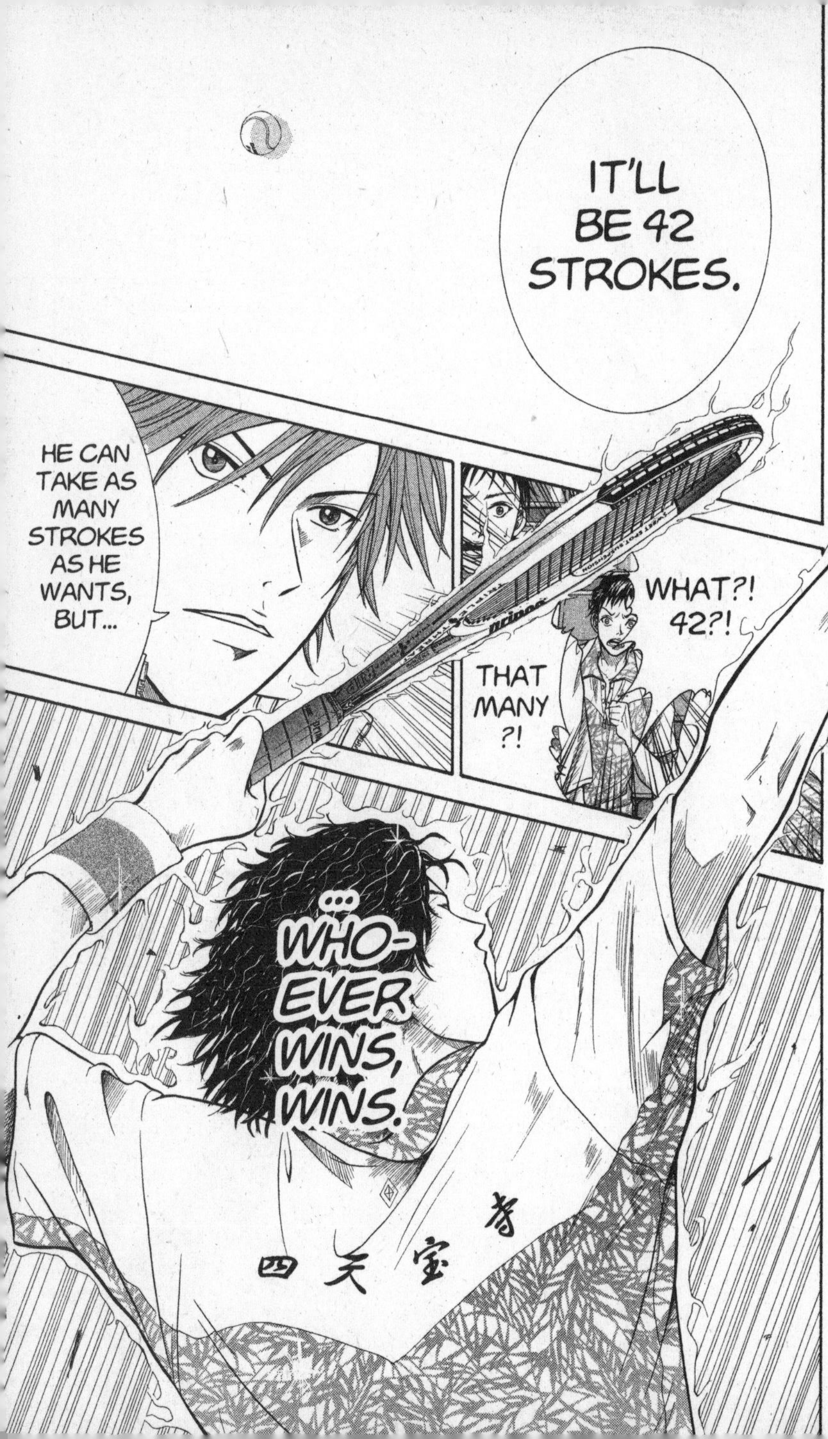
IT'LL BE 42 STROKES.
WHAT?! 42?!
THAT MANY ?!
HE CAN TAKE AS MANY STROKES AS HE WANTS, BUT...
...WHO-EVER WINS, WINS.
四天宝寺

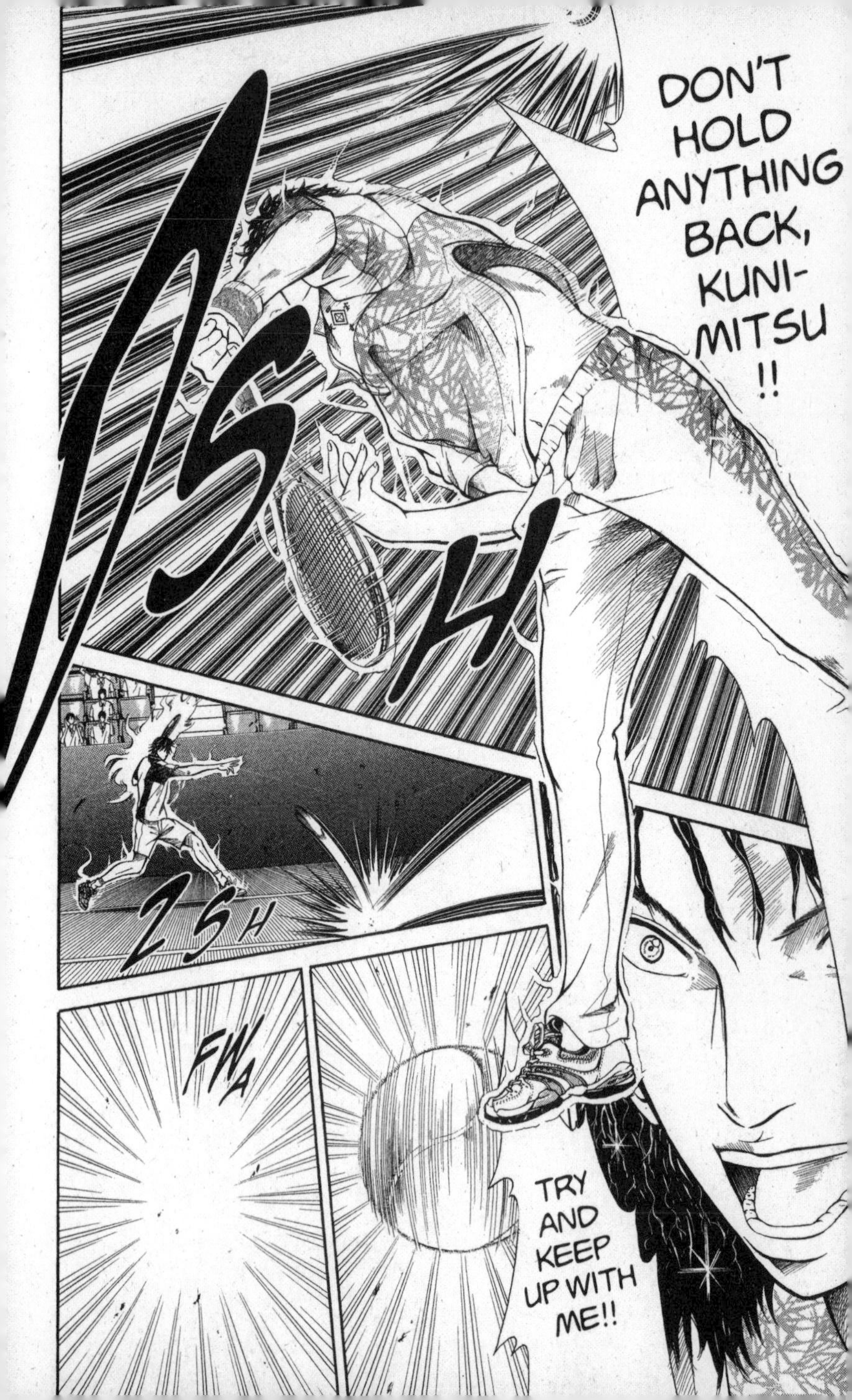
DON'T HOLD ANYTHING BACK, KUNI-MITSU !!
ZSH
ZSH
TRY AND KEEP UP WITH ME!!
FWA

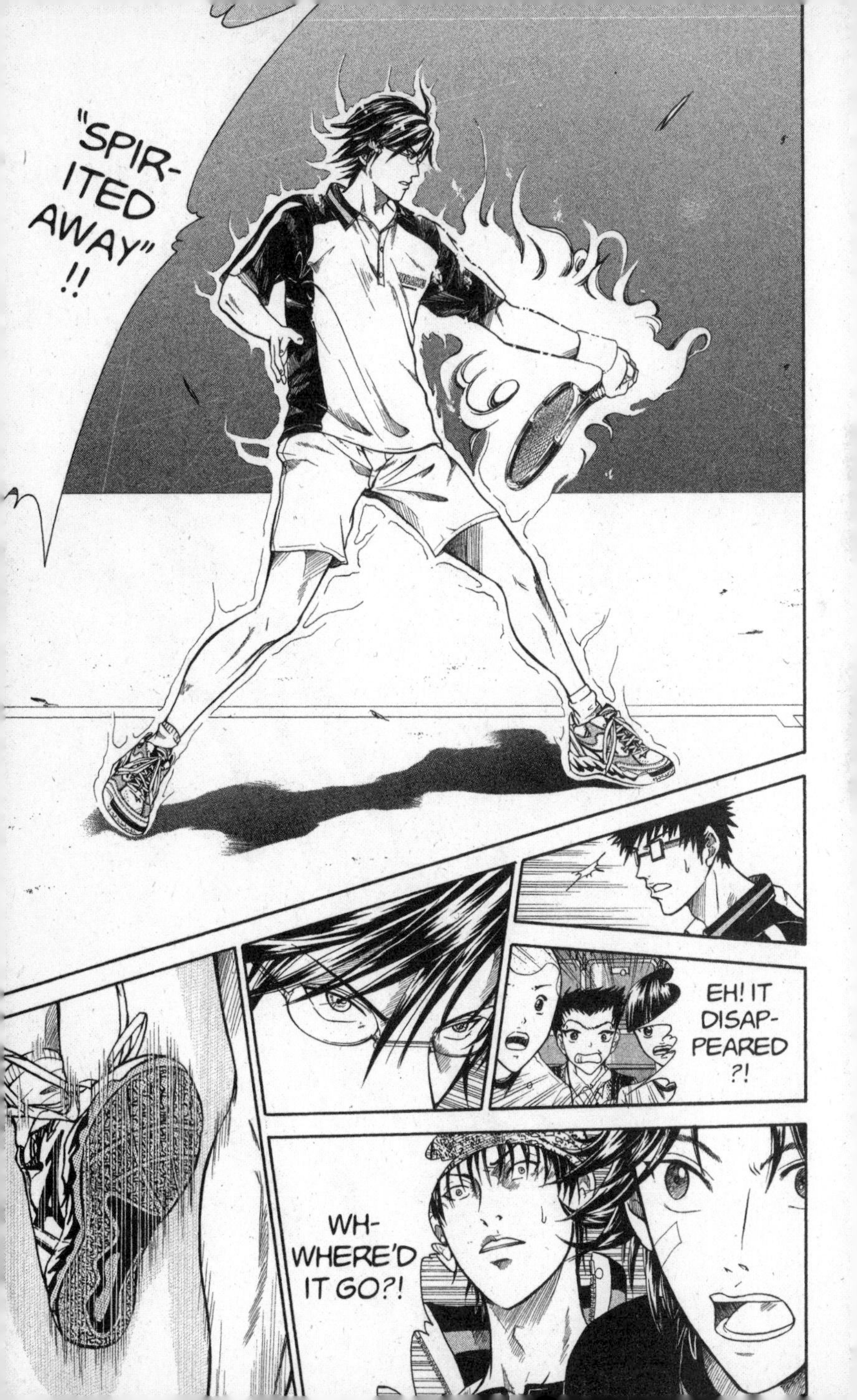
"SPIRITED AWAY"!!
EH! IT DISAPPEARED?!
WH-WHERE'D IT GO?!

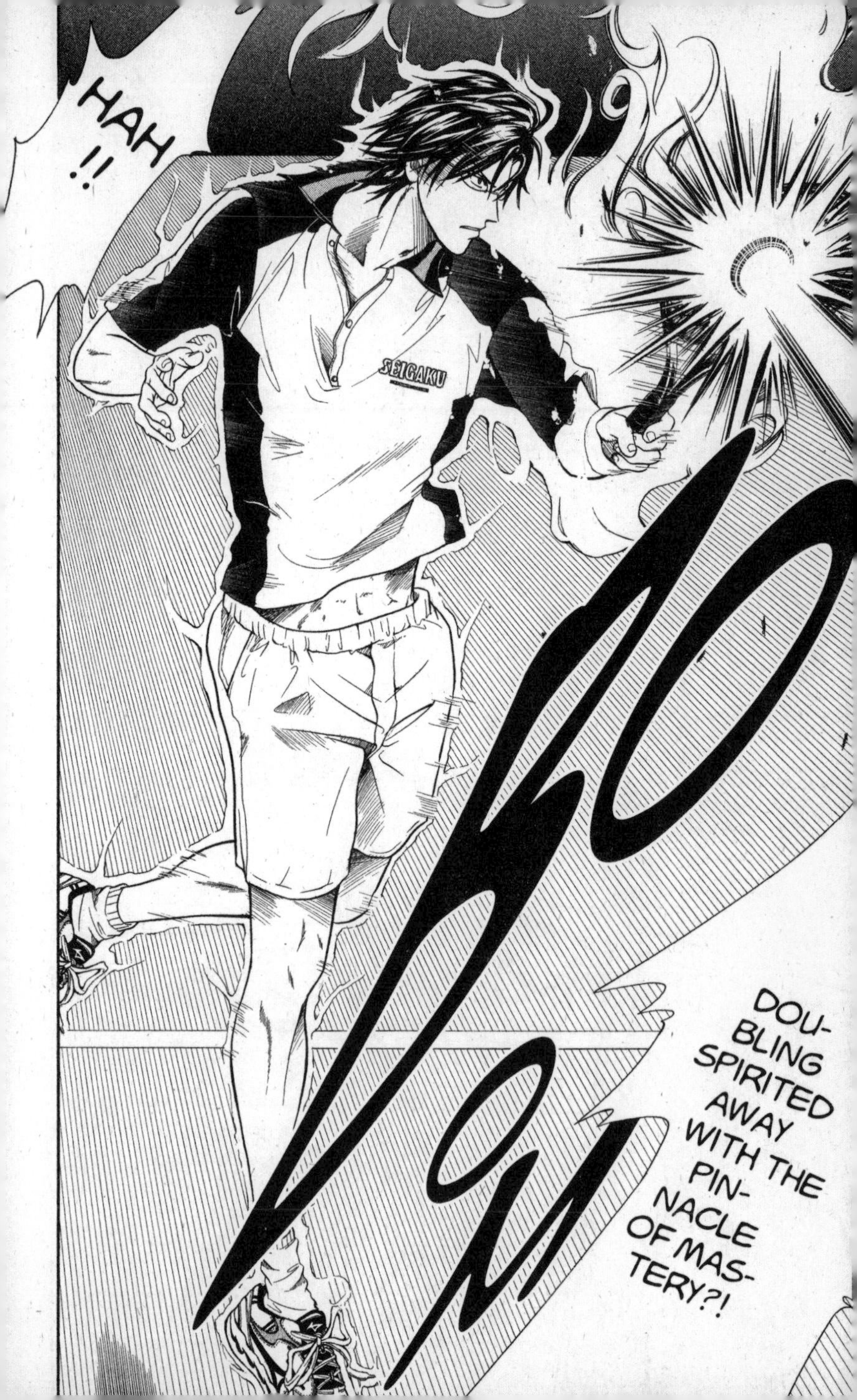
HAH!!
DOUBLING SPIRITED AWAY WITH THE PINNACLE OF MASTERY?!

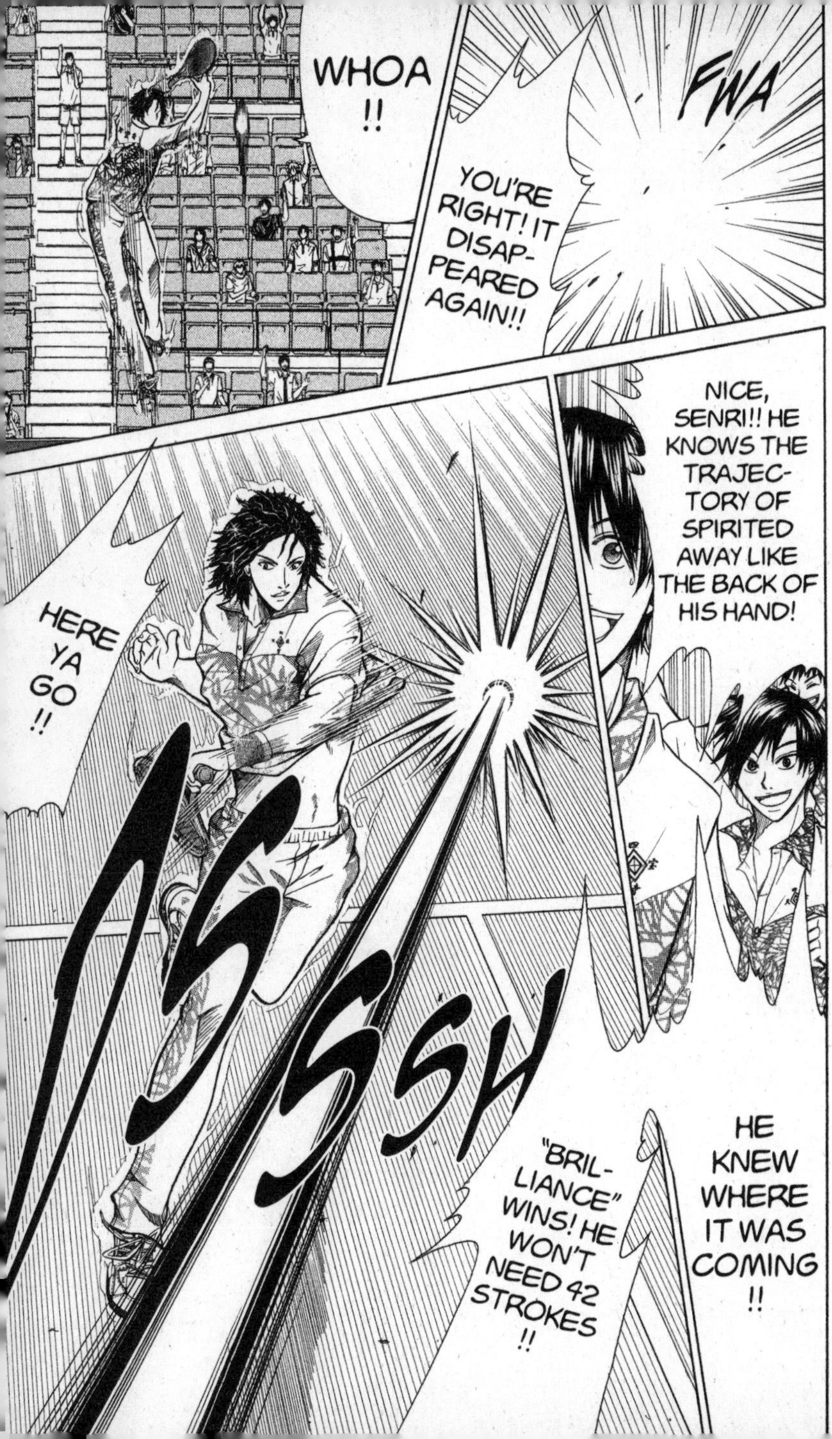
FWA
YOU'RE RIGHT!! IT DISAPPEARED AGAIN!!
WHOA!!
NICE, SENRI!! HE KNOWS THE TRAJECTORY OF SPIRITED AWAY LIKE THE BACK OF HIS HAND!
HERE YA GO!!
SSSH
HE KNEW WHERE IT WAS COMING!!
"BRILLIANCE" WINS! HE WON'T NEED 42 STROKES!!

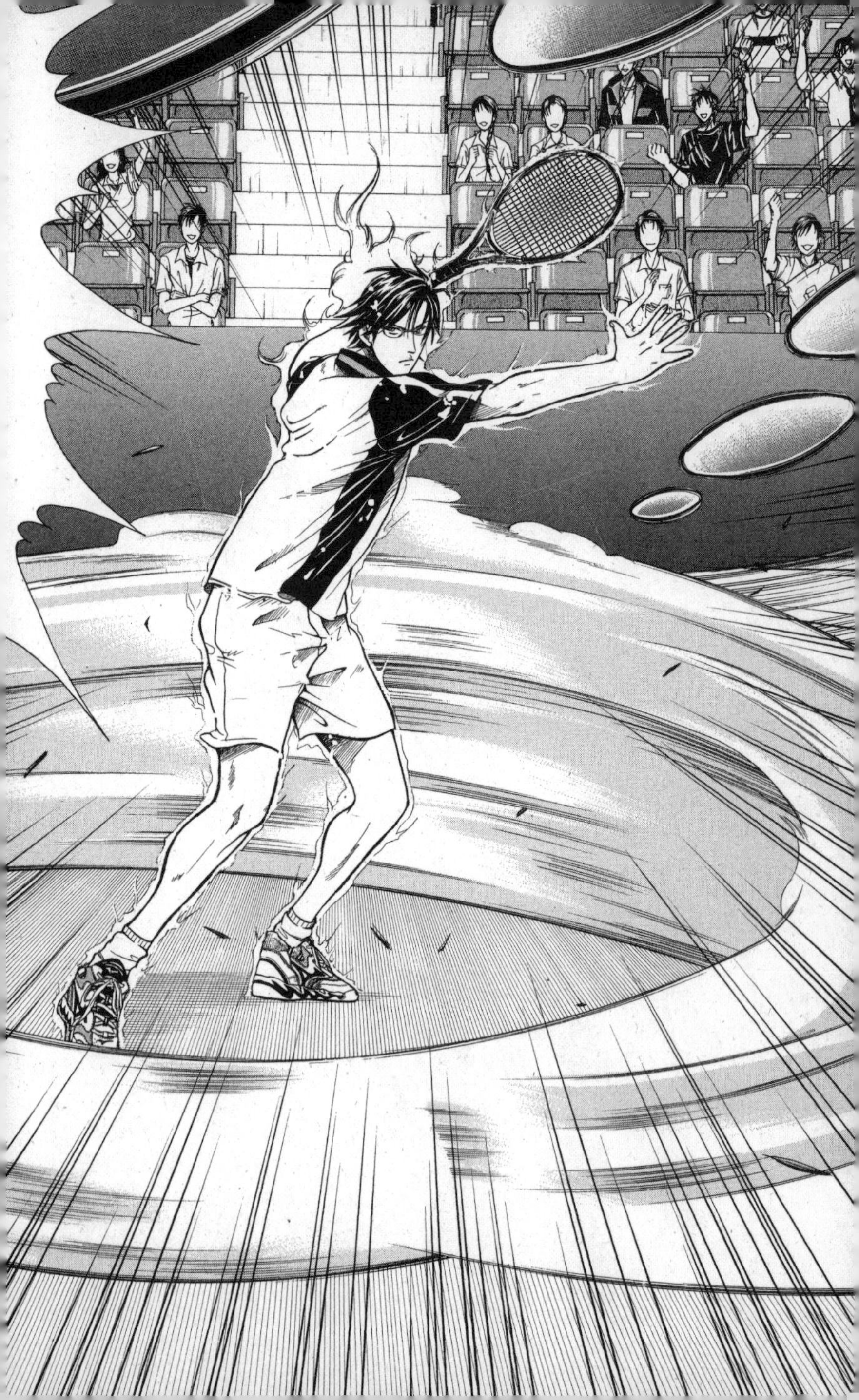

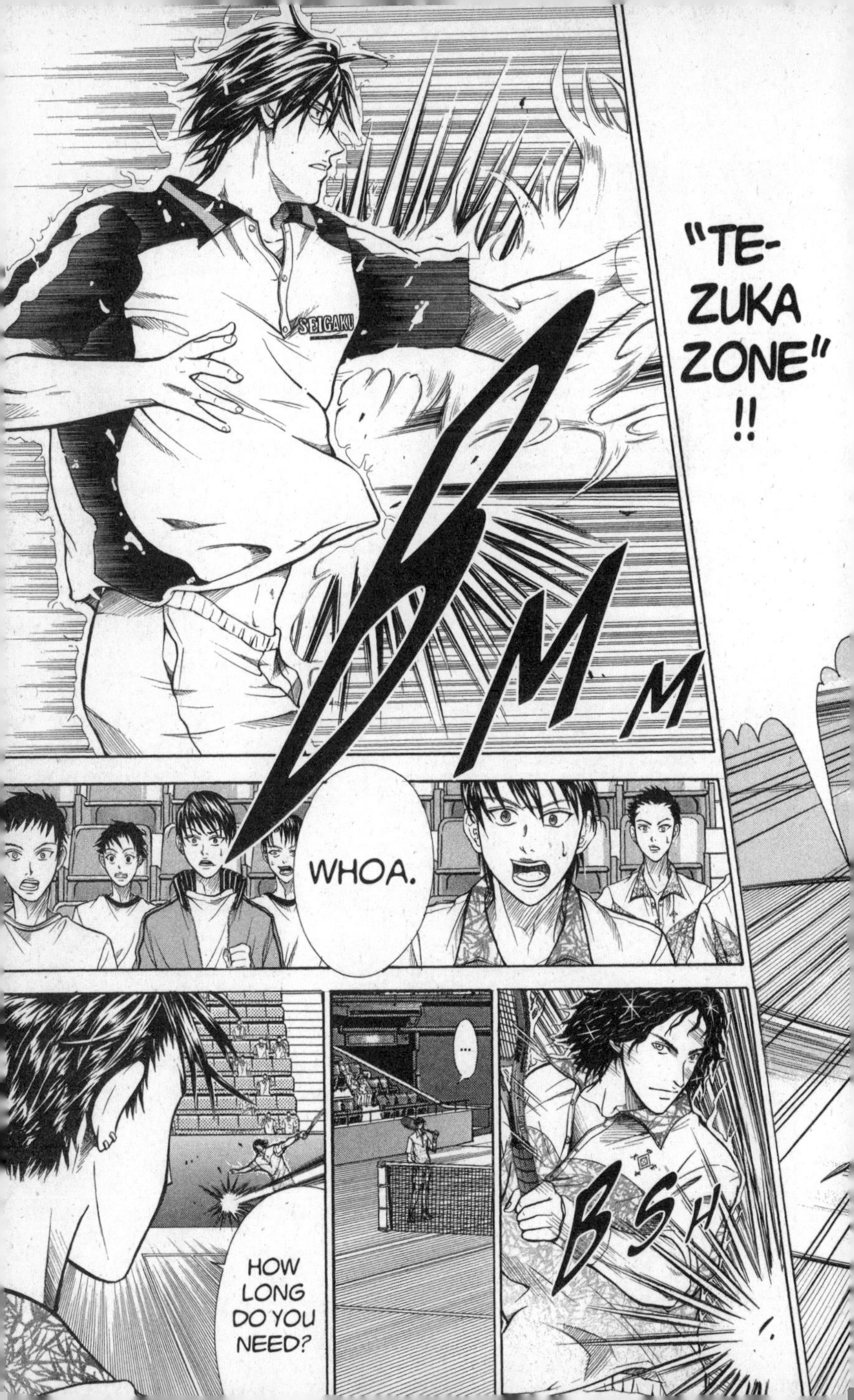
"TE-
ZUKA
ZONE"
!!
SMMM
WHOA.
BSH
...
HOW LONG DO YOU NEED?

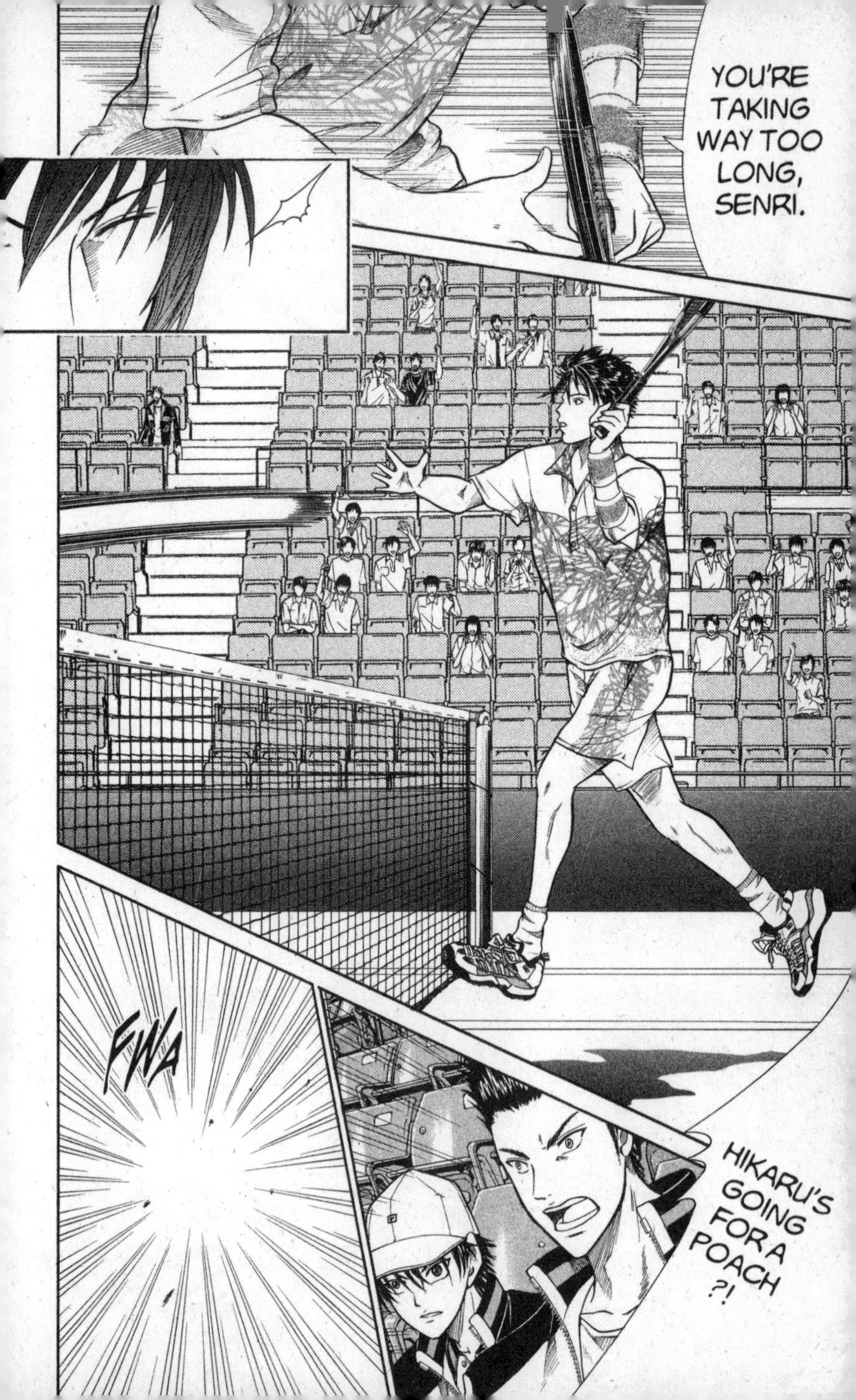
YOU'RE TAKING WAY TOO LONG, SENRI.
FWA
HIKARU'S GOING FOR A POACH ?!

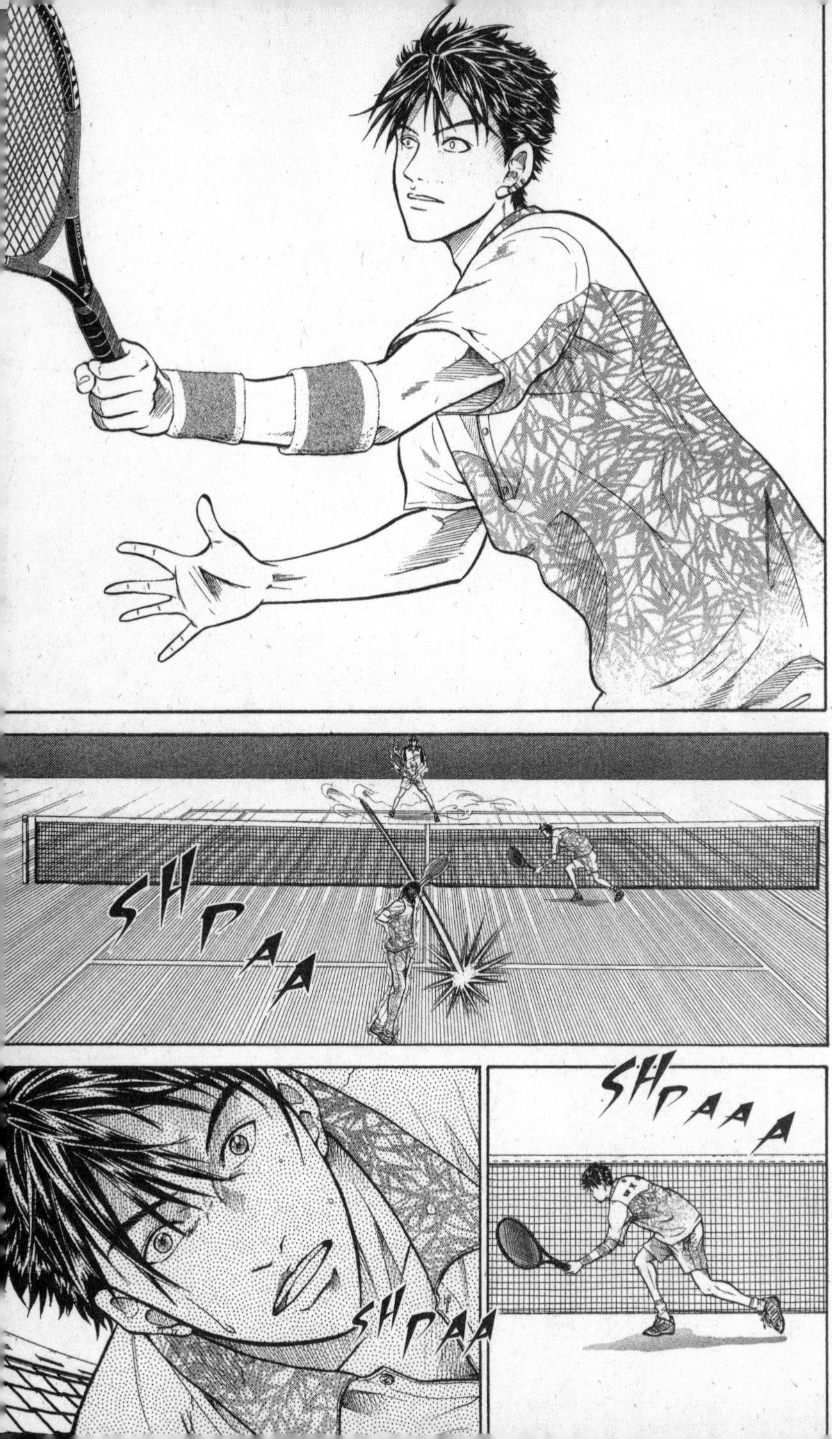
SHPAA
SHPAAA
SHPAA

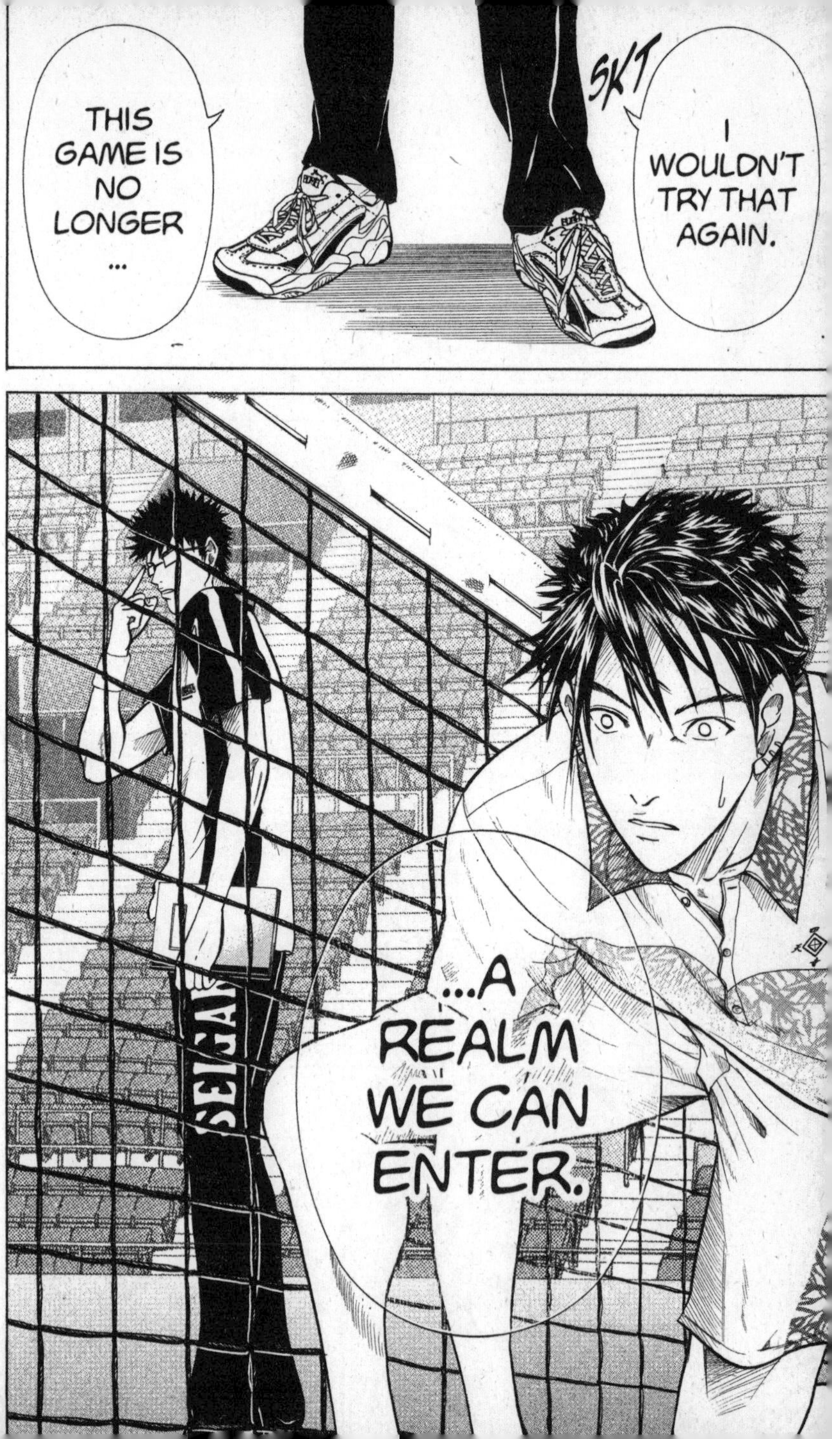
SKT
I WOULDN'T TRY THAT AGAIN.
THIS GAME IS NO LONGER ...
...A REALM WE CAN ENTER.

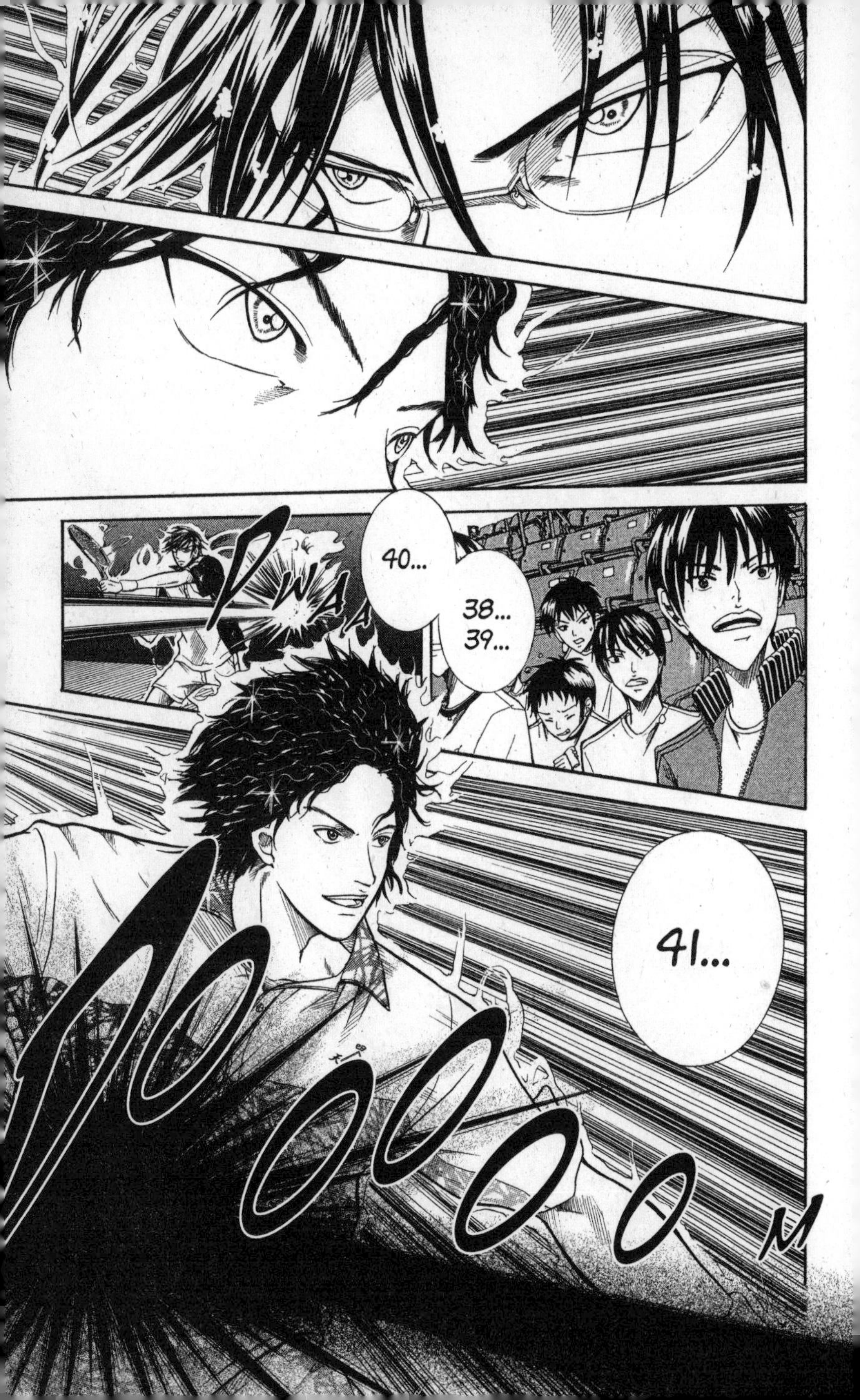
38...
39...
40...
DWAA
41...

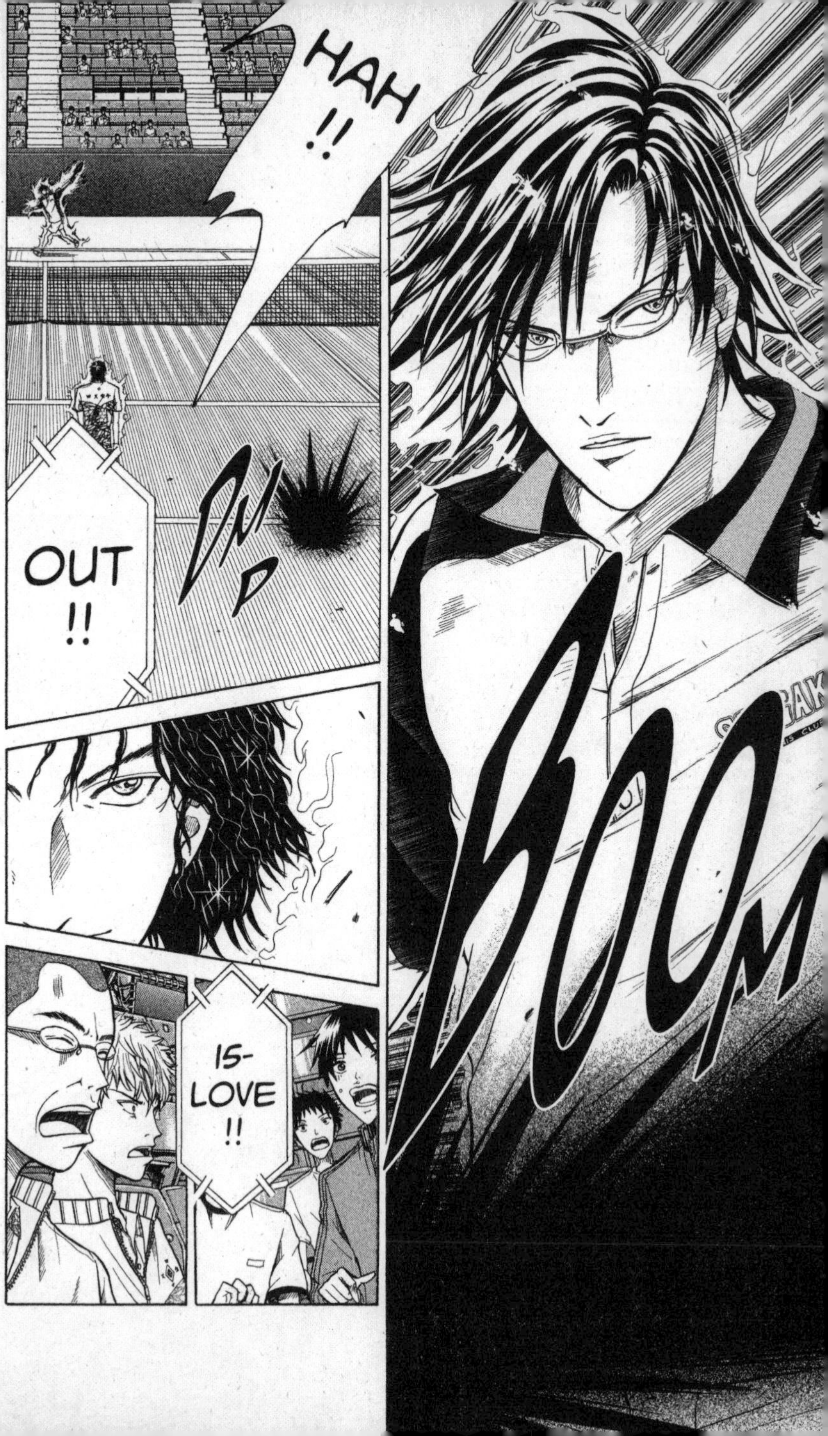
HAH!!
OUT!!
15-LOVE!!

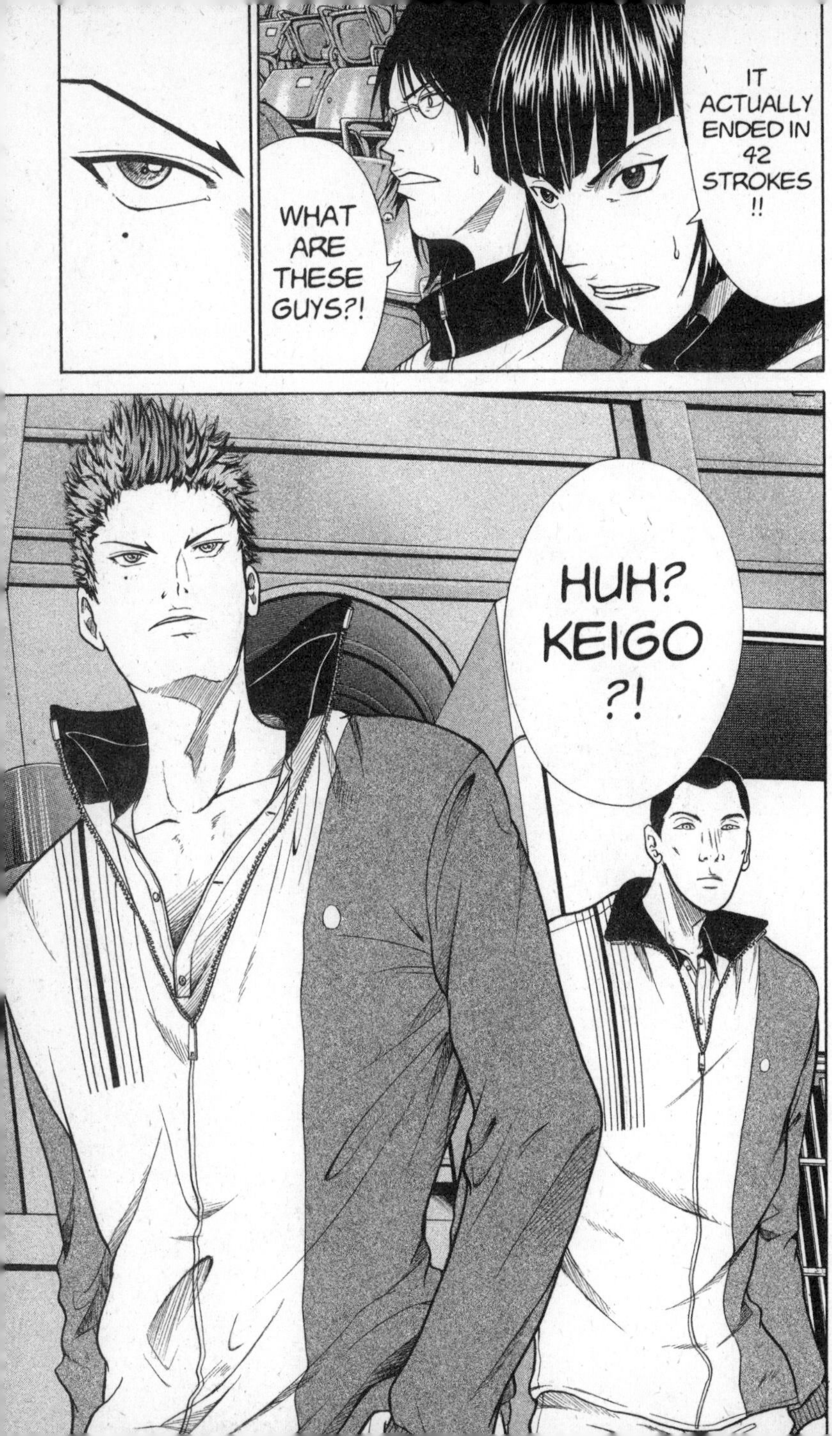
IT ACTUALLY ENDED IN 42 STROKES!!
WHAT ARE THESE GUYS?!
HUH? KEIGO?!

テニスの王子様

THE PRINCE OF TENNIS

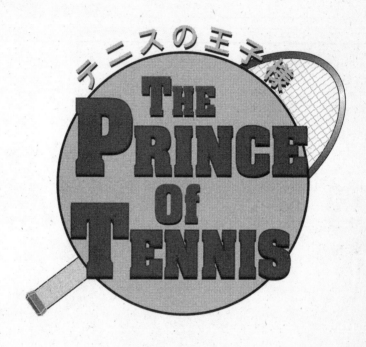

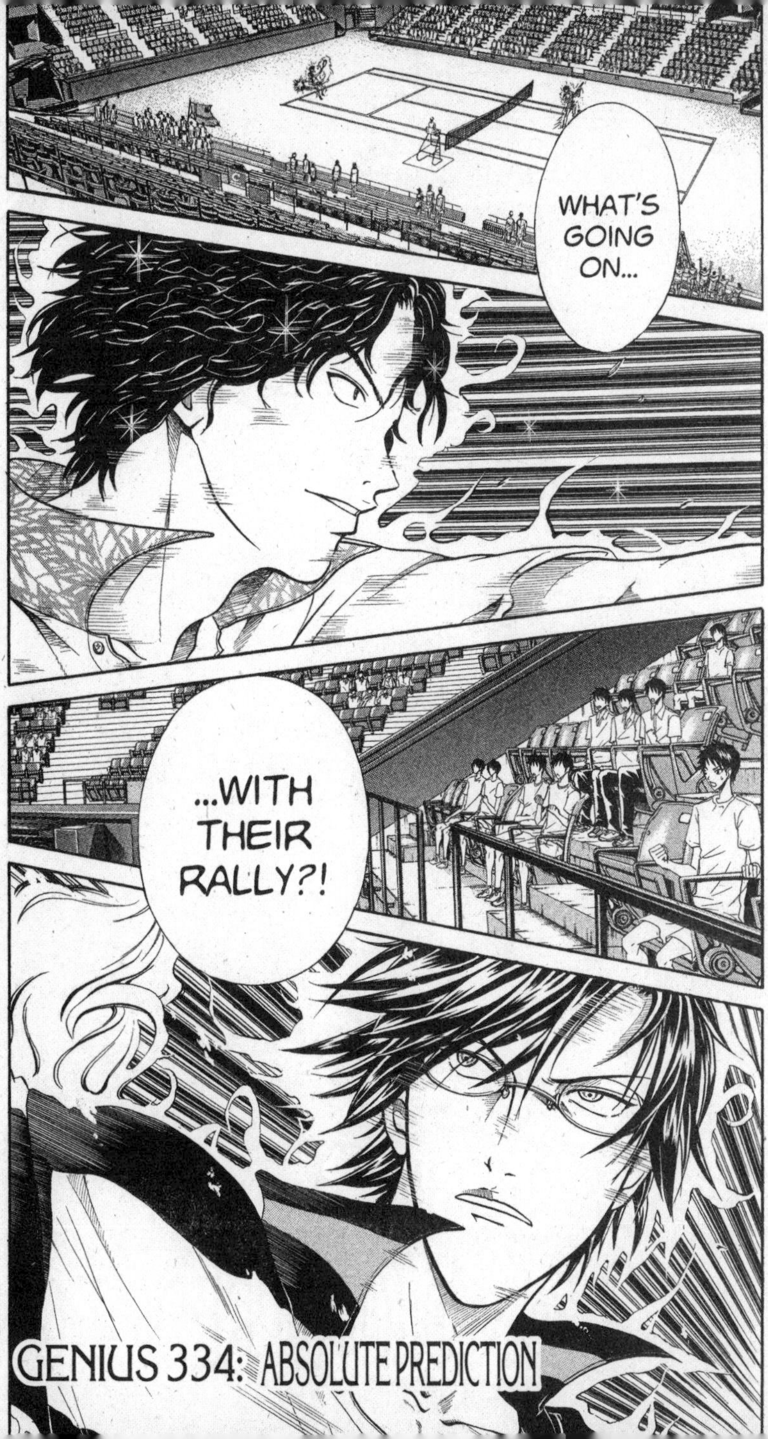
WHAT'S GOING ON...
...WITH THEIR RALLY?!
GENIUS 334: ABSOLUTE PREDICTION

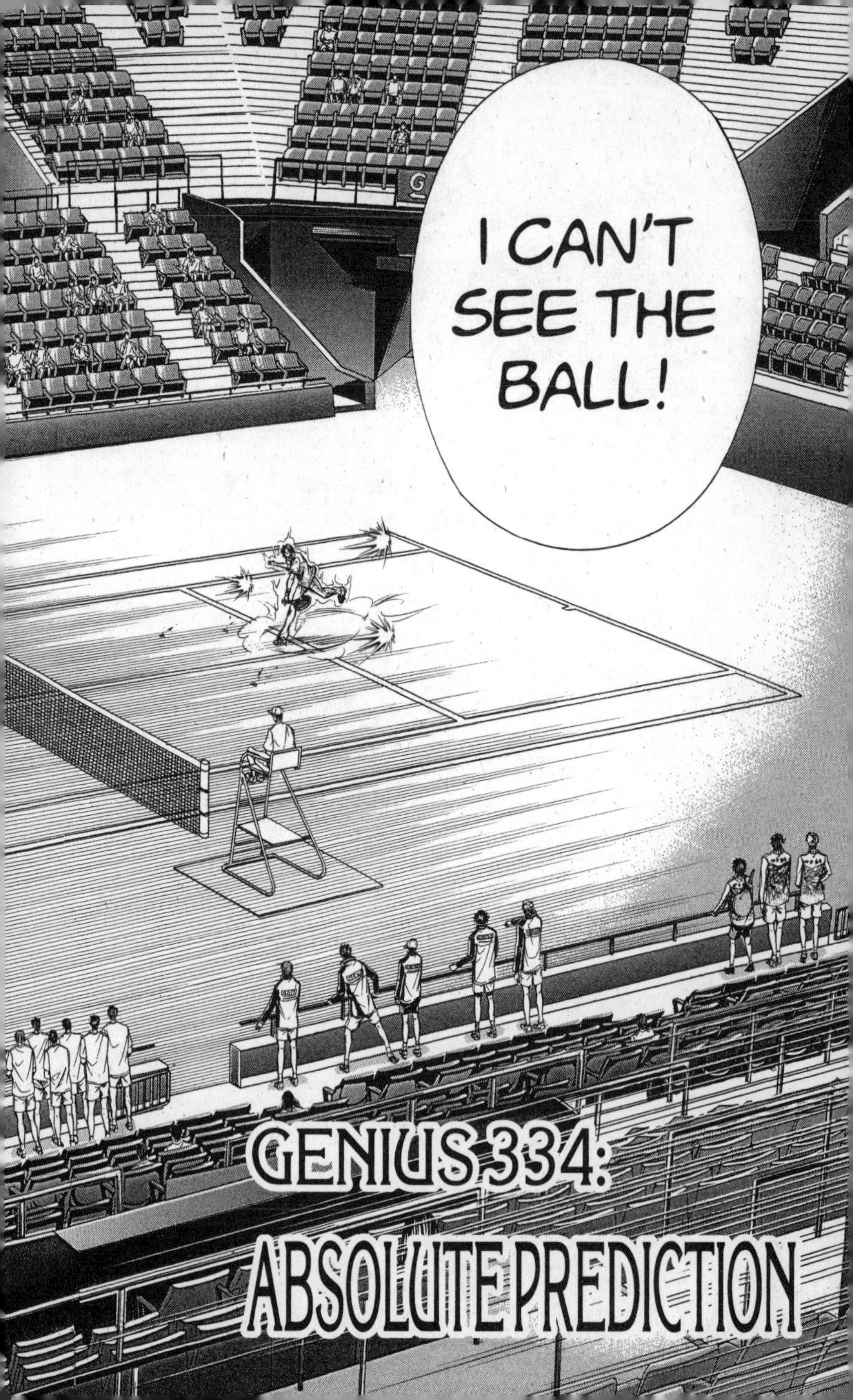
I CAN'T SEE THE BALL!
GENIUS 334:
ABSOLUTE PREDICTION

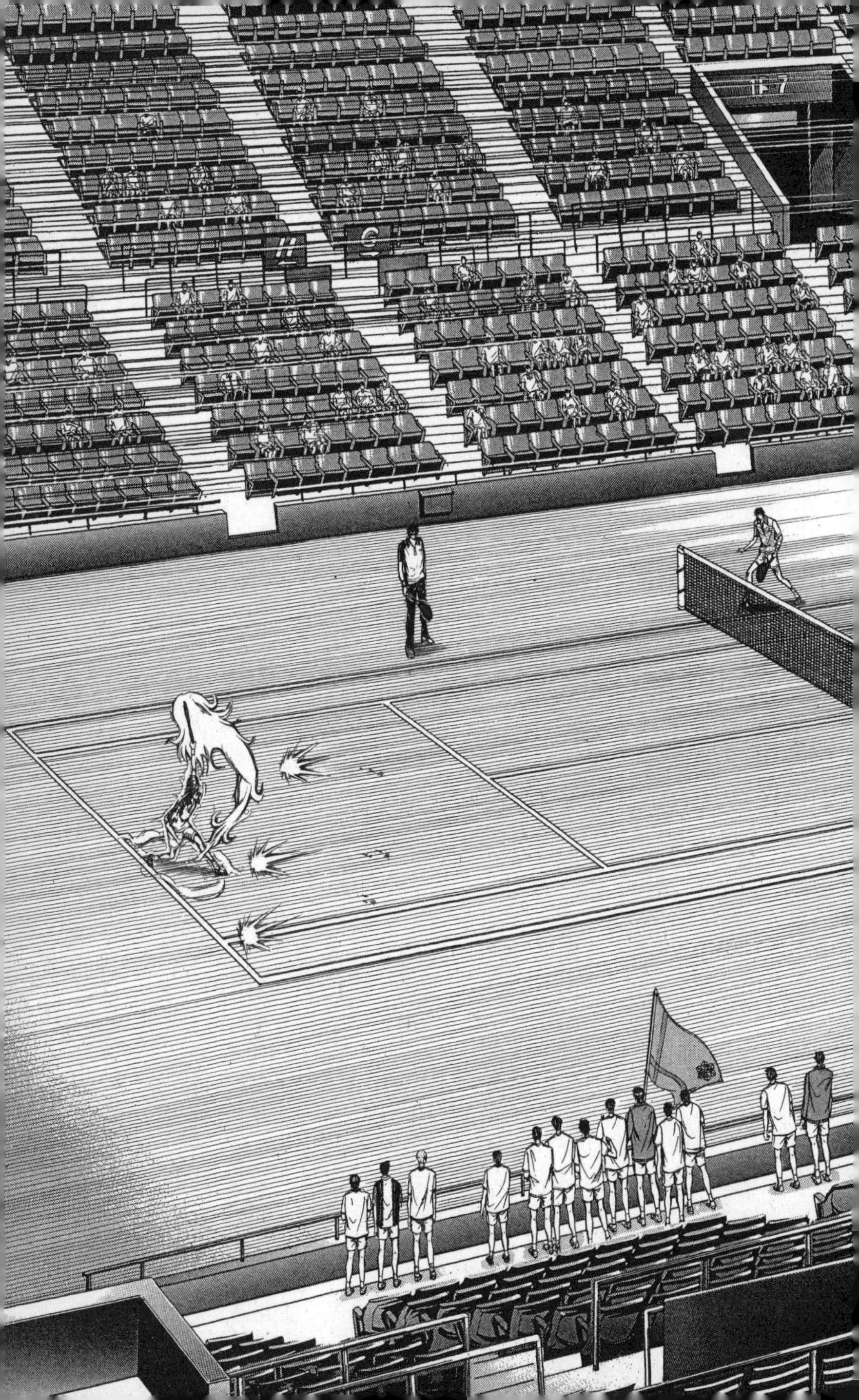

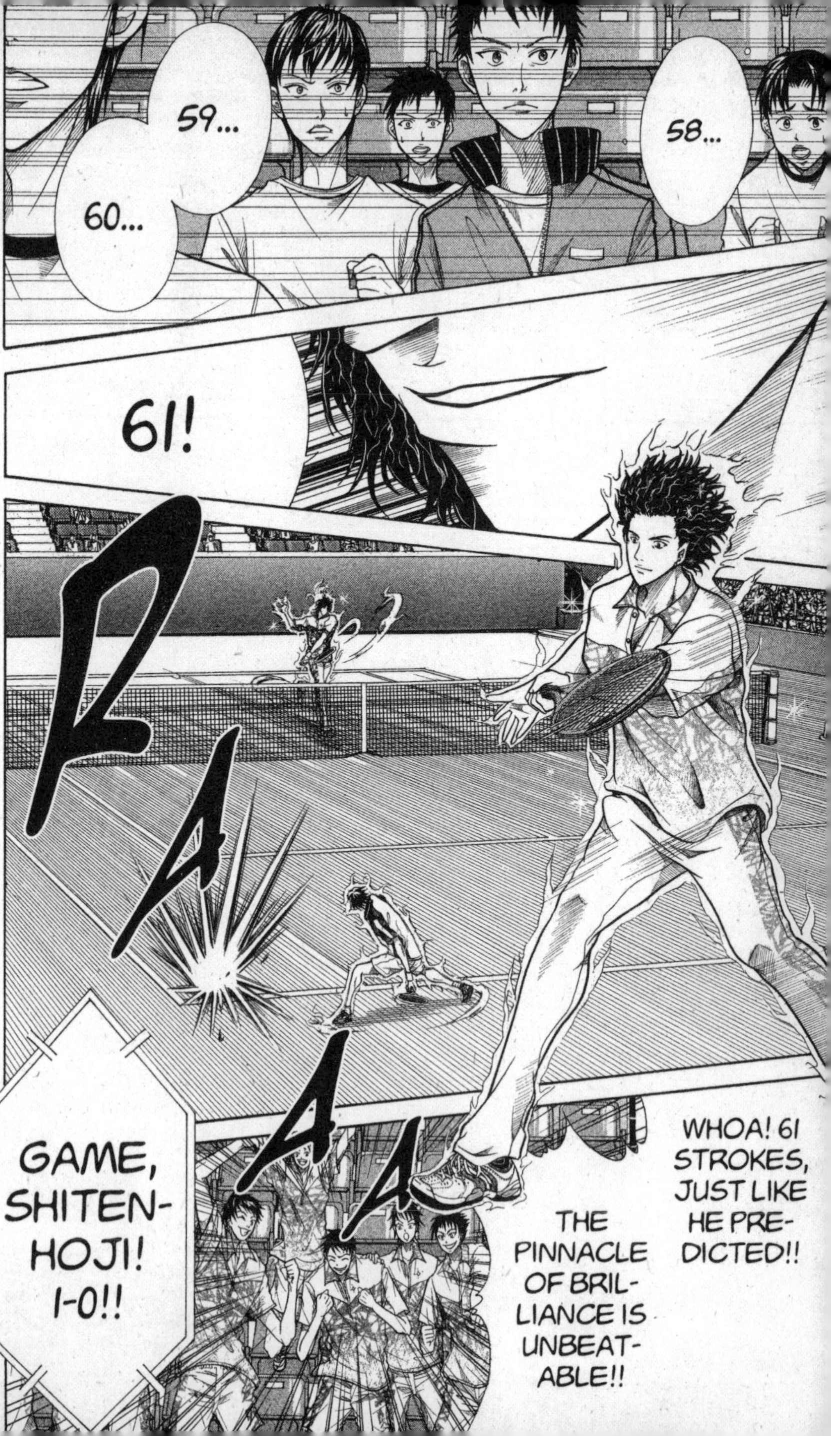
58...
59...
60...
61!
WHOA! 61 STROKES, JUST LIKE HE PRE-DICTED!!
THE PINNACLE OF BRIL-LIANCE IS UNBEAT-ABLE!!
GAME, SHITEN-HOJI! 1-0!!

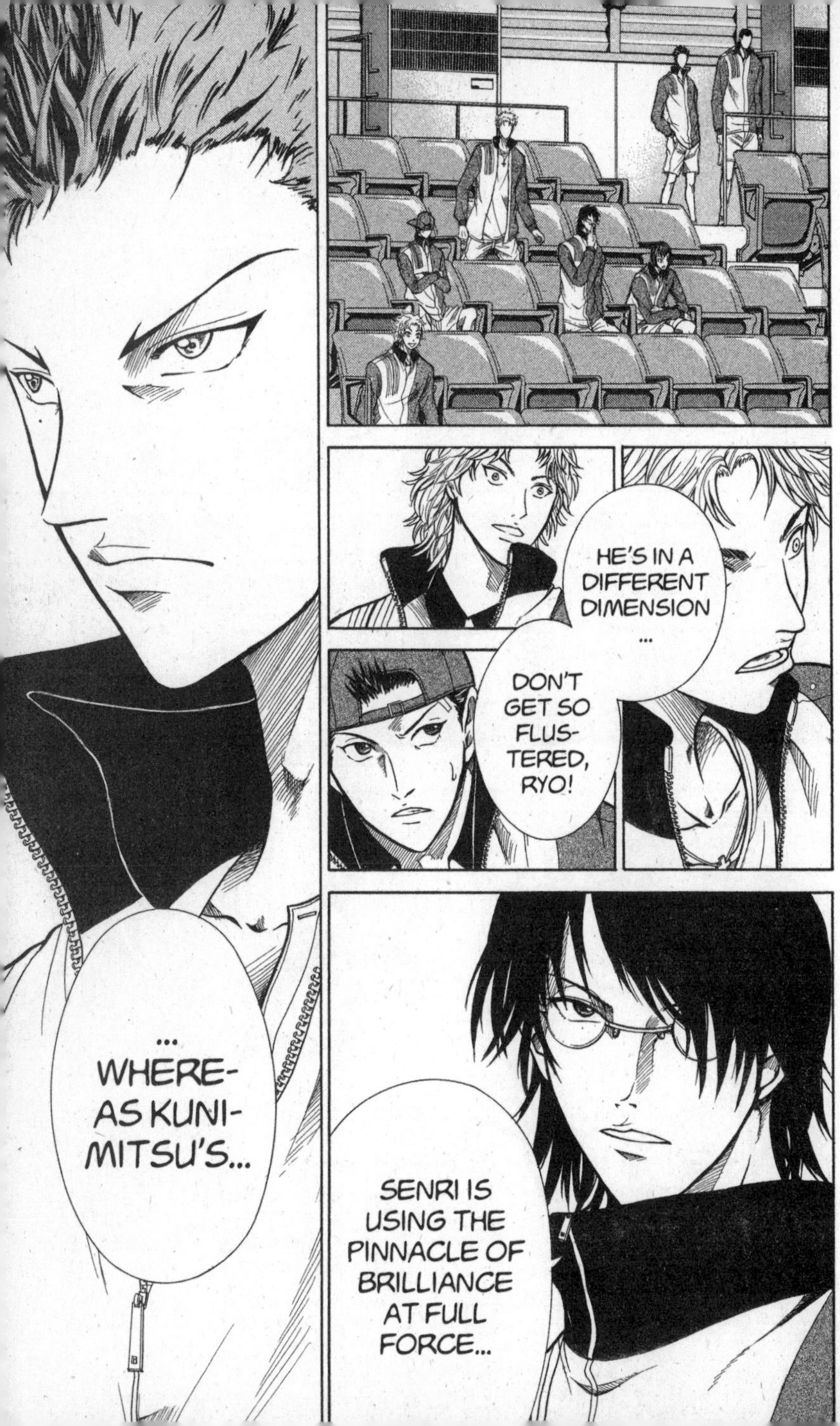
HE'S IN A DIFFERENT DIMENSION ...
DON'T GET SO FLUS-TERED, RYO!
SENRI IS USING THE PINNACLE OF BRILLIANCE AT FULL FORCE...
... WHERE-AS KUNI-MITSU'S...

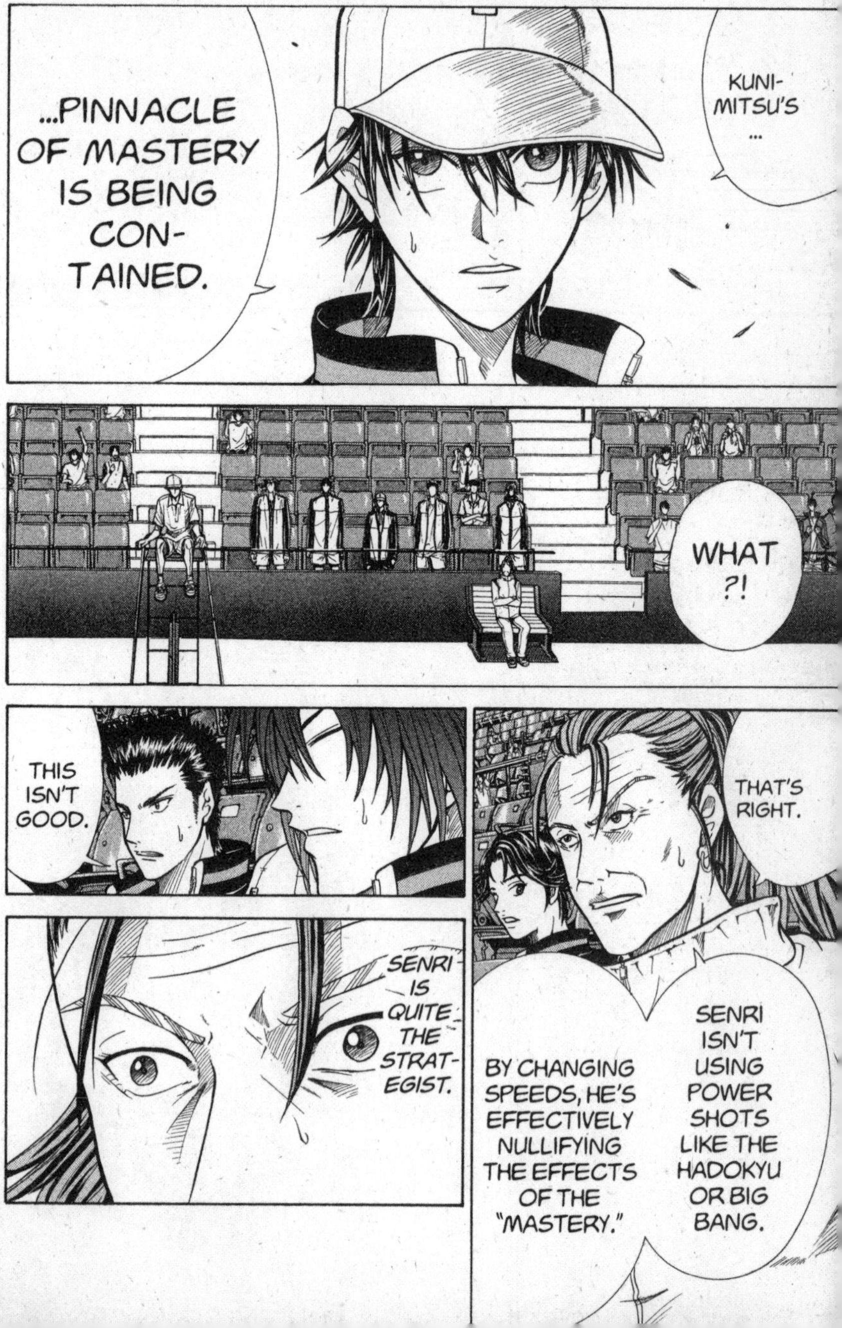
KUNI-MITSU'S ...
...PINNACLE OF MASTERY IS BEING CON-TAINED.
WHAT ?!
THAT'S RIGHT.
SENRI ISN'T USING POWER SHOTS LIKE THE HADOKYU OR BIG BANG.
BY CHANGING SPEEDS, HE'S EFFECTIVELY NULLIFYING THE EFFECTS OF THE "MASTERY."
THIS ISN'T GOOD.
SENRI IS QUITE THE STRAT-EGIST.

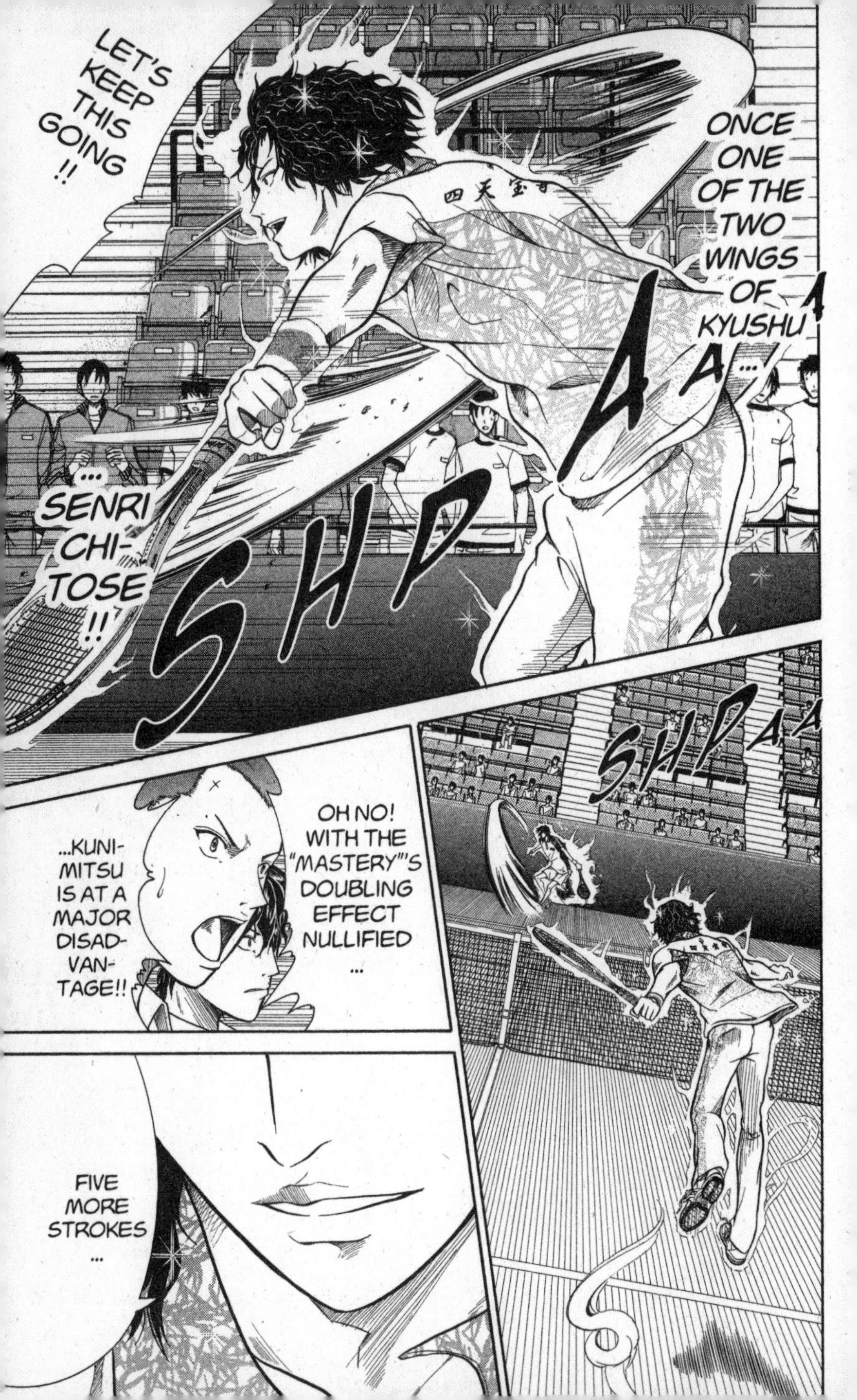

ONCE ONE OF THE TWO WINGS OF KYUSHU
...
LET'S KEEP THIS GOING!!
SHDAAA...
...SENRI CHITOSE!!
SHDAA
OH NO! WITH THE "MASTERY"'S DOUBLING EFFECT NULLIFIED...
...KUNIMITSU IS AT A MAJOR DISADVANTAGE!!
FIVE MORE STROKES...

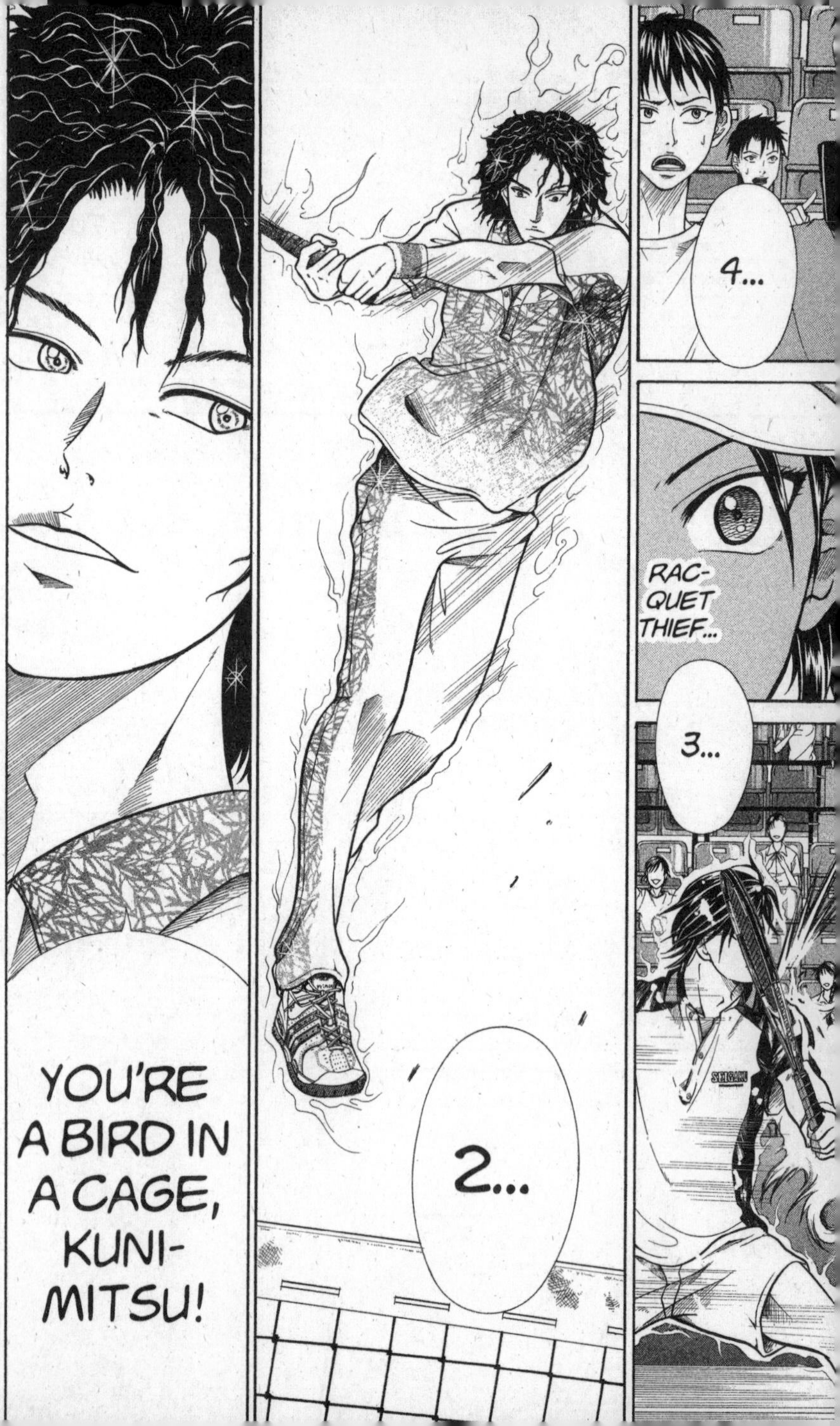
4...
RAC-
QUET
THIEF...
3...
SEIGAKU
2...
YOU'RE A BIRD IN A CAGE, KUNI- MITSU!

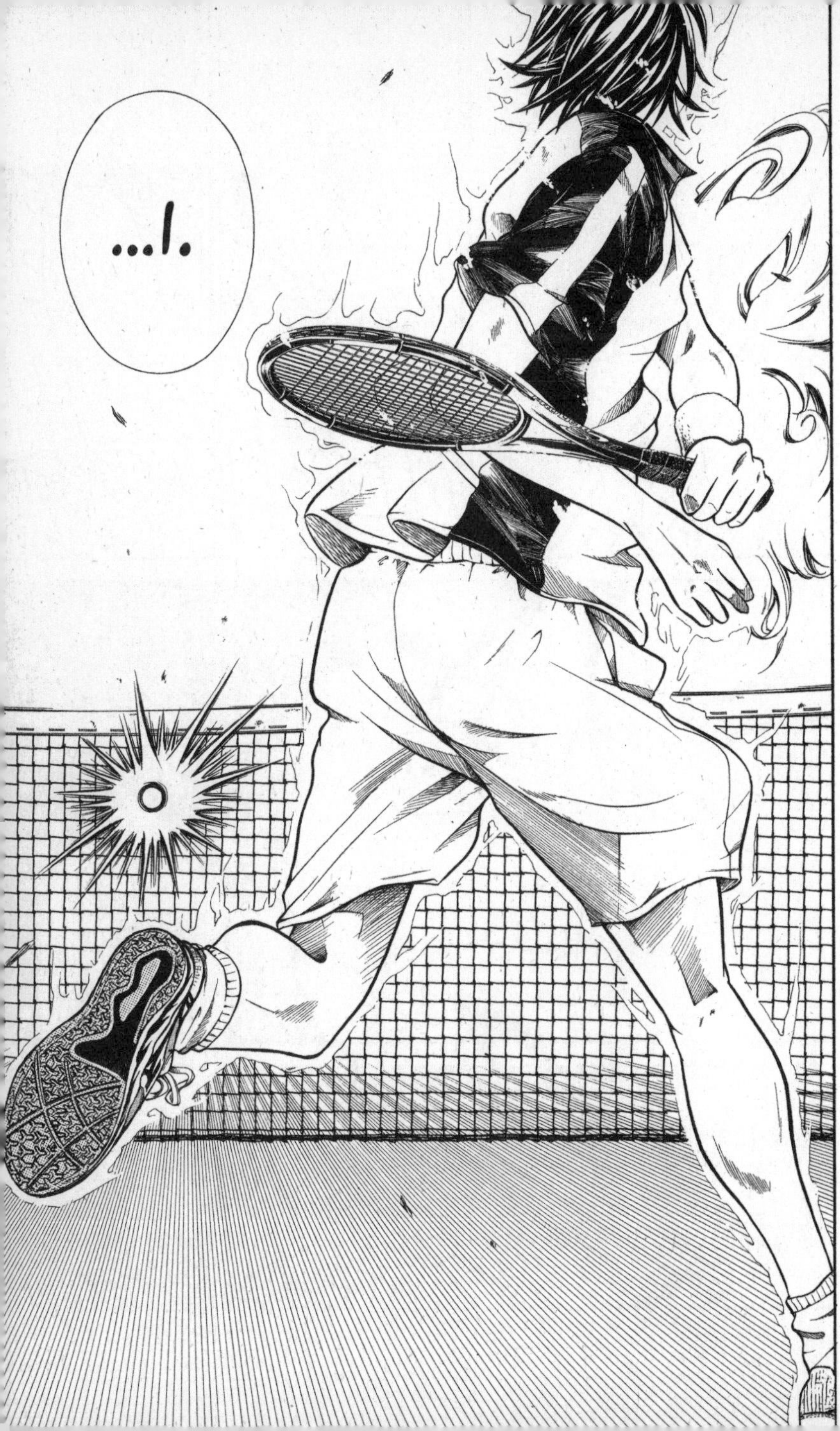
...!

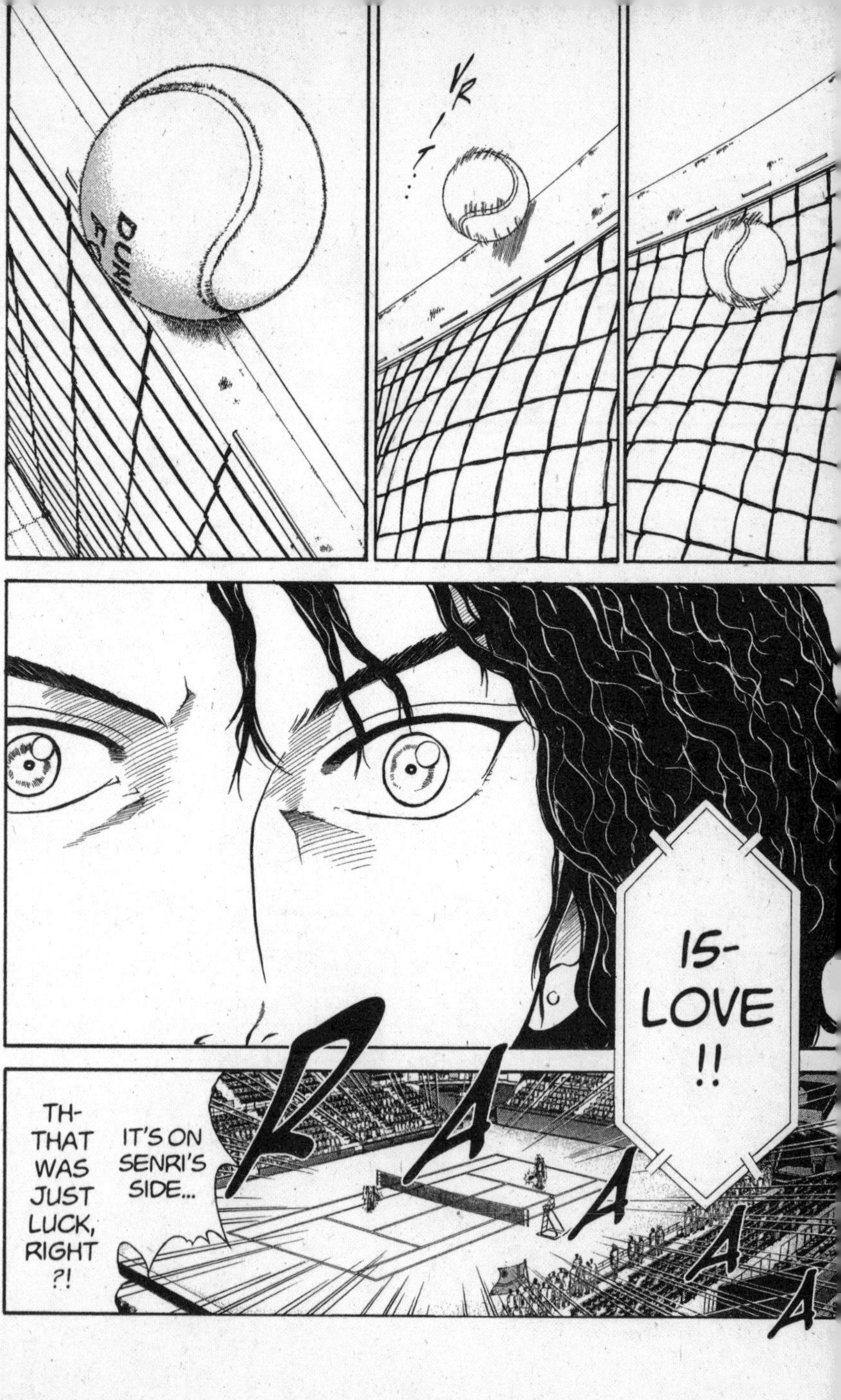
VRI-T...
15-LOVE!!
BAAAAA
IT'S ON SENRI'S SIDE...
TH-THAT WAS JUST LUCK, RIGHT?!

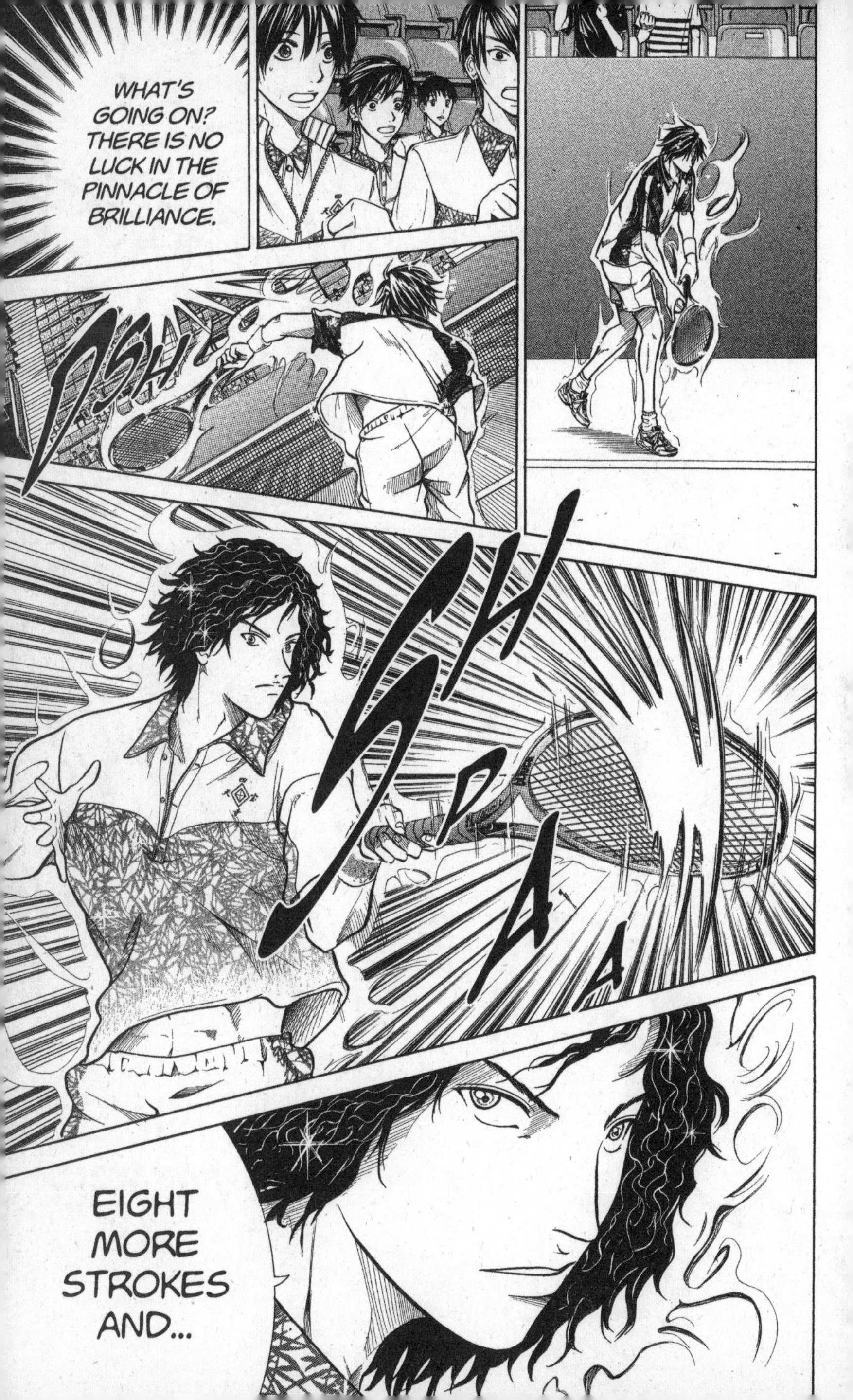
WHAT'S GOING ON? THERE IS NO LUCK IN THE PINNACLE OF BRILLIANCE.
DASH
EIGHT MORE STROKES AND...

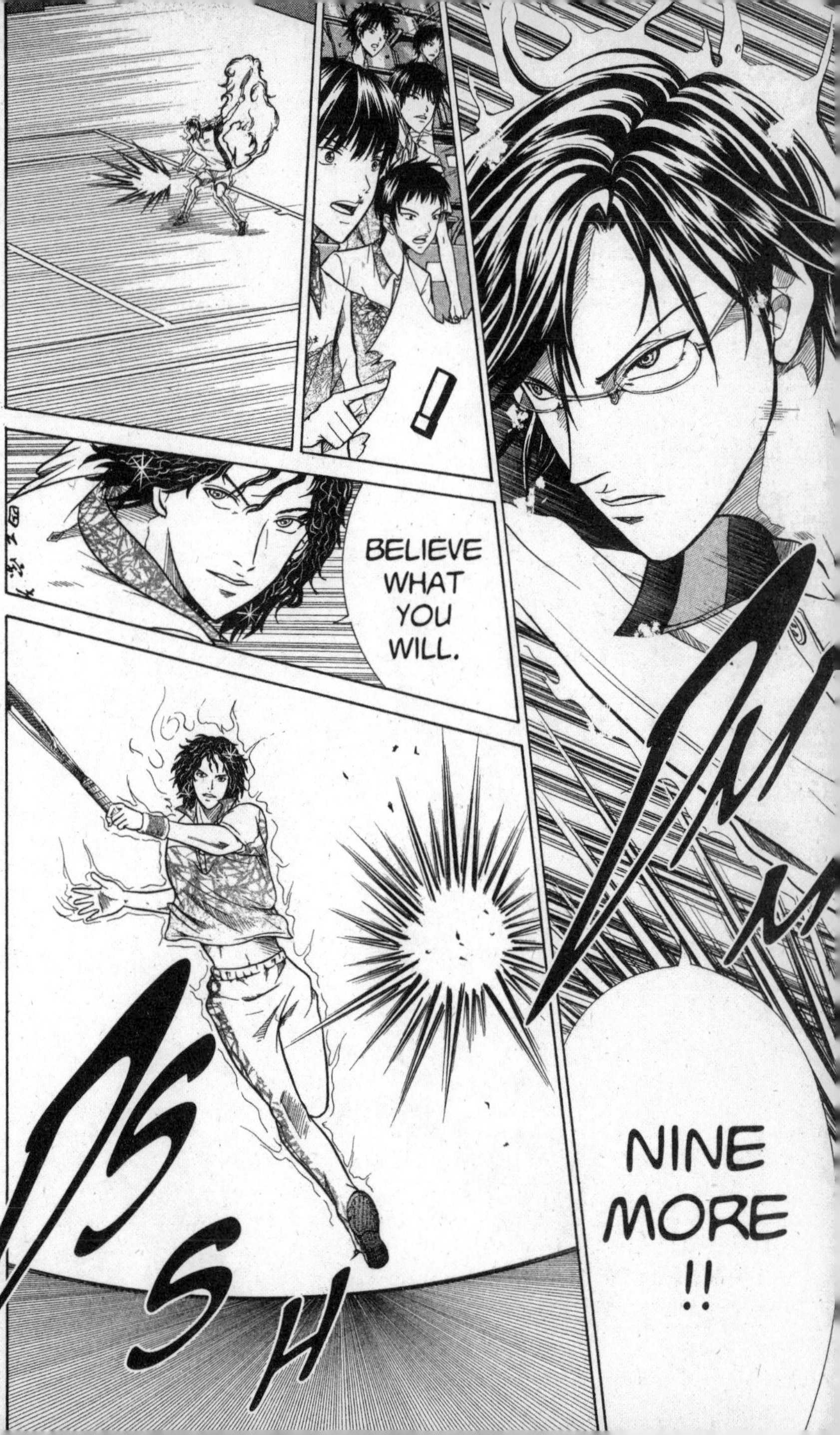
NINE MORE !!
!
BELIEVE WHAT YOU WILL.

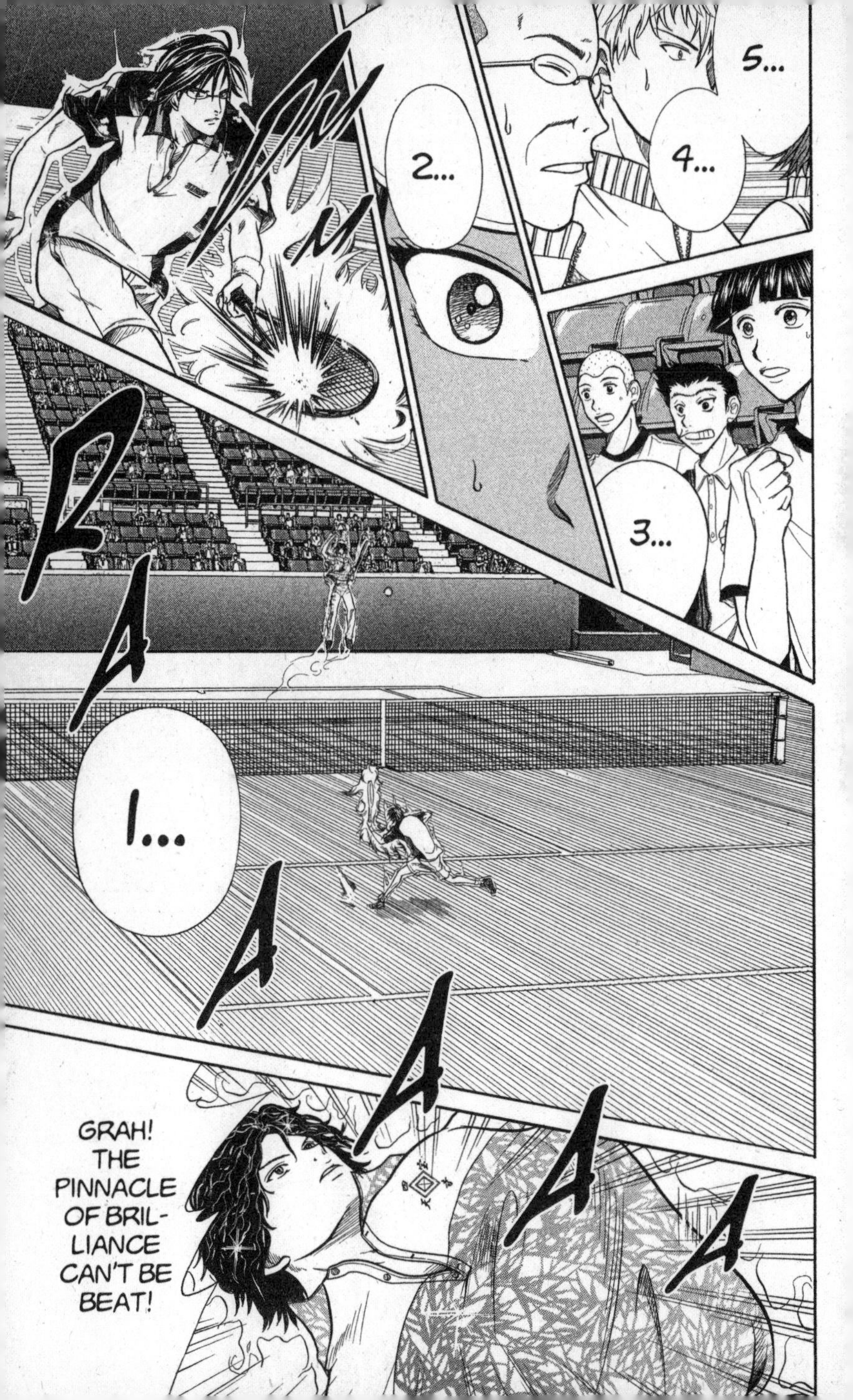
5...
4...
3...
2...
I...
GRAH! THE PINNACLE OF BRIL-LIANCE CAN'T BE BEAT!

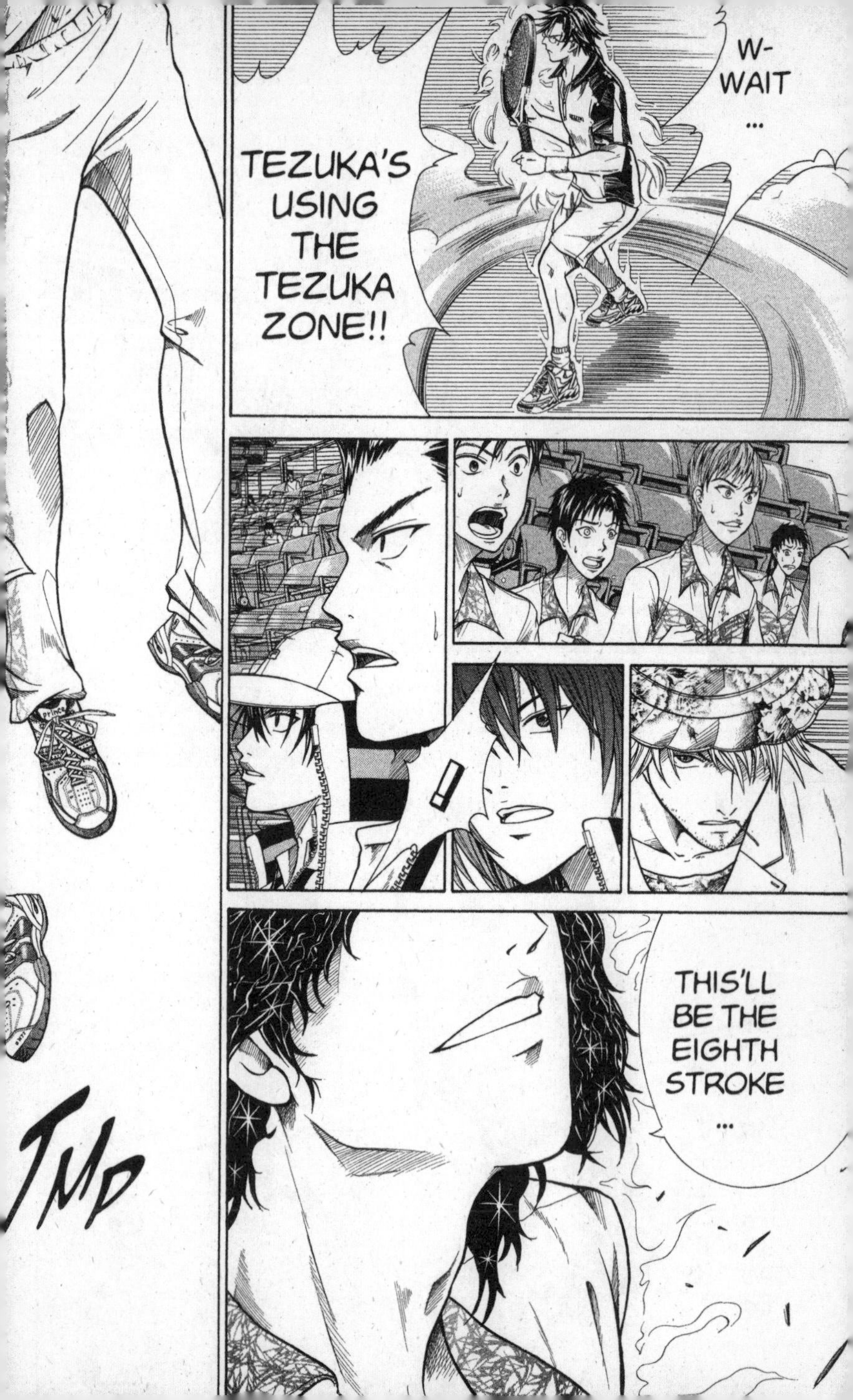
W-WAIT ...
TEZUKA'S USING THE TEZUKA ZONE!!
!
THIS'LL BE THE EIGHTH STROKE ...
TMP

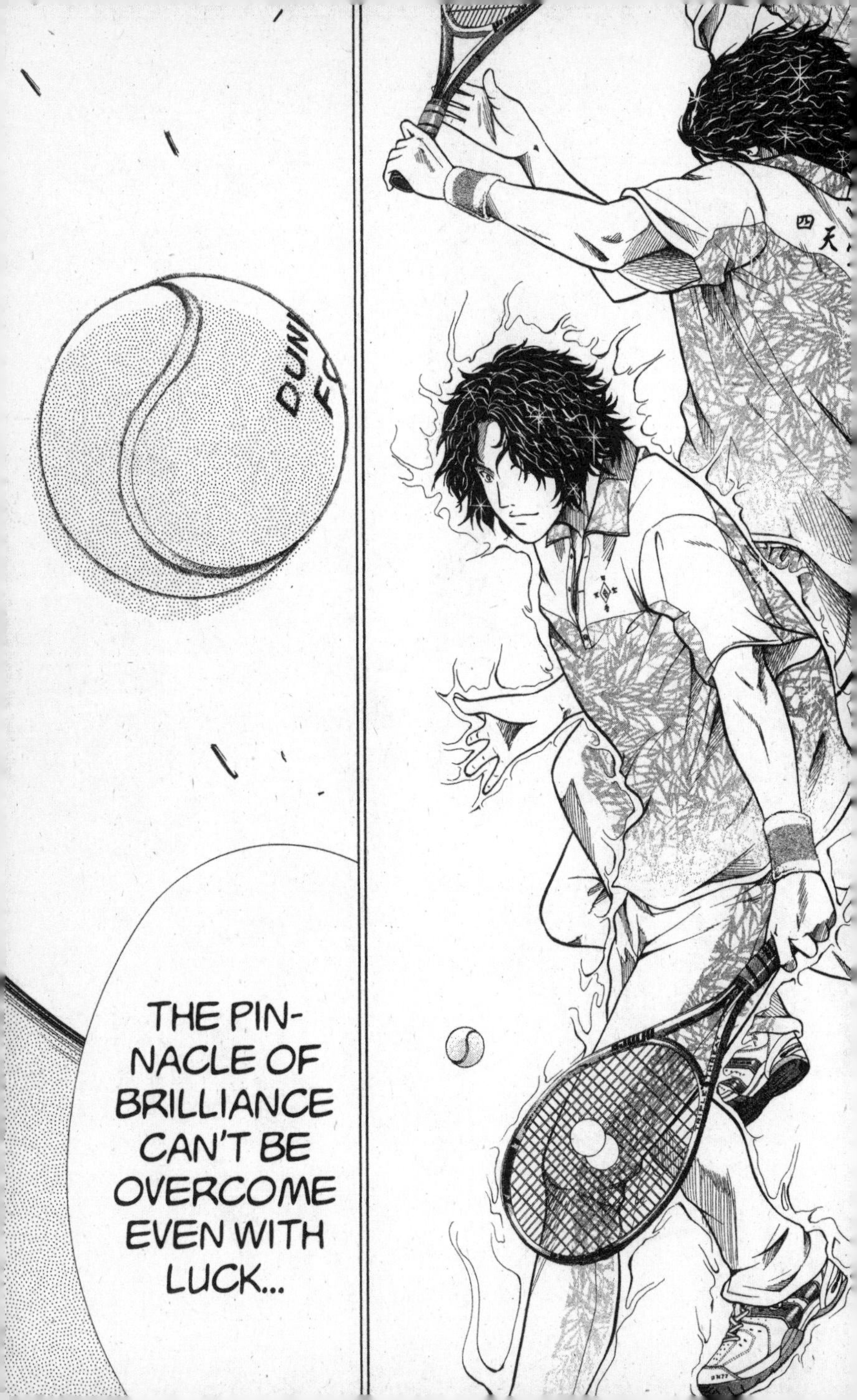
THE PIN-
NACLE OF
BRILLIANCE
CAN'T BE
OVERCOME
EVEN WITH
LUCK...

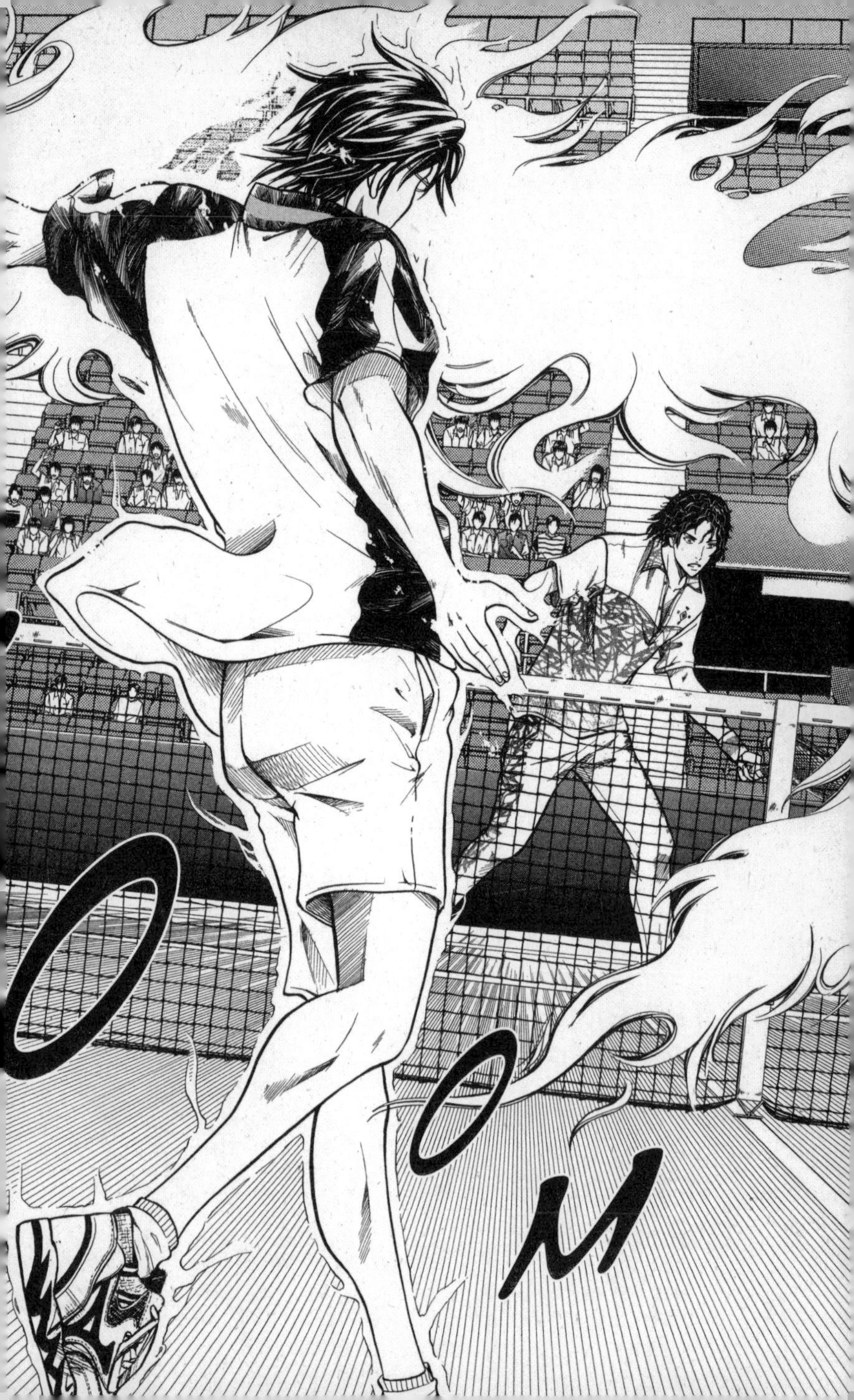
OOM

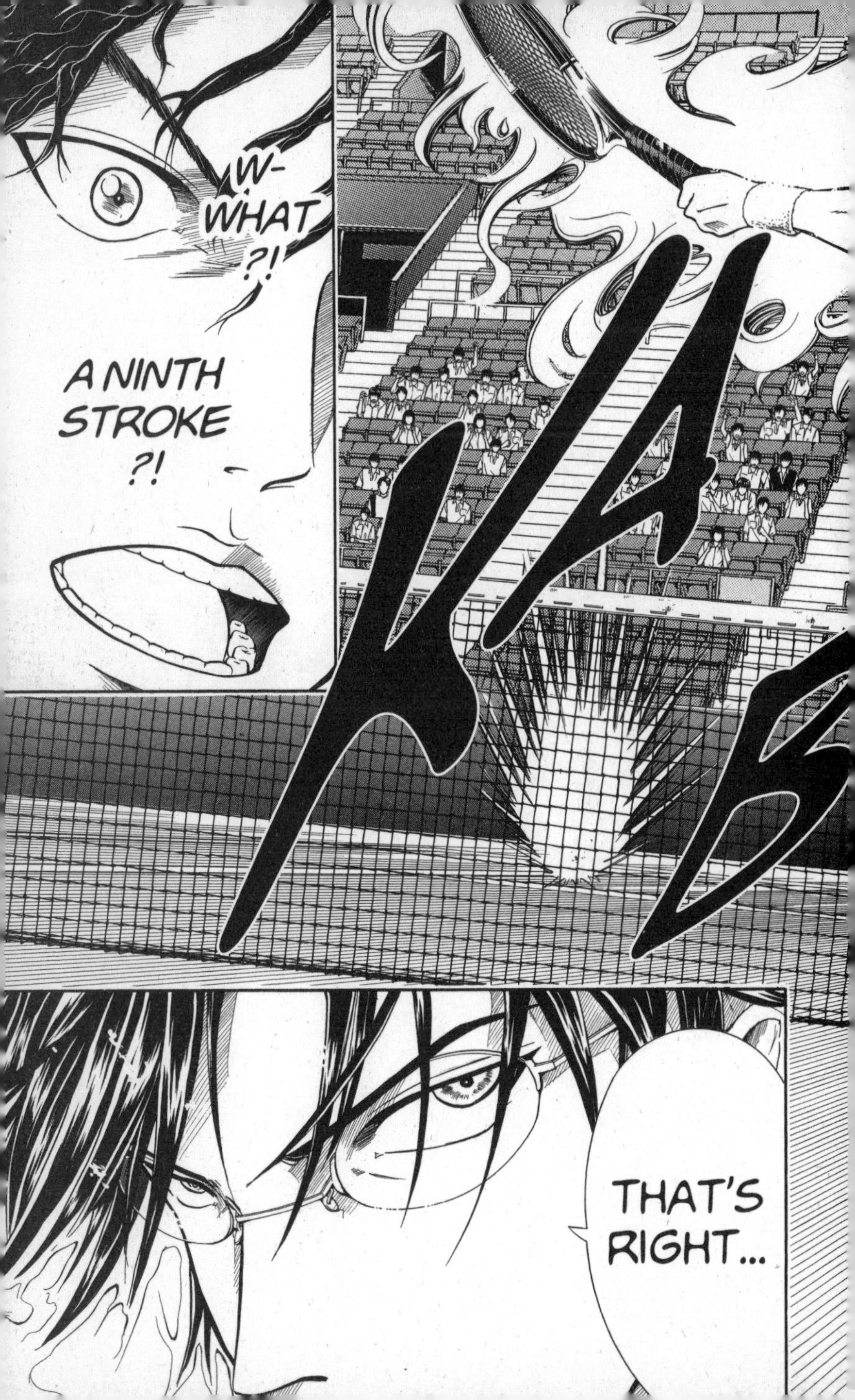
W-WHAT ?!
A NINTH STROKE ?!
THAT'S RIGHT...

テニスの王子様

THE PRINCE OF TENNIS

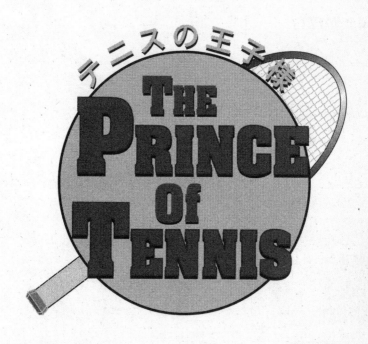

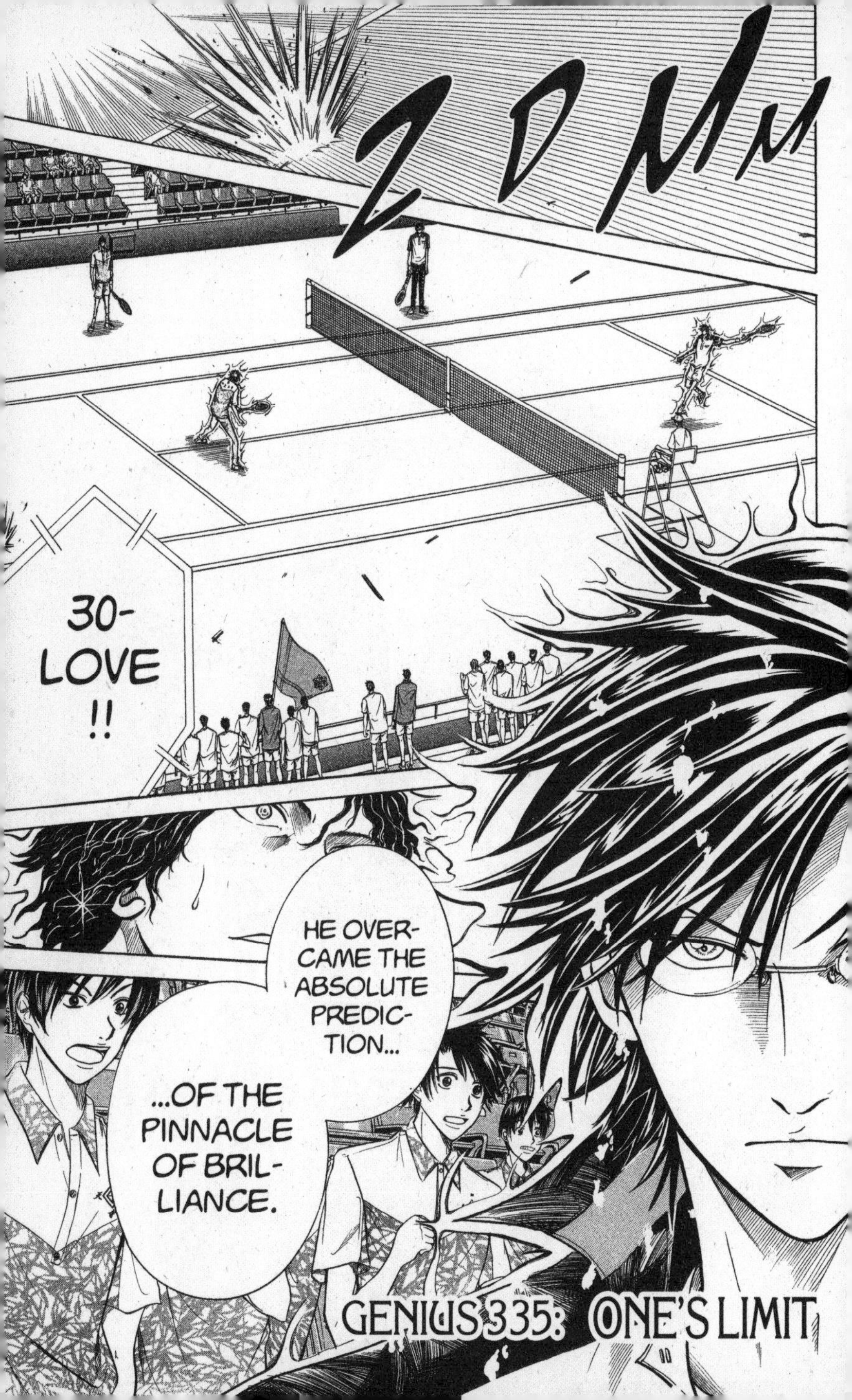
ZDMM
30-LOVE!!
HE OVER-CAME THE ABSOLUTE PREDIC-TION...
...OF THE PINNACLE OF BRIL-LIANCE.
GENIUS 335: ONE'S LIMIT

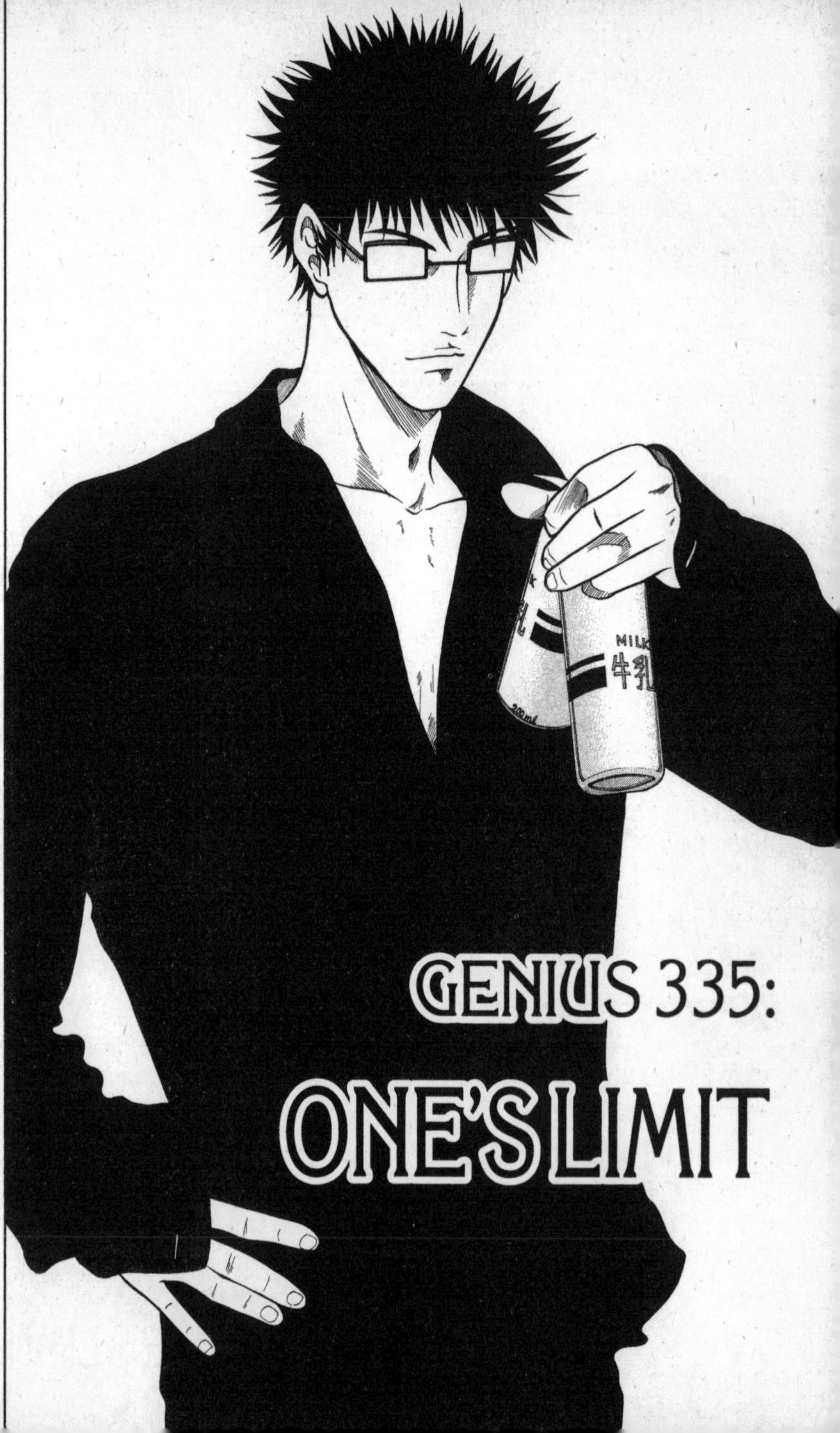
MILK
牛乳
GENIUS 335:
ONE'S LIMIT

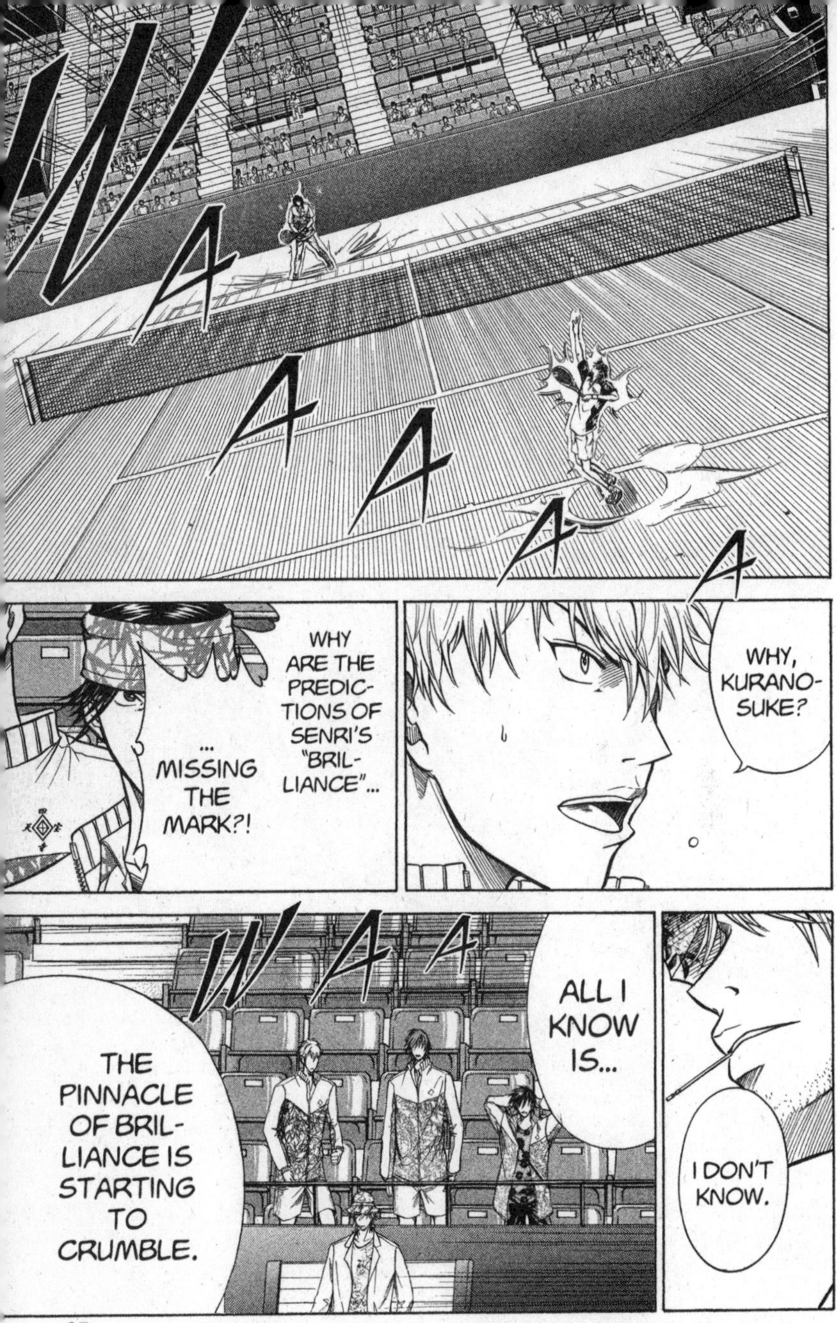
WAAAAAAA
WHY, KURANOSUKE?
WHY ARE THE PREDICTIONS OF SENRI'S "BRILLIANCE"...
...MISSING THE MARK?!
ALL I KNOW IS...
I DON'T KNOW.
WAA
THE PINNACLE OF BRILLIANCE IS STARTING TO CRUMBLE.

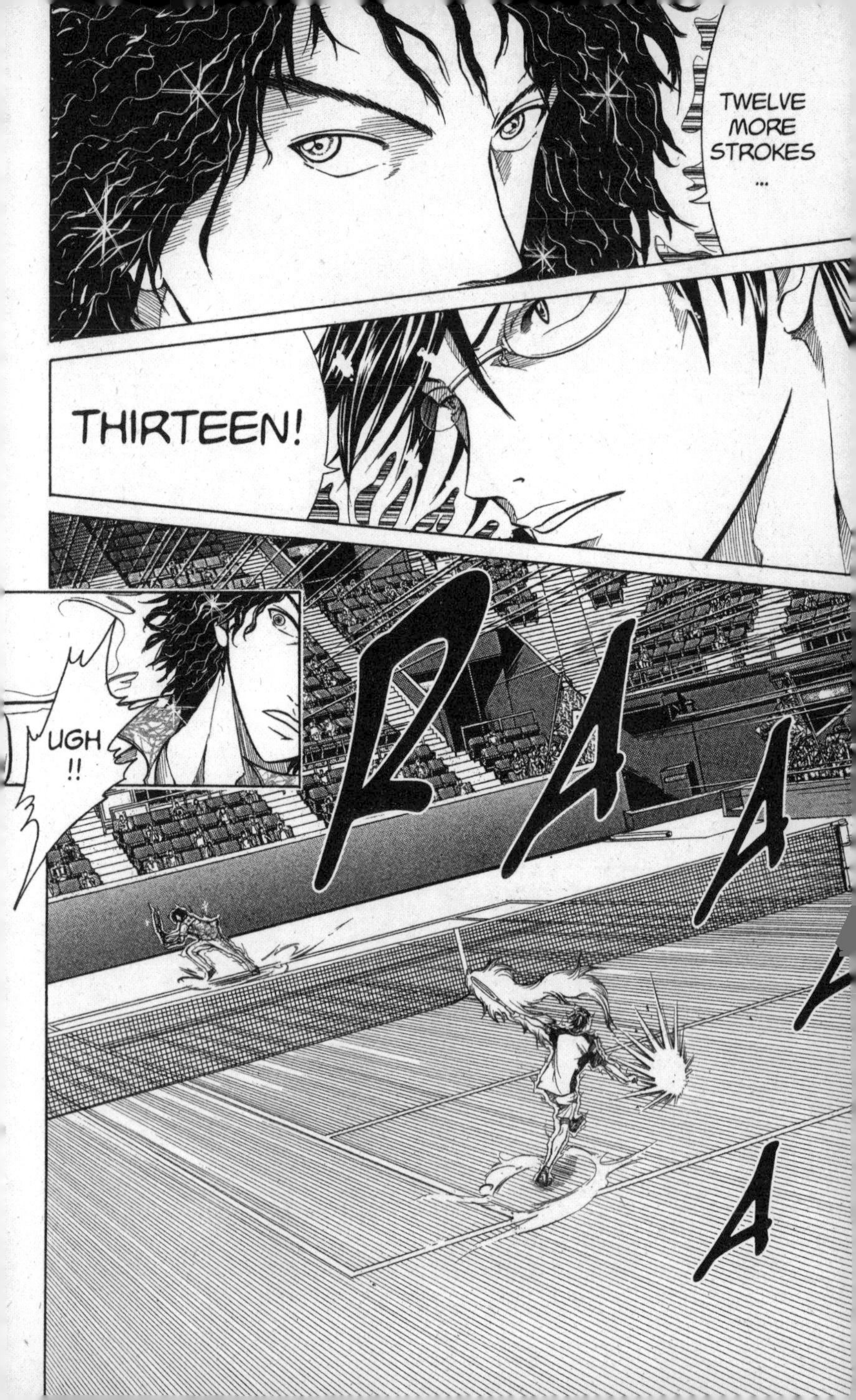
TWELVE MORE STROKES ...
THIRTEEN!
UGH !!
RAAAA

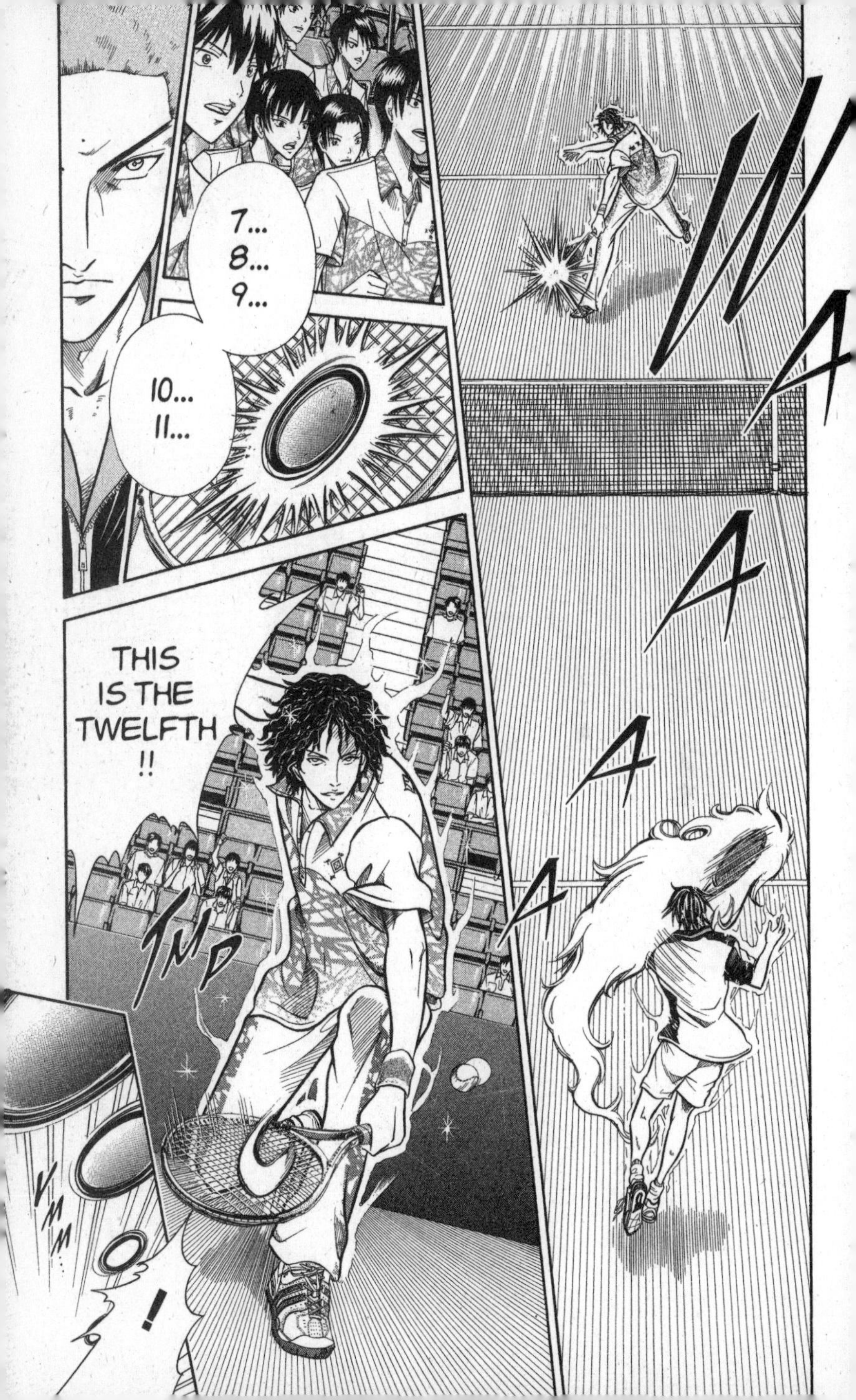
WAAAAA
7...
8...
9...
10...
11...
THIS IS THE TWELFTH!!
VMMMO
!

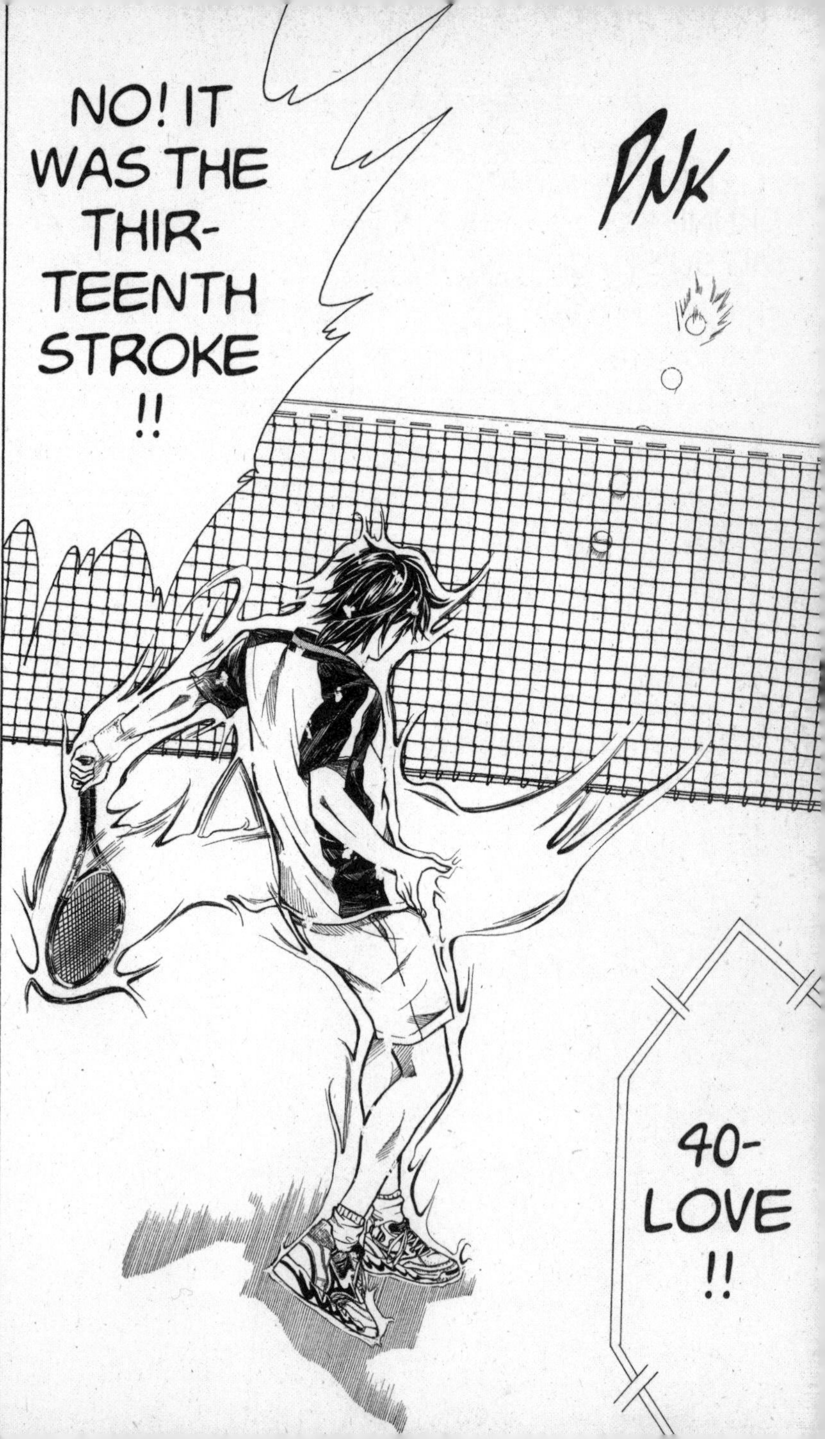
NO! IT WAS THE THIR-TEENTH STROKE !!
PNK
40-LOVE !!

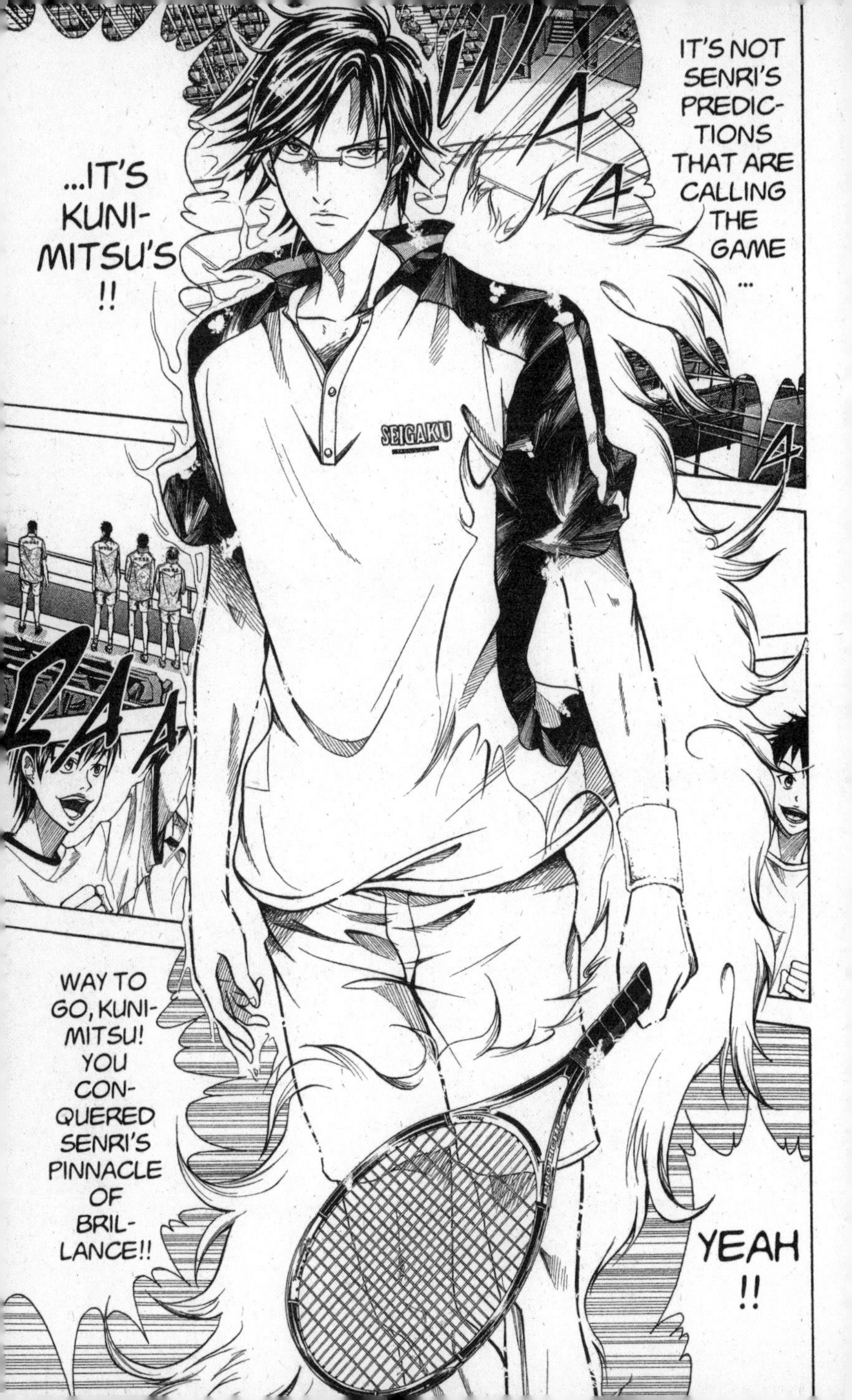
IT'S NOT SENRI'S PREDICTIONS THAT ARE CALLING THE GAME...
...IT'S KUNIMITSU'S!!
YEAH!!
WAY TO GO, KUNIMITSU! YOU CONQUERED SENRI'S PINNACLE OF BRILLANCE!!

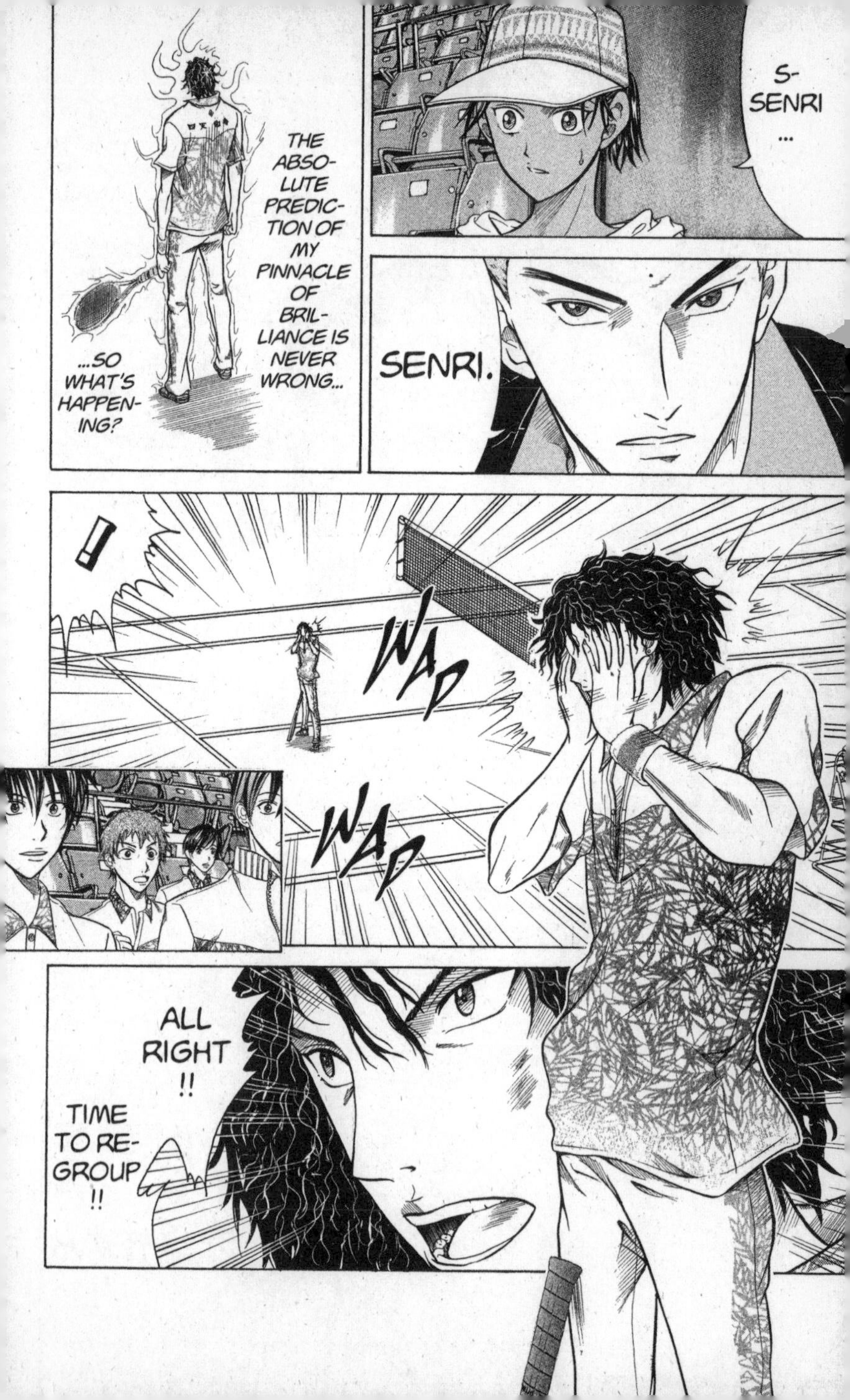
S-SENRI ...
SENRI.
THE ABSOLUTE PREDICTION OF MY PINNACLE OF BRILLIANCE IS NEVER WRONG...
...SO WHAT'S HAPPENING?
!
WAD
WAD
ALL RIGHT !!
TIME TO REGROUP !!

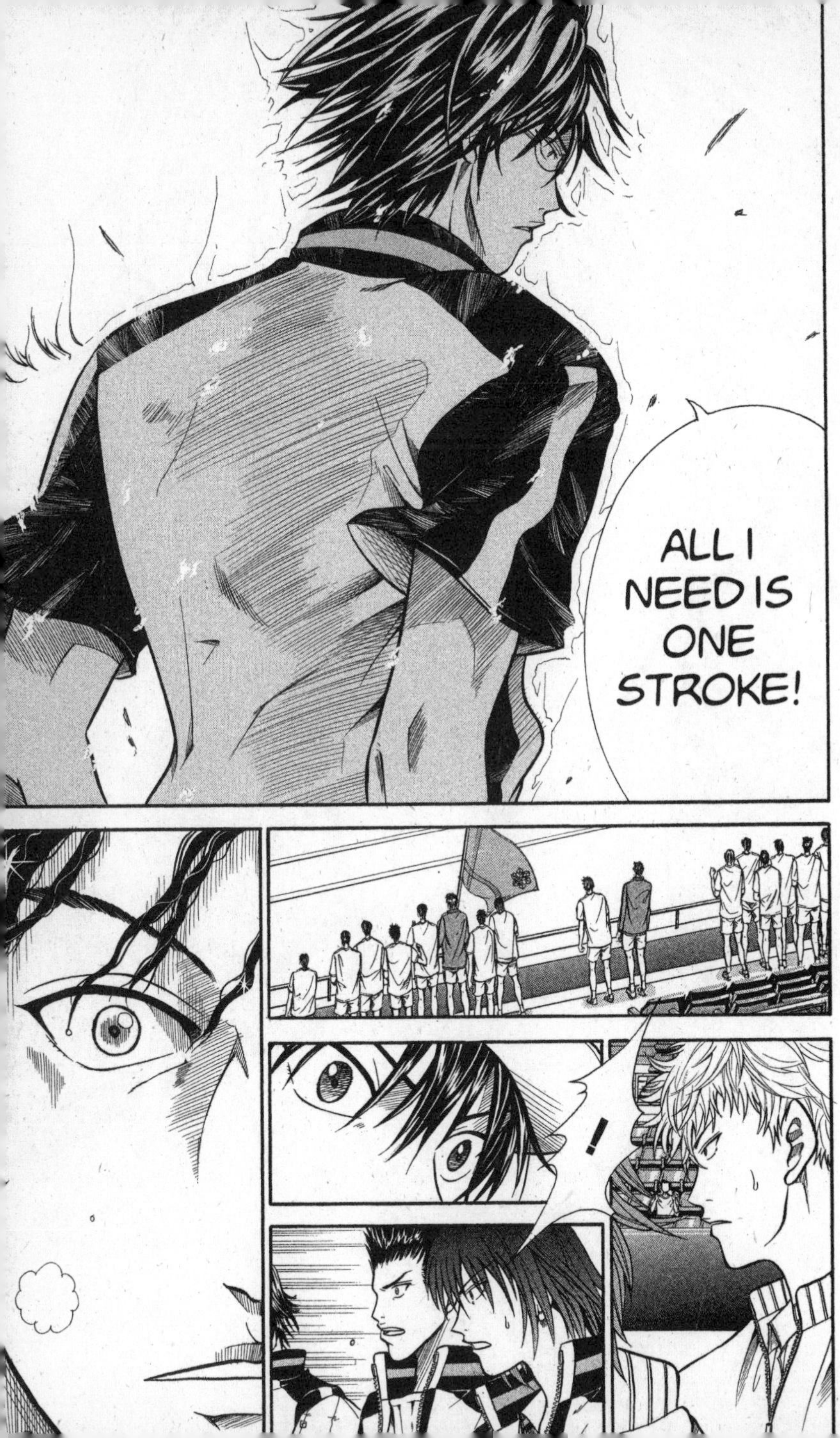
ALL I NEED IS ONE STROKE!
!

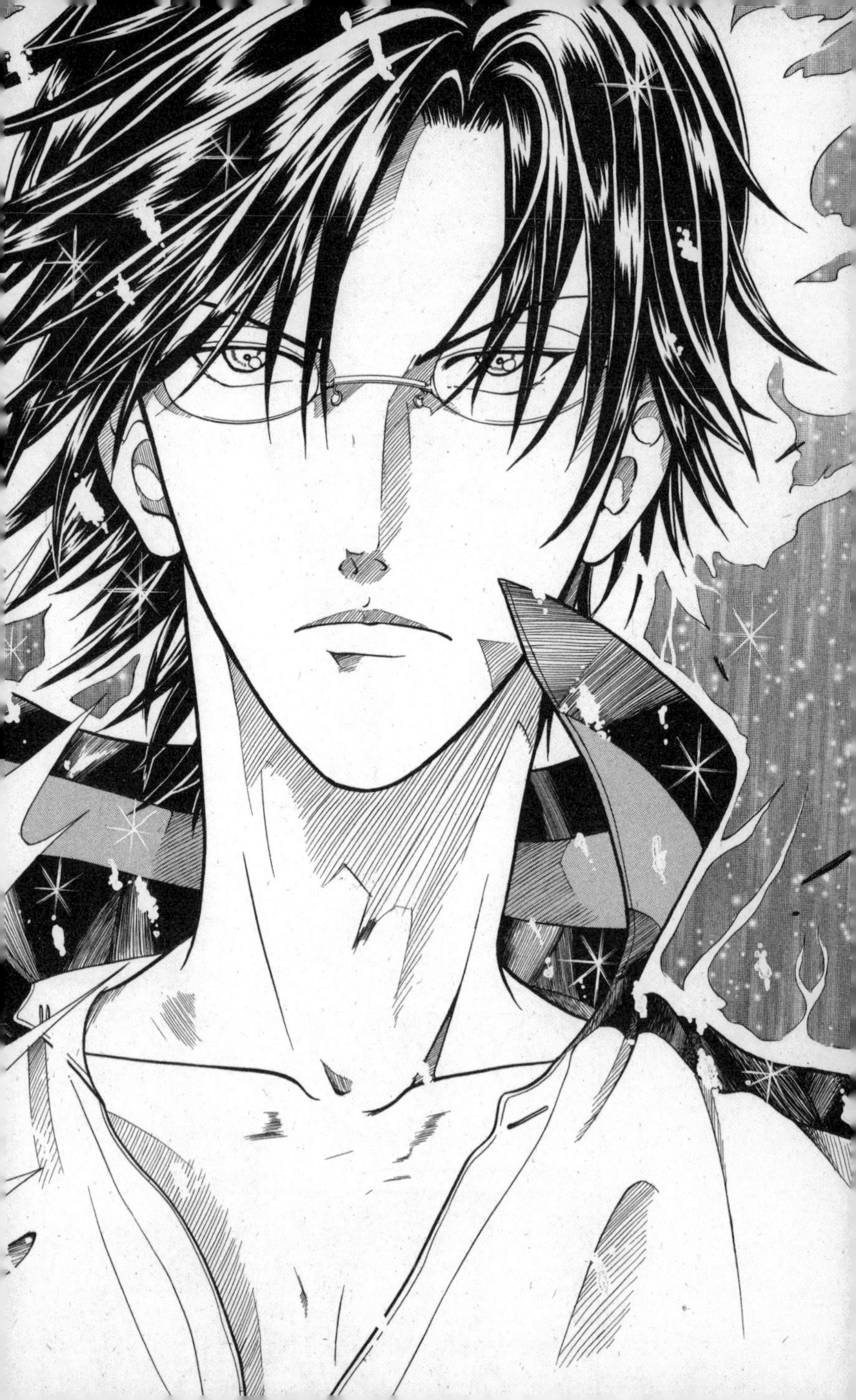

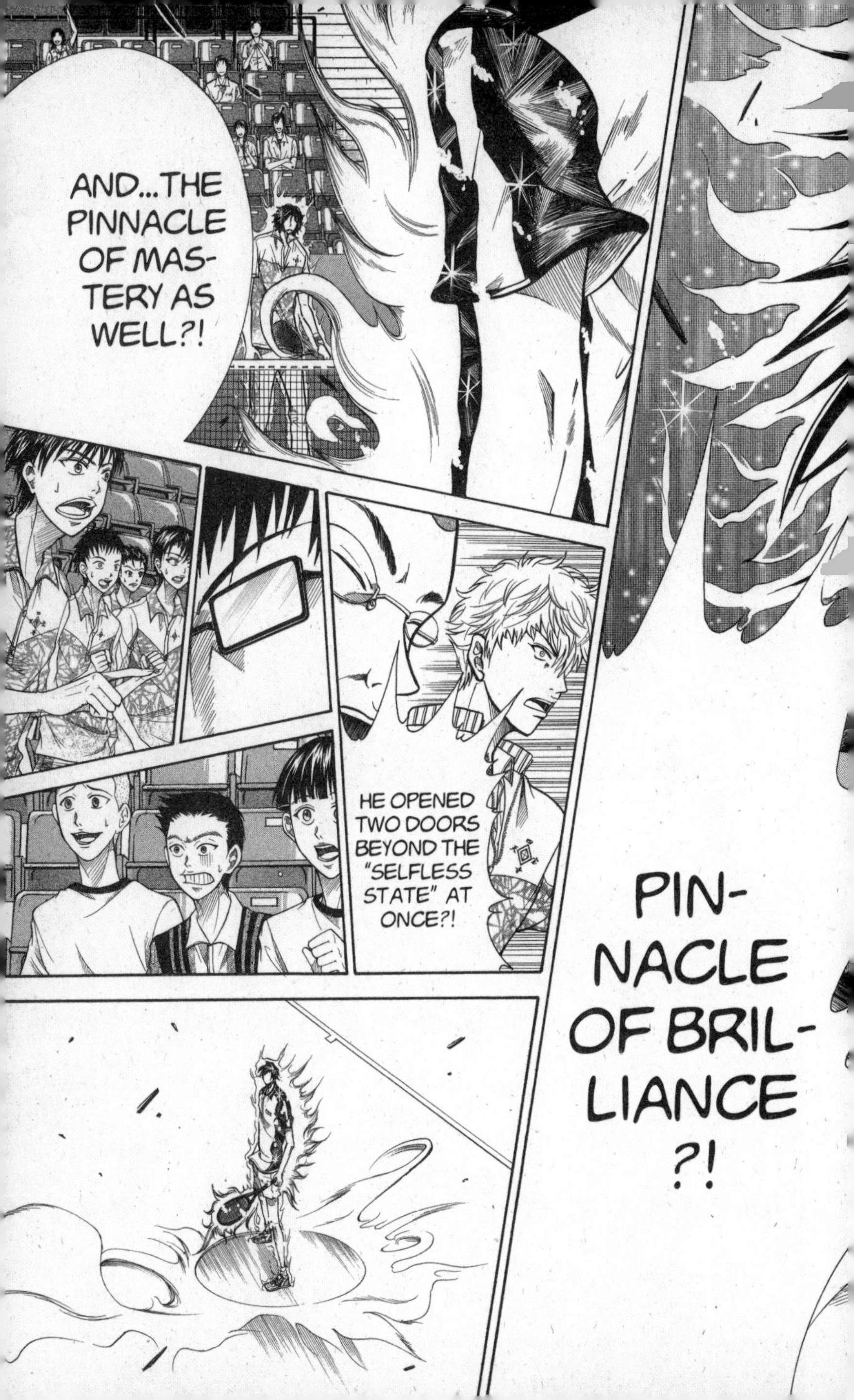
PIN-NACLE OF BRIL-LIANCE ?!
AND...THE PINNACLE OF MAS-TERY AS WELL?!
HE OPENED TWO DOORS BEYOND THE "SELFLESS STATE" AT ONCE?!

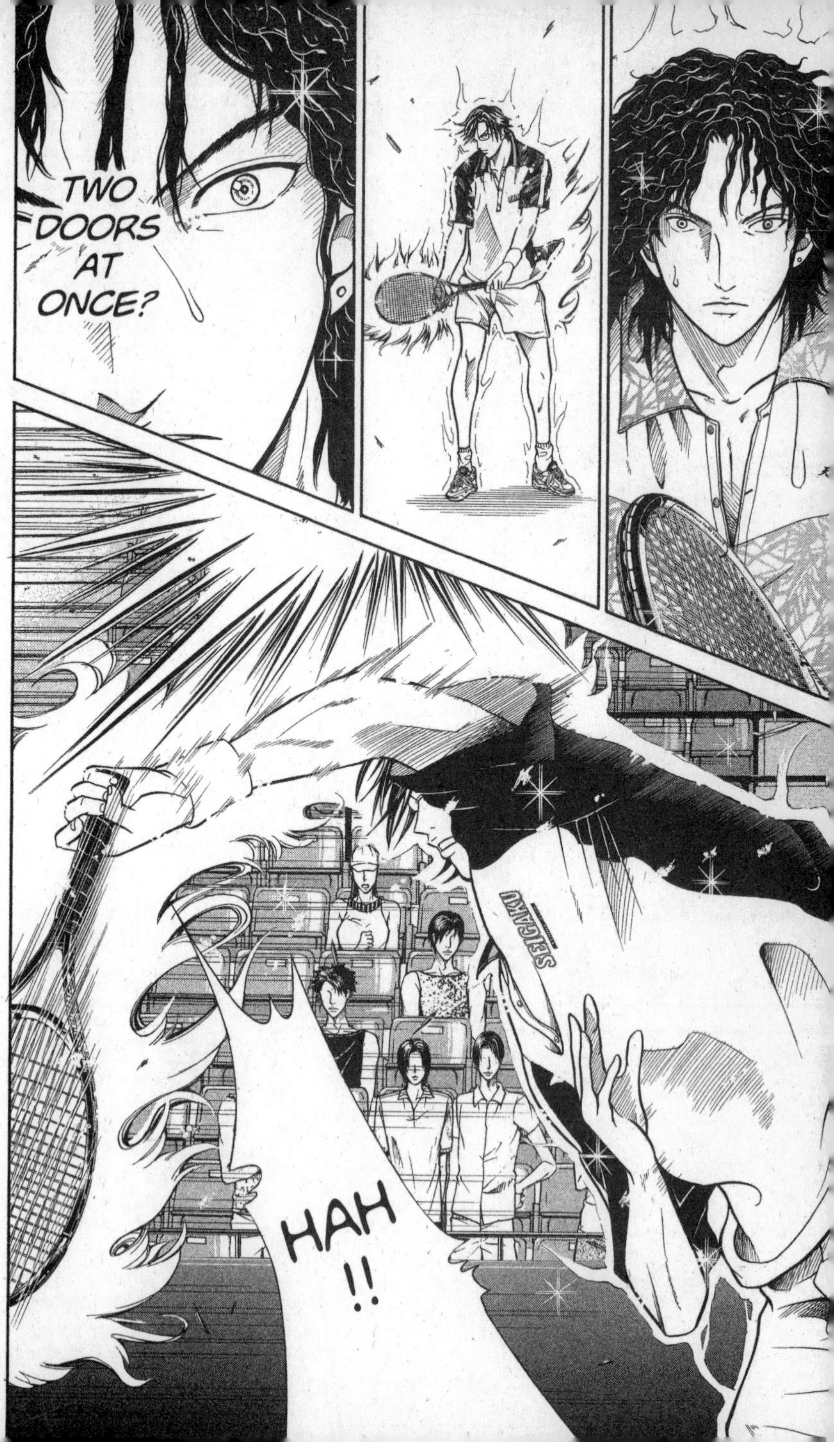
TWO DOORS AT ONCE?
SEIGAKU
HAH !!

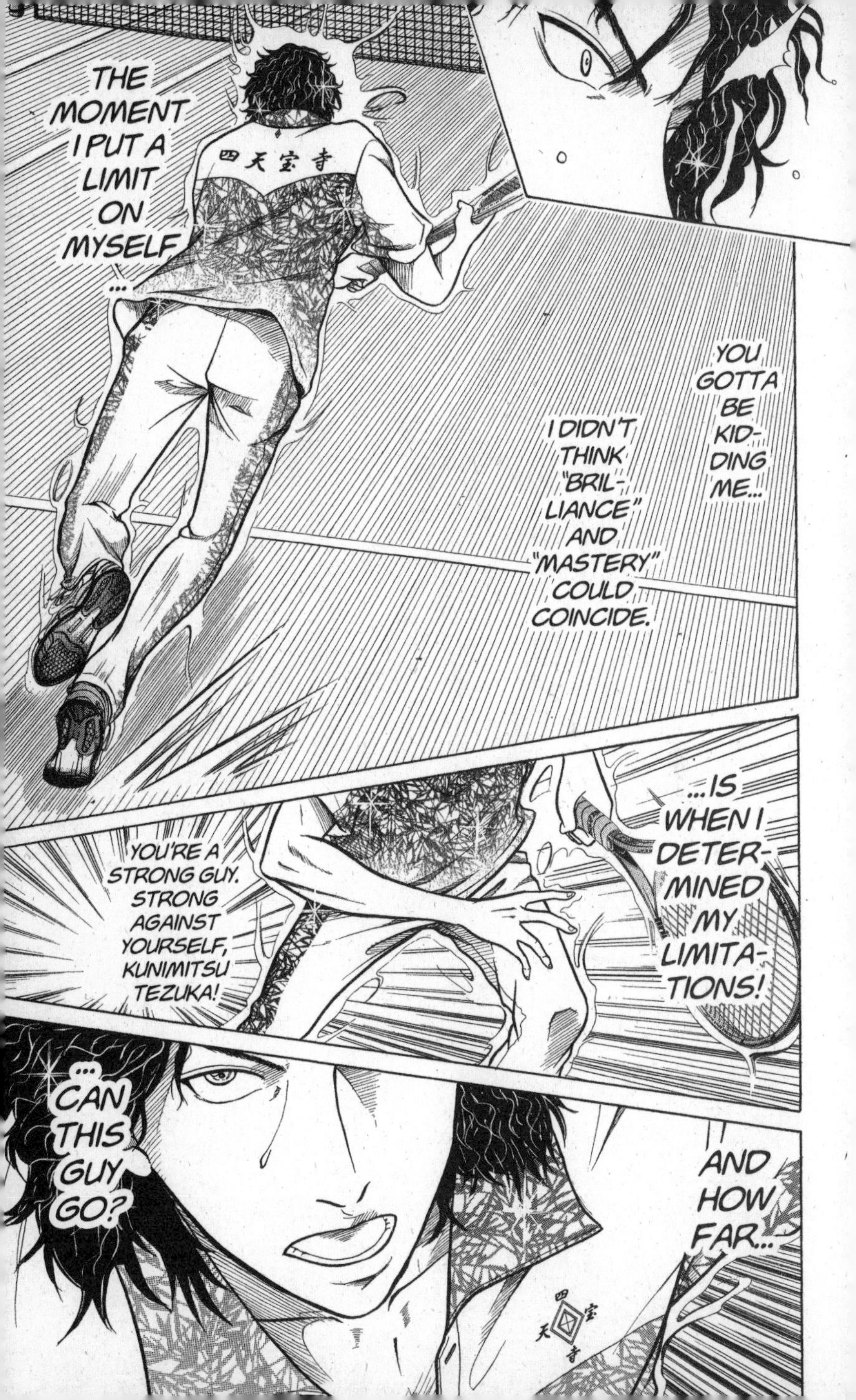
YOU GOTTA BE KIDDING ME...
I DIDN'T THINK "BRILLIANCE" AND "MASTERY" COULD COINCIDE.
THE MOMENT I PUT A LIMIT ON MYSELF...
四天宝寺
...IS WHEN I DETERMINED MY LIMITATIONS!
YOU'RE A STRONG GUY. STRONG AGAINST YOURSELF, KUNIMITSU TEZUKA!
AND HOW FAR...
...CAN THIS GUY GO?

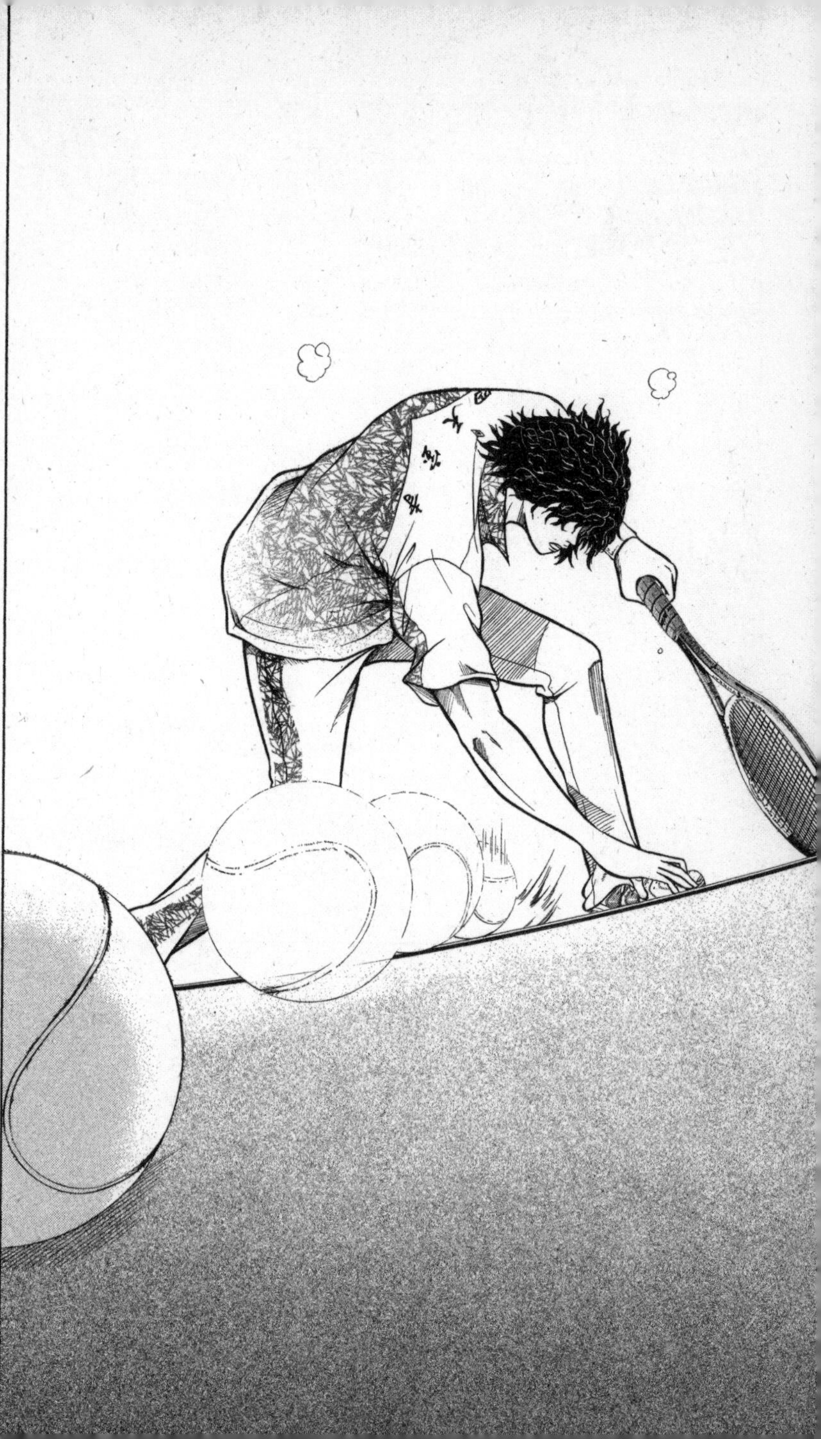

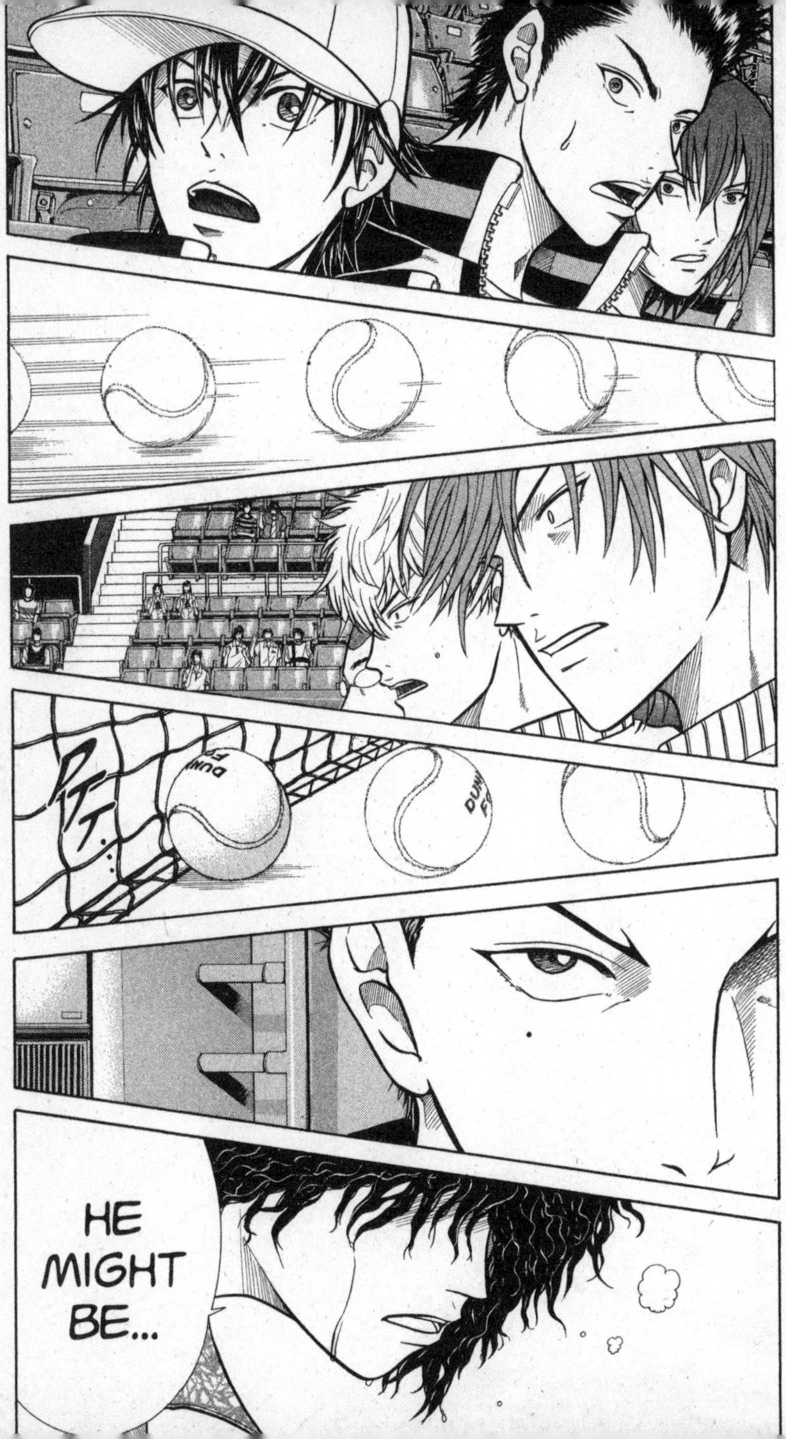
PTT...
HE MIGHT BE...

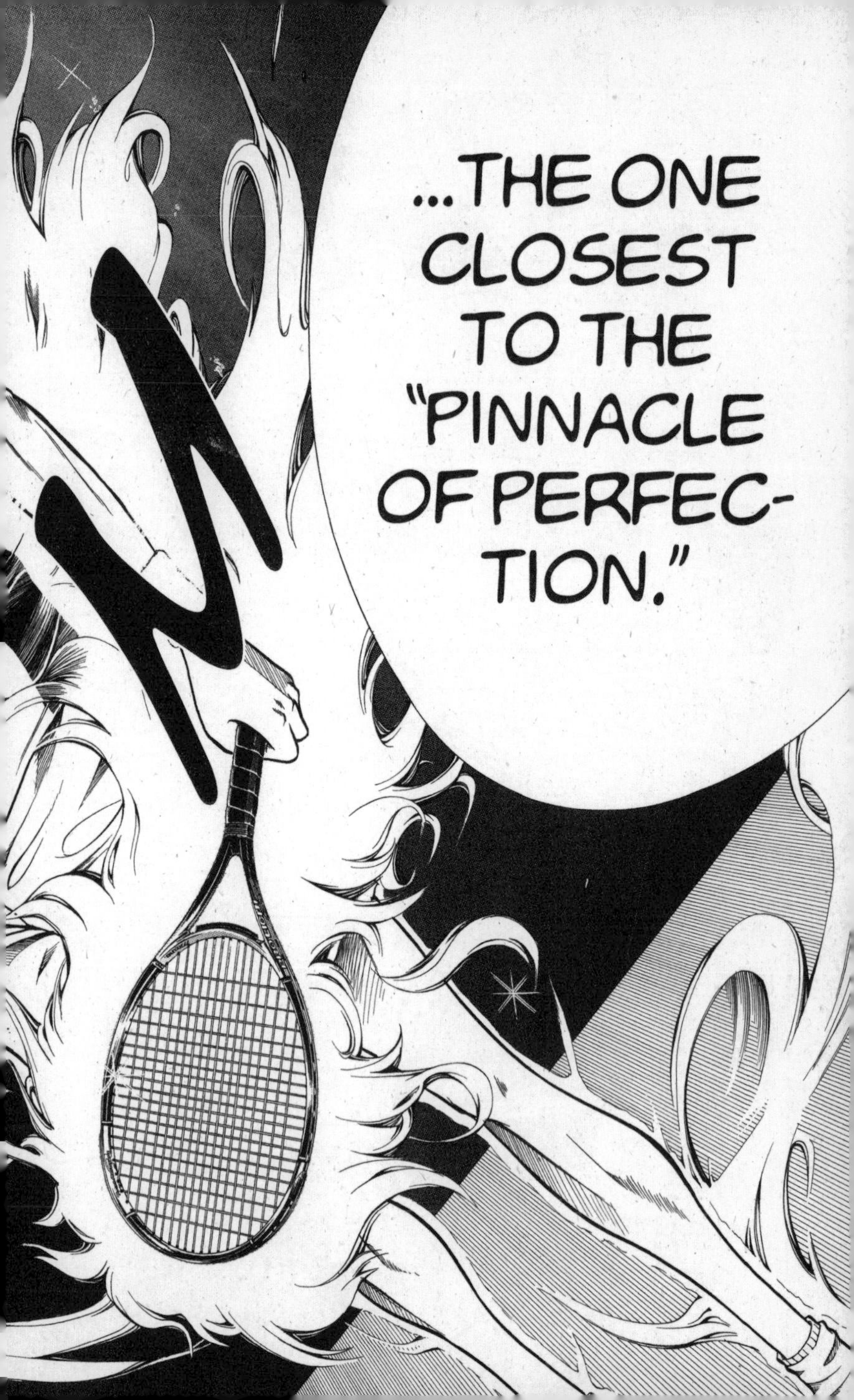
...THE ONE CLOSEST TO THE "PINNACLE OF PERFECTION."

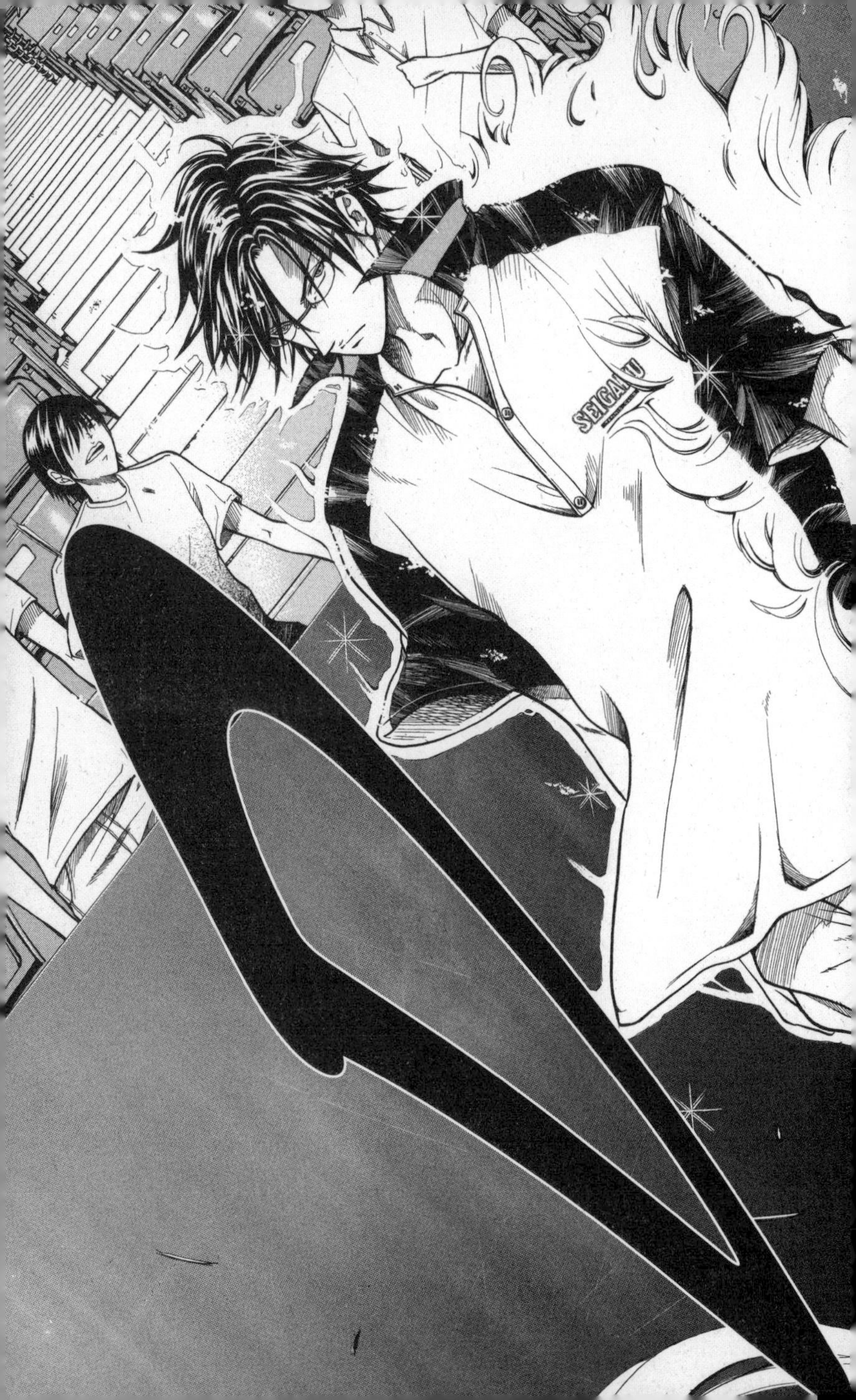
SEIGAKU

テニスの王子様

THE PRINCE OF TENNIS

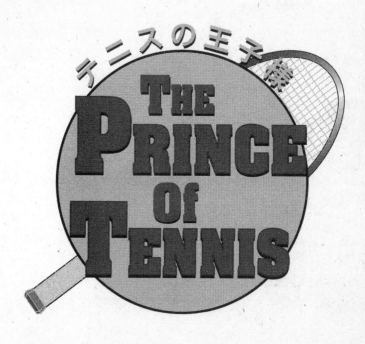

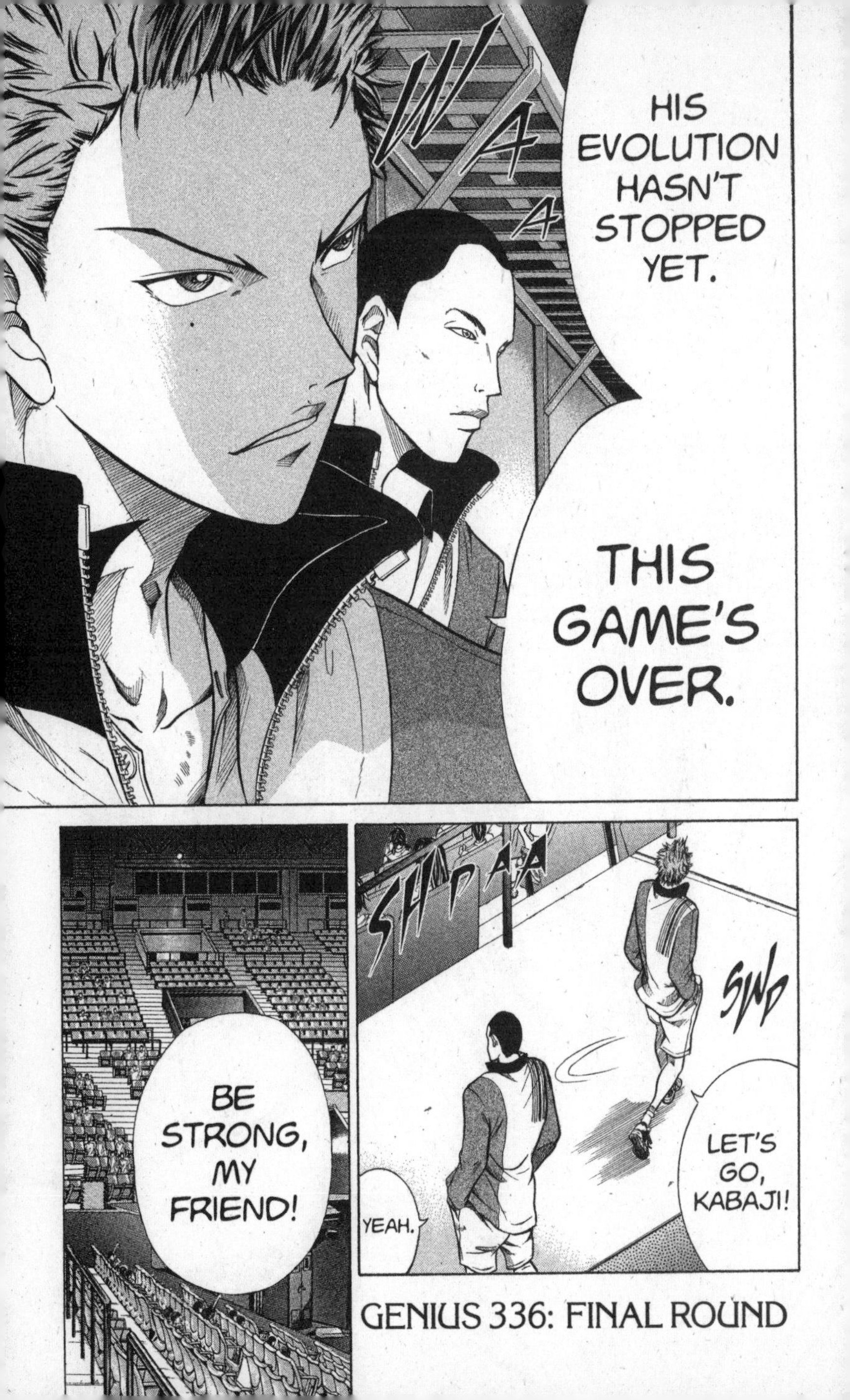
WAA
HIS EVOLUTION HASN'T STOPPED YET.
THIS GAME'S OVER.
SHDAA
SWD
LET'S GO, KABAJI!
YEAH.
BE STRONG, MY FRIEND!

GENIUS 336: FINAL ROUND

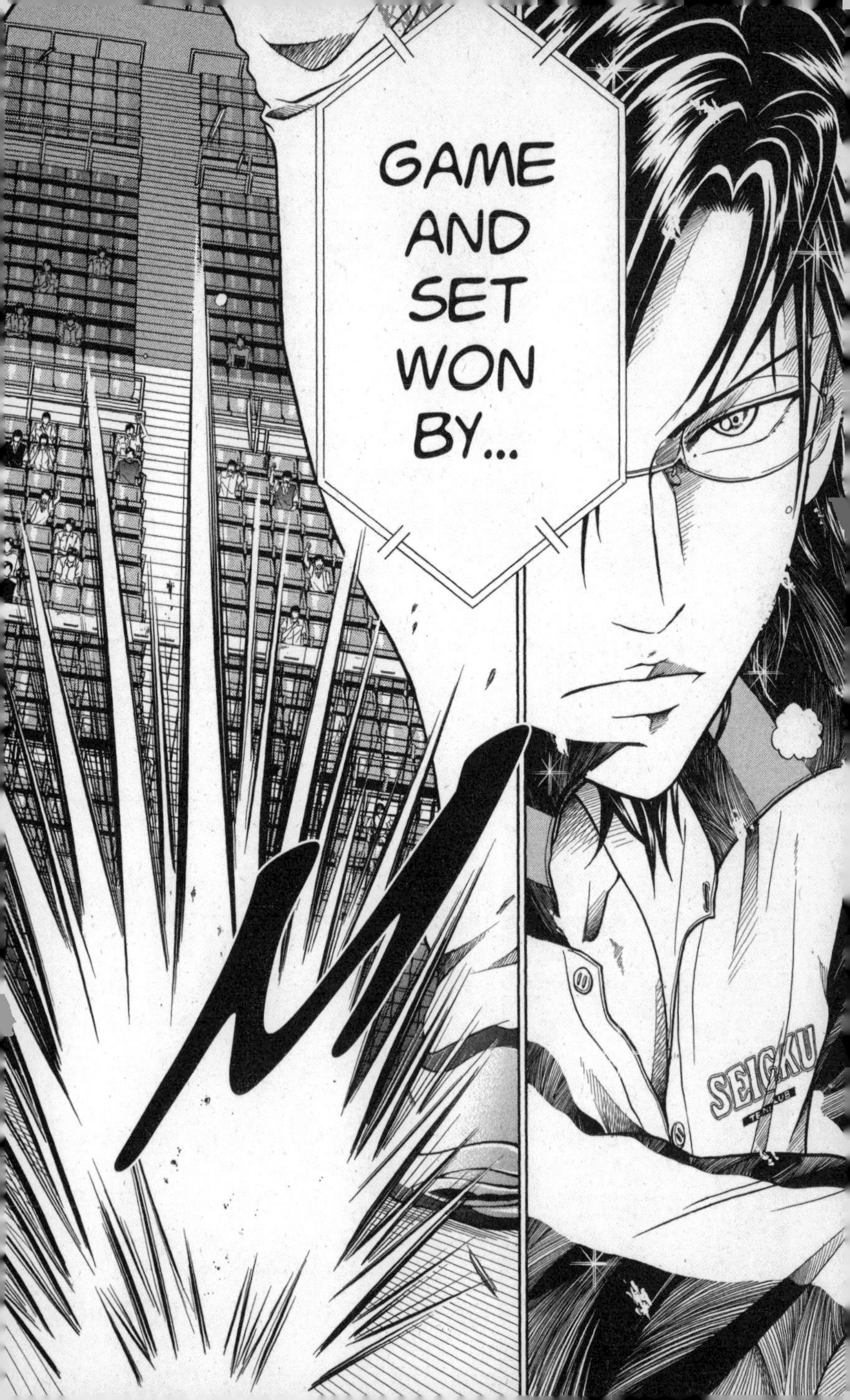
GAME AND SET WON BY...
SEIGAKU

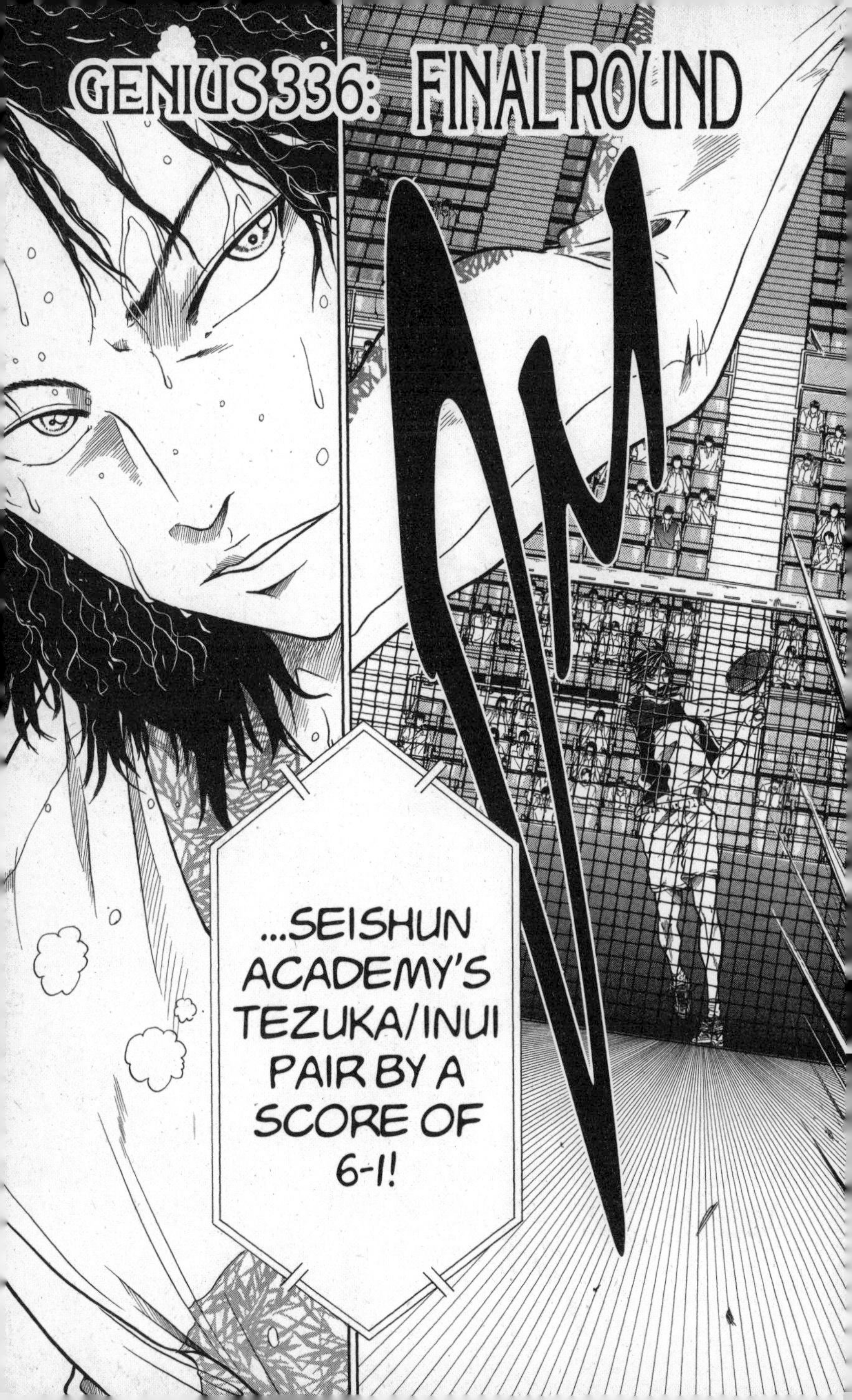
GENIUS 336: FINAL ROUND
...SEISHUN ACADEMY'S TEZUKA/INUI PAIR BY A SCORE OF 6-1!

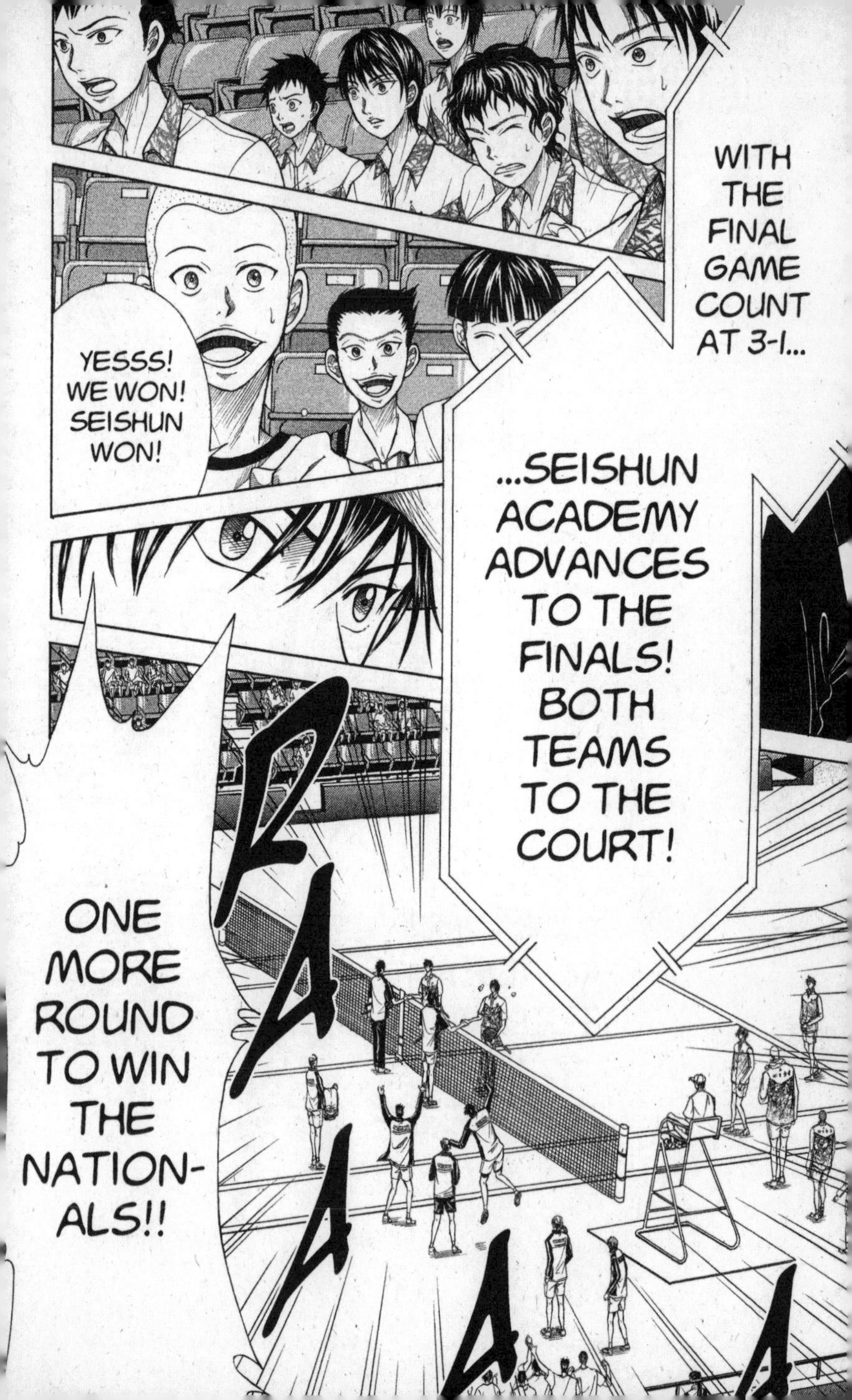
WITH THE FINAL GAME COUNT AT 3-1...
YESSS! WE WON! SEISHUN WON!
...SEISHUN ACADEMY ADVANCES TO THE FINALS! BOTH TEAMS TO THE COURT!
ONE MORE ROUND TO WIN THE NATION-ALS!!

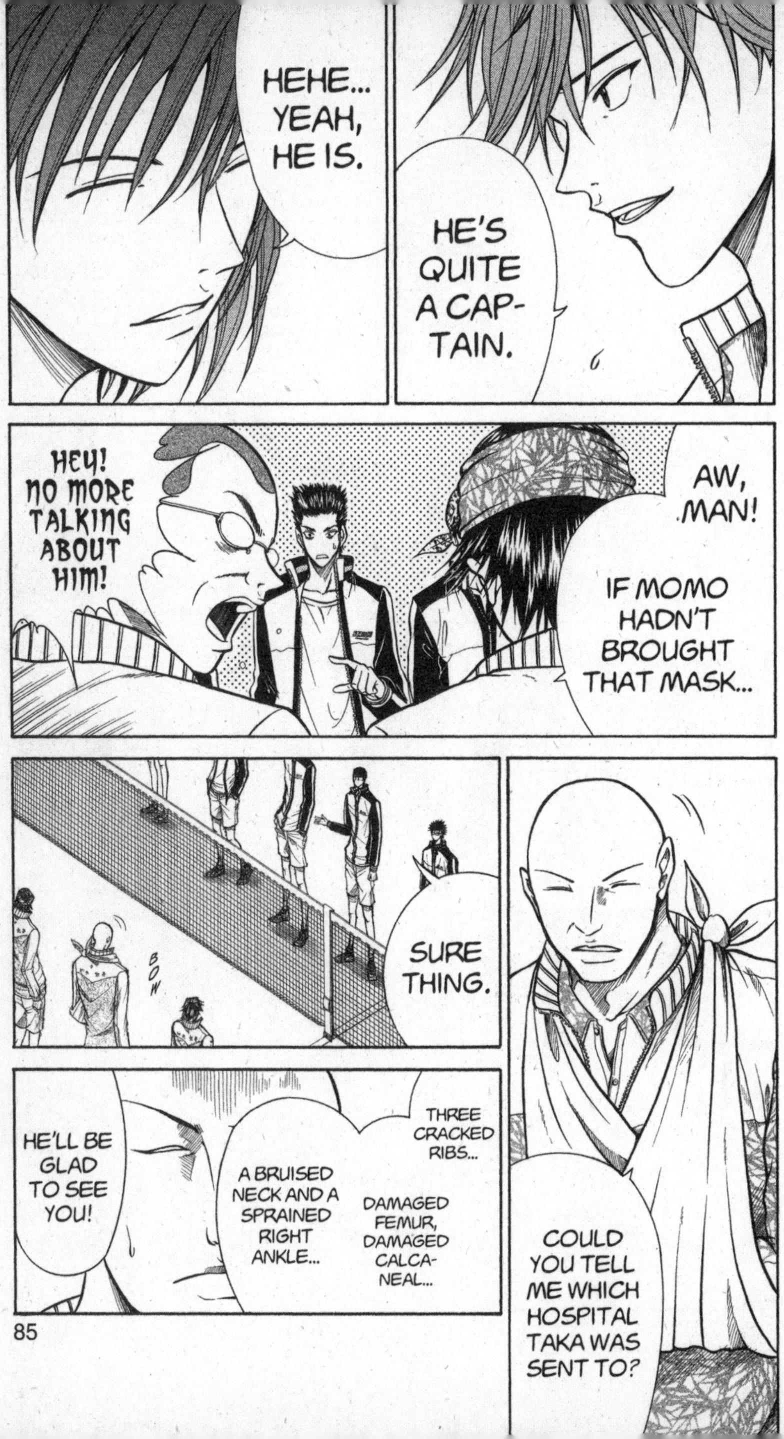
HE'S QUITE A CAP-TAIN.
HEHE... YEAH, HE IS.
AW, MAN!
IF MOMO HADN'T BROUGHT THAT MASK...
HEY! NO MORE TALKING ABOUT HIM!
COULD YOU TELL ME WHICH HOSPITAL TAKA WAS SENT TO?
SURE THING.
BOW
THREE CRACKED RIBS...
DAMAGED FEMUR, DAMAGED CALCA-NEAL...
A BRUISED NECK AND A SPRAINED RIGHT ANKLE...
HE'LL BE GLAD TO SEE YOU!

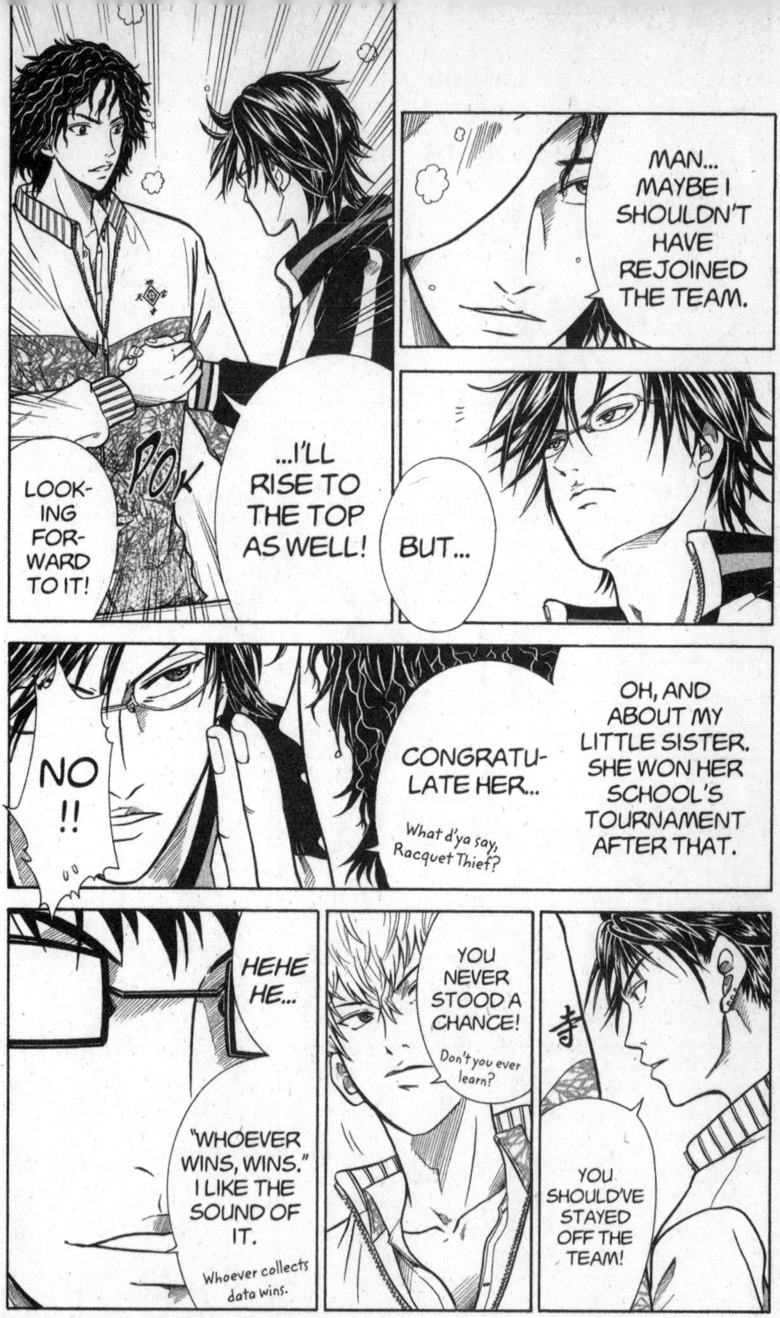
MAN... MAYBE I SHOULDN'T HAVE REJOINED THE TEAM.
BUT...
...I'LL RISE TO THE TOP AS WELL!
POK
LOOKING-ING FOR-WARD TO IT!
OH, AND ABOUT MY LITTLE SISTER. SHE WON HER SCHOOL'S TOURNAMENT AFTER THAT.
CONGRATULATE HER...
What d'ya say, Racquet Thief?
NO !!
YOU SHOULD'VE STAYED OFF THE TEAM!
YOU NEVER STOOD A CHANCE!
Don't you ever learn?
HEHE HE...
"WHOEVER WINS, WINS." I LIKE THE SOUND OF IT.
Whoever collects data wins.

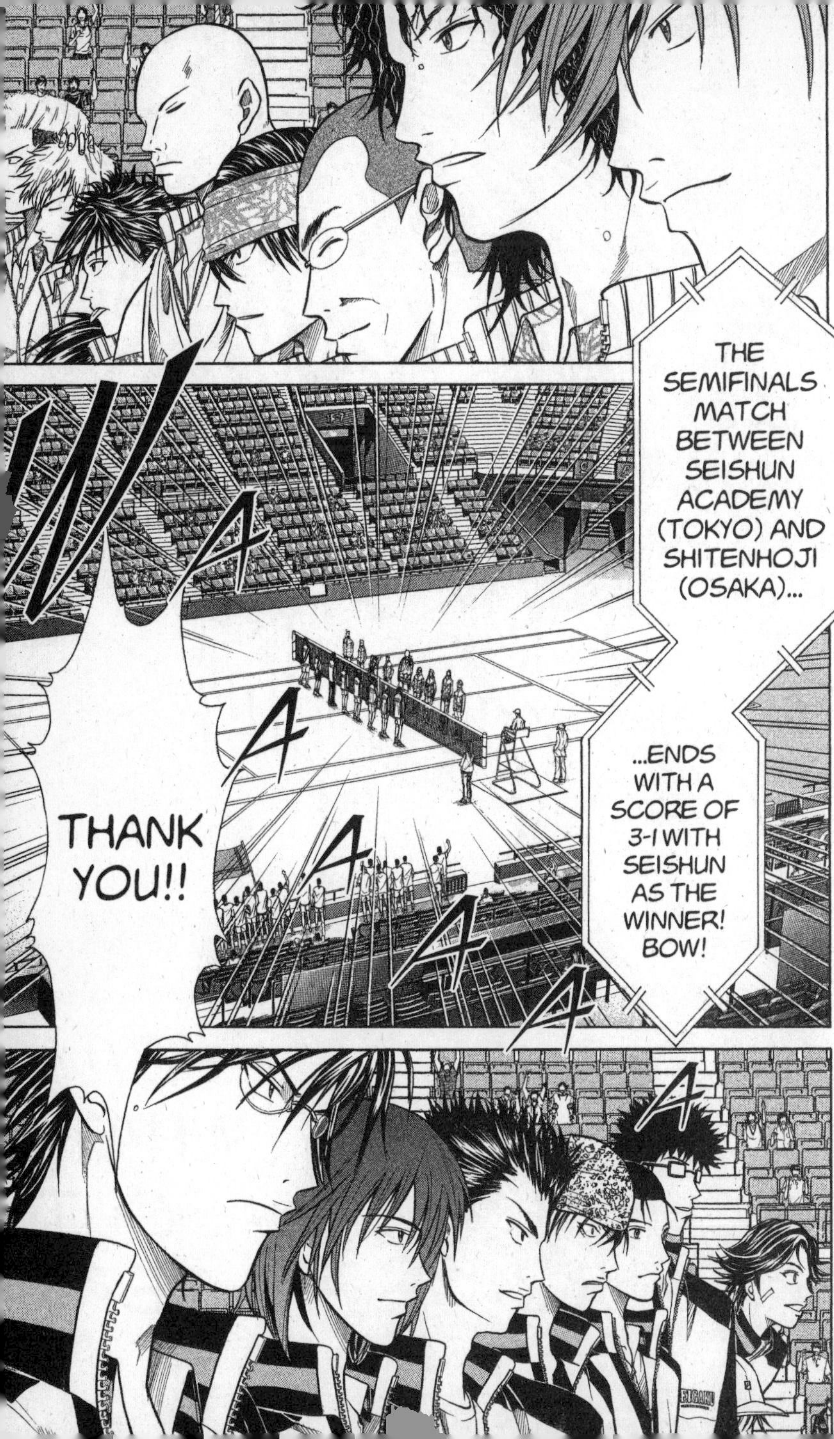
THE SEMIFINALS MATCH BETWEEN SEISHUN ACADEMY (TOKYO) AND SHITENHOJI (OSAKA)...
...ENDS WITH A SCORE OF 3-1 WITH SEISHUN AS THE WINNER! BOW!
THANK YOU!!
WAAAAAA

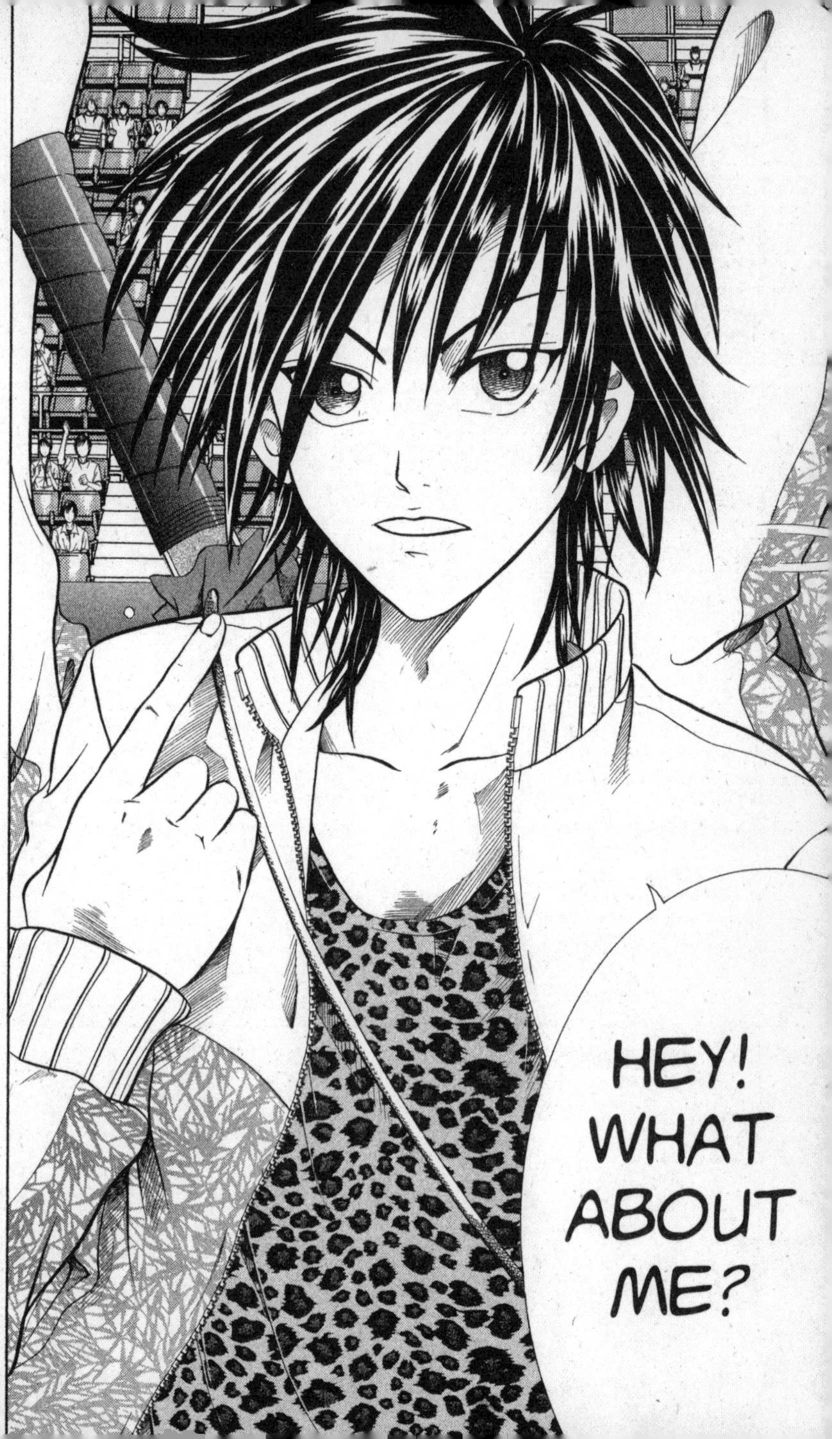
HEY! WHAT ABOUT ME?

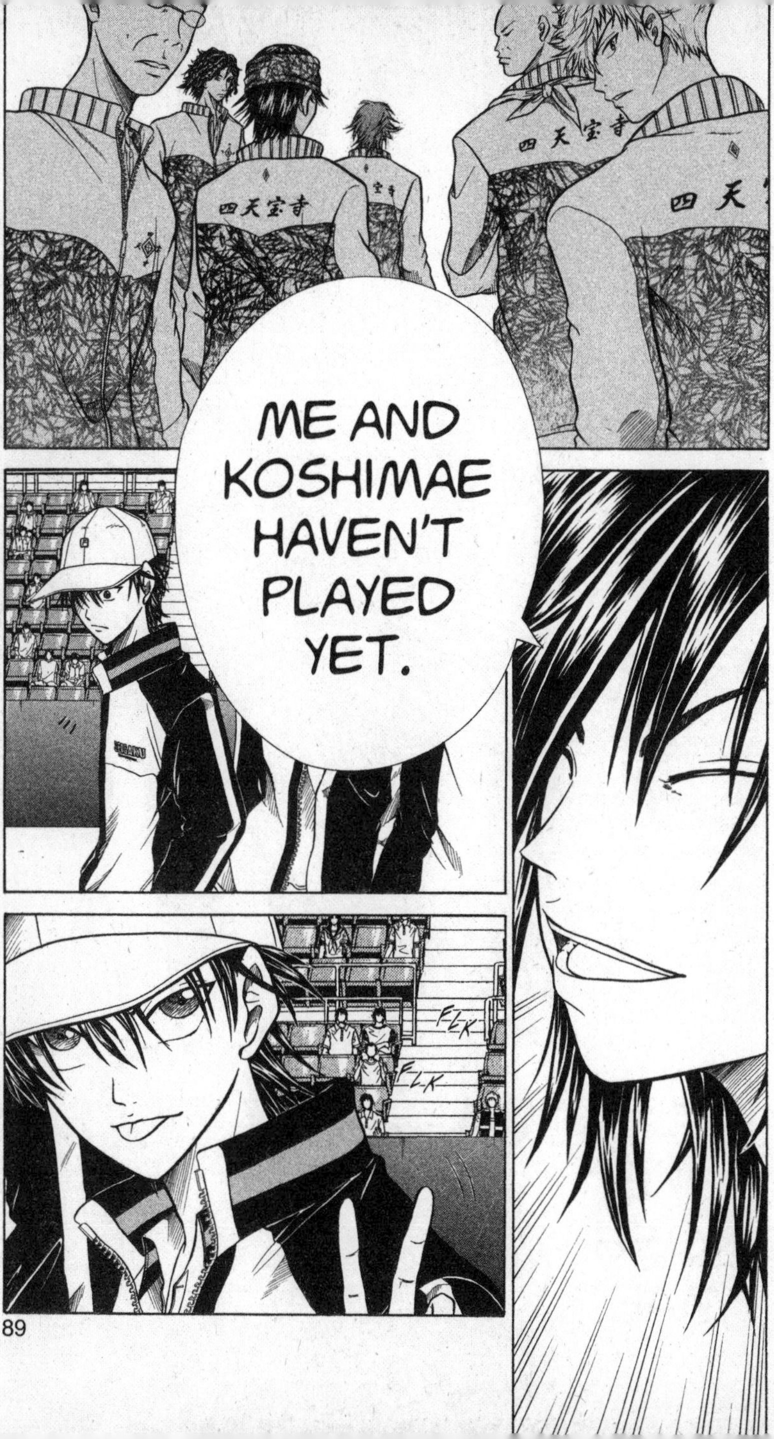
ME AND KOSHIMAE HAVEN'T PLAYED YET.
FLK
FLK

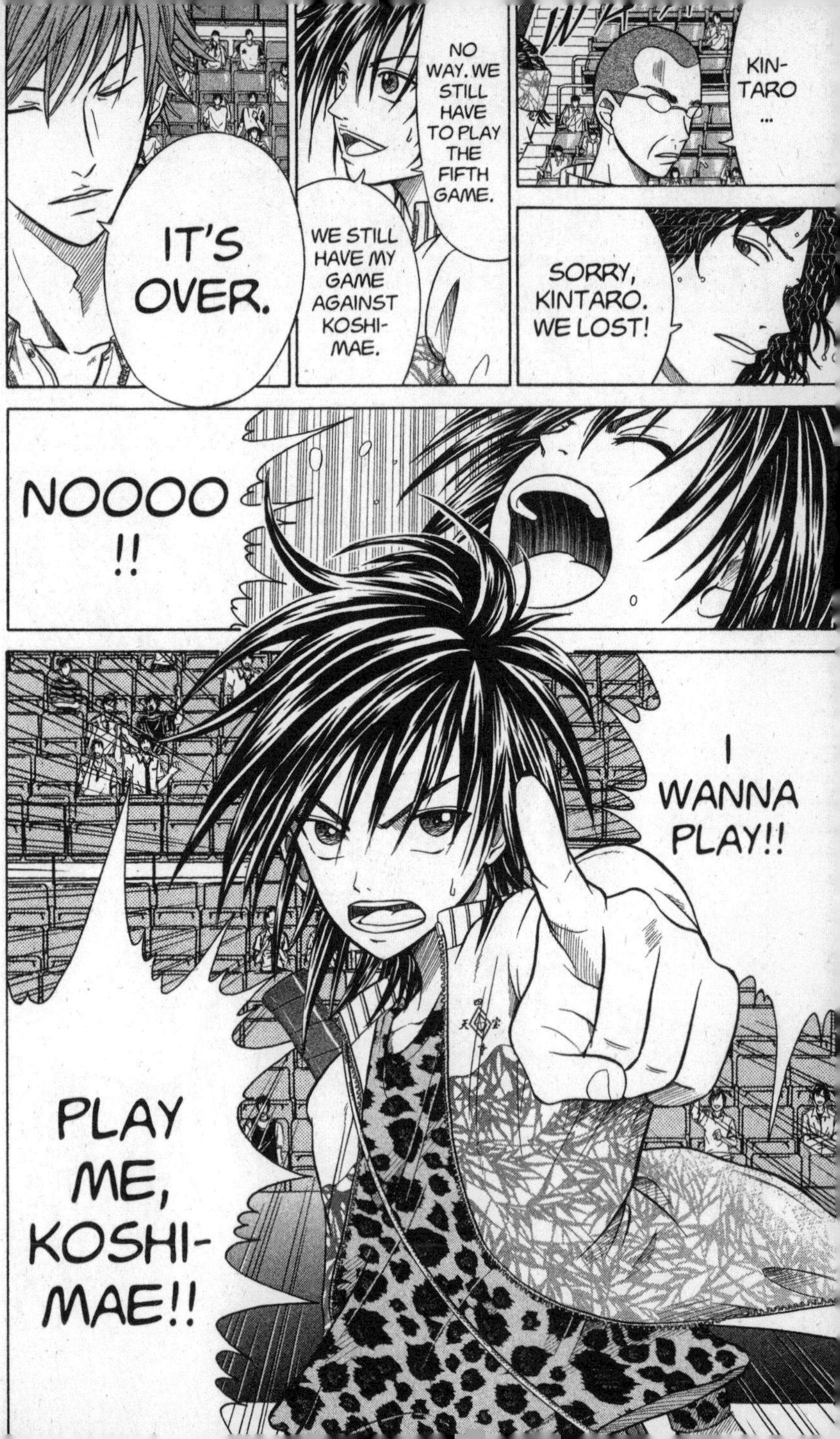
KIN-TARO ...
SORRY, KINTARO. WE LOST!
NO WAY. WE STILL HAVE TO PLAY THE FIFTH GAME.
WE STILL HAVE MY GAME AGAINST KOSHI-MAE.
IT'S OVER.
NOOOO !!
I WANNA PLAY!!
PLAY ME, KOSHI-MAE!!

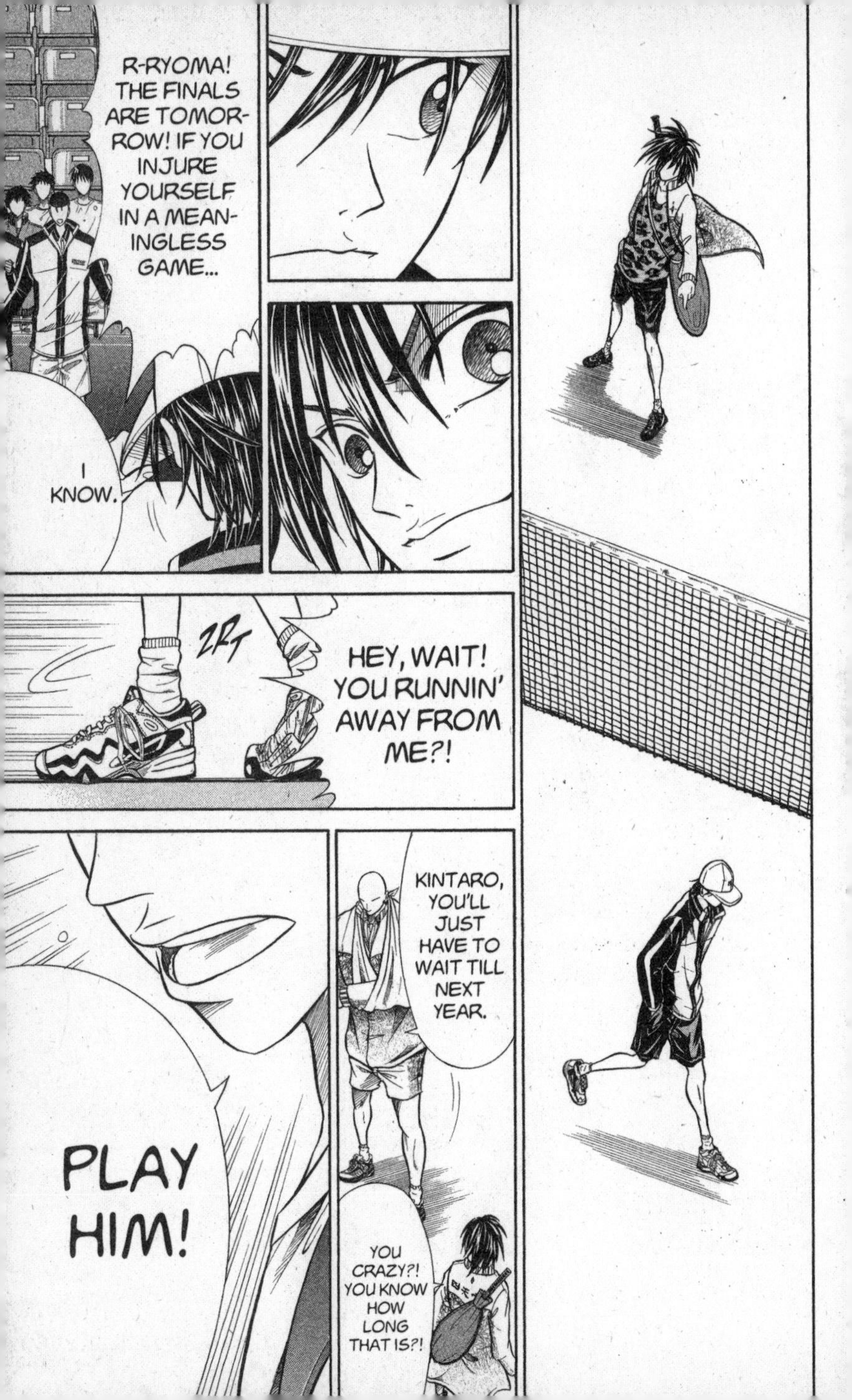
R-RYOMA! THE FINALS ARE TOMOR-ROW! IF YOU INJURE YOURSELF IN A MEAN-INGLESS GAME...
I KNOW.
HEY, WAIT! YOU RUNNIN' AWAY FROM ME?!
ZRT
KINTARO, YOU'LL JUST HAVE TO WAIT TILL NEXT YEAR.
YOU CRAZY?! YOU KNOW HOW LONG THAT IS?!
PLAY HIM!

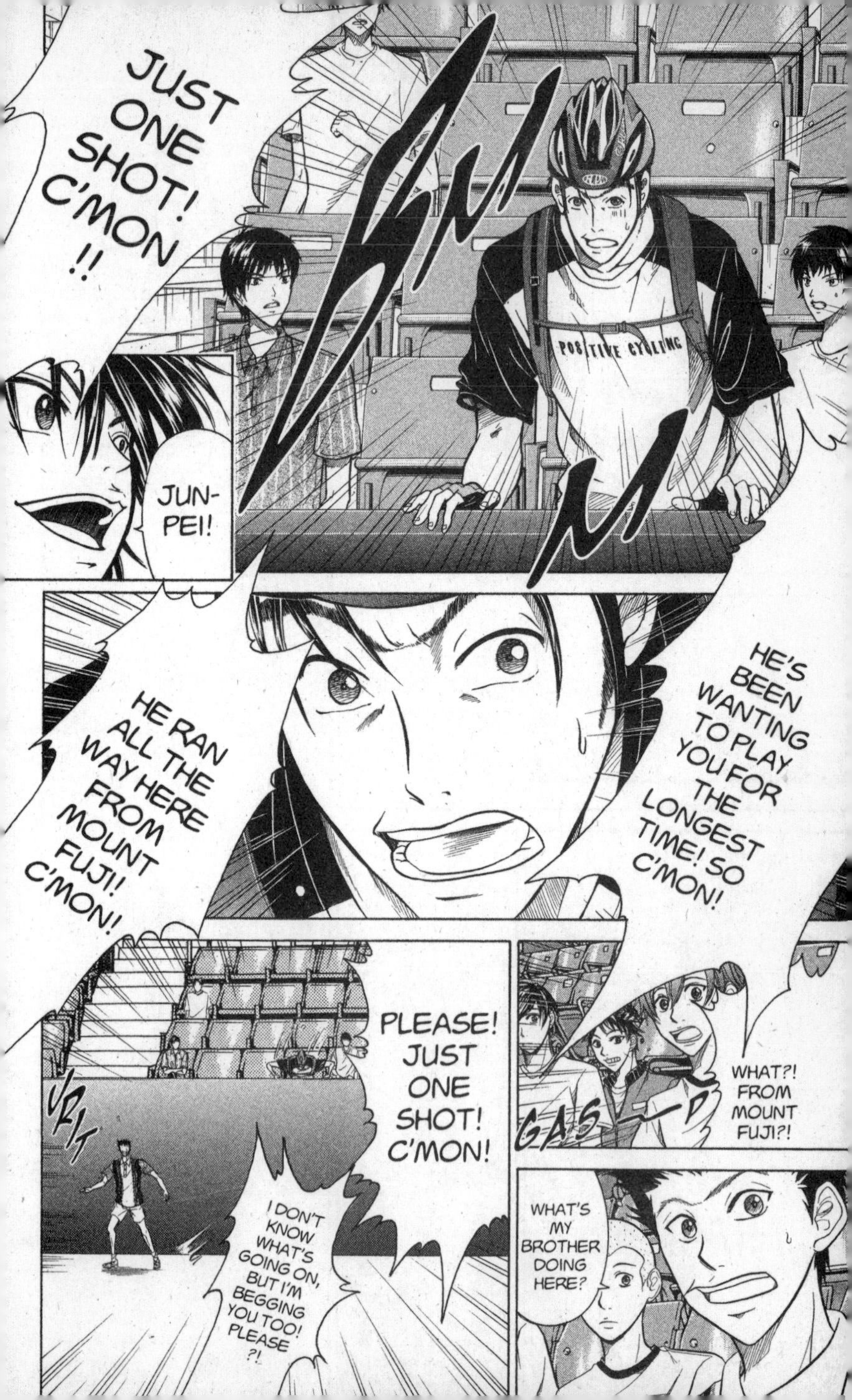
JUST ONE SHOT! C'MON!!
JUN-PEI!
HE'S BEEN WANTING TO PLAY YOU FOR THE LONGEST TIME! SO C'MON!
HE RAN ALL THE WAY HERE FROM MOUNT FUJI!! C'MON!
WHAT?! FROM MOUNT FUJI?!
WHAT'S MY BROTHER DOING HERE?
PLEASE! JUST ONE SHOT! C'MON!
I DON'T KNOW WHAT'S GOING ON, BUT I'M BEGGING YOU TOO! PLEASE?!

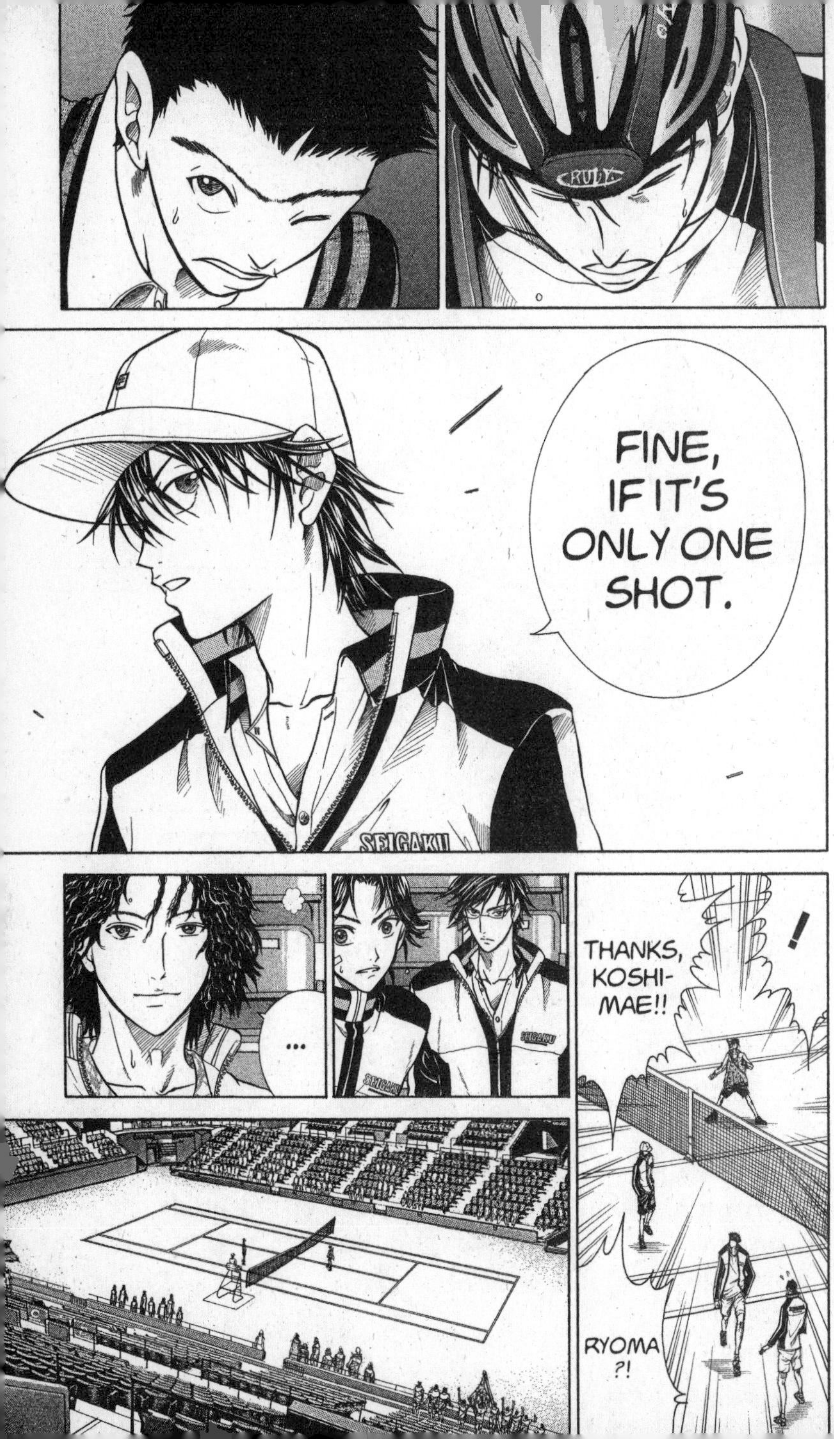
FINE, IF IT'S ONLY ONE SHOT.
!
THANKS, KOSHI-MAE!!
RYOMA ?!
...

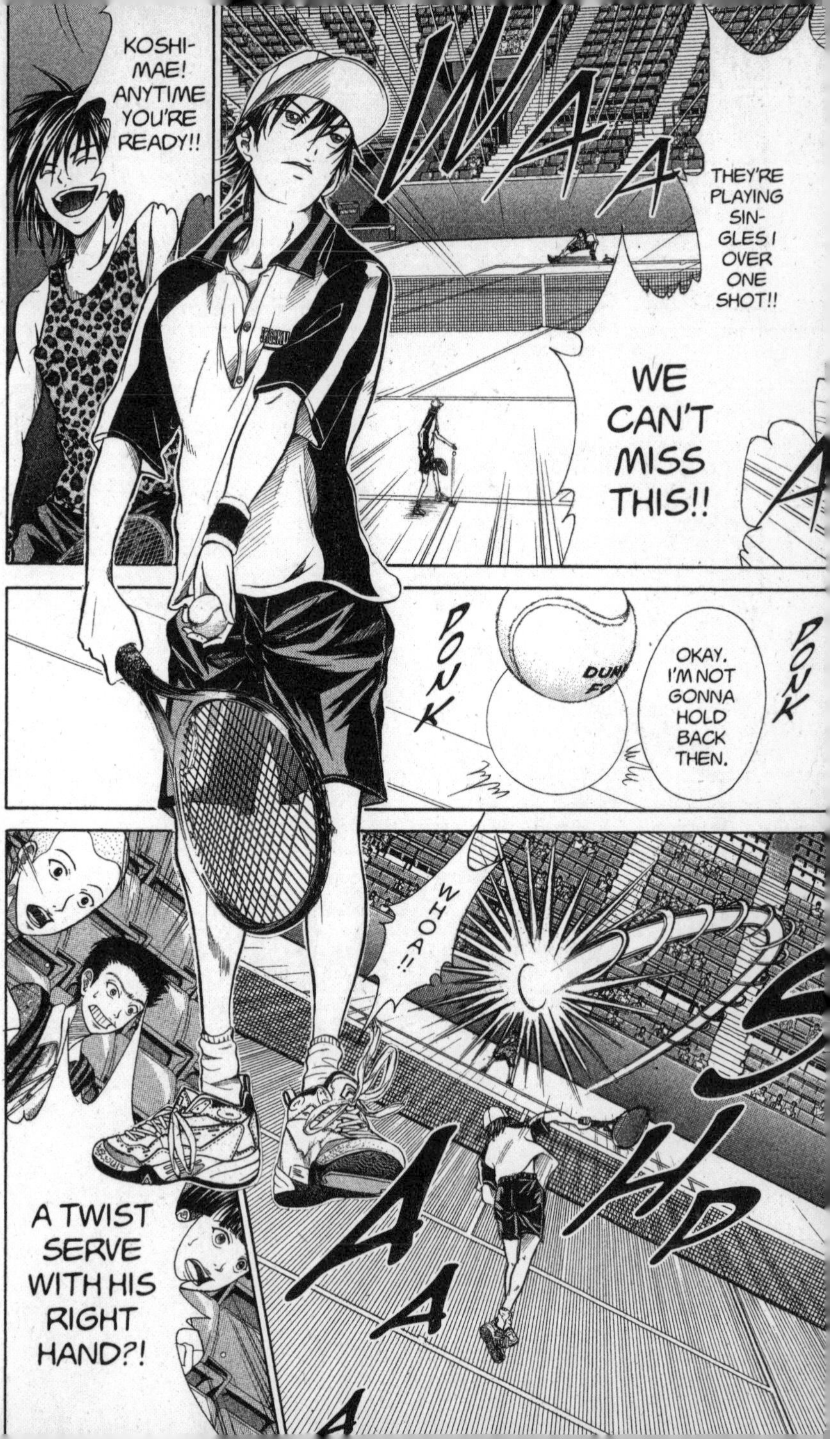
WAA
THEY'RE PLAYING SIN-GLES 1 OVER ONE SHOT!!
WE CAN'T MISS THIS!!
KOSHI-MAE! ANYTIME YOU'RE READY!!
DONK
OKAY. I'M NOT GONNA HOLD BACK THEN.
DONK
WHOA!!
A TWIST SERVE WITH HIS RIGHT HAND?!

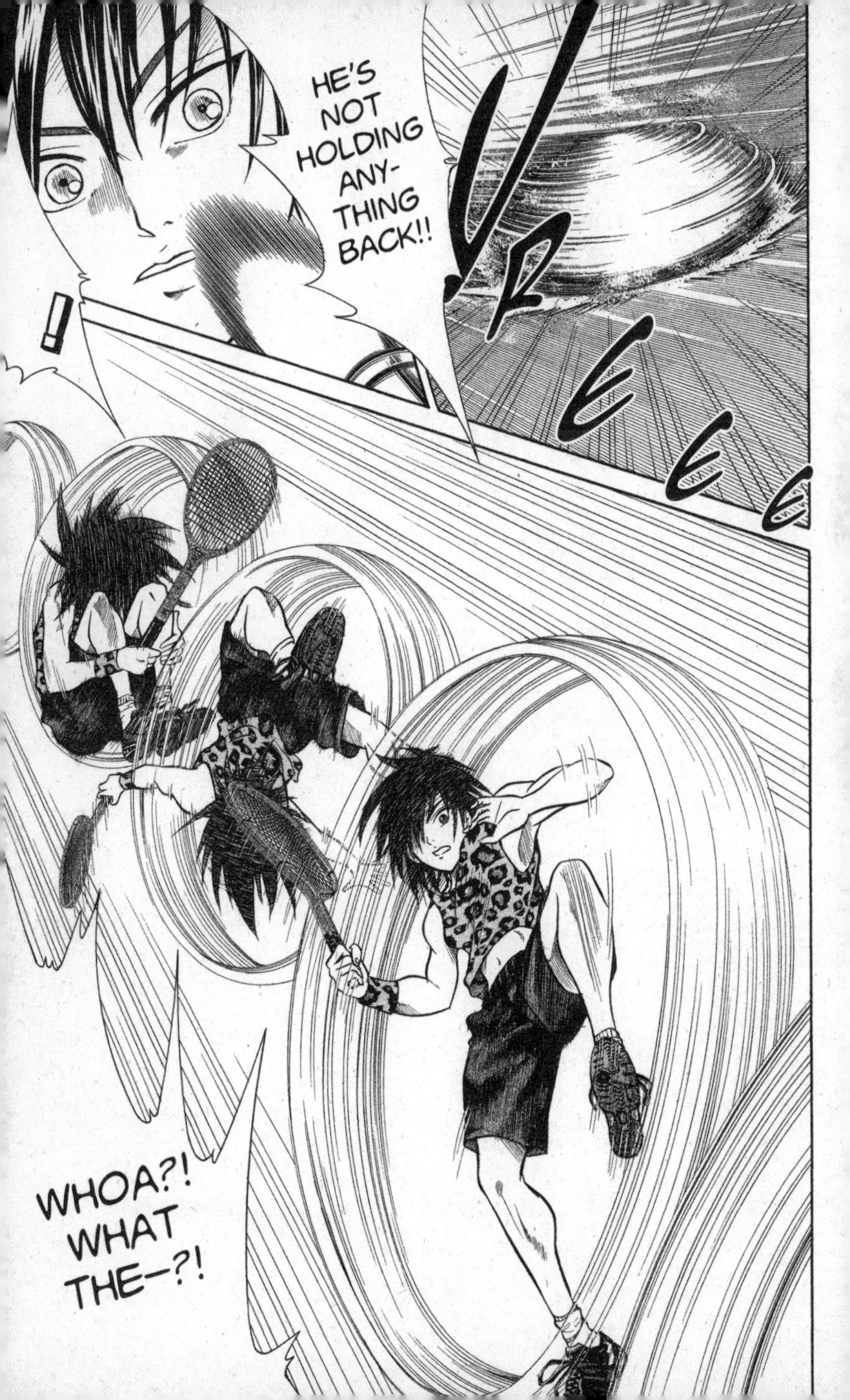

HE'S NOT HOLDING ANY-THING BACK!!
!
VREEEEE
WHOA?! WHAT THE--?!

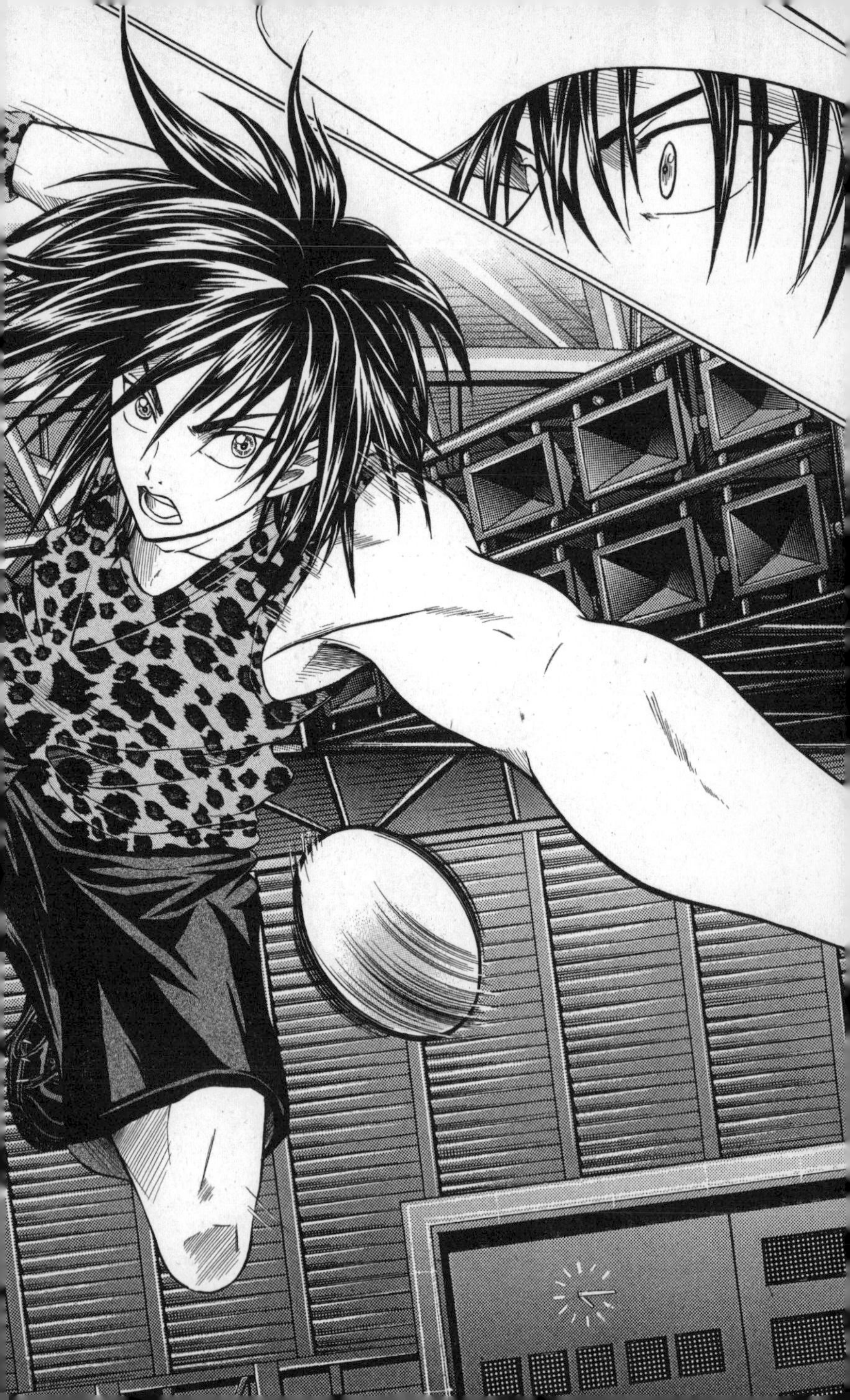

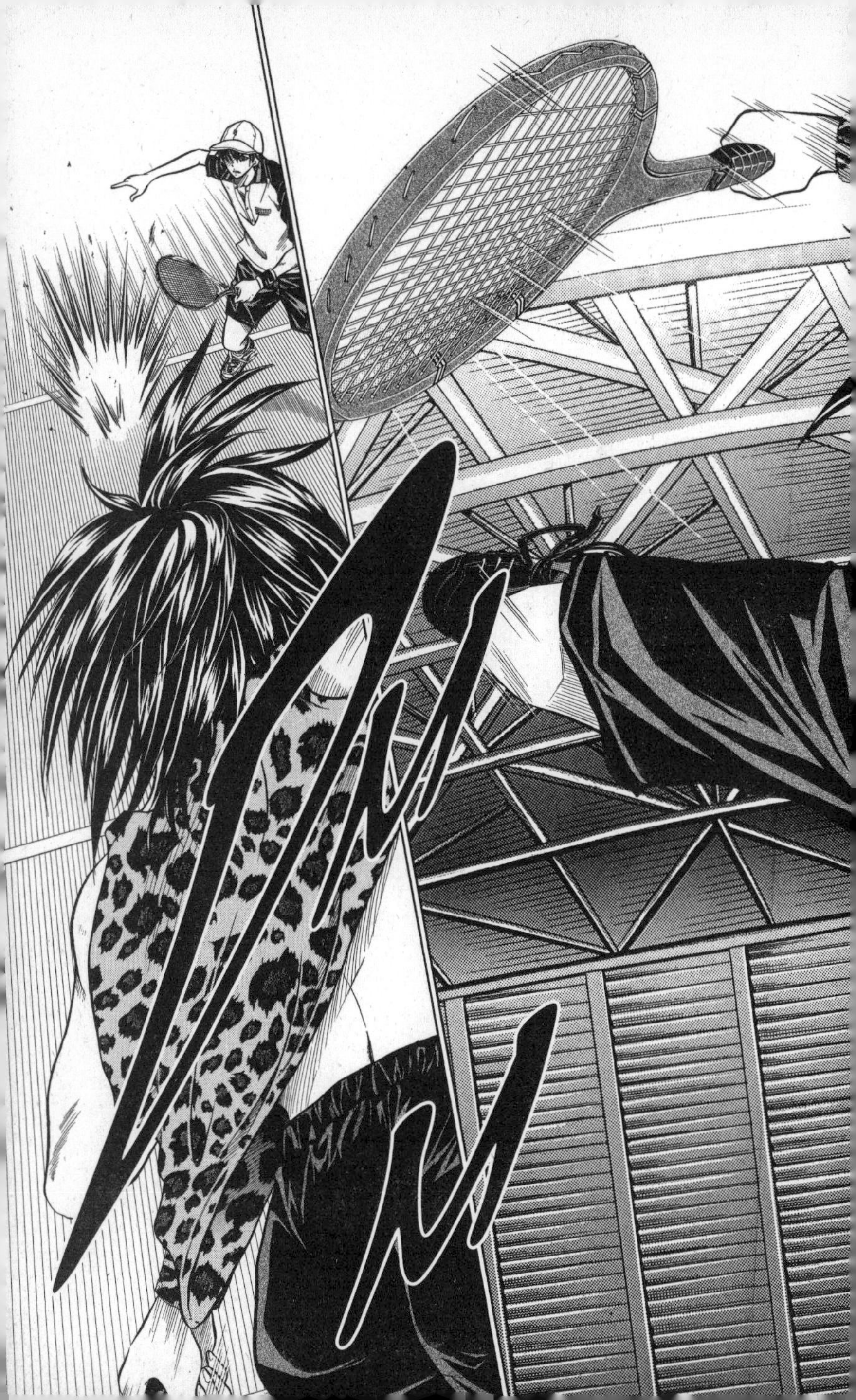

テニスの王子様

THE PRINCE OF TENNIS

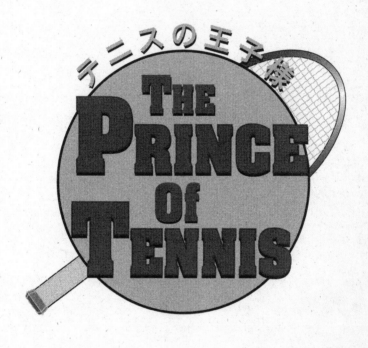

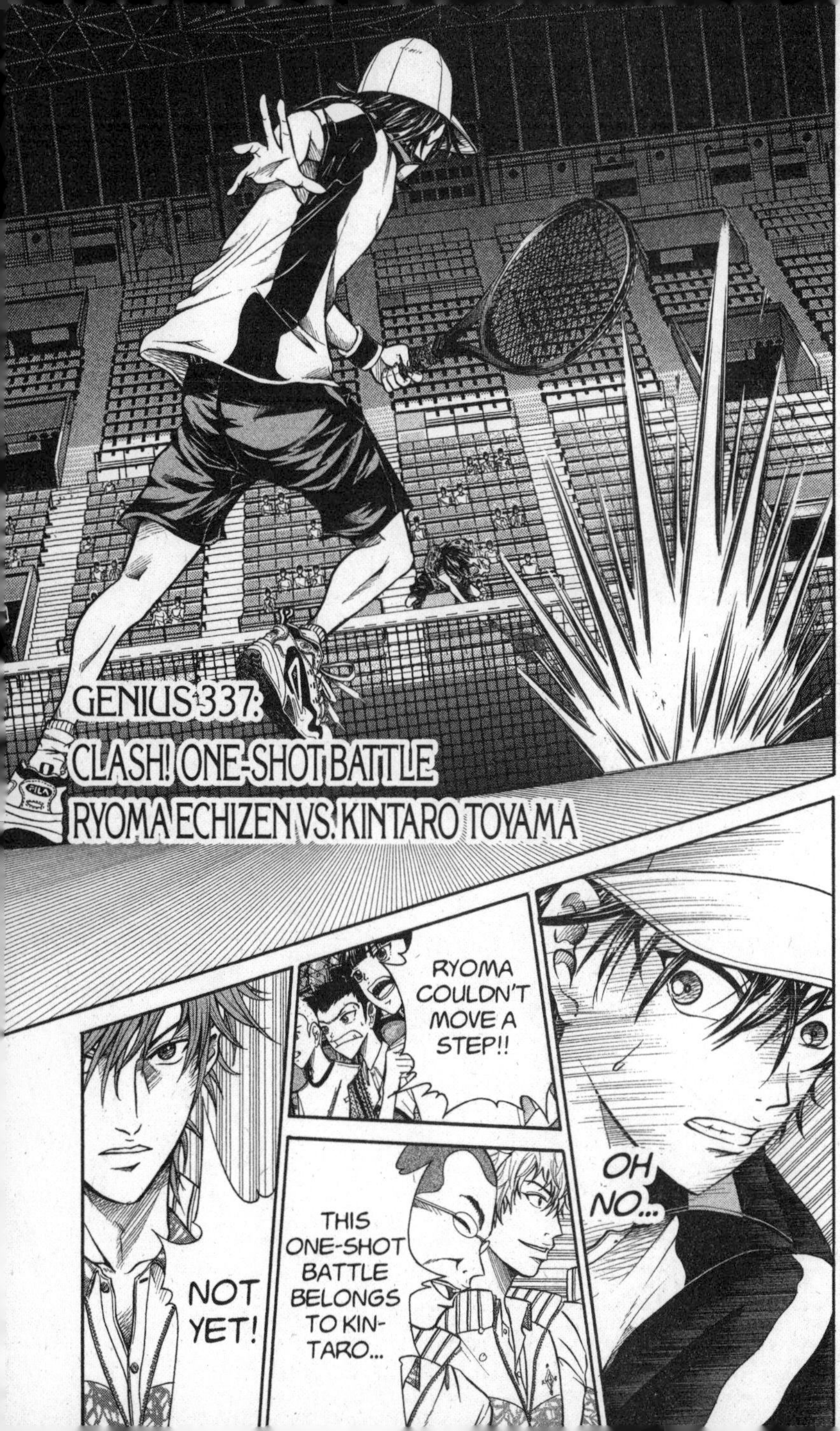
GENIUS 337:
CLASH! ONE-SHOT BATTLE
RYOMA ECHIZEN VS. KINTARO TOYAMA
OH NO...
RYOMA COULDN'T MOVE A STEP!!
THIS ONE-SHOT BATTLE BELONGS TO KIN-TARO...
NOT YET!

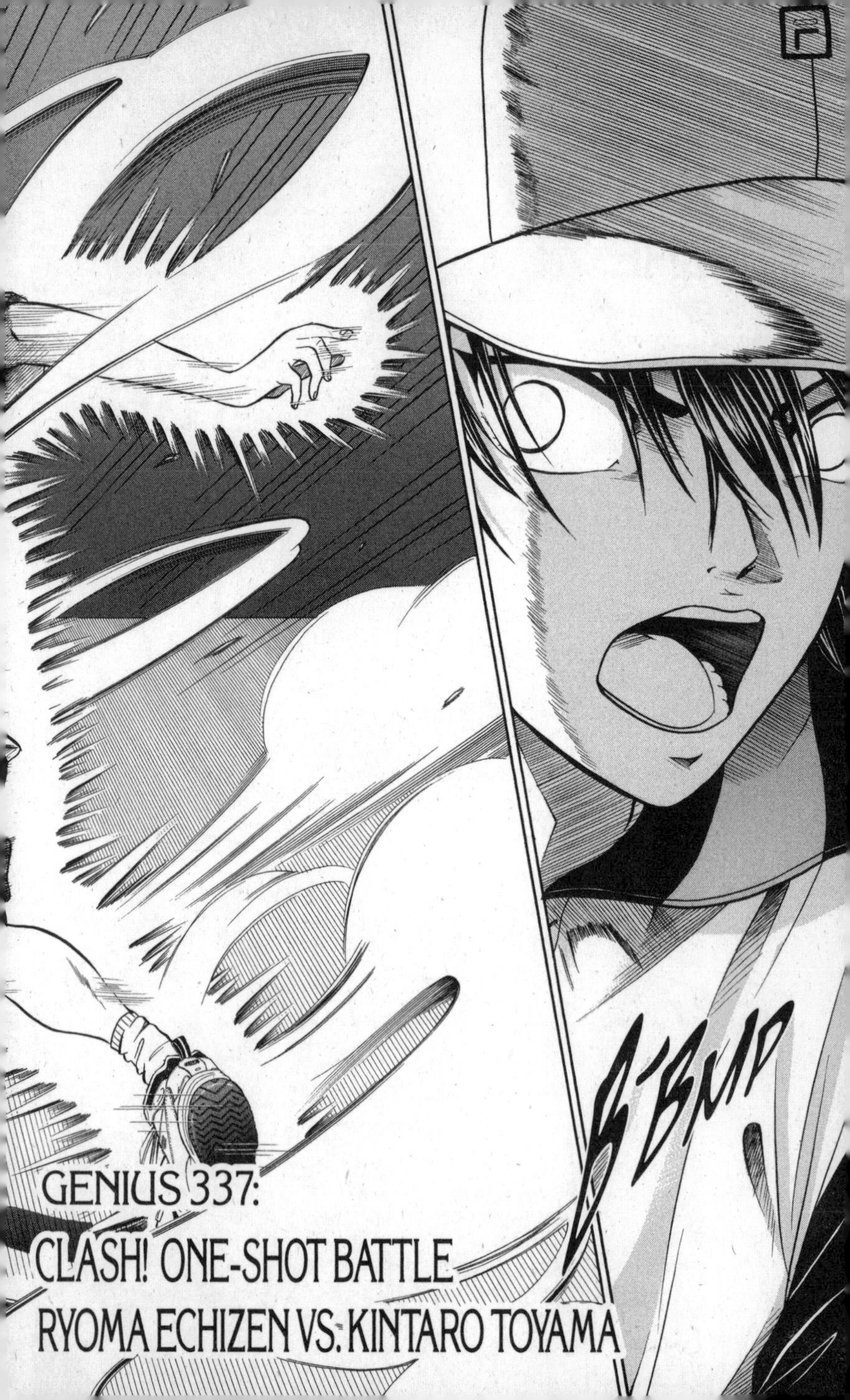

GENIUS 337:
CLASH! ONE-SHOT BATTLE
RYOMA ECHIZEN VS. KINTARO TOYAMA

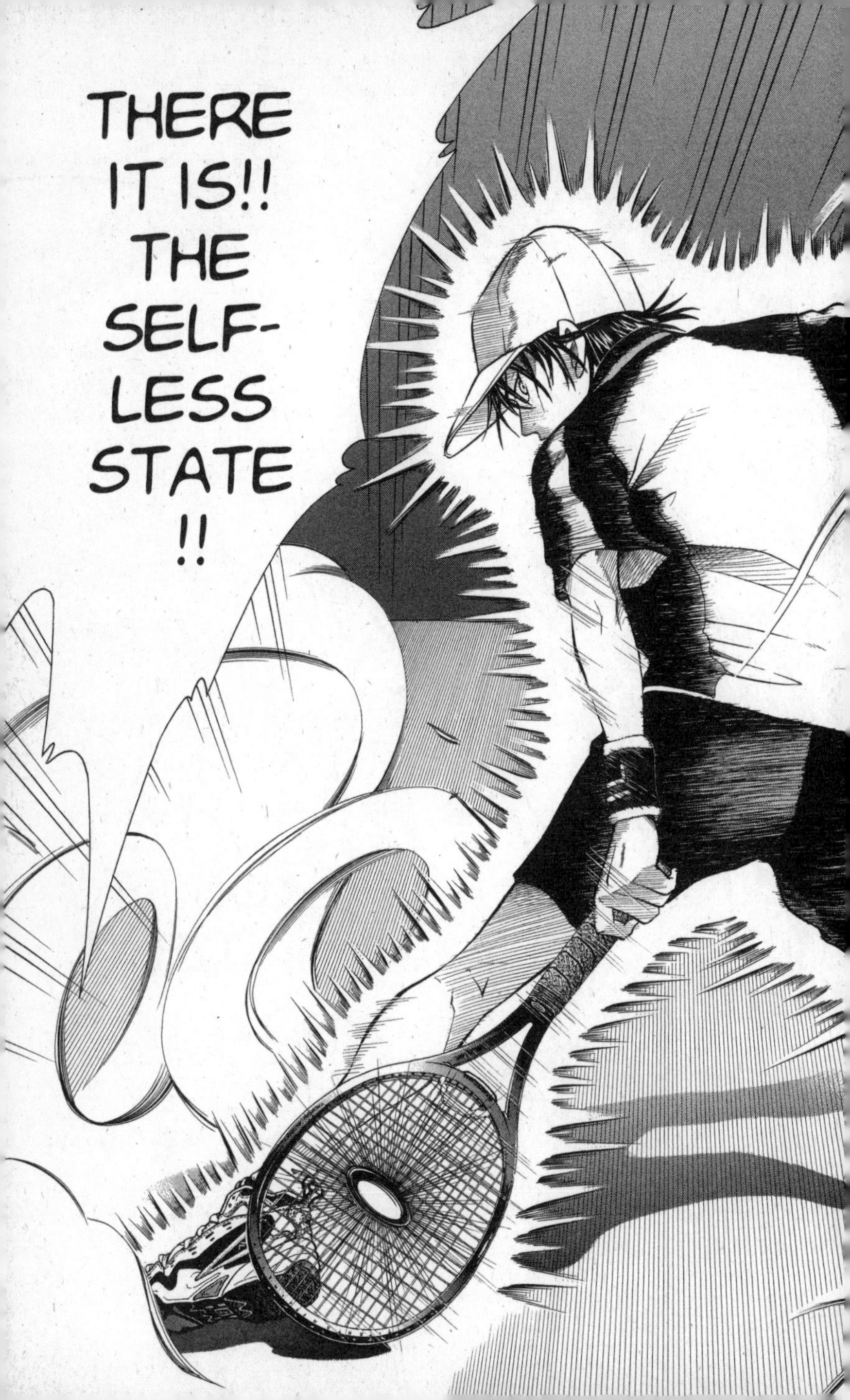
THERE IT IS!! THE SELF-LESS STATE !!

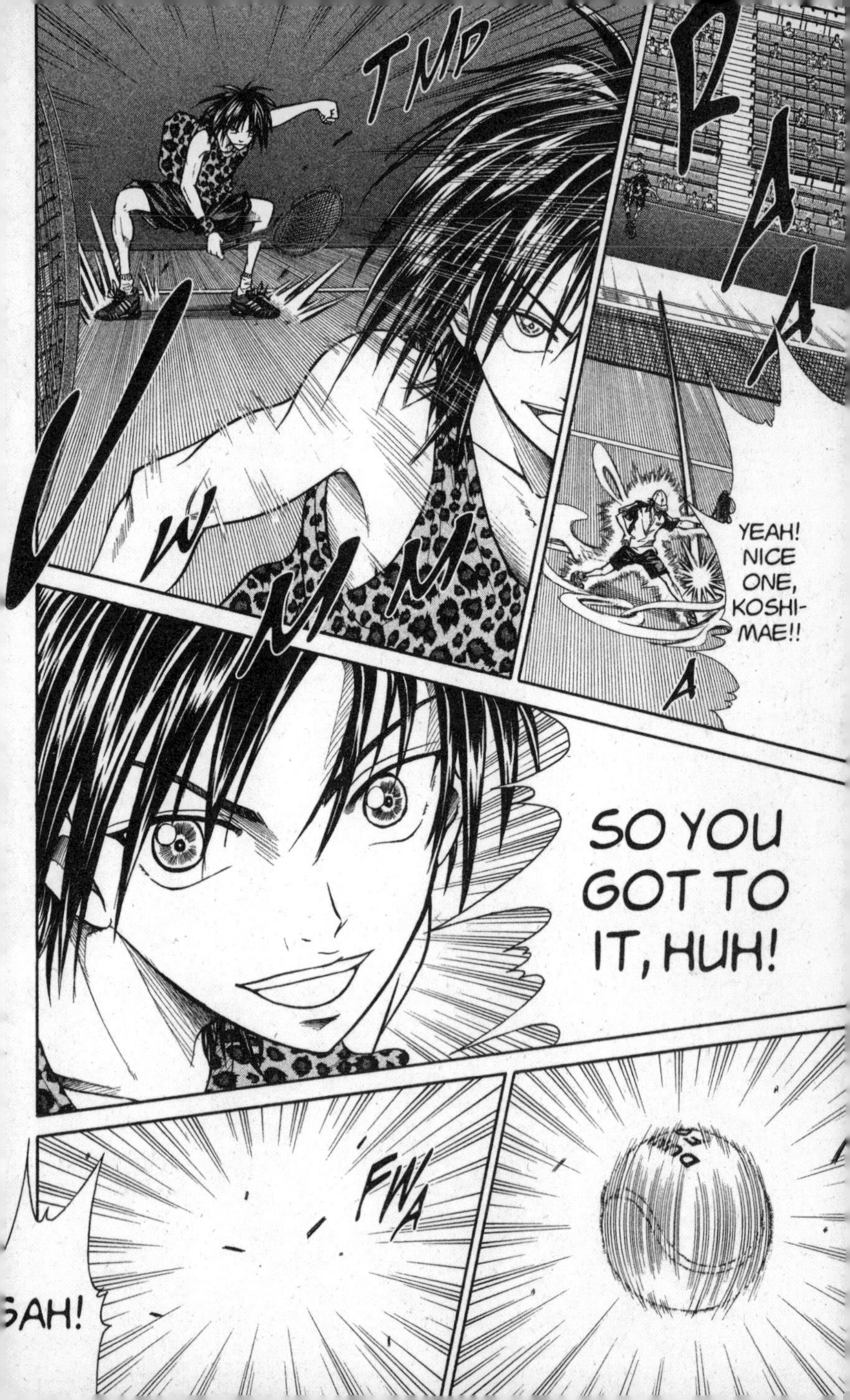
YEAH! NICE ONE, KOSHI-MAE!!
TMP
SO YOU GOT TO IT, HUH!
FWA

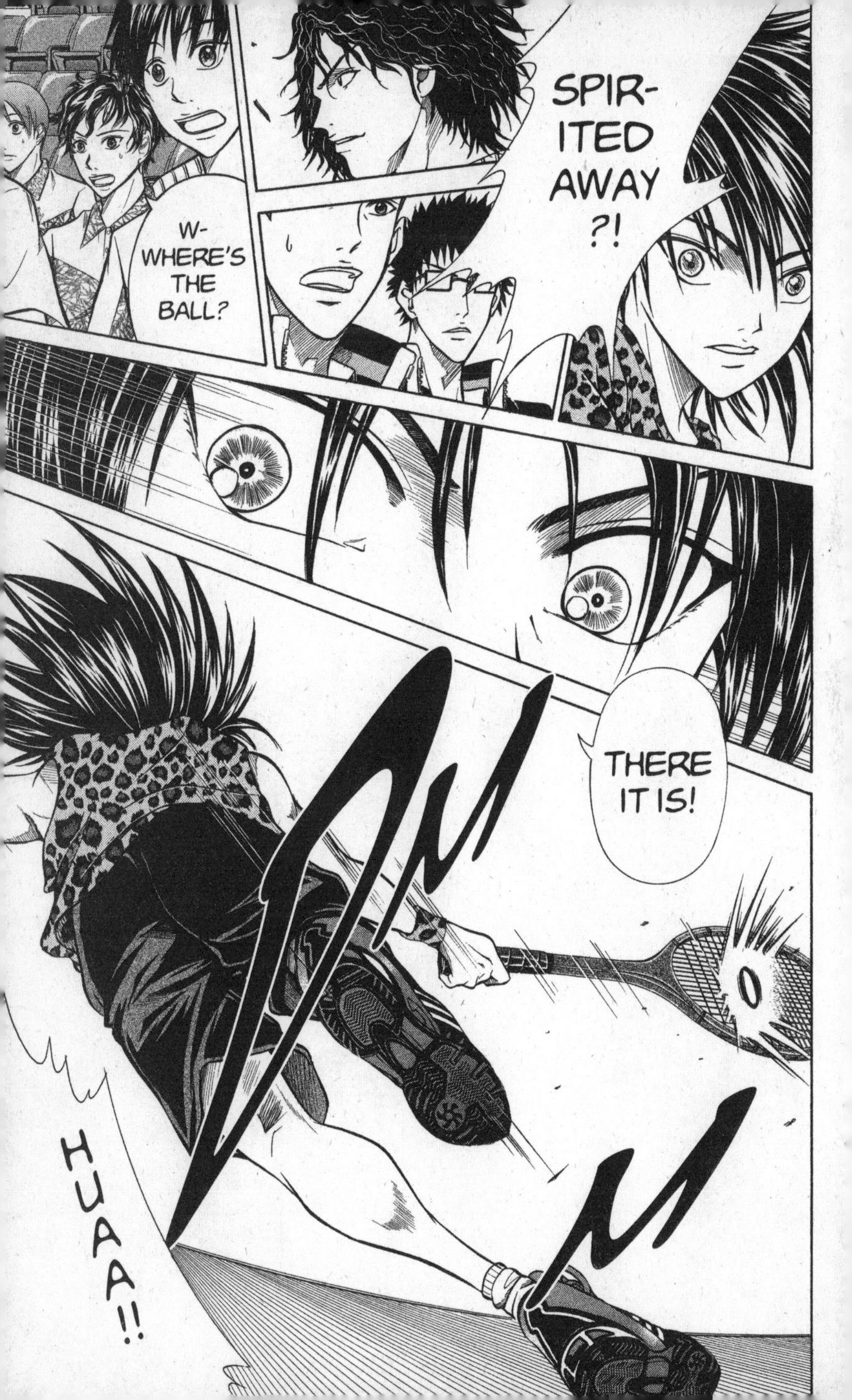
SPIR-ITED AWAY?!
W-WHERE'S THE BALL?
THERE IT IS!
HUAA!!

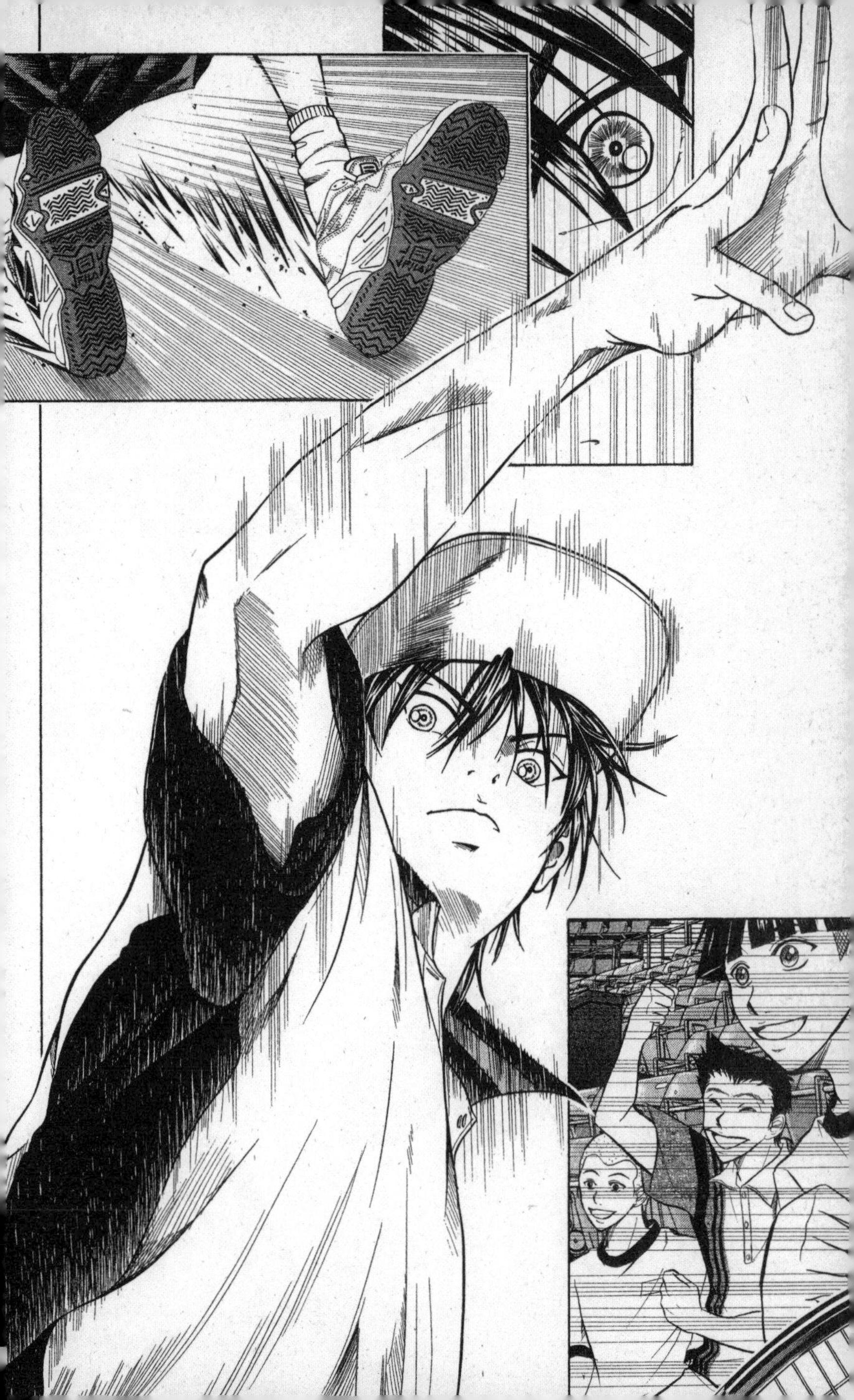

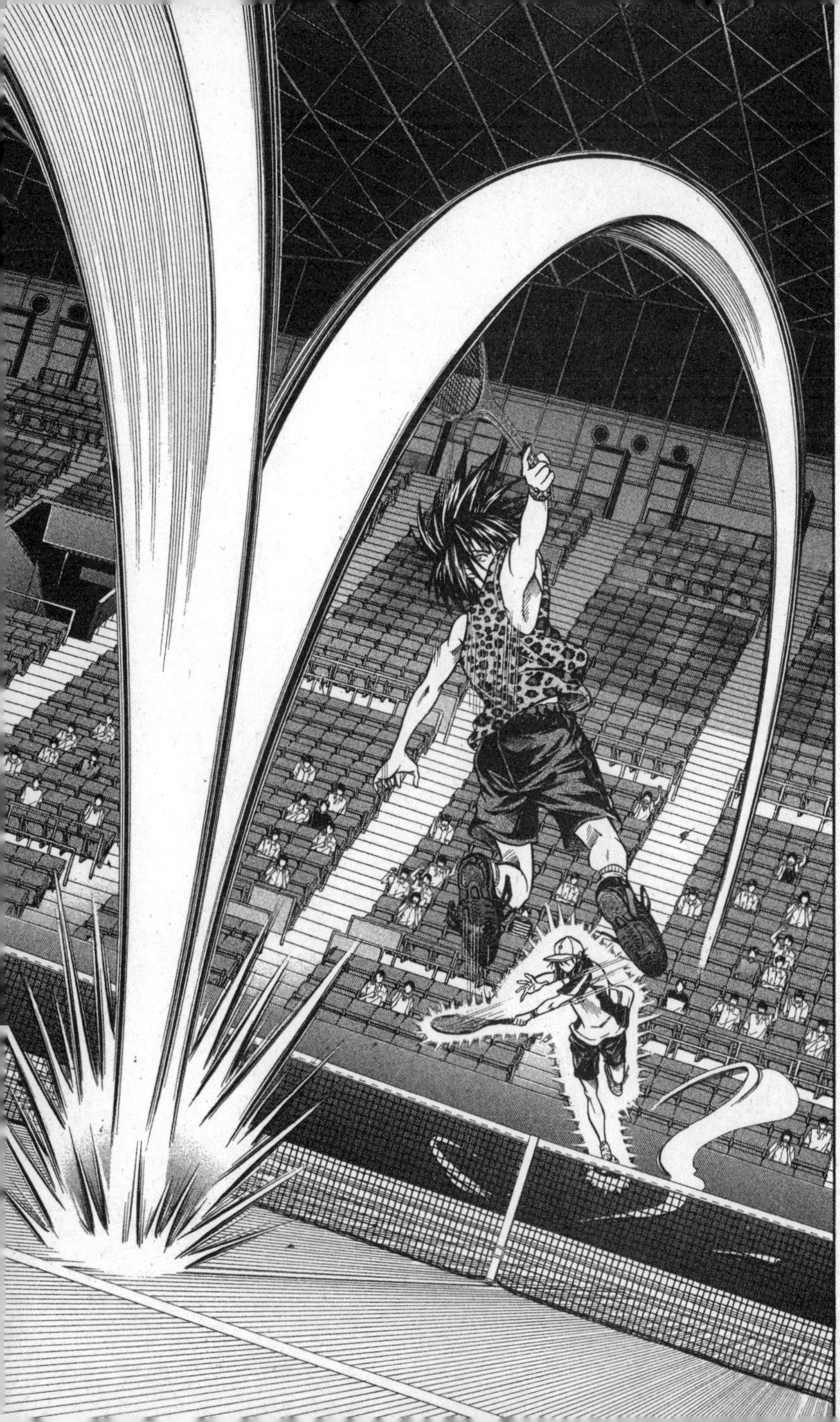

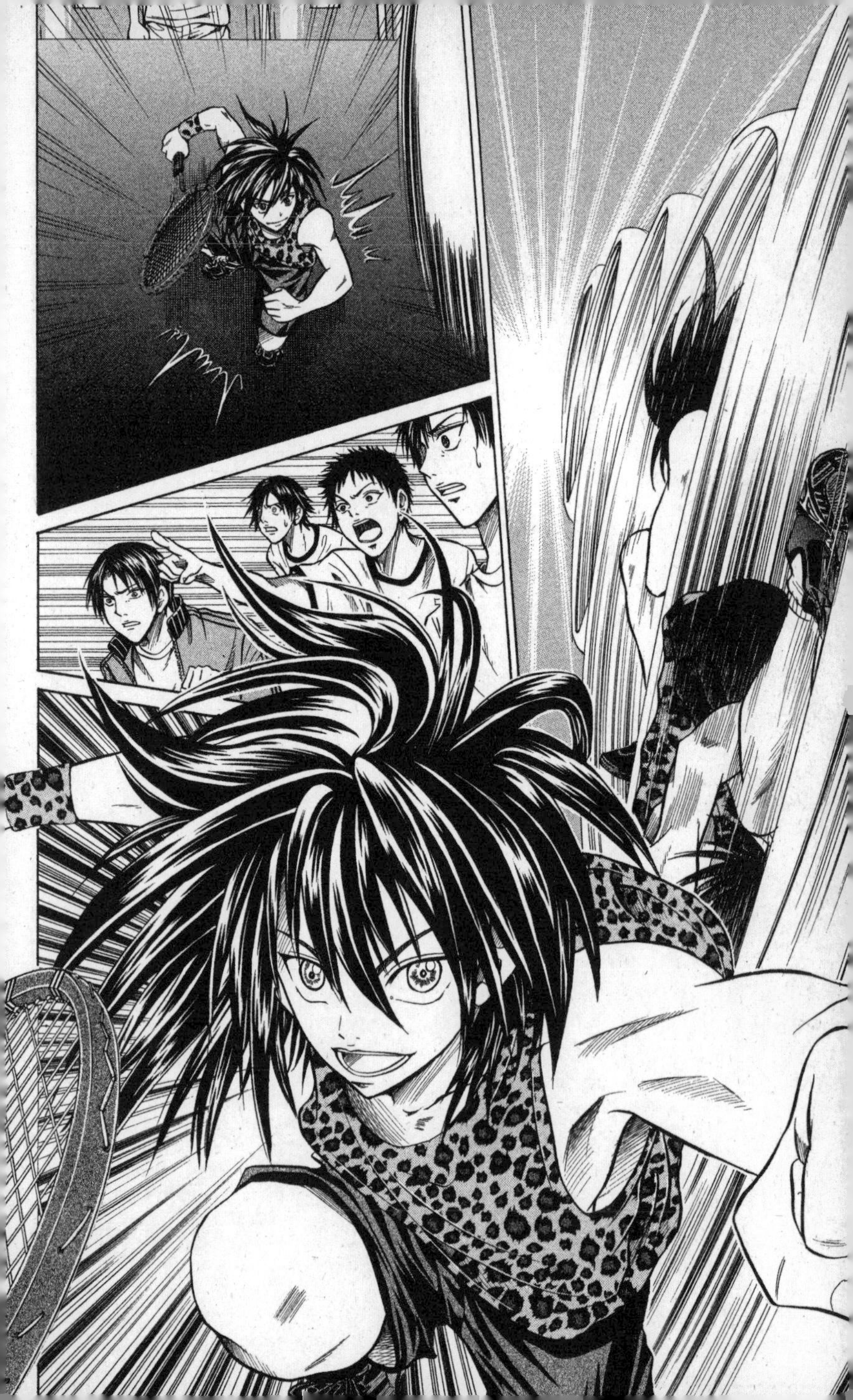

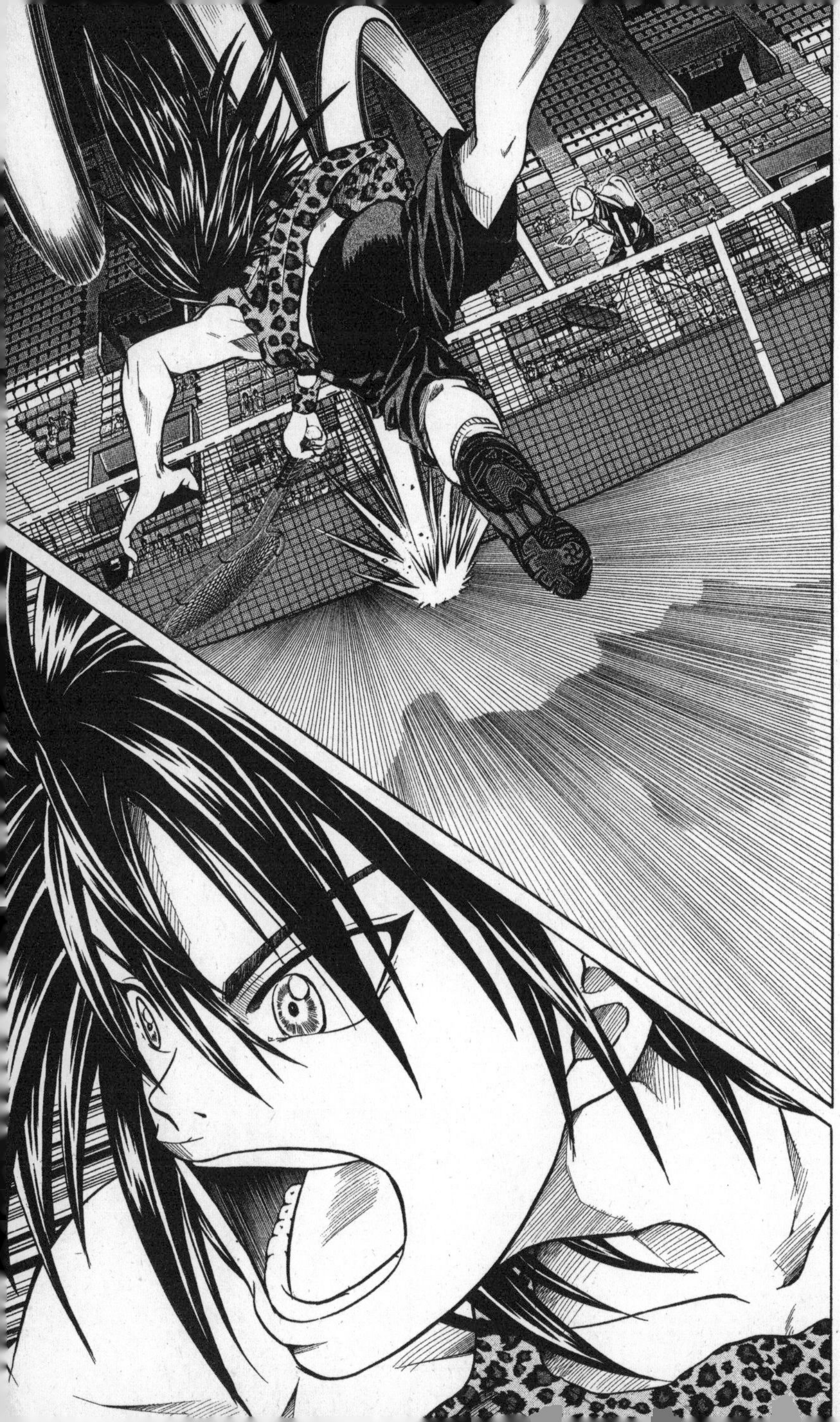

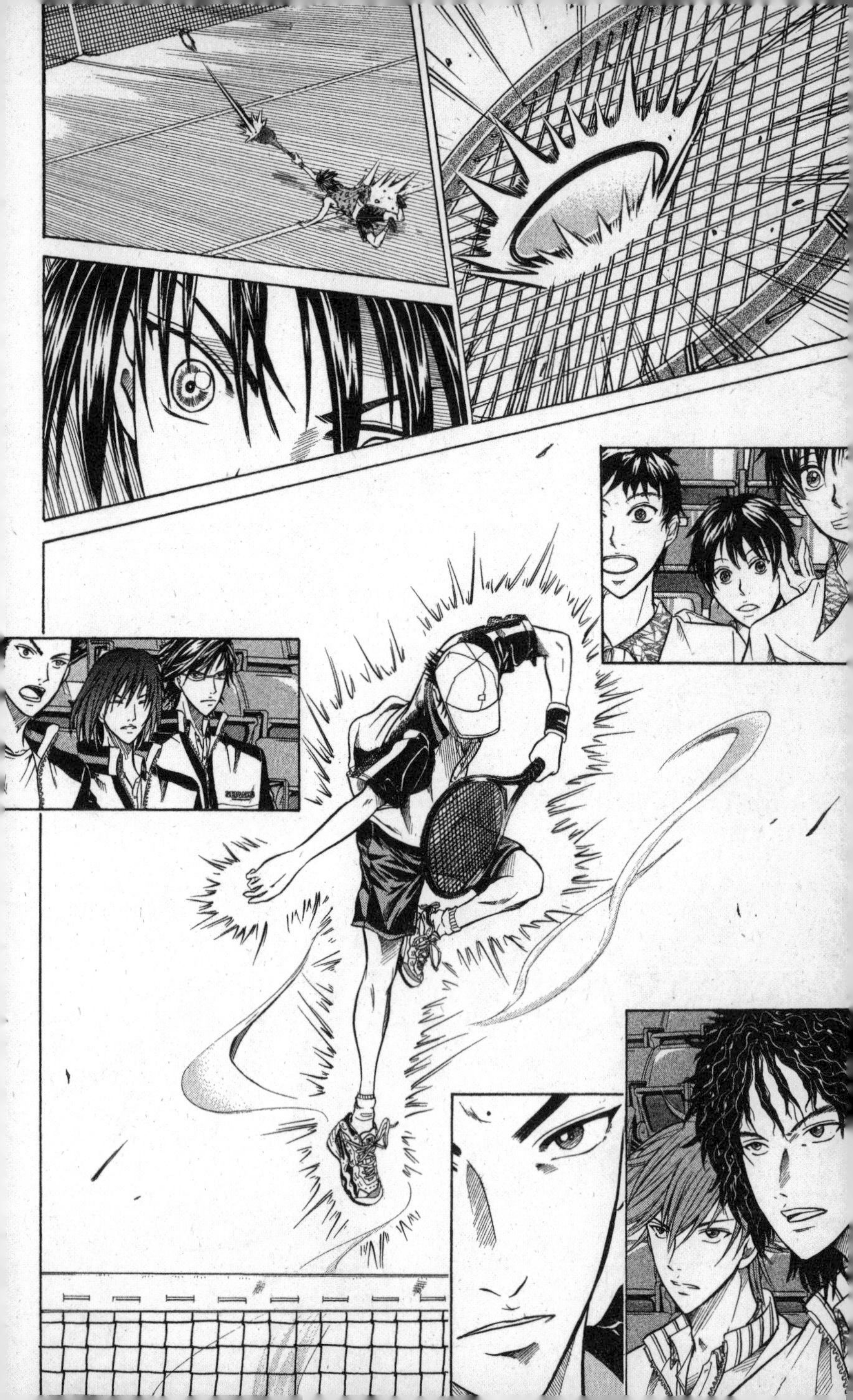

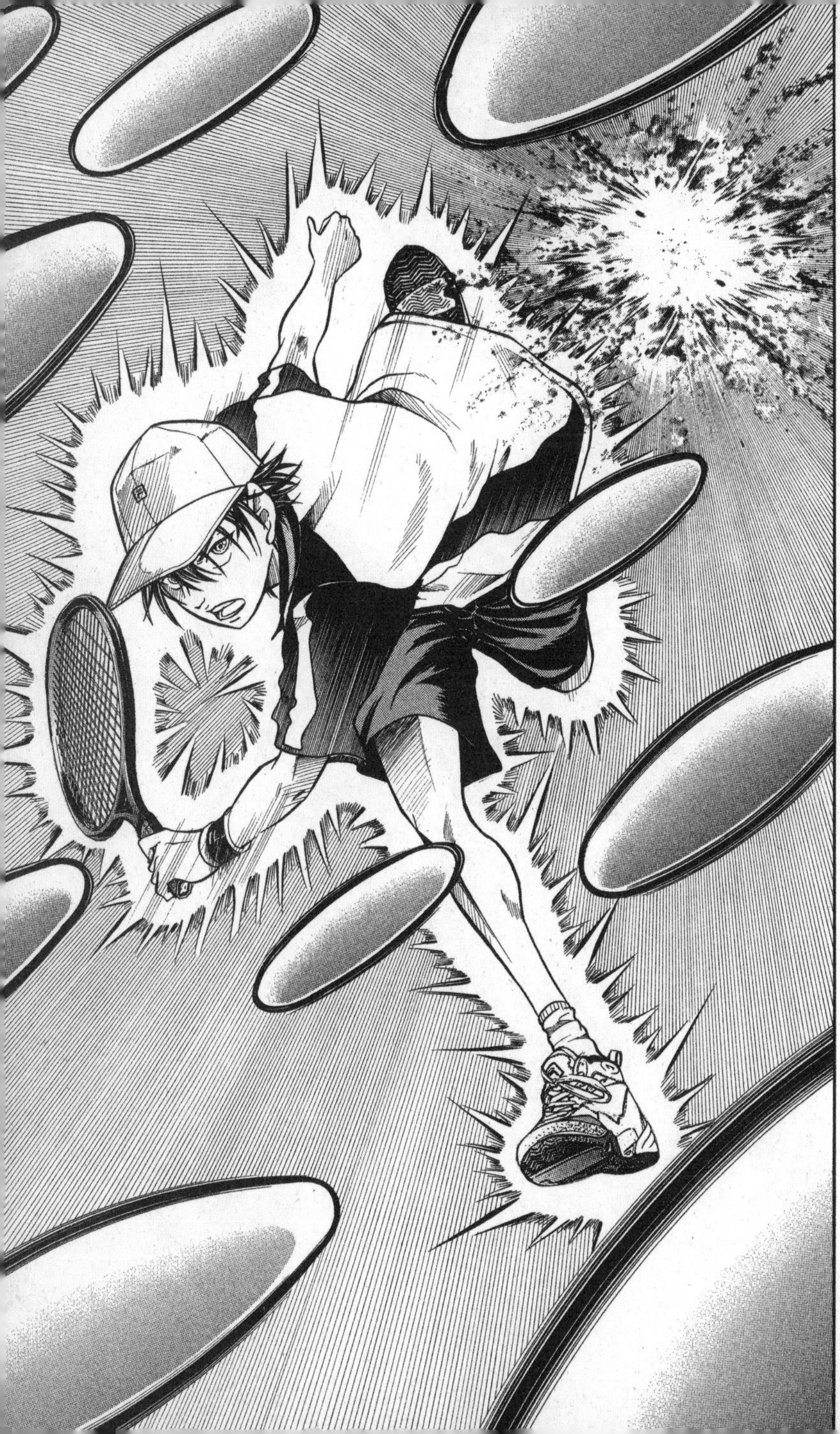

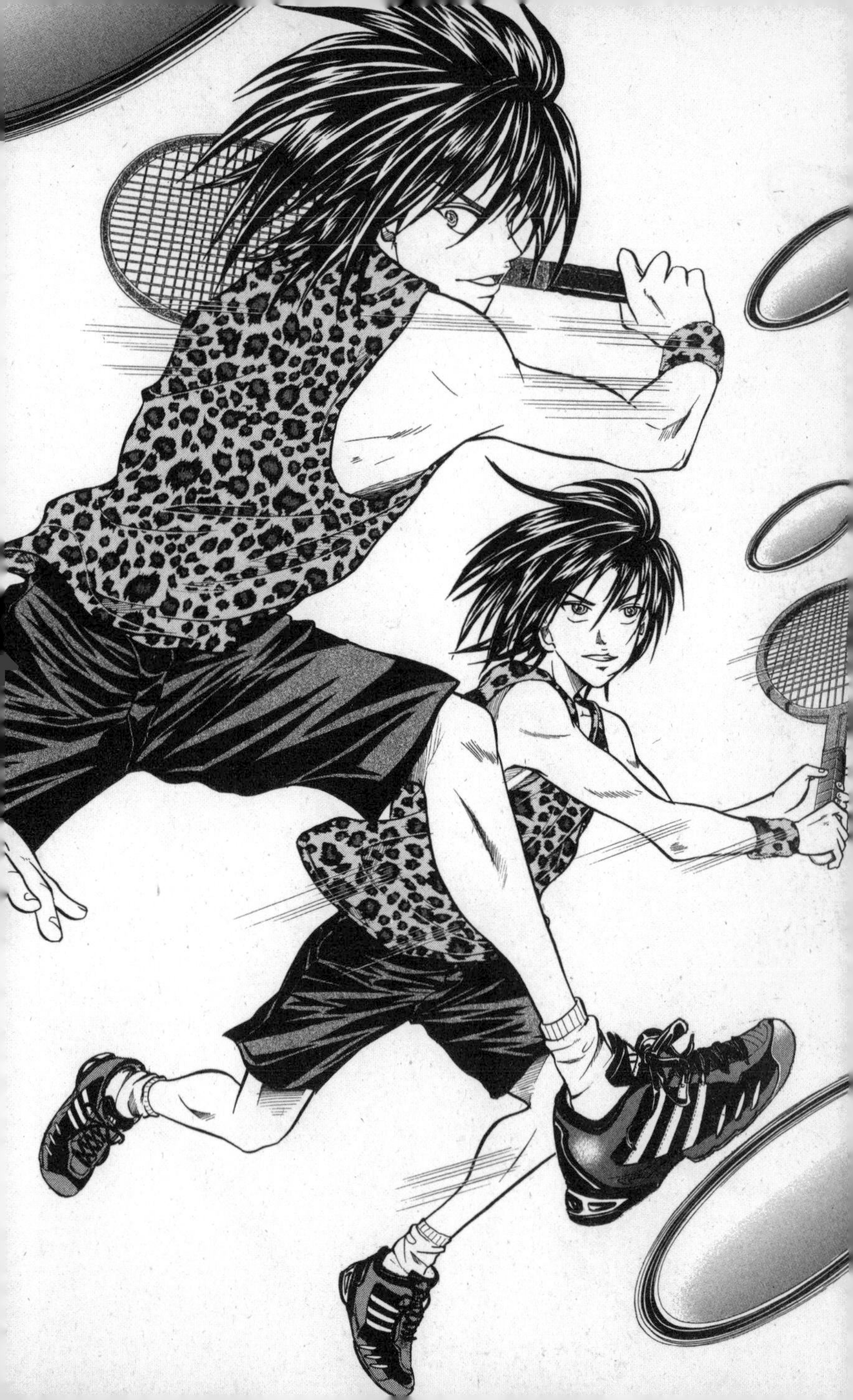

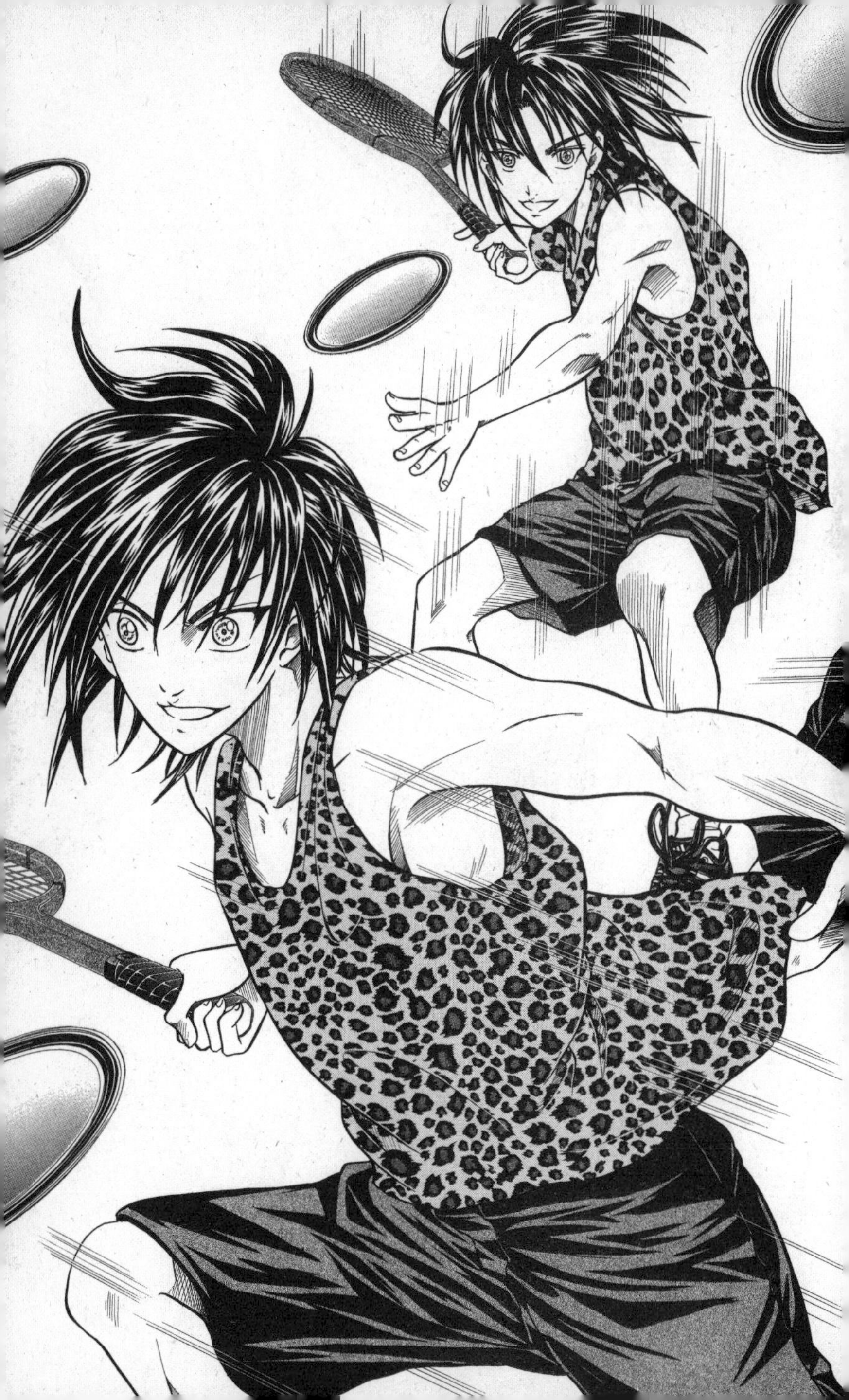

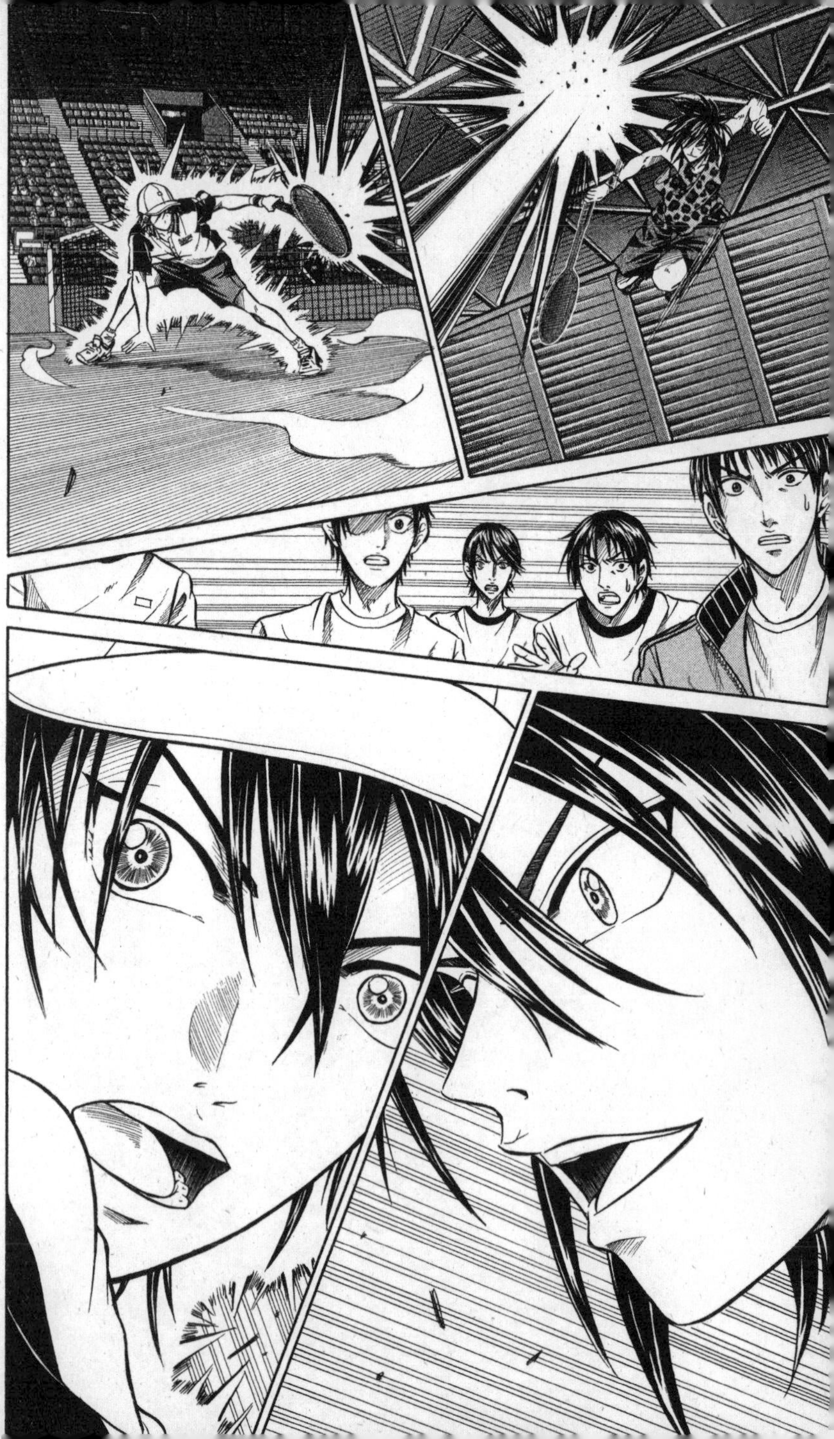

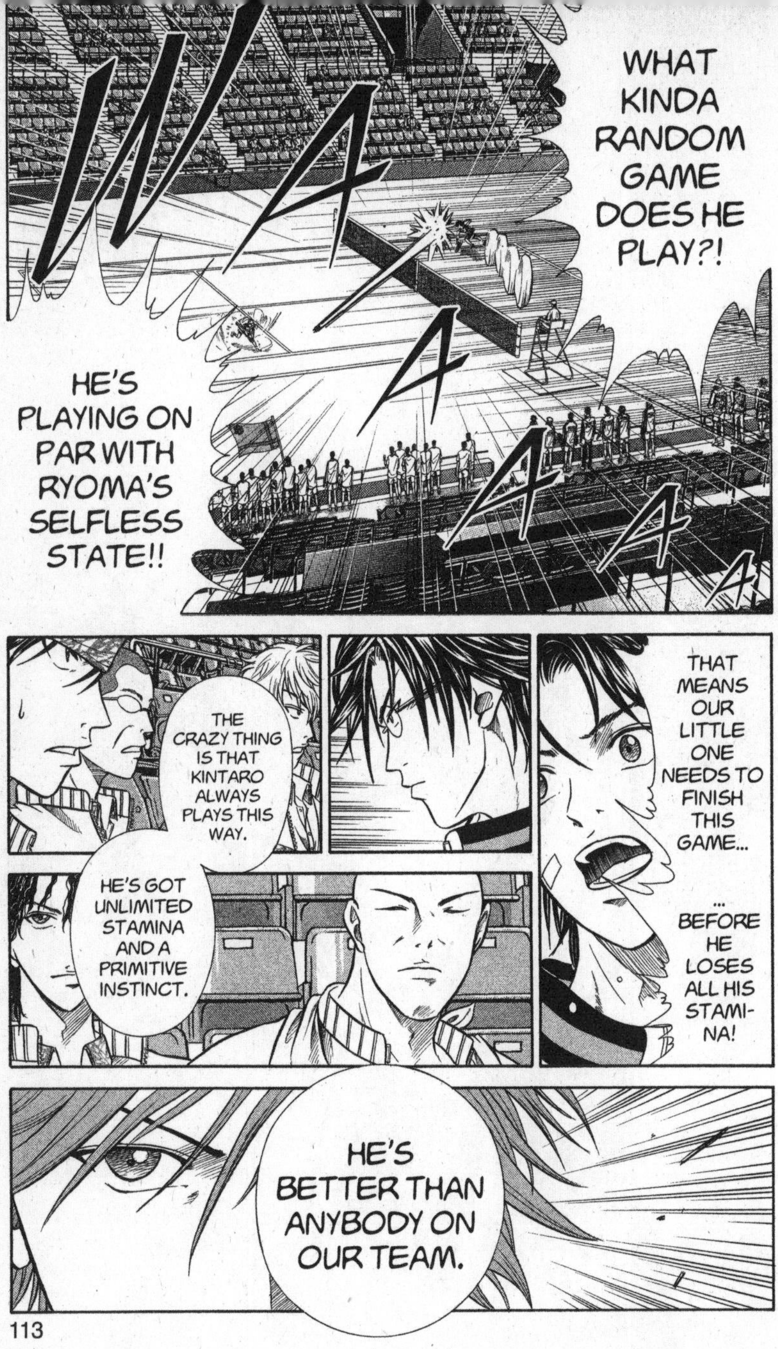
WHAT KINDA RANDOM GAME DOES HE PLAY?!
WAAAAAA
HE'S PLAYING ON PAR WITH RYOMA'S SELFLESS STATE!!
THAT MEANS OUR LITTLE ONE NEEDS TO FINISH THIS GAME...
...BEFORE HE LOSES ALL HIS STAMINA!
THE CRAZY THING IS THAT KINTARO ALWAYS PLAYS THIS WAY.
HE'S GOT UNLIMITED STAMINA AND A PRIMITIVE INSTINCT.
HE'S BETTER THAN ANYBODY ON OUR TEAM.

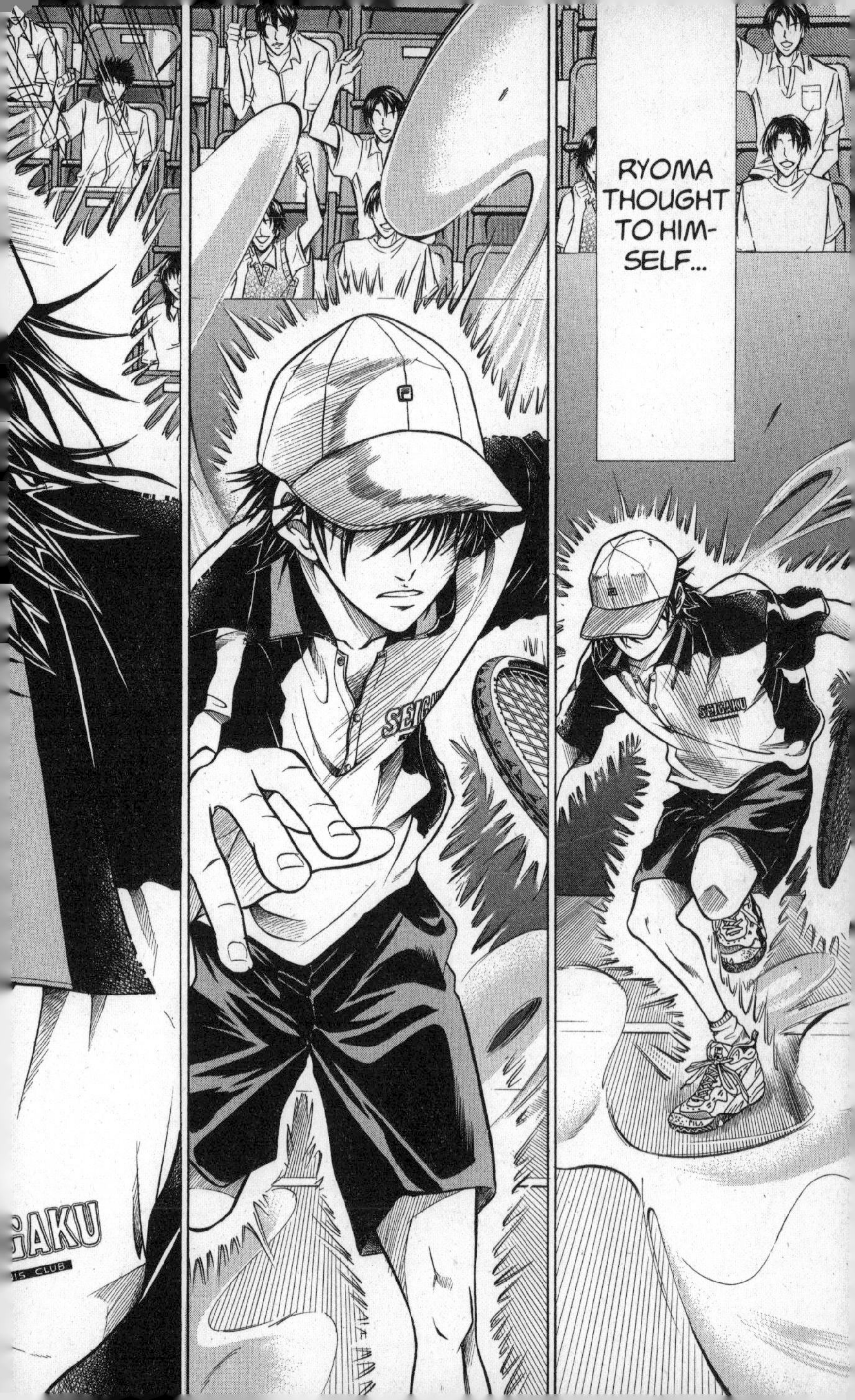
RYOMA THOUGHT TO HIM-SELF...
SEIGAKU
SEIGAKU
GAKU

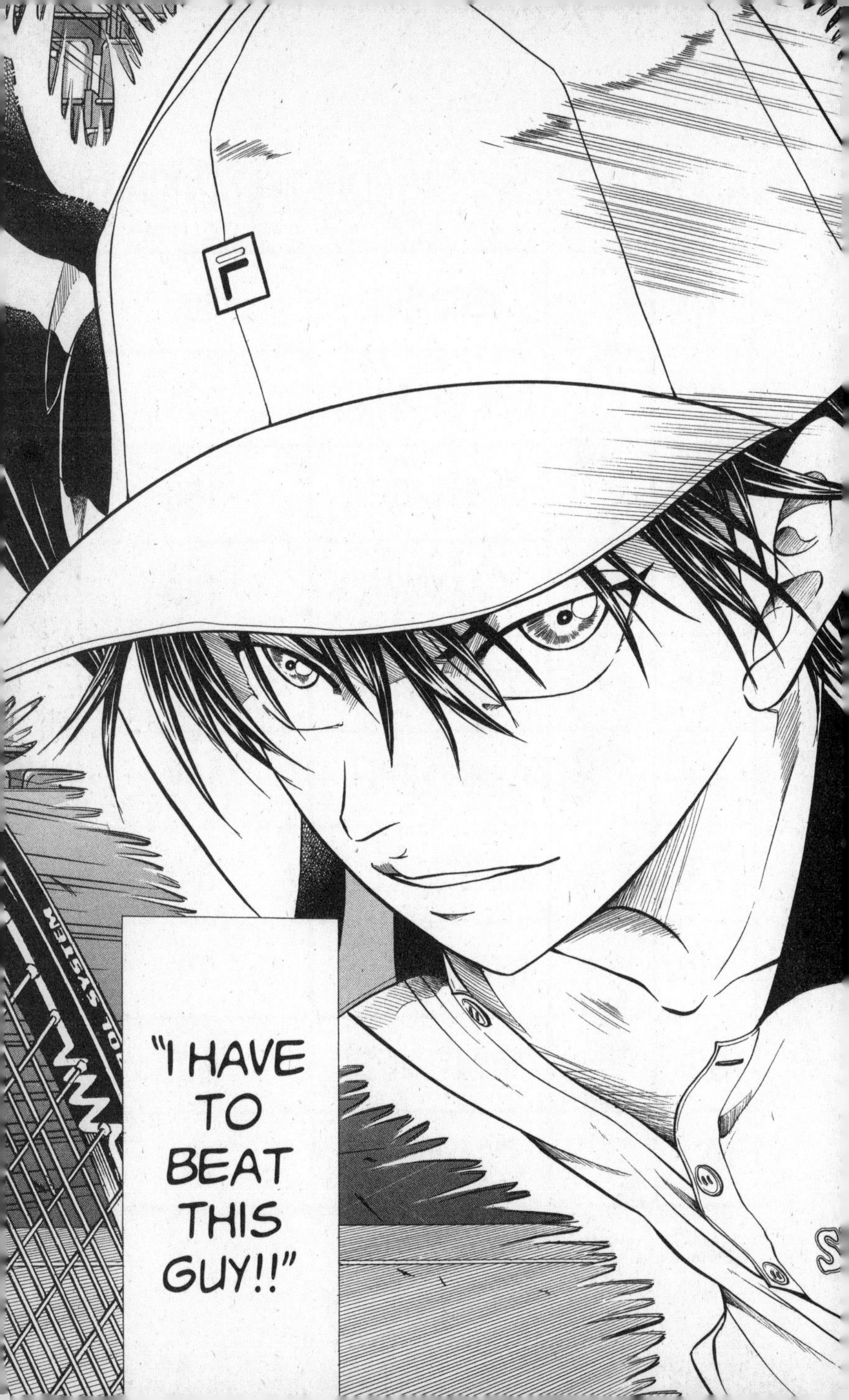
"I HAVE TO BEAT THIS GUY!!"

2007

VALENTINE'S DAY CHOCOLATE RANKING 1

1ST	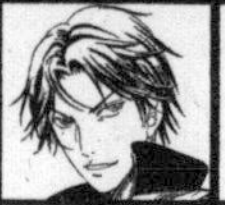	KEIGO ATOBE	807
2ND	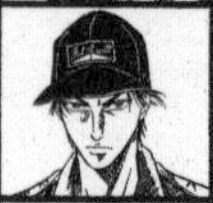	GENICHIRO SANADA	231
3RD	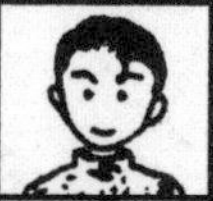	TAKESHI KONOMI	158
4TH	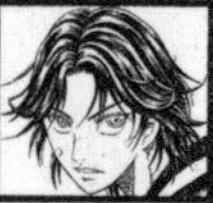	EIJI KIKUMARU	120
5TH	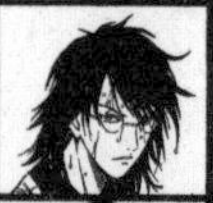	YUUSHI OSHITARI	112
6TH	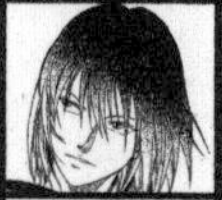	SHUSUKE FUJI	105
7TH	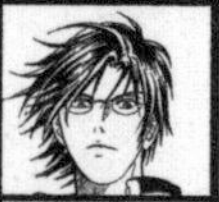	KUMINITSU TEZUKA	84
8TH	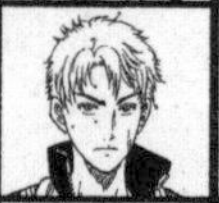	OHTORI CHOTARO	79
9TH	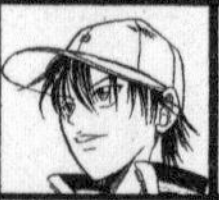	RYOMA ECHIZEN	69
10TH	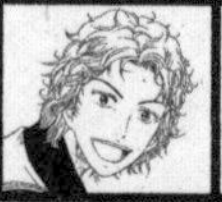	JIRO AKUTAGAWA	63

CONTINUED ON PAGE 134

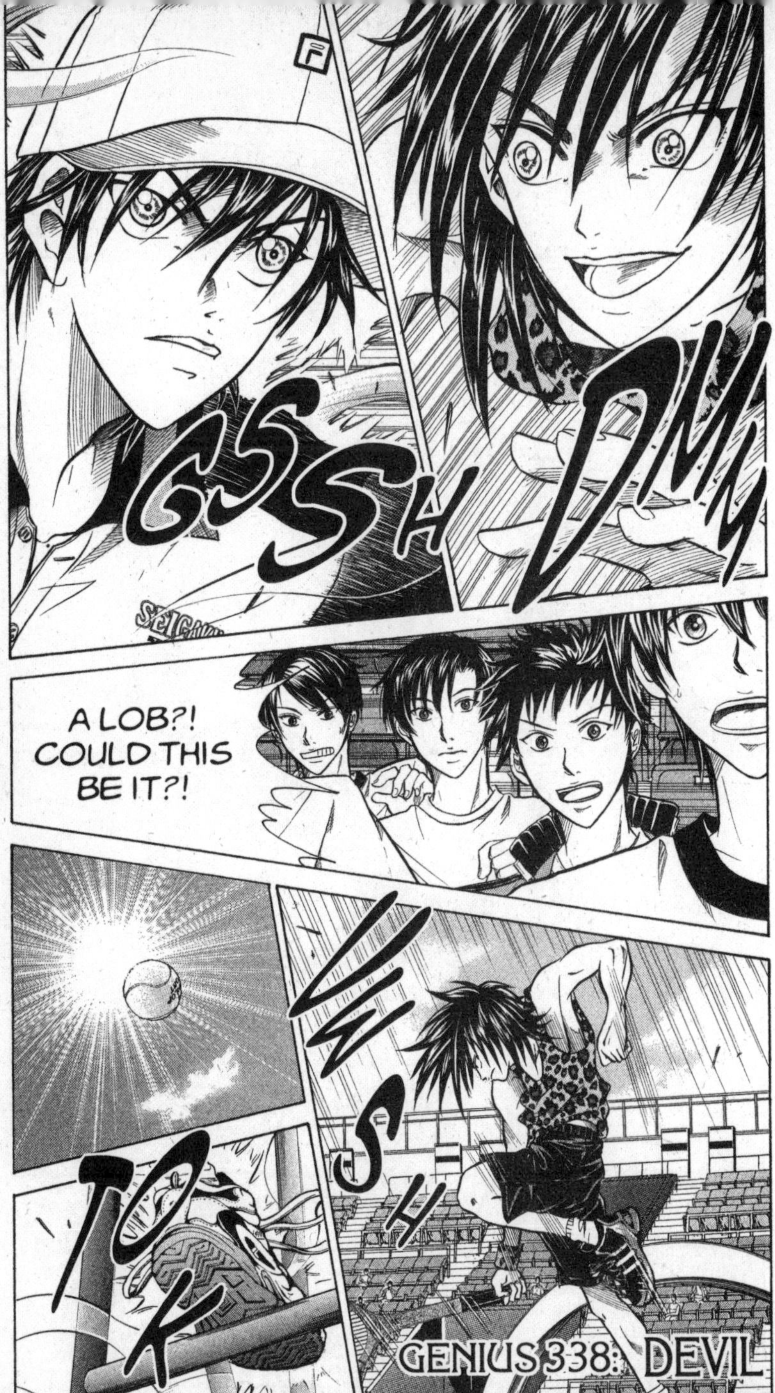
DMM
GSSH
A LOB?! COULD THIS BE IT?!
WHSH
TOK
GENIUS 338: DEVIL

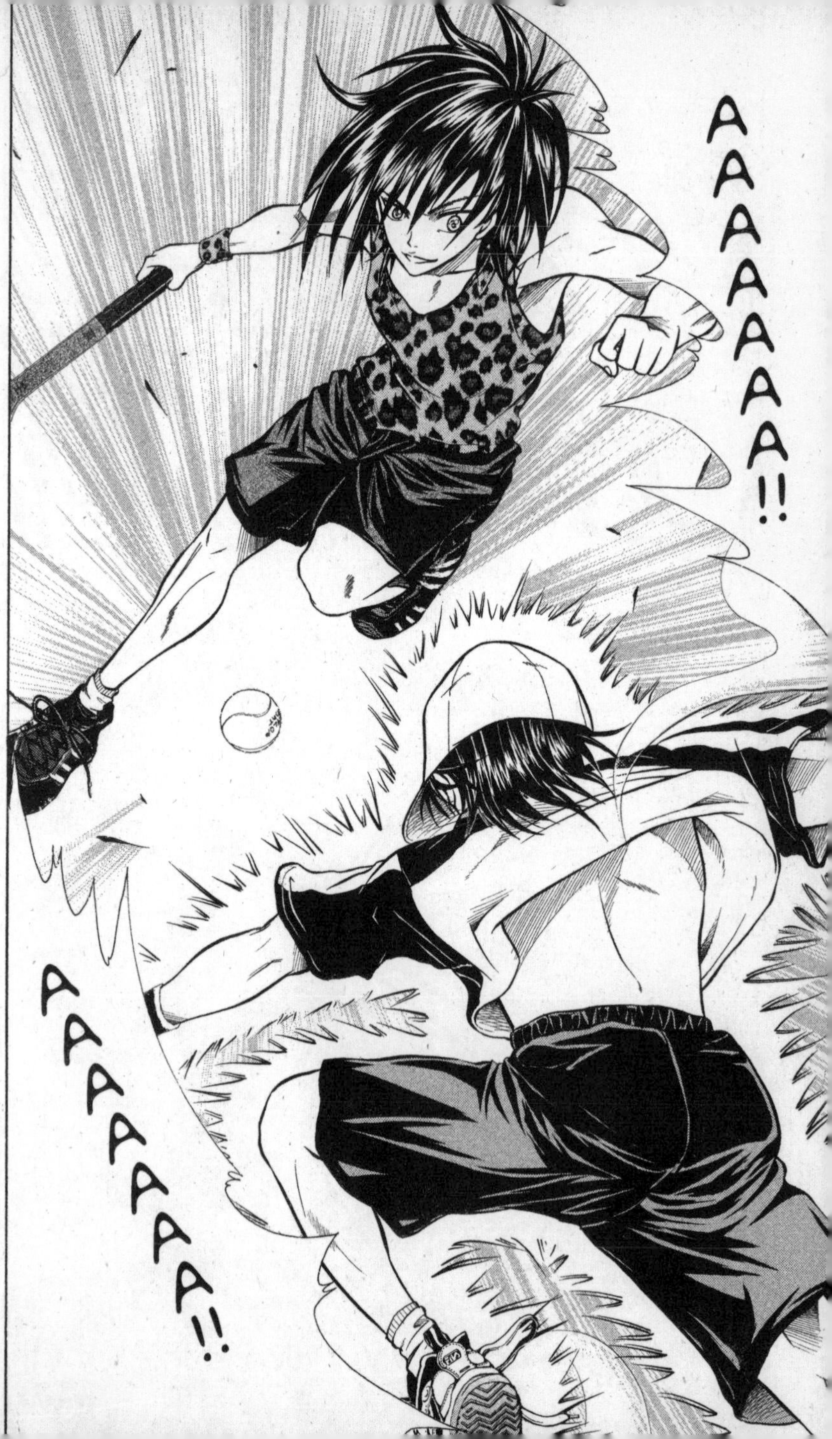
AAAAAAA!!
AAAAAAA!!

READ THIS WAY

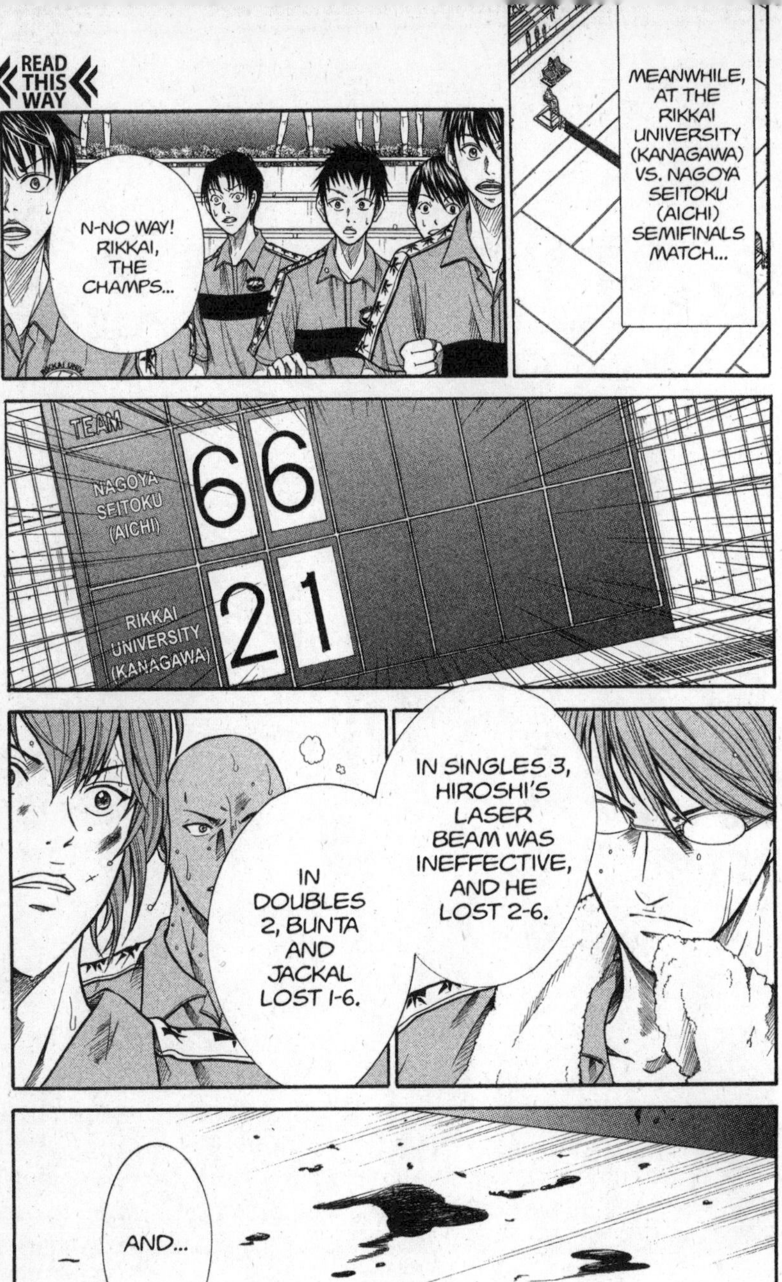
MEANWHILE, AT THE RIKKAI UNIVERSITY (KANAGAWA) VS. NAGOYA SEITOKU (AICHI) SEMIFINALS MATCH...
N-NO WAY! RIKKAI, THE CHAMPS...
TEAM
NAGOYA SEITOKU (AICHI)
6 6
RIKKAI UNIVERSITY (KANAGAWA)
2 1
IN SINGLES 3, HIROSHI'S LASER BEAM WAS INEFFECTIVE, AND HE LOST 2-6.
IN DOUBLES 2, BUNTA AND JACKAL LOST 1-6.
AND...

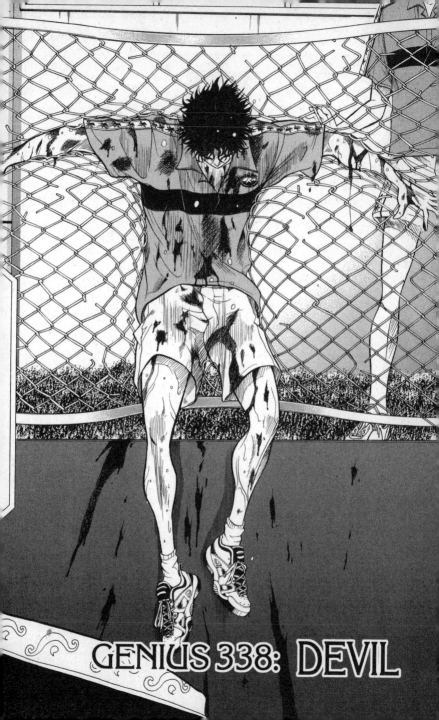

GENIUS 338: DEVIL

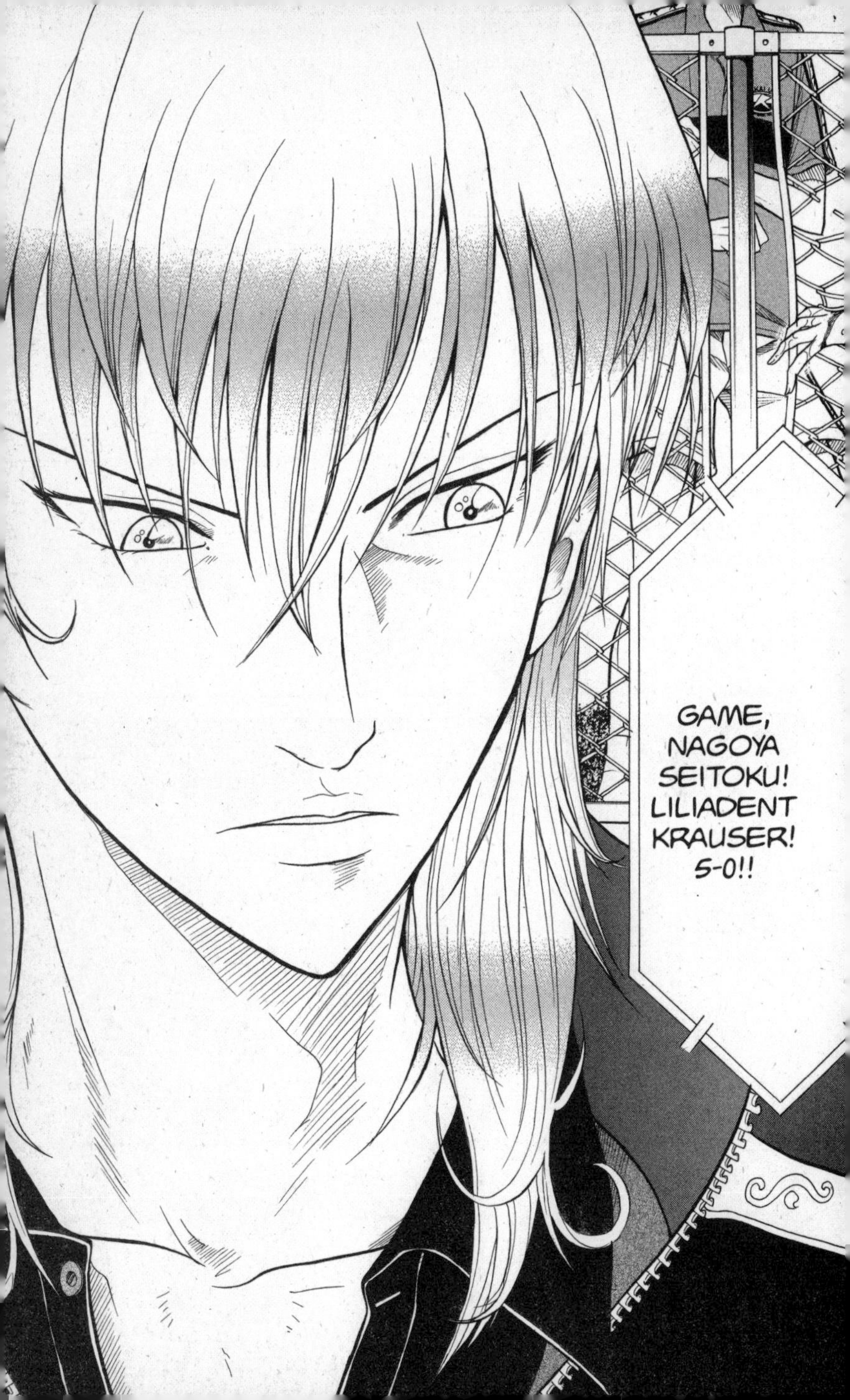
GAME, NAGOYA SEITOKU! LILIADENT KRAUSER! 5-0!!

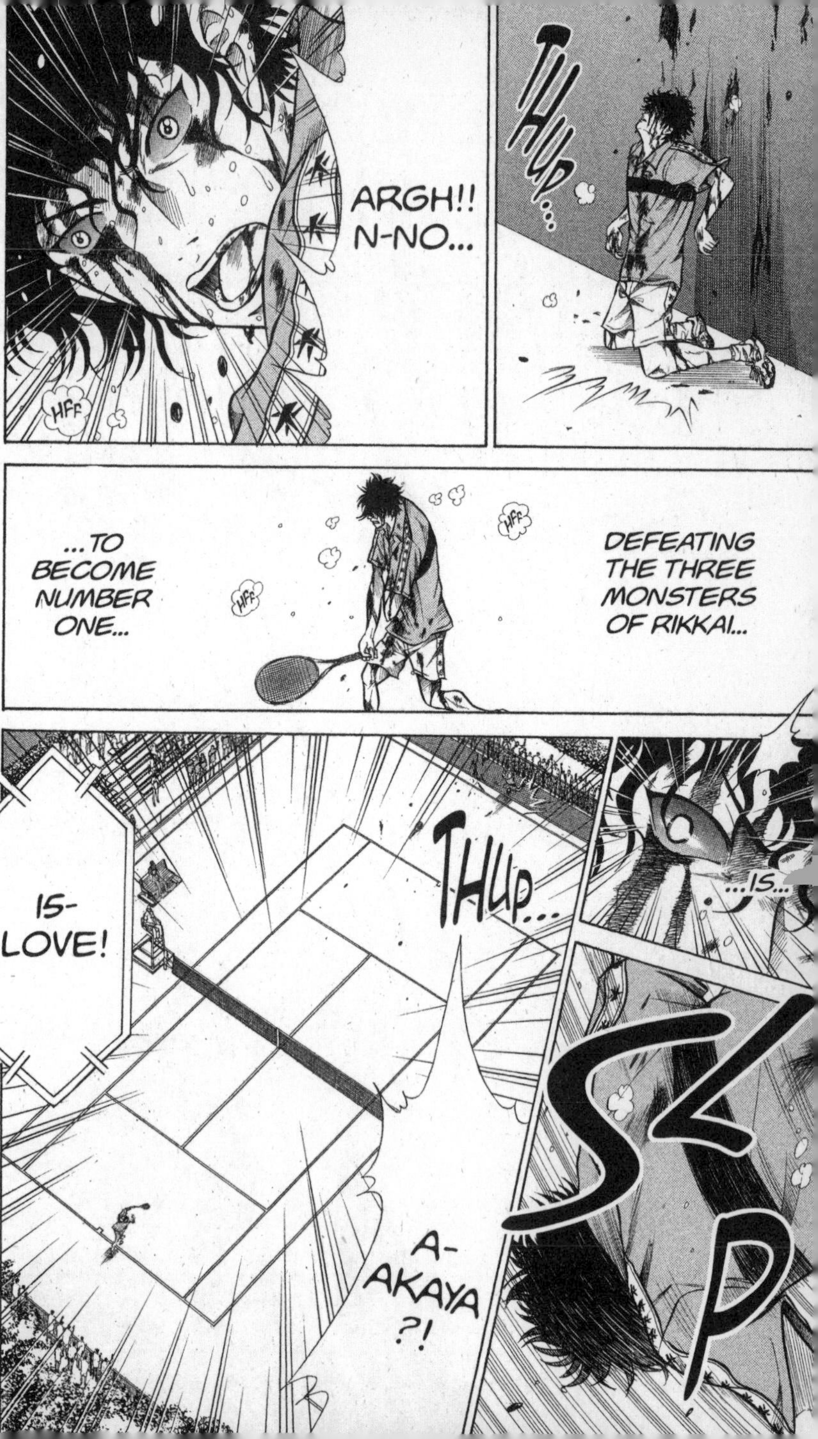
THUP...
ARGH!! N-NO...
HFF
DEFEATING THE THREE MONSTERS OF RIKKAI...
...TO BECOME NUMBER ONE...
HFF
HFF
...IS...
THUP...
IS-LOVE!
A-AKAYA?!

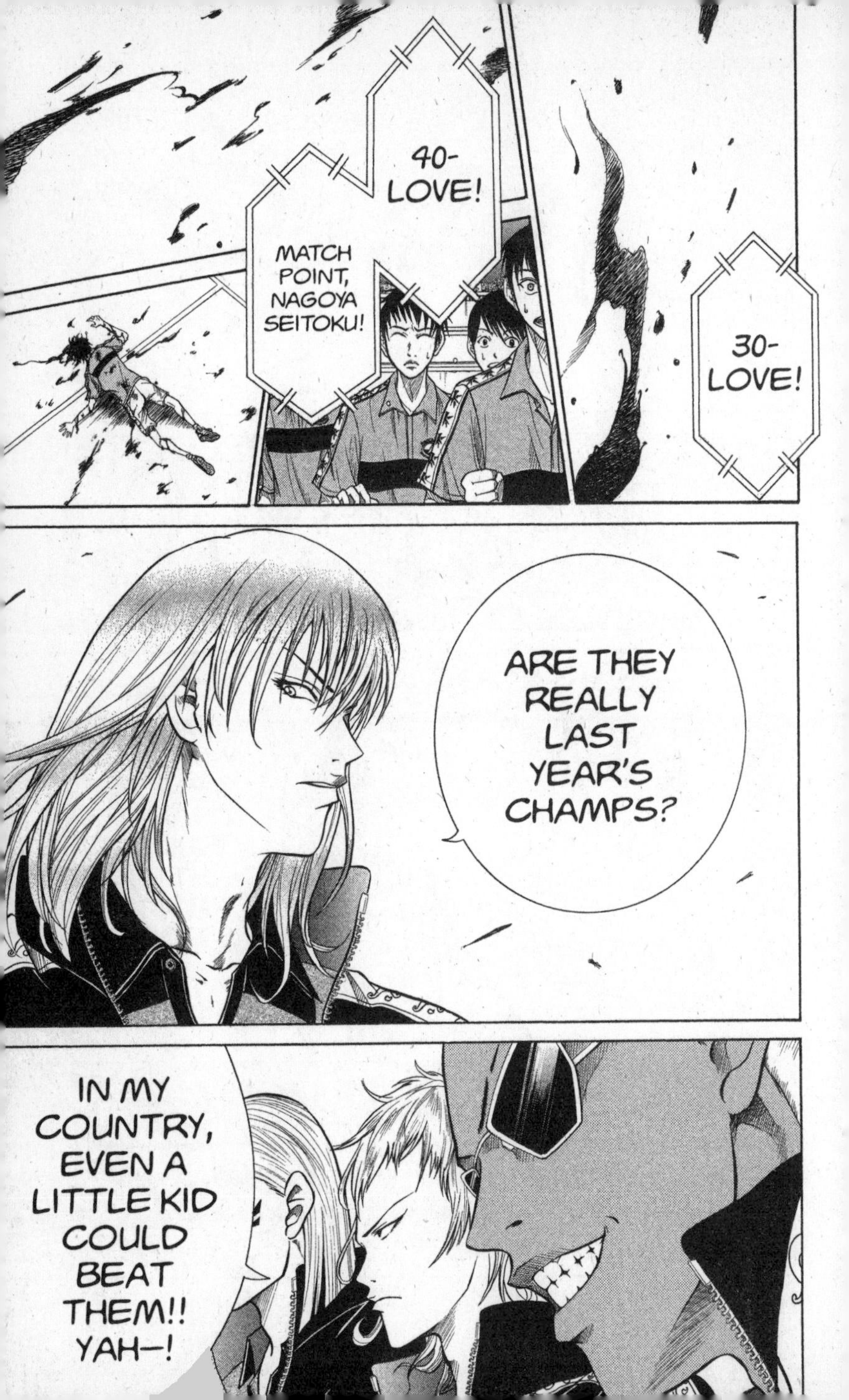
30-LOVE!
40-LOVE!
MATCH POINT, NAGOYA SEITOKU!
ARE THEY REALLY LAST YEAR'S CHAMPS?
IN MY COUNTRY, EVEN A LITTLE KID COULD BEAT THEM!! YAH—!

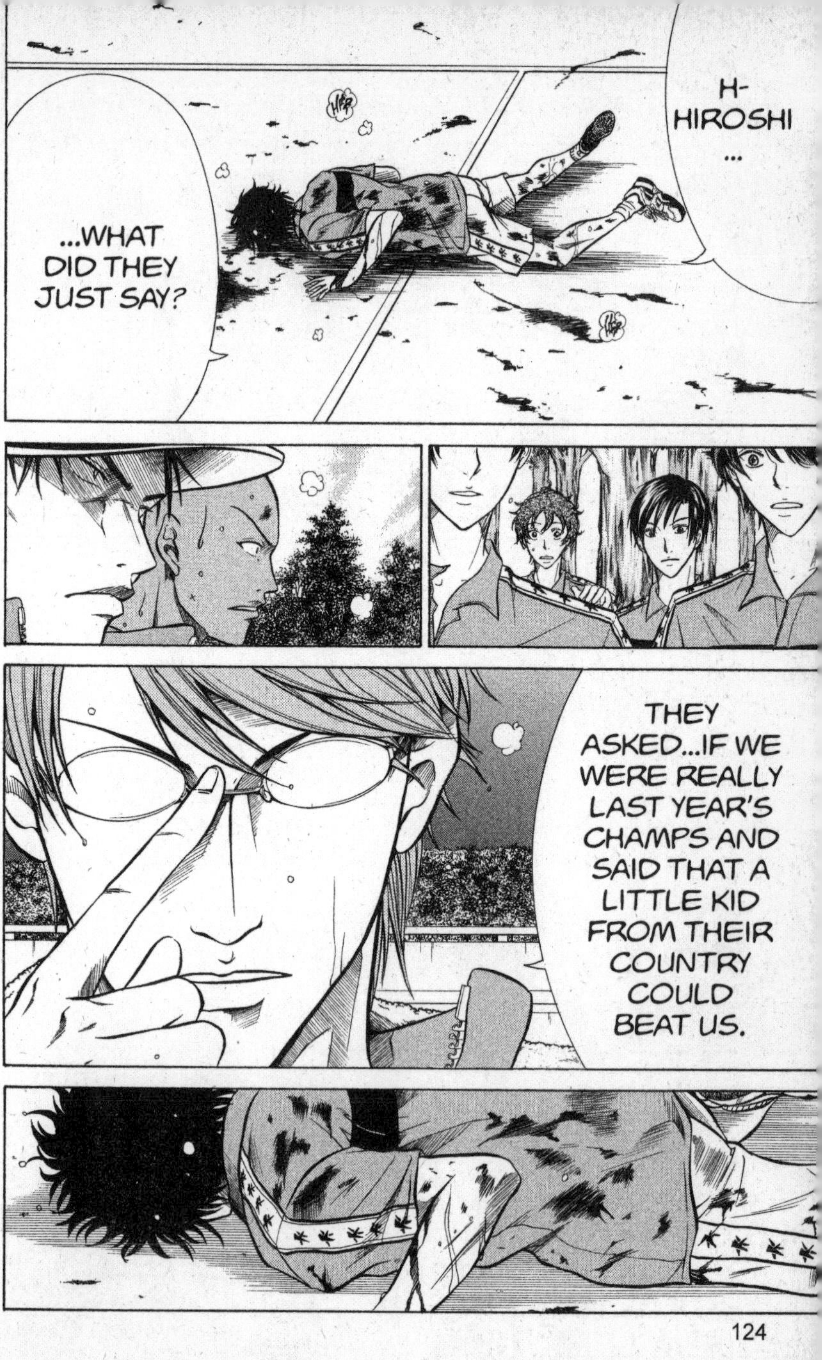
H- HIROSHI ...
...WHAT DID THEY JUST SAY?
THEY ASKED...IF WE WERE REALLY LAST YEAR'S CHAMPS AND SAID THAT A LITTLE KID FROM THEIR COUNTRY COULD BEAT US.

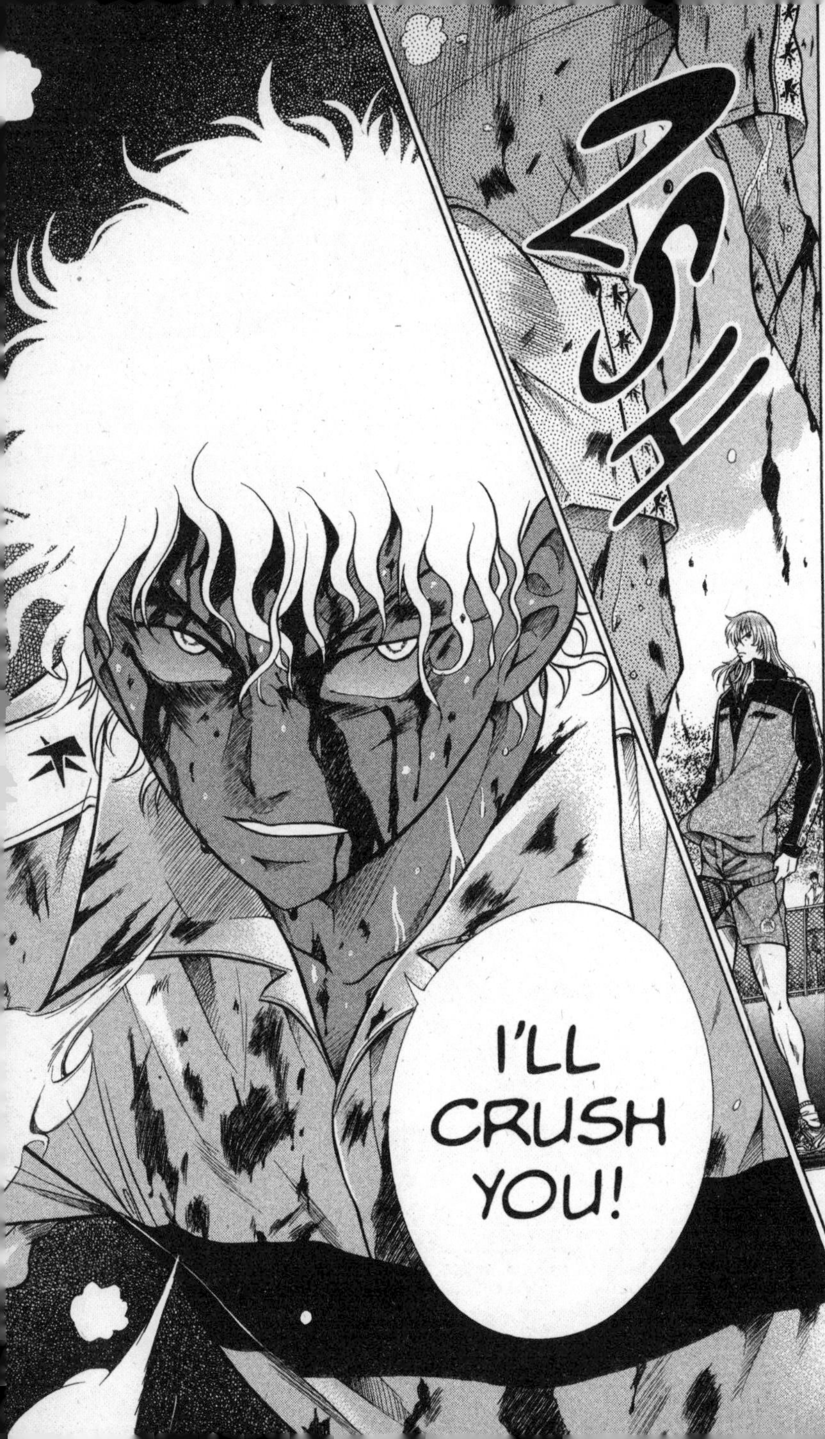
SWISH
I'LL CRUSH YOU!

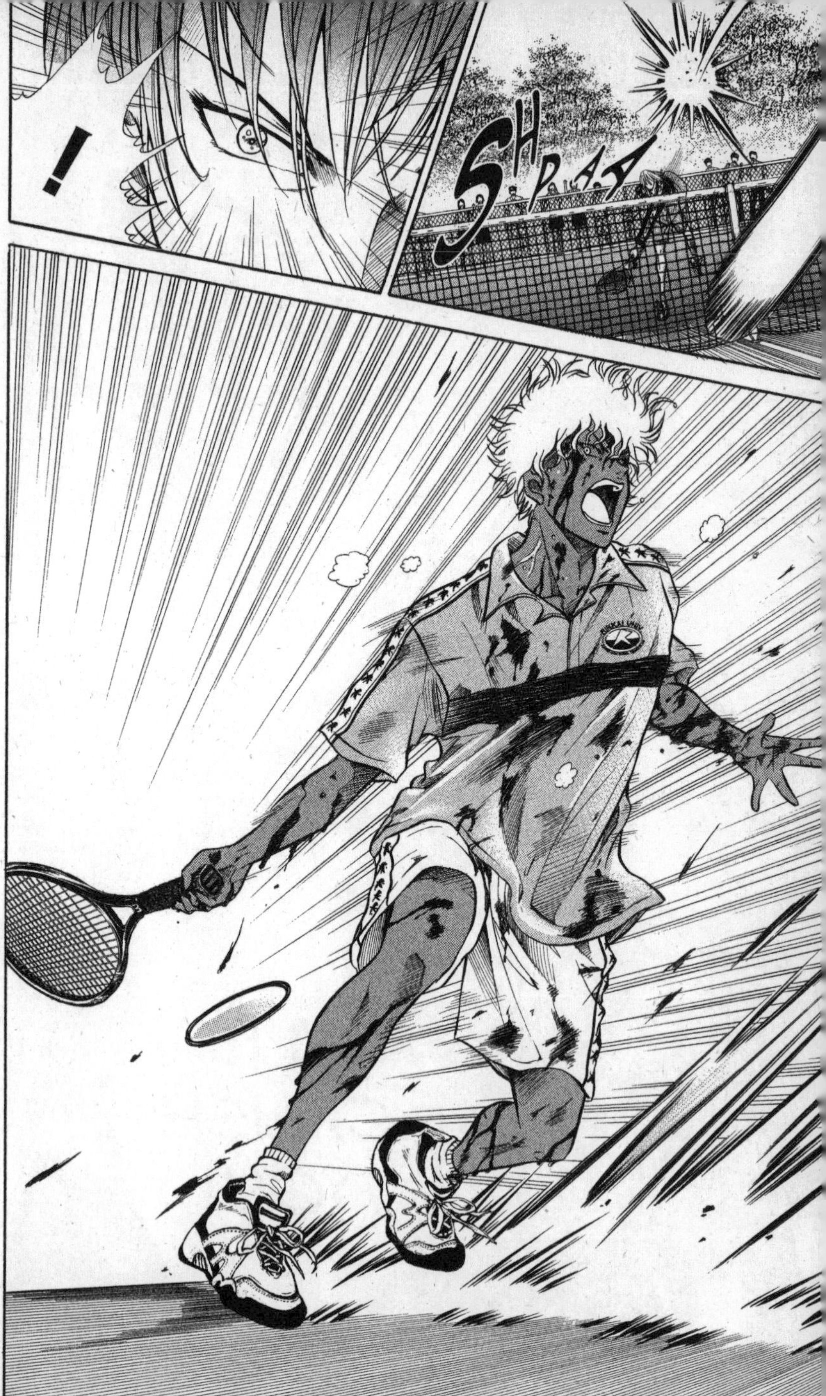
SHPAA
!

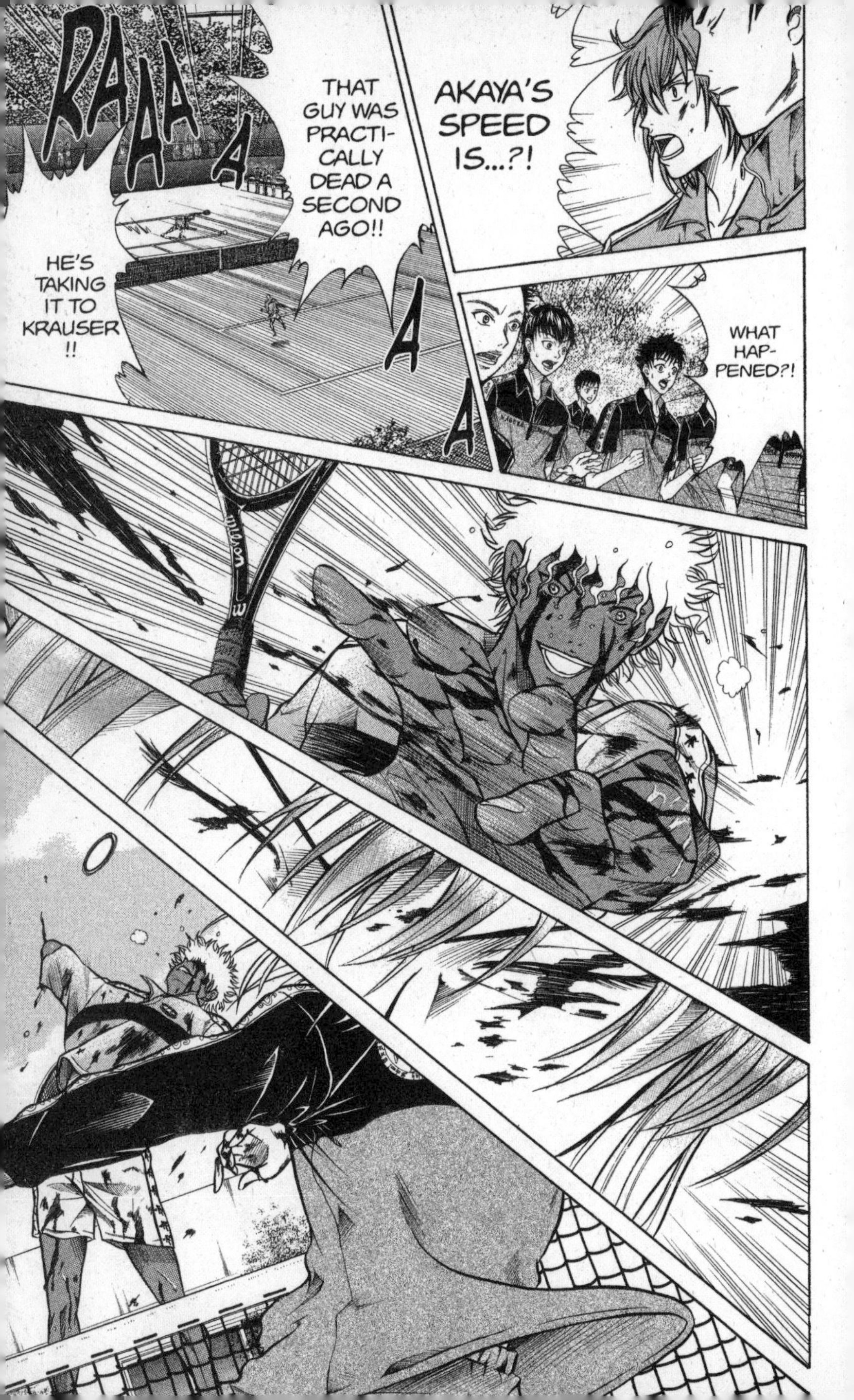
AKAYA'S SPEED IS...?!
RAAAAAA
THAT GUY WAS PRACTICALLY DEAD A SECOND AGO!!
HE'S TAKING IT TO KRAUSER!!
WHAT HAPPENED?!

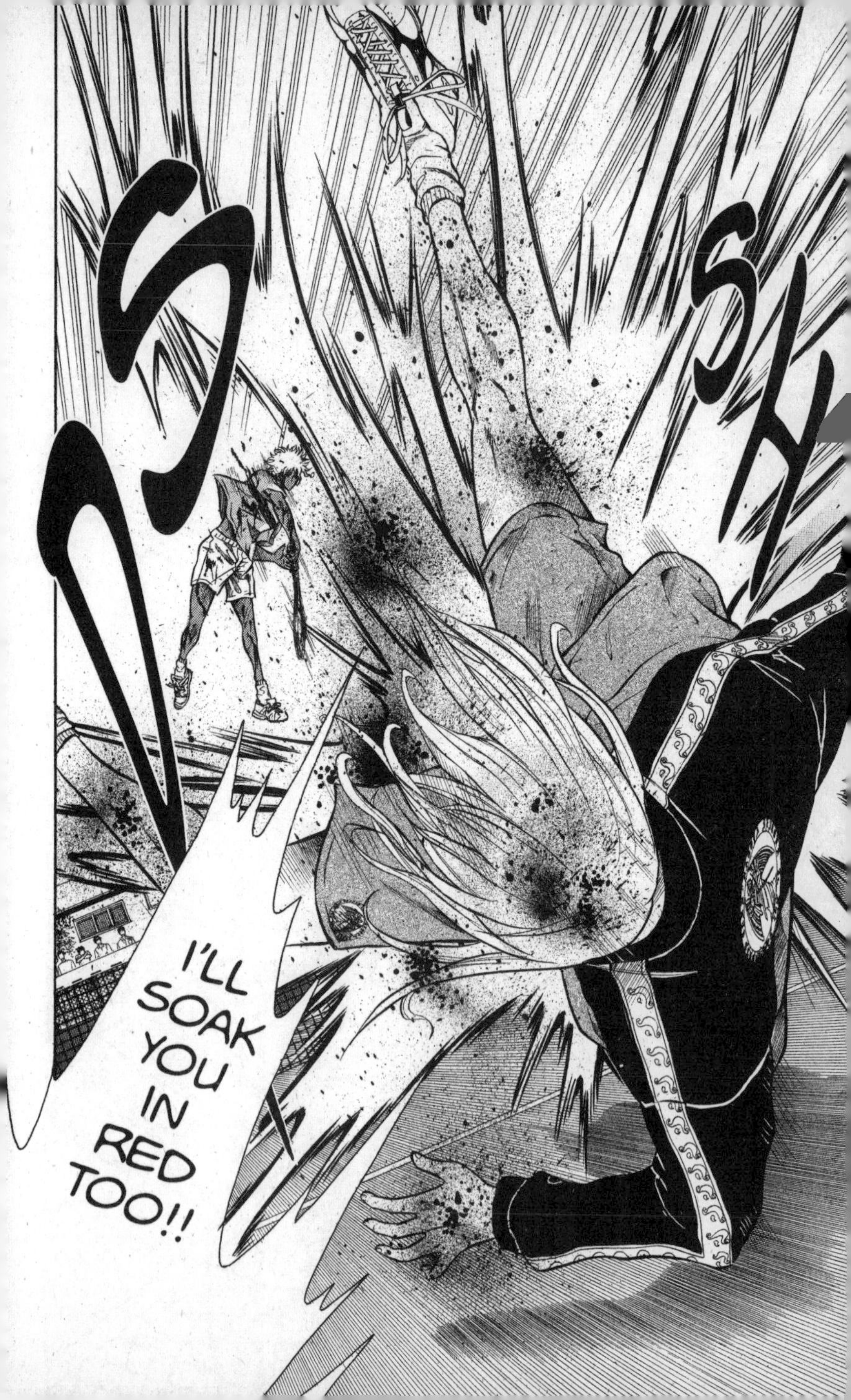
SH
I'LL SOAK YOU IN RED TOO!!

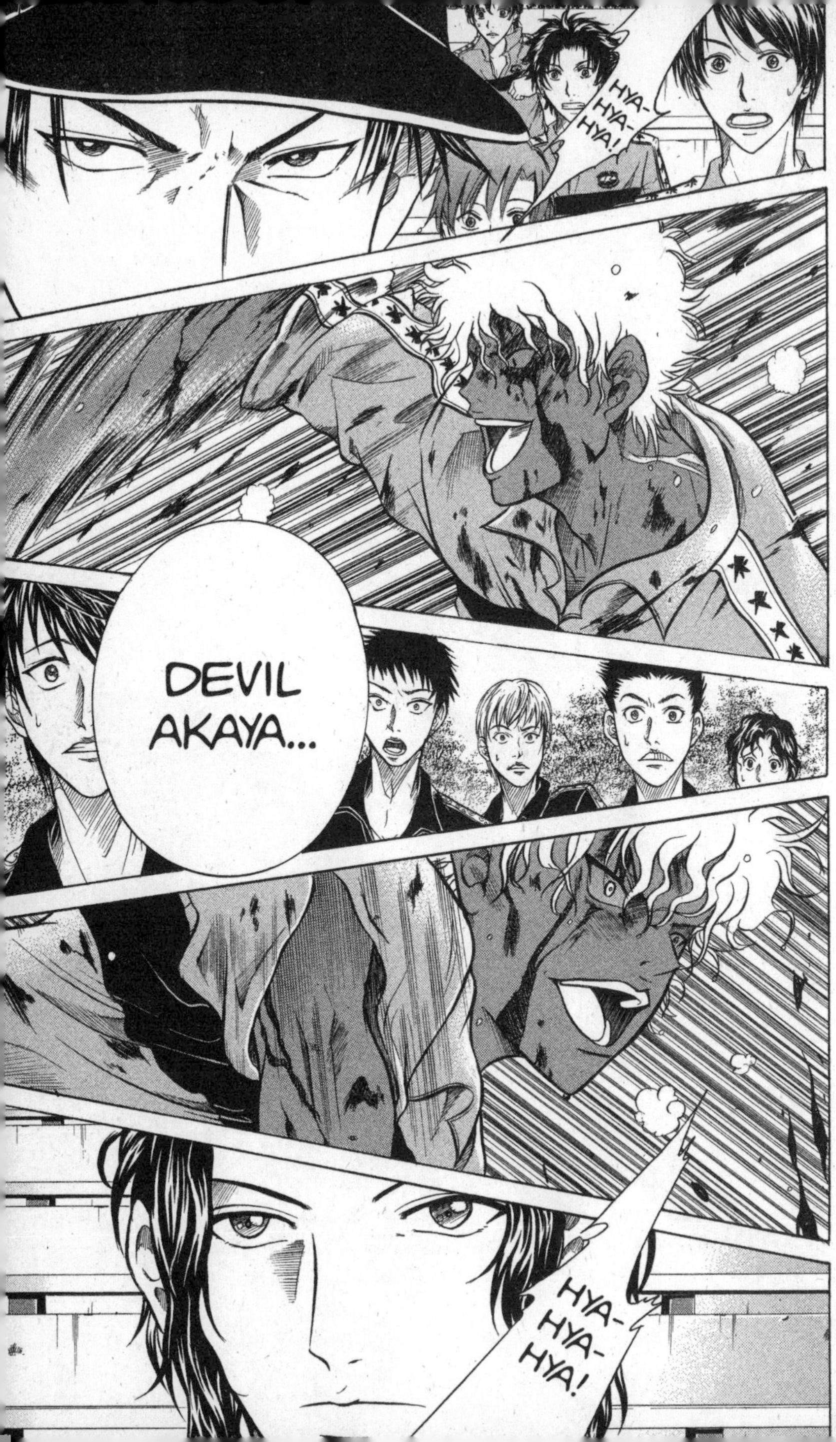
HYA-HYA-HYA!
DEVIL AKAYA...
HYA-HYA-HYA!

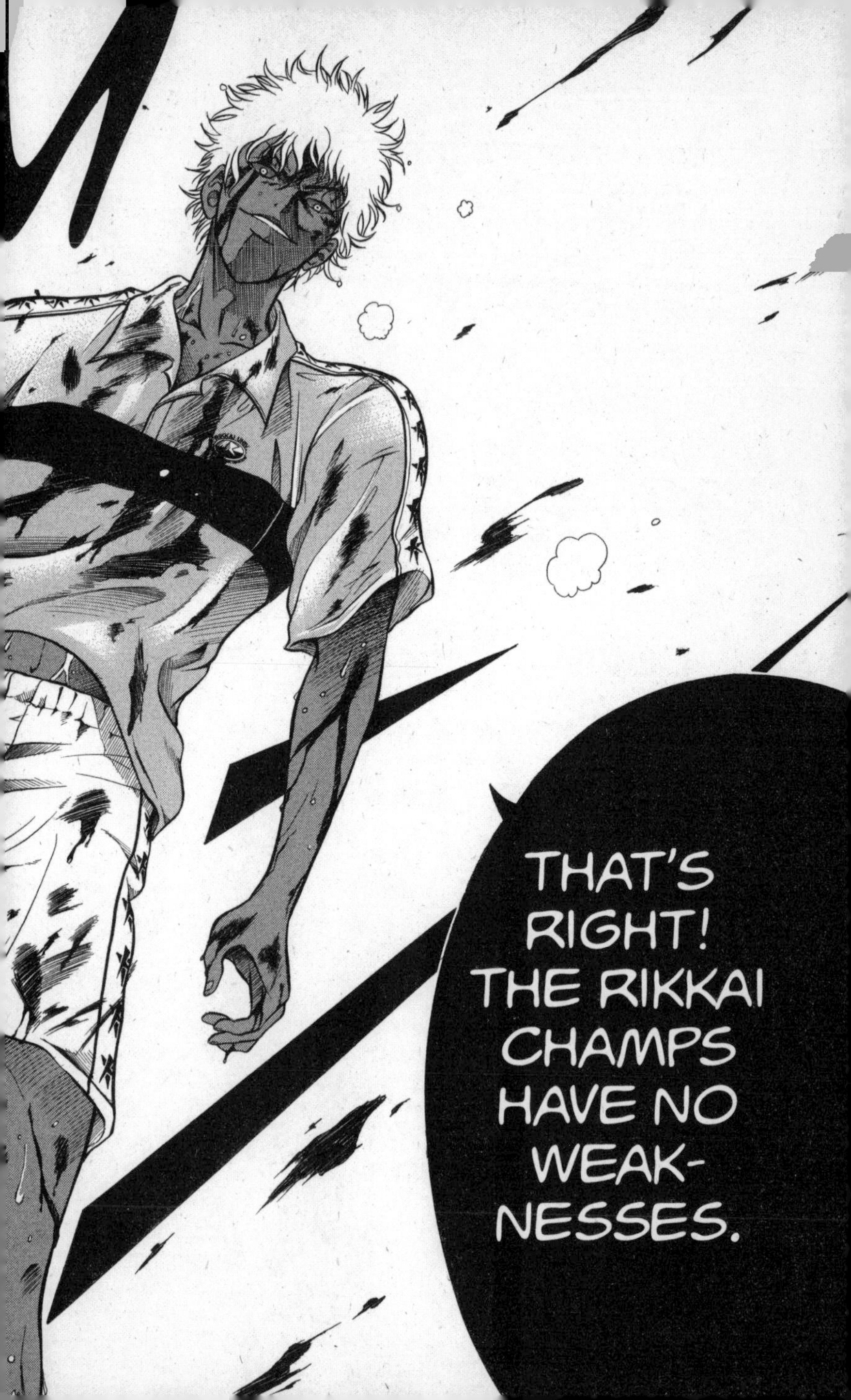
THAT'S RIGHT! THE RIKKAI CHAMPS HAVE NO WEAK-NESSES.

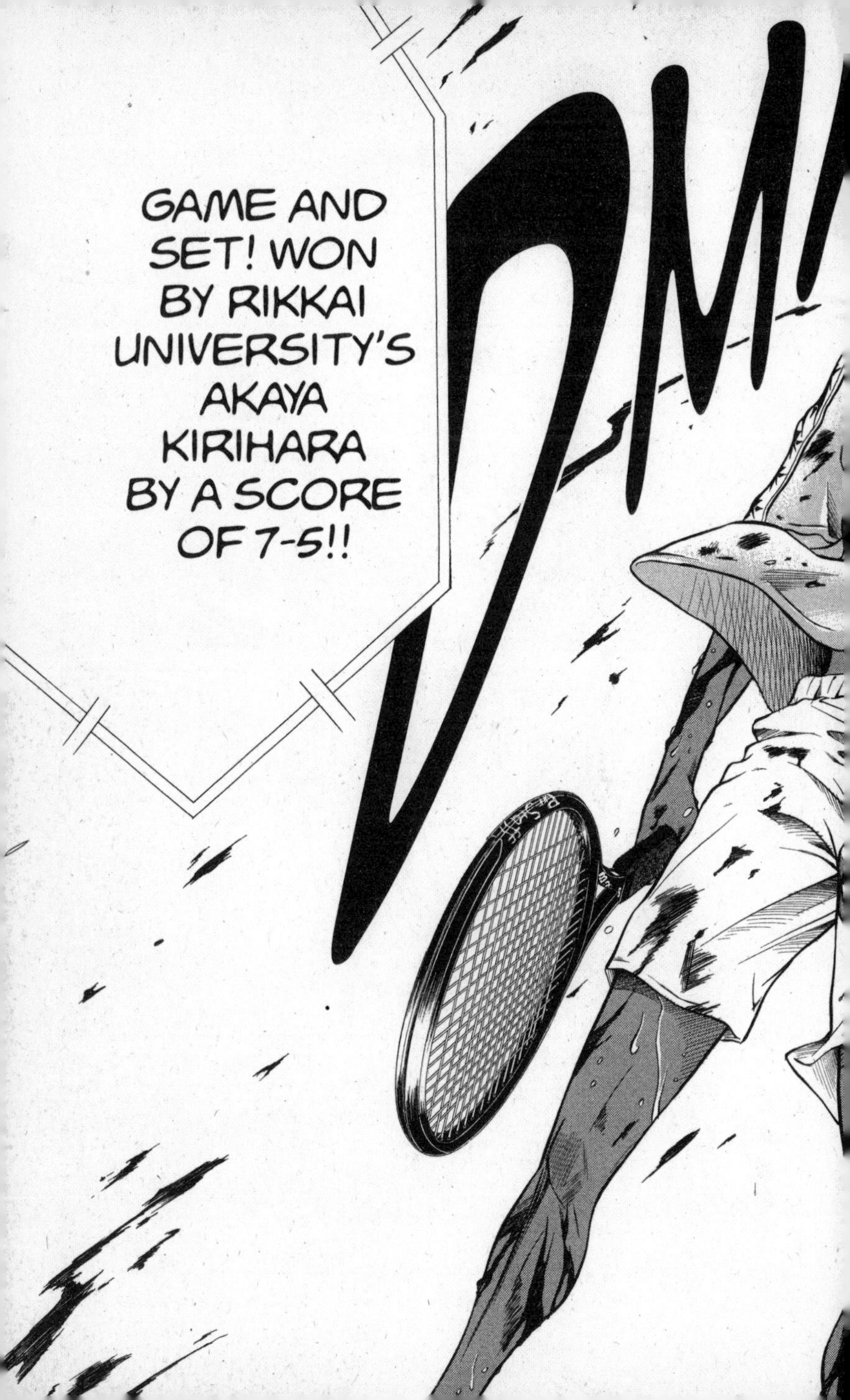
GAME AND SET! WON BY RIKKAI UNIVERSITY'S AKAYA KIRIHARA BY A SCORE OF 7-5!!

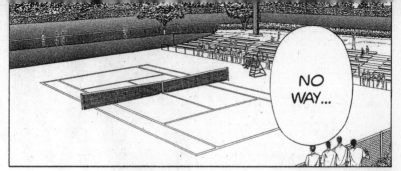

NO WAY...

"I CAN'T BELIEVE WE LOST TO AN ISLAND NATION OF TENNIS AMATEURS"...

...THAT'S WHAT YOU'RE GOING TO SAY.

RIGHT?

?!

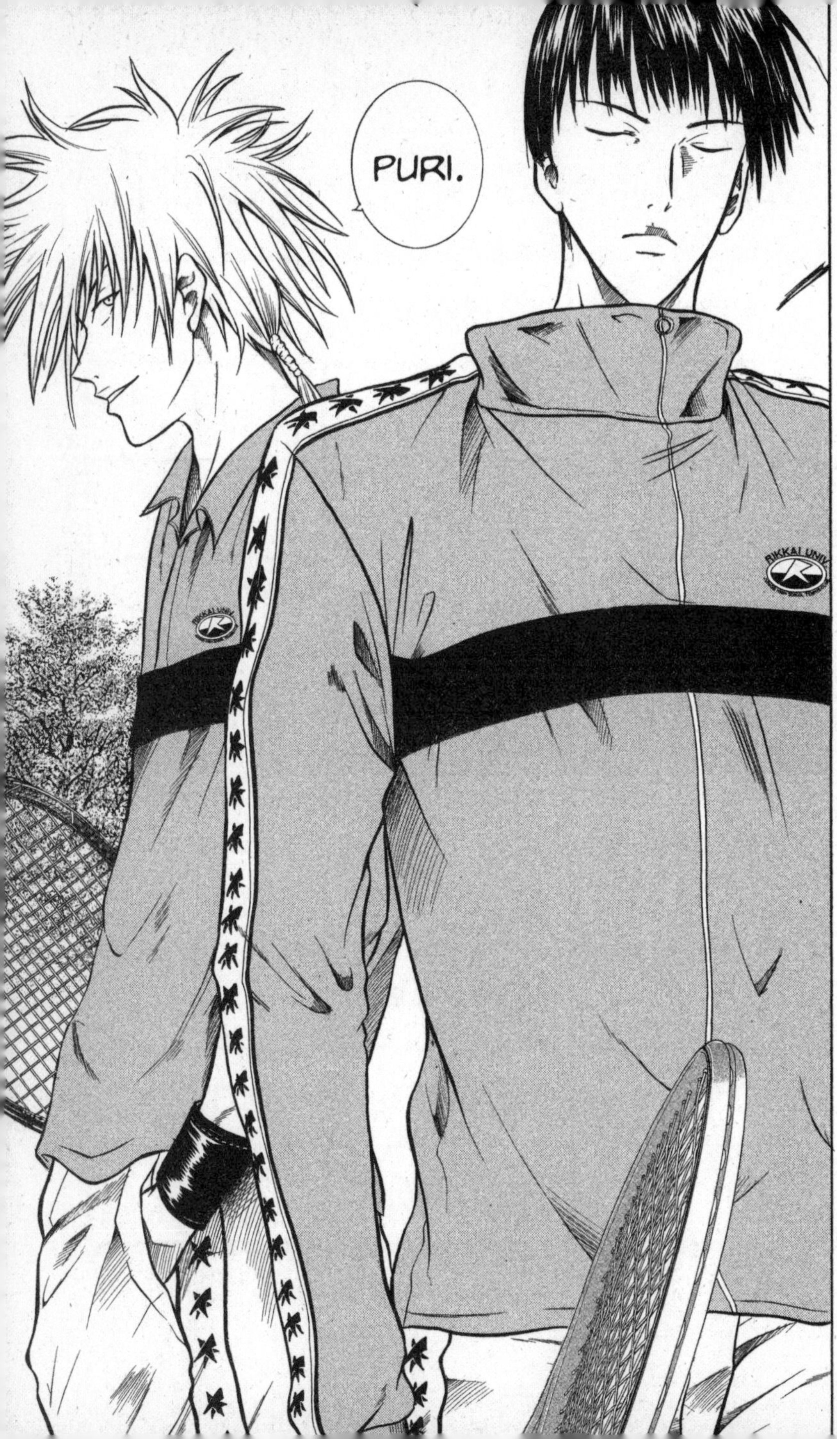
PURI.
RIKKAI UNIV

2007

VALENTINE'S DAY CHOCOLATE RANKING 2

10TH	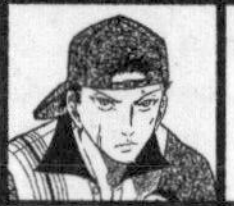	RYO SHISHIDO	63
10TH	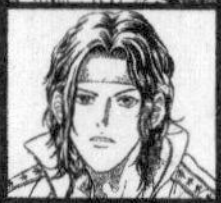	SEIICHI YUKIMURA	63
13TH	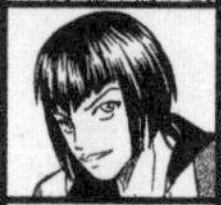	GAKUTO MUKAHI	56
14TH	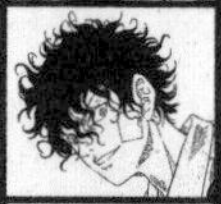	AKAYA KIRIHARA	42
15TH	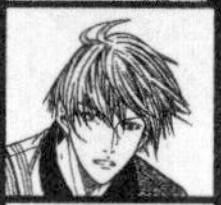	WAKASHI HIYOSHI	40
16TH	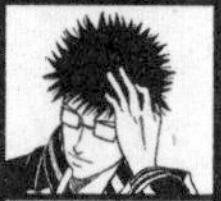	SADAHARU INUI	36
17TH	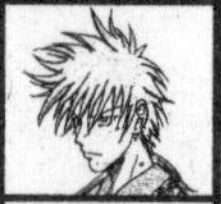	MASAHARU NIO	34
17TH	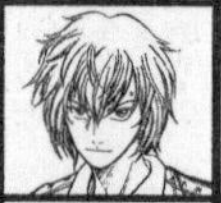	BUNTA MARUI	34
19TH	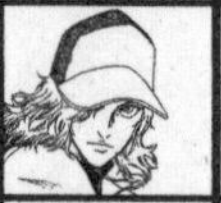	YUJIRO KAI	31
20TH	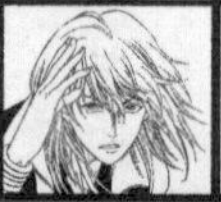	RIN HIRAKOBA	29

CONTINUED ON PAGE 152

GAME AND SET! WON BY RIKKAI'S NIO/YANAGI PAIR BY A SCORE OF 6-1!!

NAGOYA SEITOKU (AICHI)	6	6	5	1
RIKKAI UNIVERSITY (KANAGAWA)	2	1	7	6

NO WAY...

SO IN THE FIRST TWO GAMES...

...YOU SWINDLED US?!

GENIUS 339: THE UPSHOT OF THE ONE-SHOT BATTLE

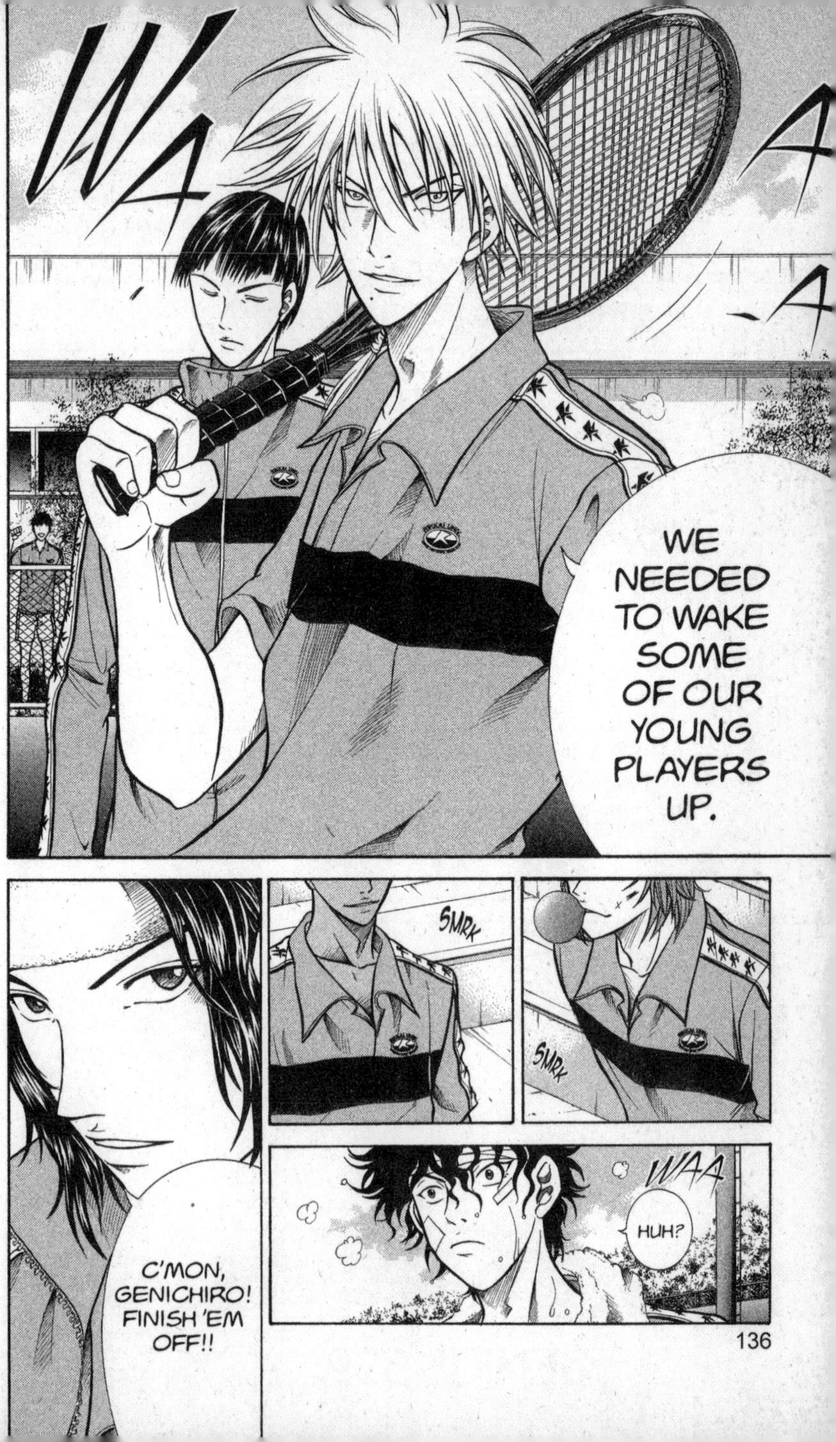
WAAAA
WE NEEDED TO WAKE SOME OF OUR YOUNG PLAYERS UP.
SMRK
SMRK
WAA
HUH?
C'MON, GENICHIRO! FINISH 'EM OFF!!

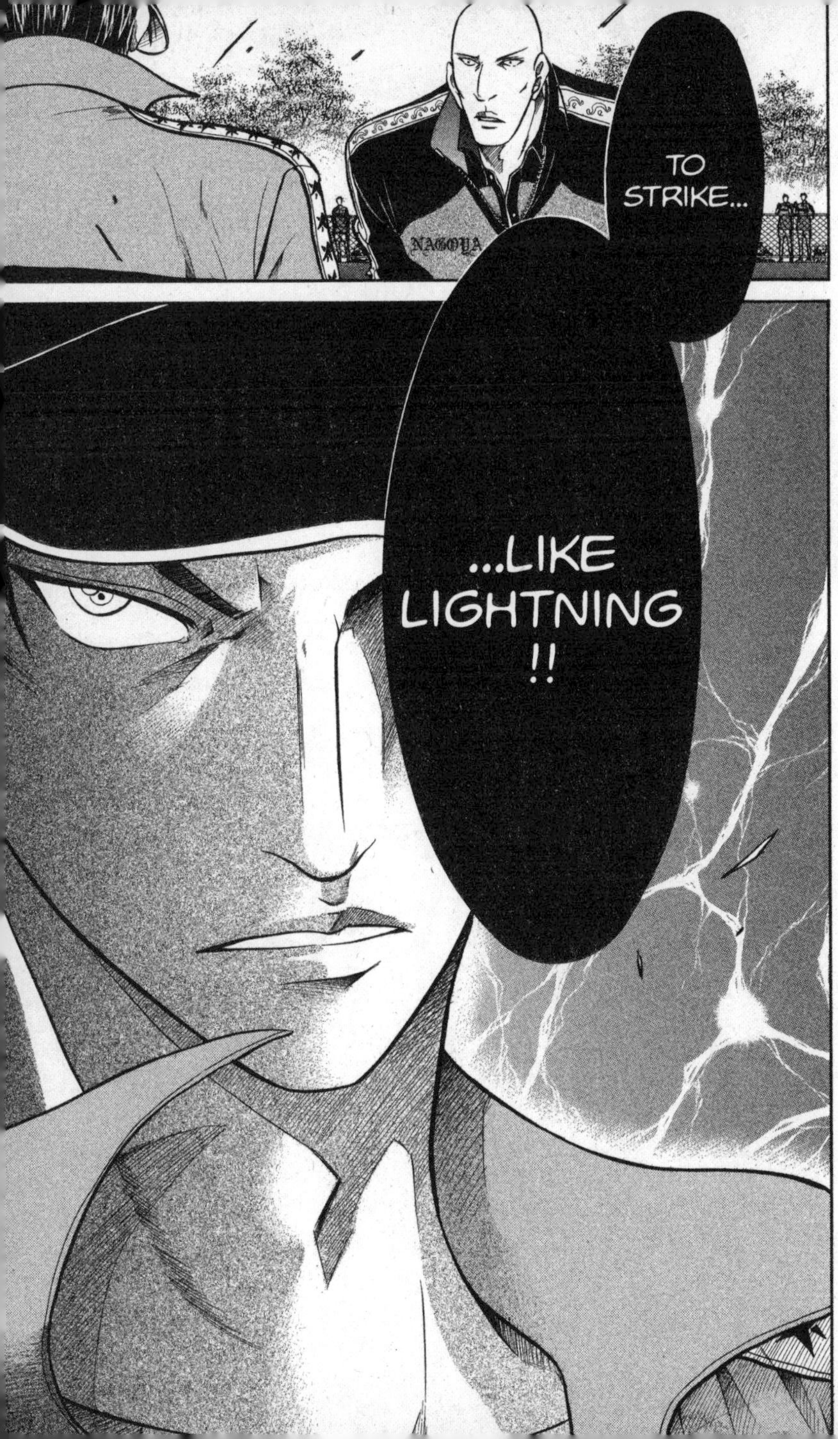
NAGOYA
TO STRIKE...
...LIKE LIGHTNING !!

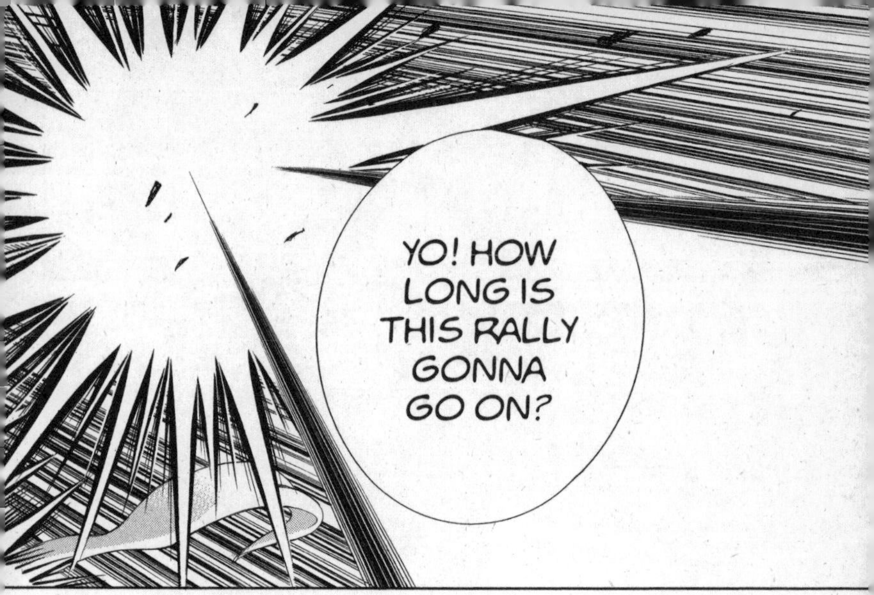
YO! HOW LONG IS THIS RALLY GONNA GO ON?

THE UPSHOT OF THE ONE-SHOT BATTLE

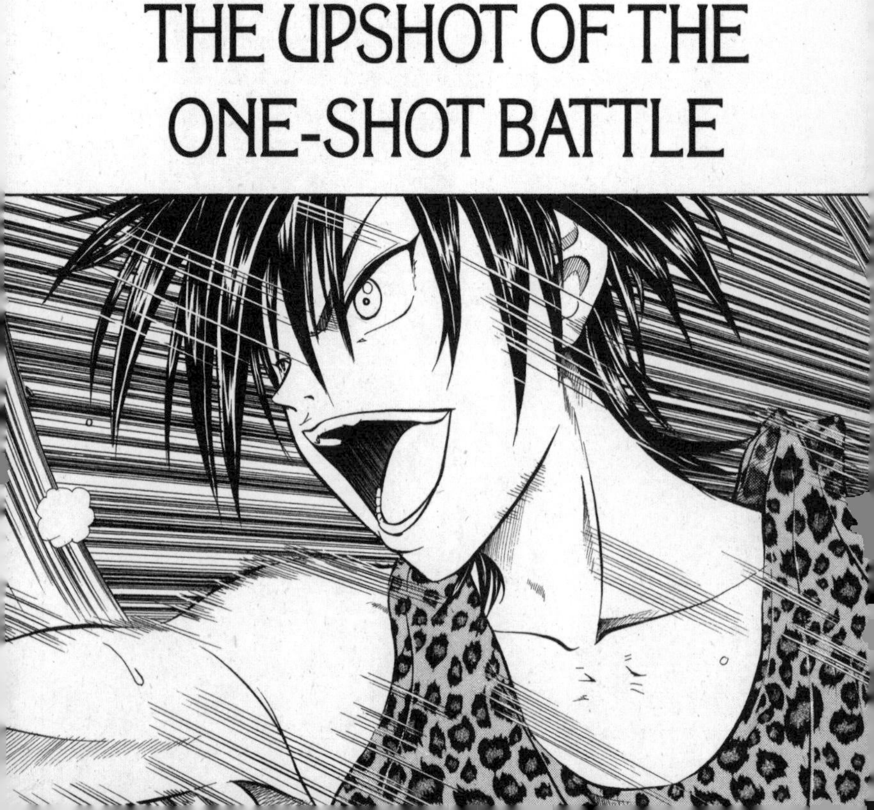

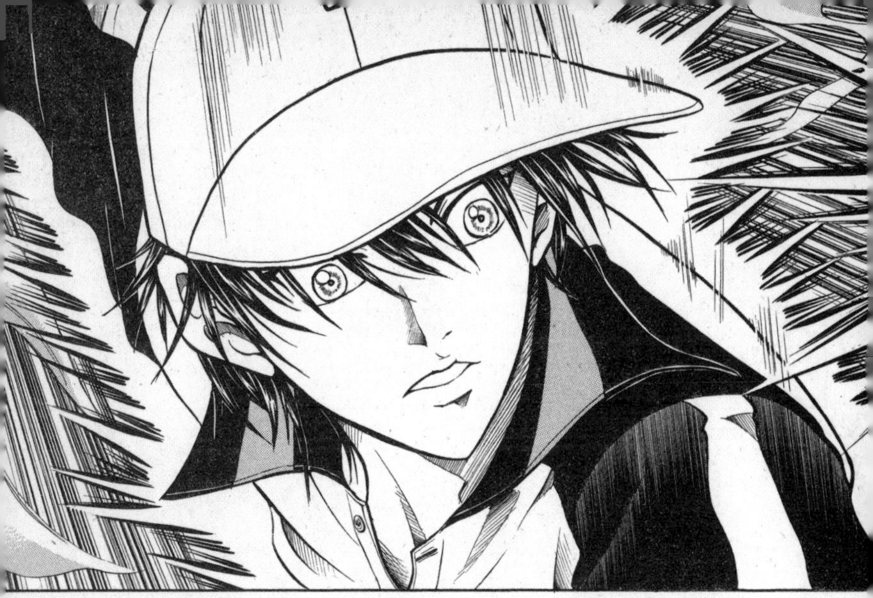

GENIUS 339:

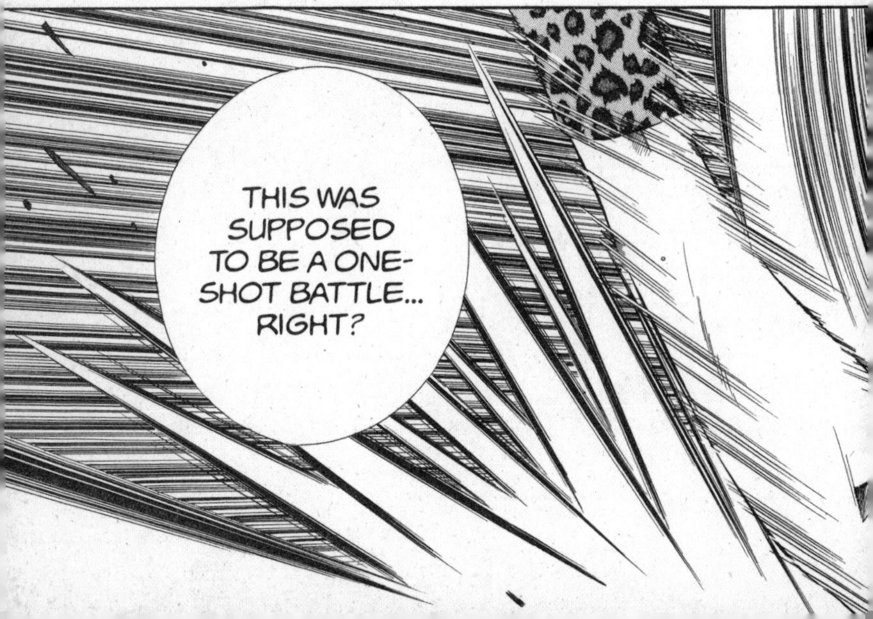
THIS WAS SUPPOSED TO BE A ONE-SHOT BATTLE... RIGHT?

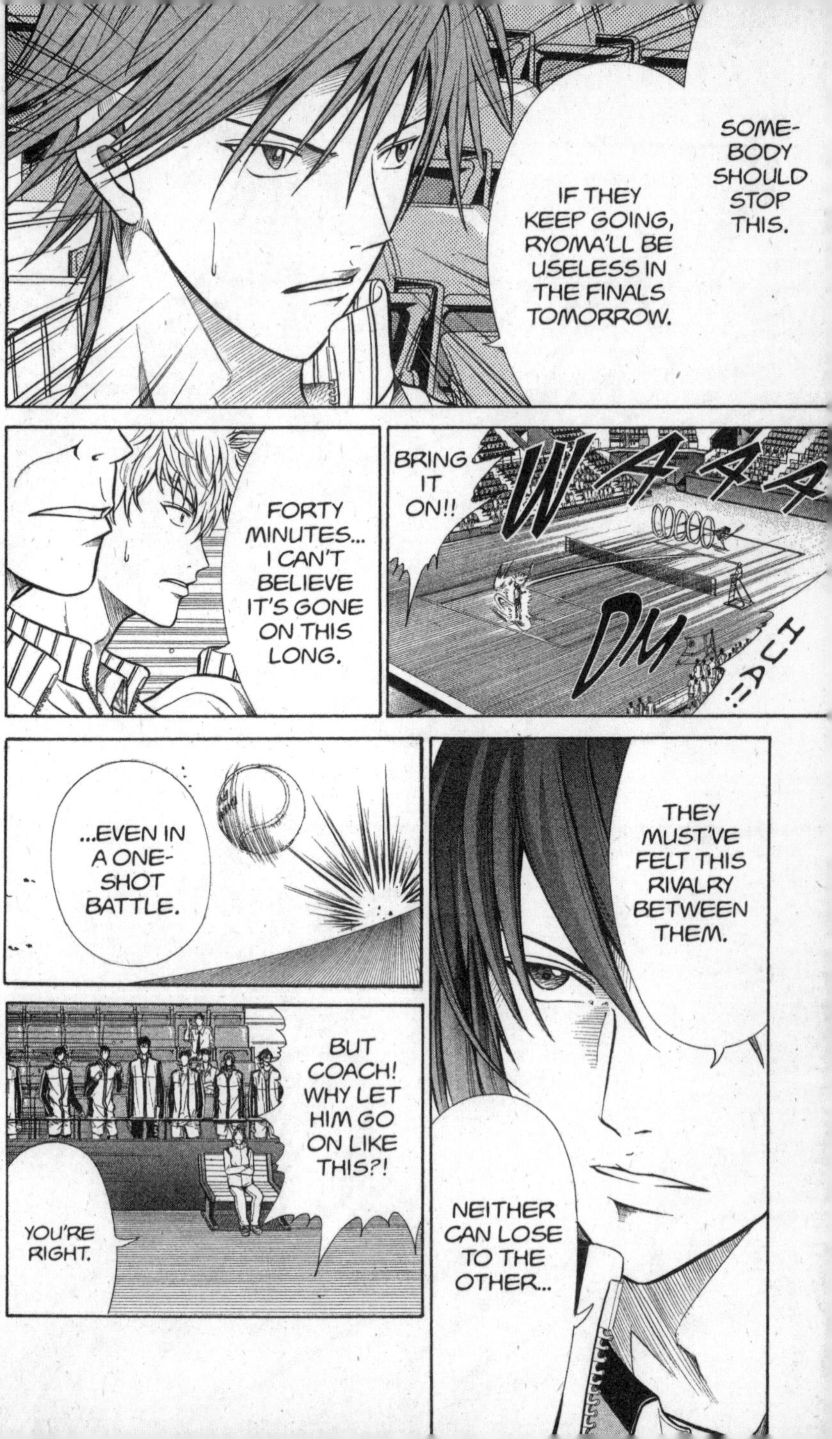
SOME-BODY SHOULD STOP THIS.
IF THEY KEEP GOING, RYOMA'LL BE USELESS IN THE FINALS TOMORROW.
BRING IT ON!!
WAAA
DM
FORTY MINUTES... I CAN'T BELIEVE IT'S GONE ON THIS LONG.
THEY MUST'VE FELT THIS RIVALRY BETWEEN THEM.
NEITHER CAN LOSE TO THE OTHER...
...EVEN IN A ONE-SHOT BATTLE.
BUT COACH! WHY LET HIM GO ON LIKE THIS?!
YOU'RE RIGHT.

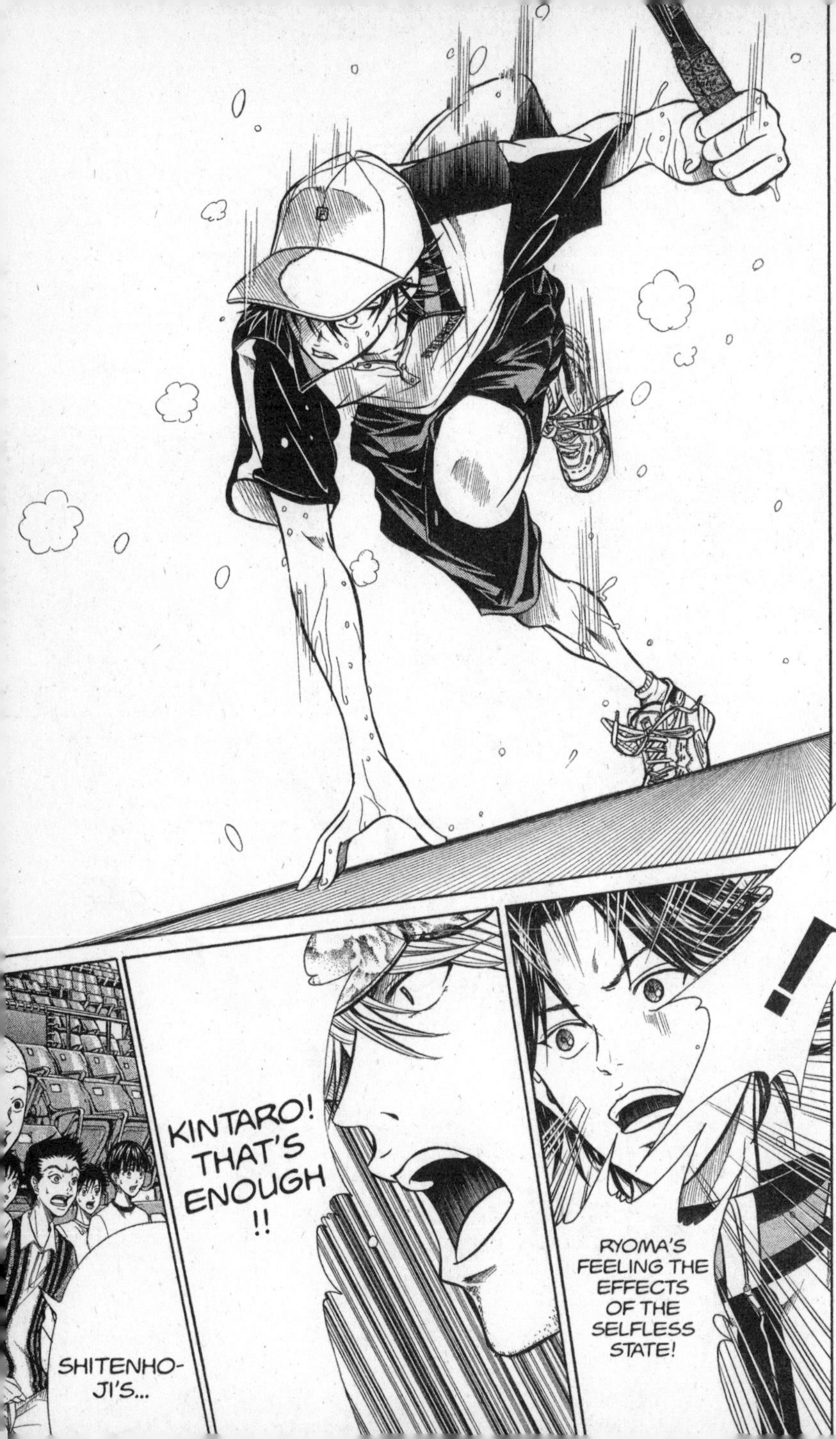
!
RYOMA'S FEELING THE EFFECTS OF THE SELFLESS STATE!
KINTARO! THAT'S ENOUGH !!
SHITENHO-JI'S...

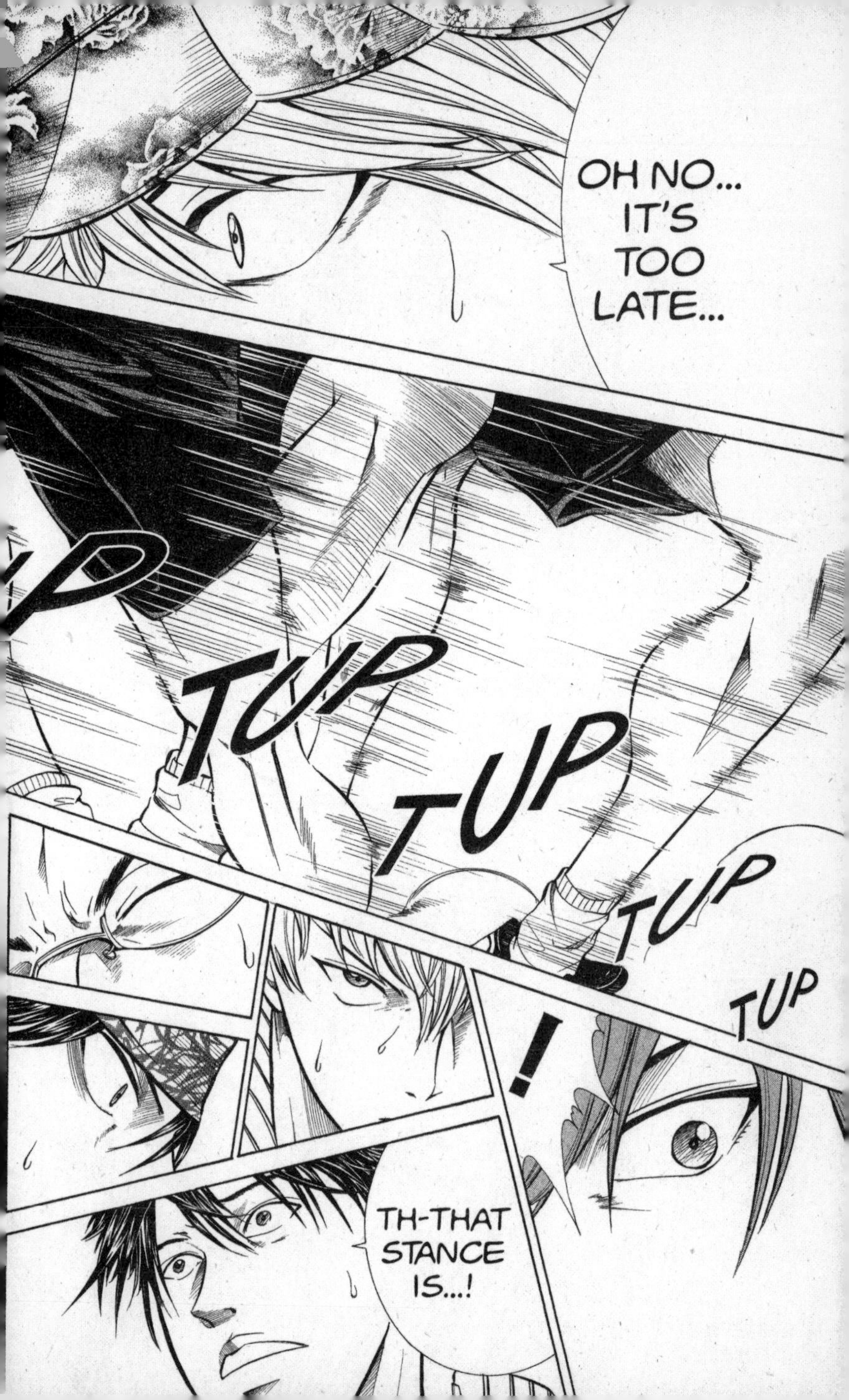
OH NO... IT'S TOO LATE...
TUP
TUP
TUP
TUP
TUP
!
TH-THAT STANCE IS...!

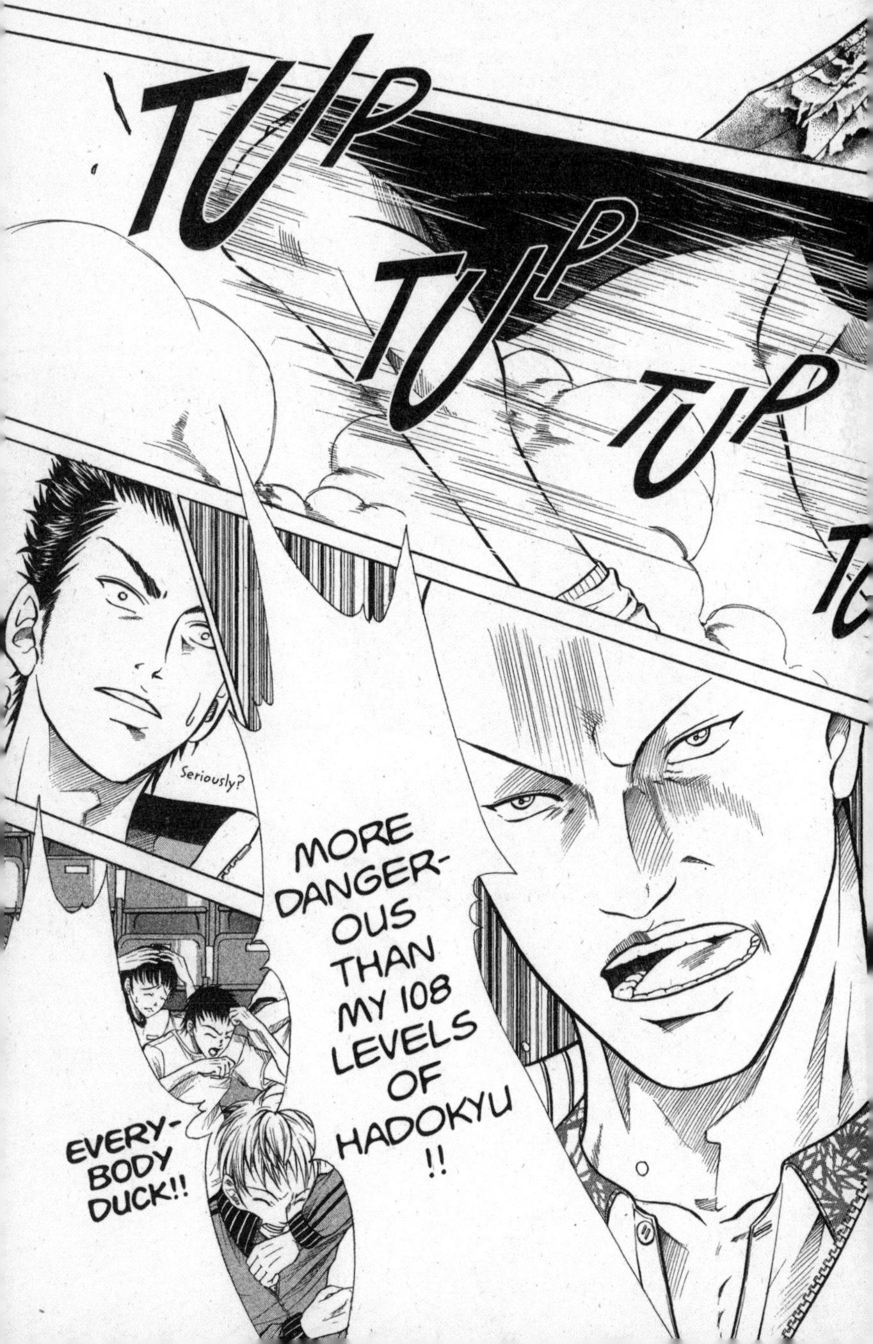
TUP
TUP
TUP
TU
MORE DANGER-OUS THAN MY 108 LEVELS OF HADOKYU !!
Seriously?
EVERY-BODY DUCK!!

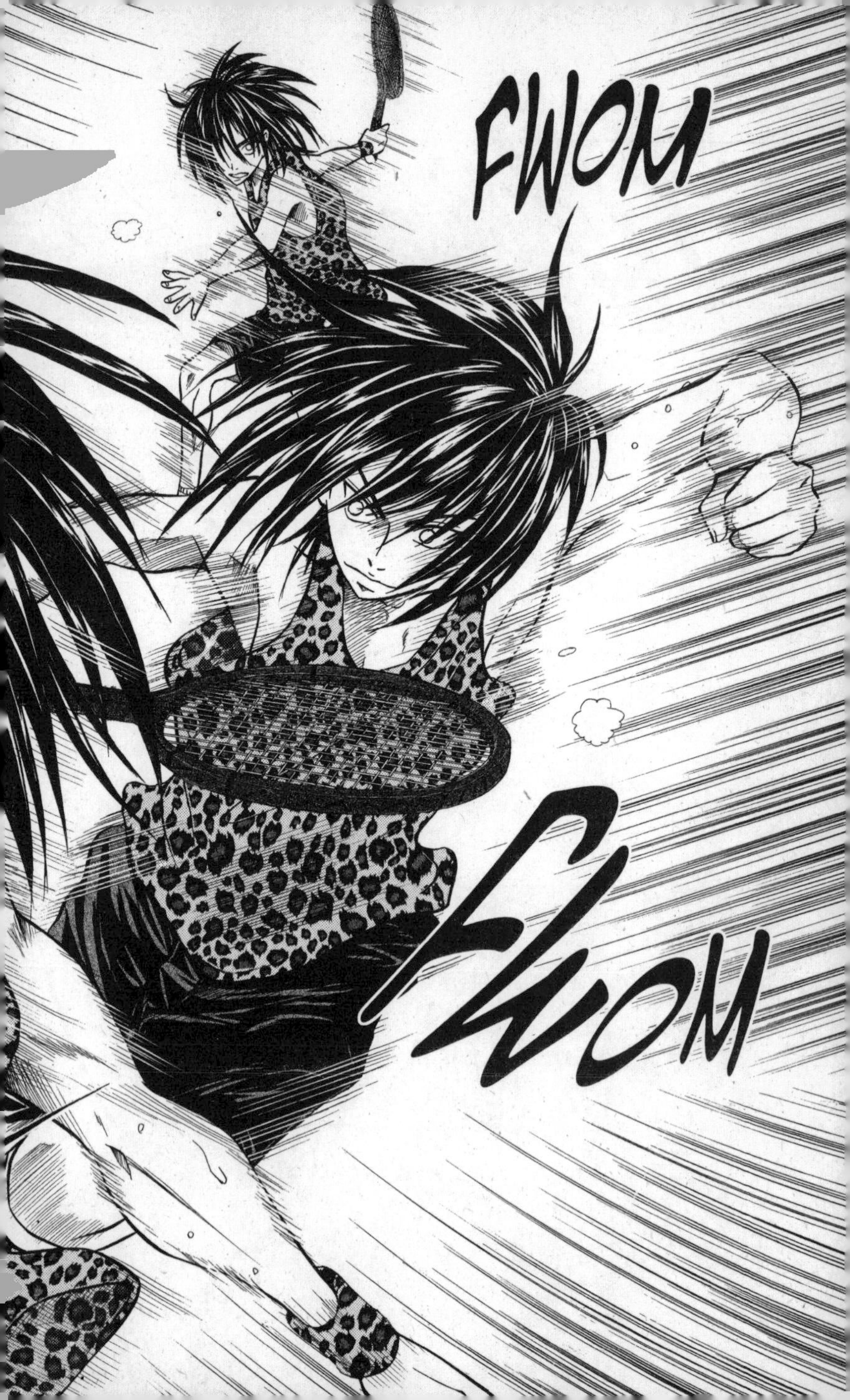
FWOM
FWOM

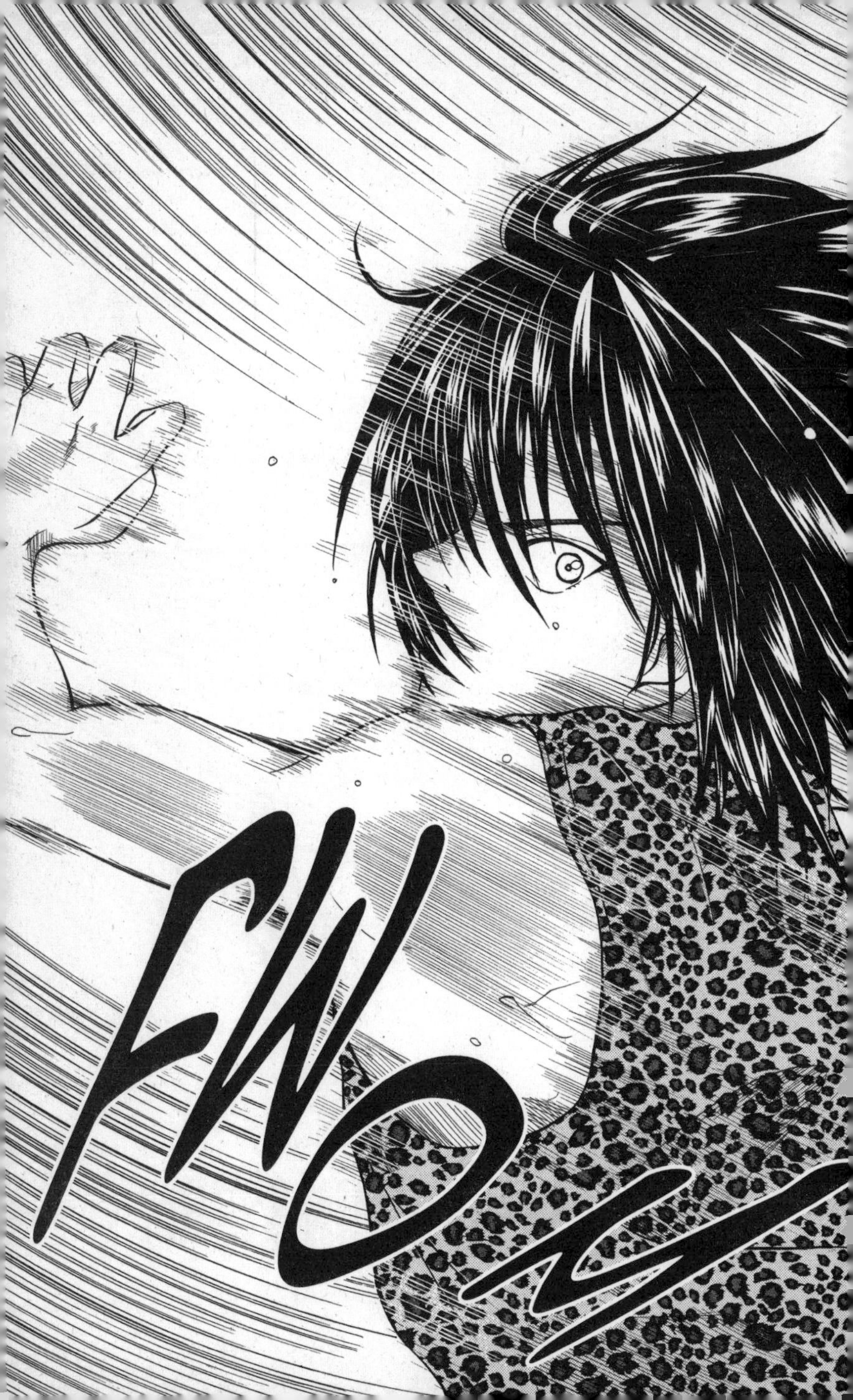
FWOOM

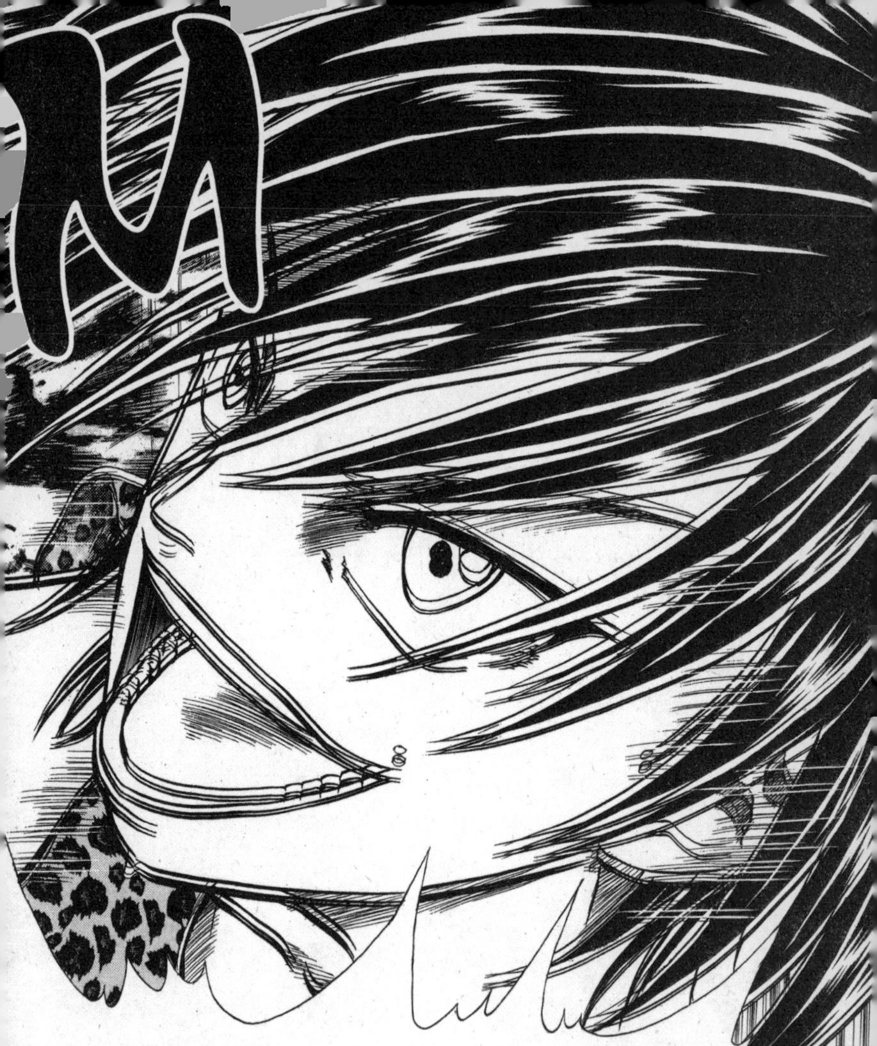
M

SWINGING **MOUNTAIN STORM**!!

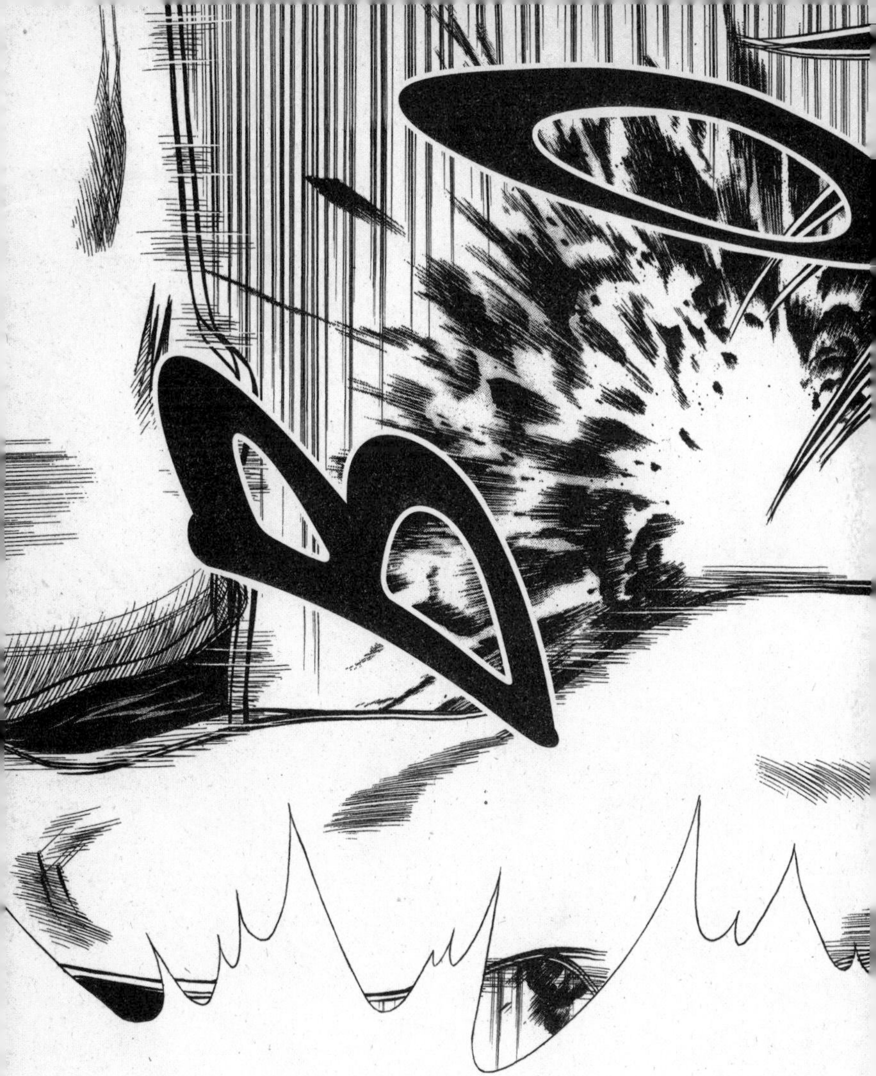

SUPER ULTRA DELICIOUS

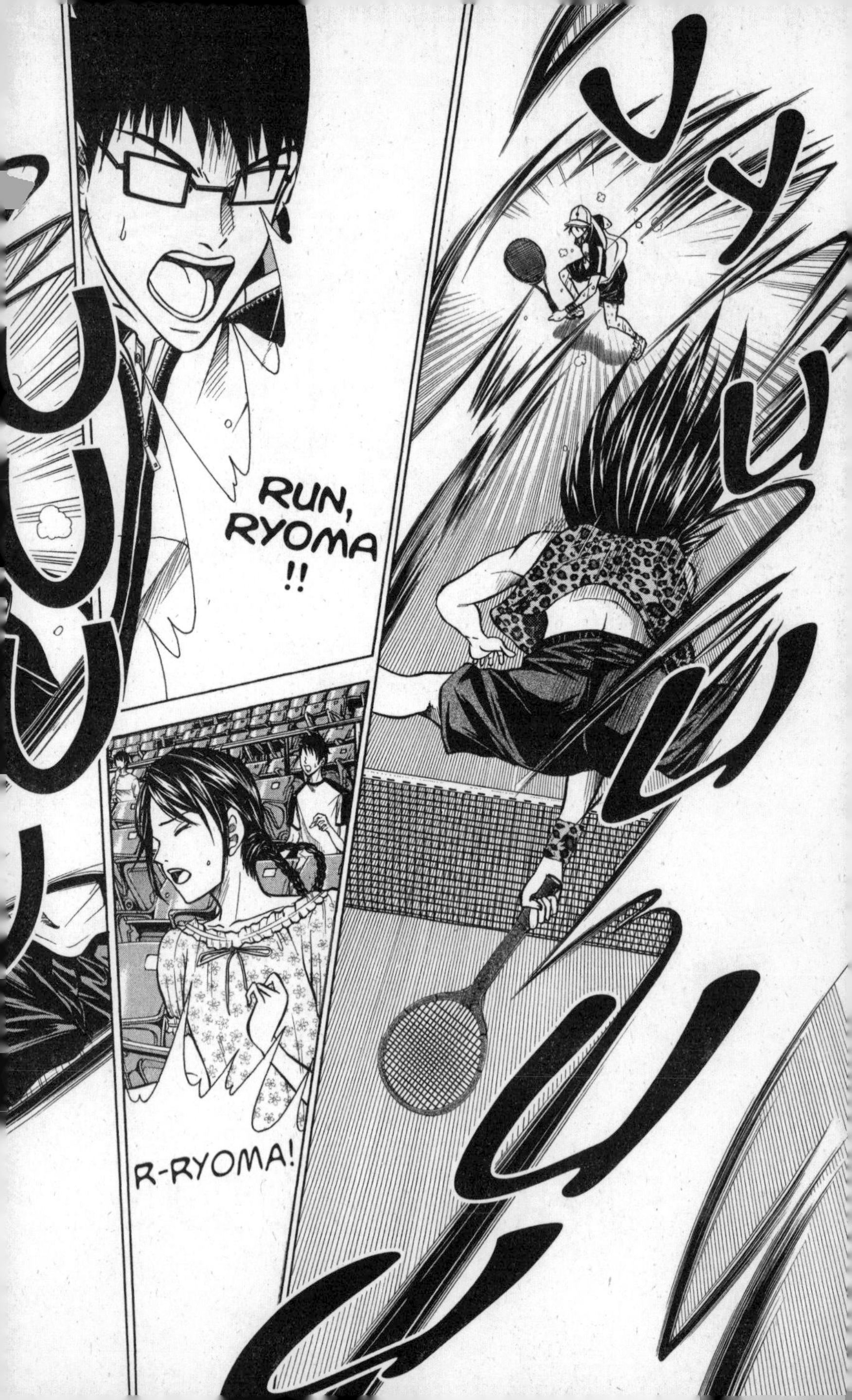
RUN, RYOMA !!
R-RYOMA!

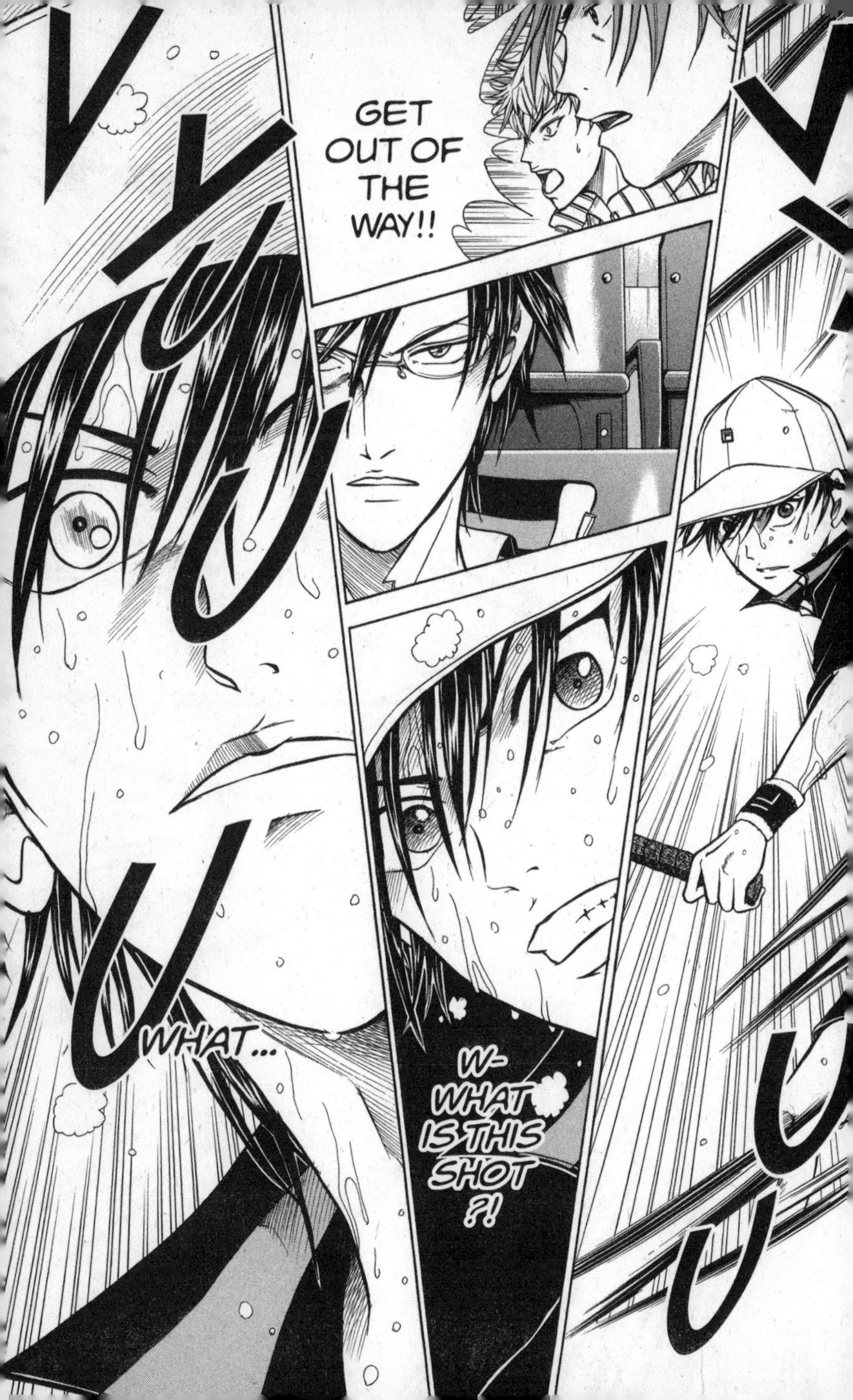
GET OUT OF THE WAY!!
W-WHAT IS THIS SHOT ?!
WHAT...

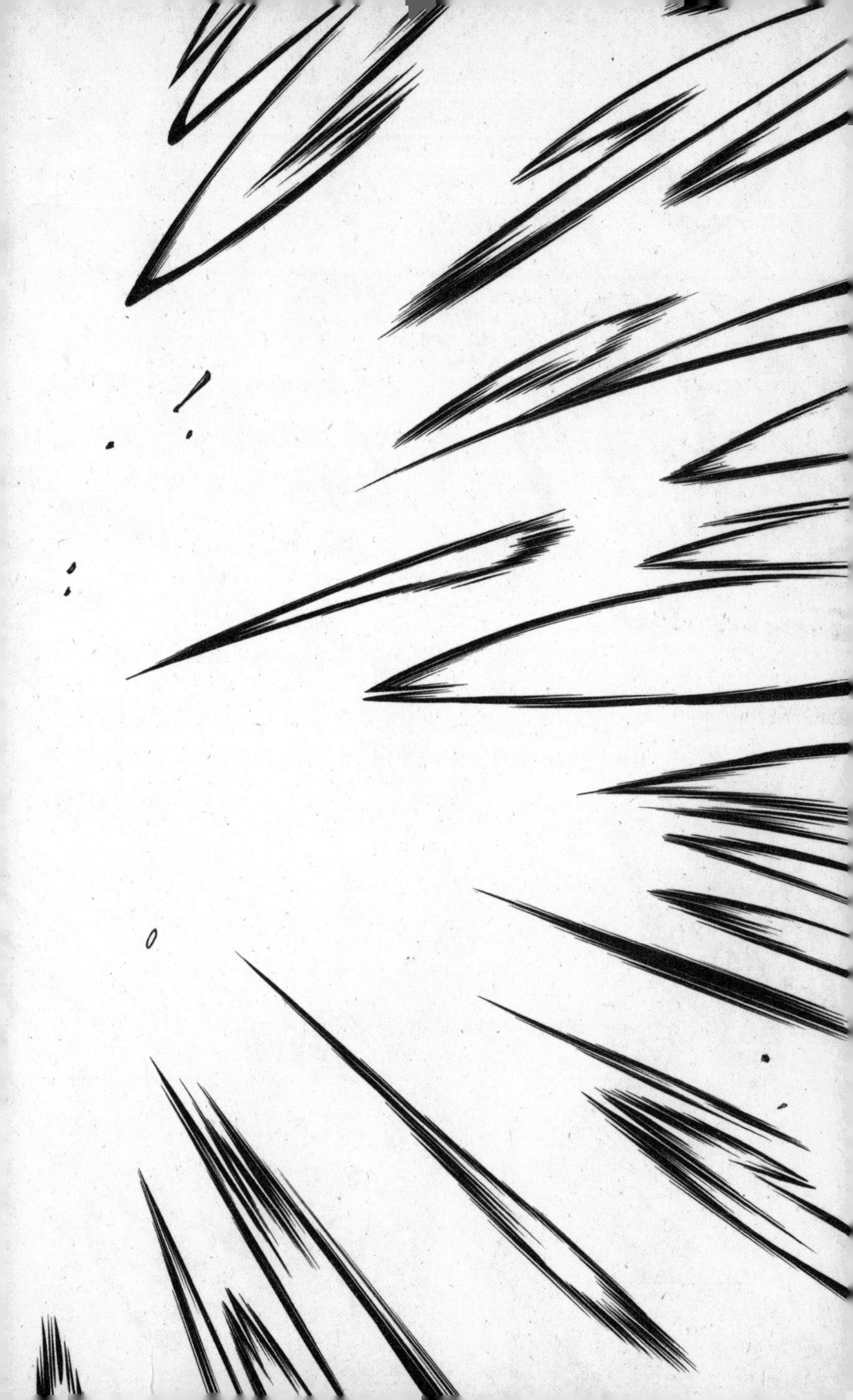

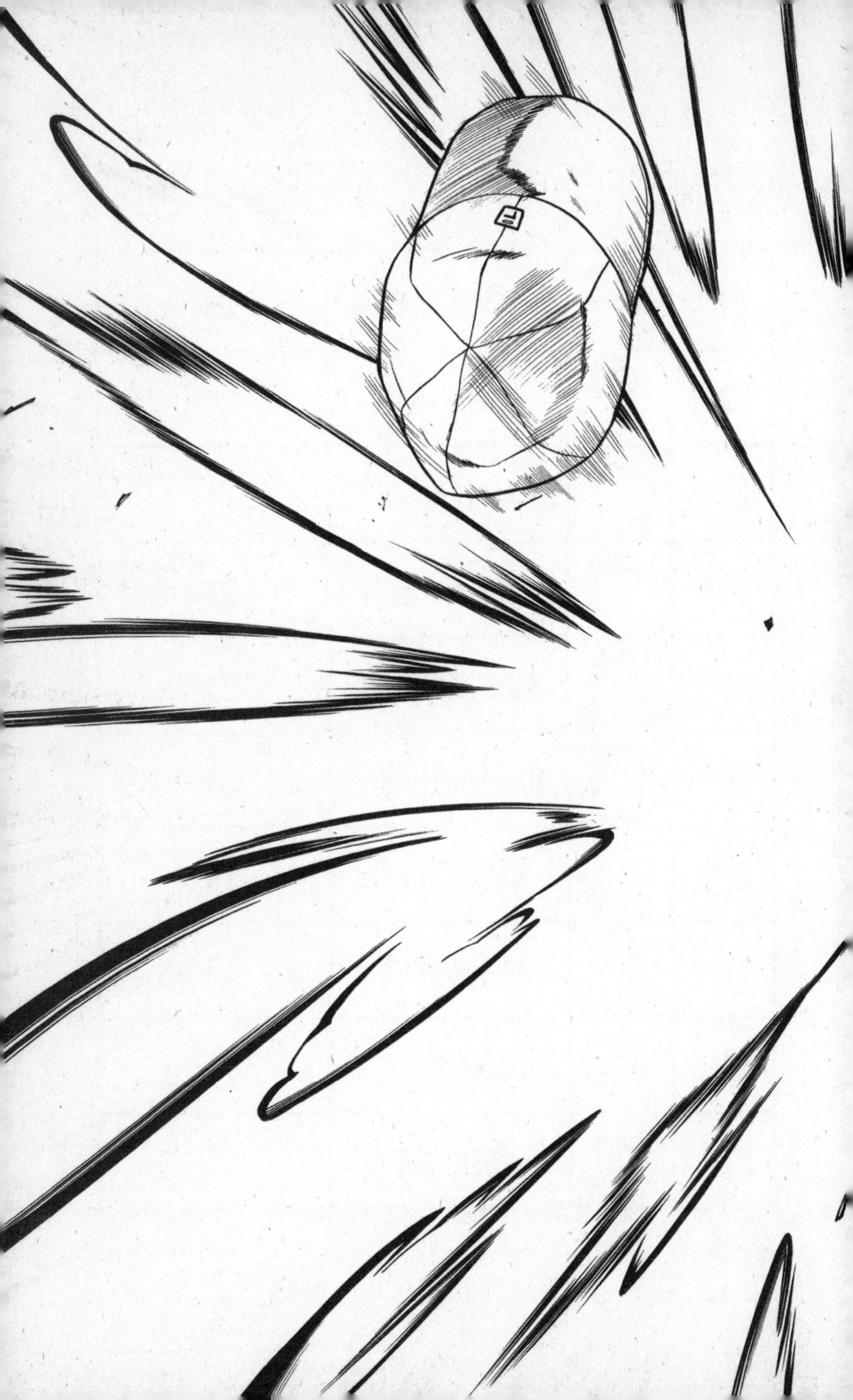

2007

VALENTINE'S DAY CHOCOLATE RANKING 3

21ST	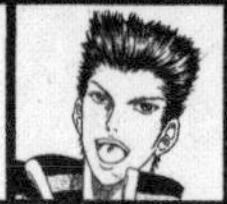	TAKESHI MOMOSHIRO	28
22ND	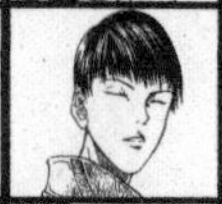	RENJI YANAGI	26
23RD	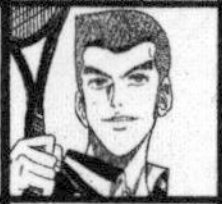	TAKASHI KAWAMURA	21
23RD	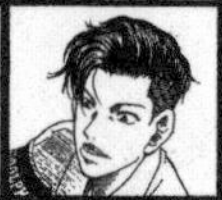	SHINYA YANAGISAWA	21
23RD	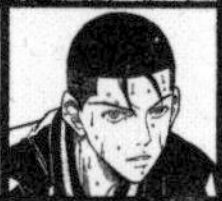	SHUICHIRO OISHI	21
26TH	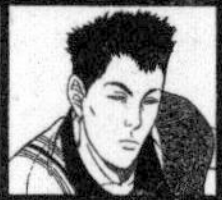	MUNEHIRO KABAJI	20
27TH	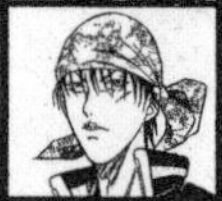	KAORU KAIDO	19
27TH	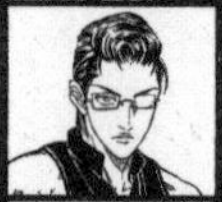	EISHIRO KITE	19
27TH	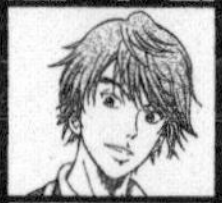	KYOSUMI SENGOKU	19
27TH	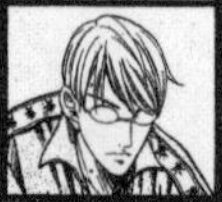	HIROSHI YAGYU	19

CONTINUED ON PAGE 170

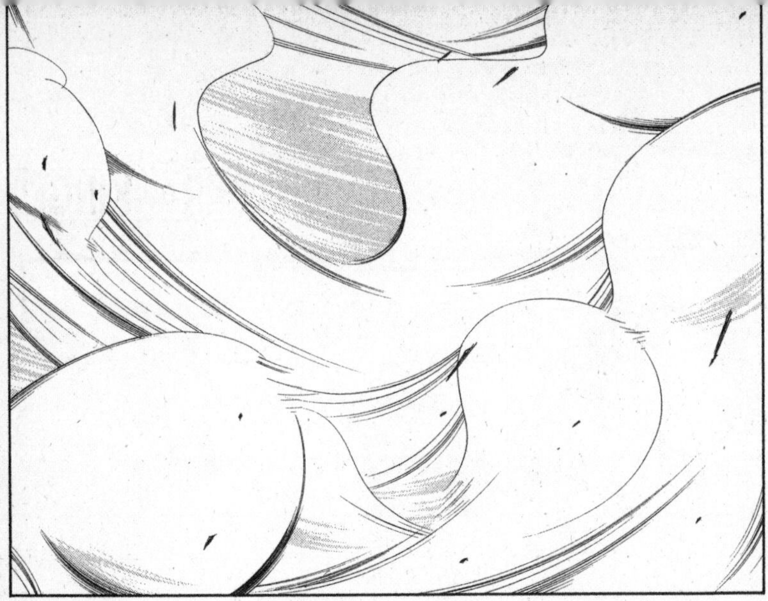

TK Works presents

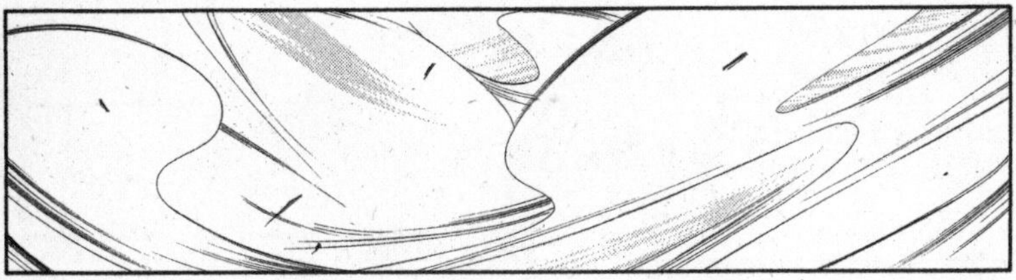

THE PRINCE OF TENNIS

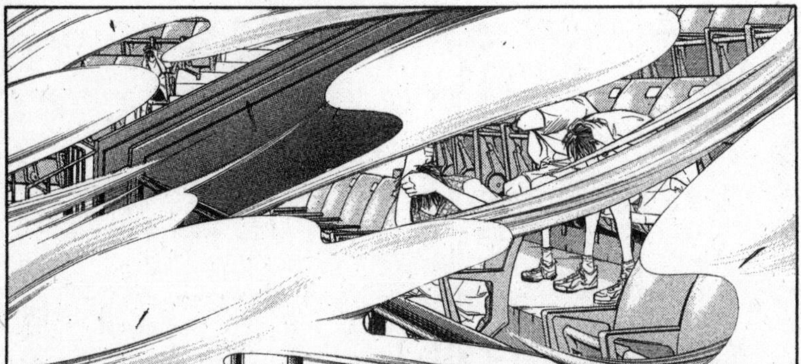

GENIUS 340: TO THE PRINCES OF TENNIS

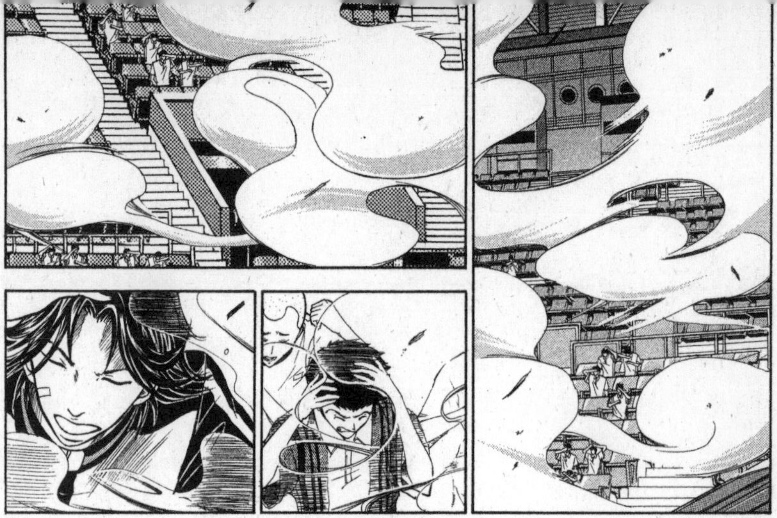

All produced by

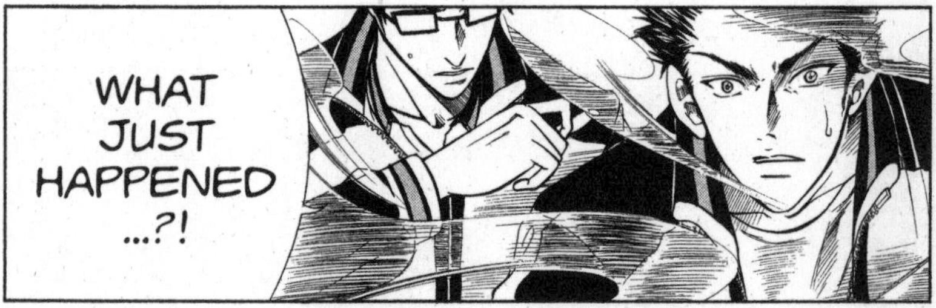
WHAT JUST HAPPENED ...?!

TAKESHI KONOMI

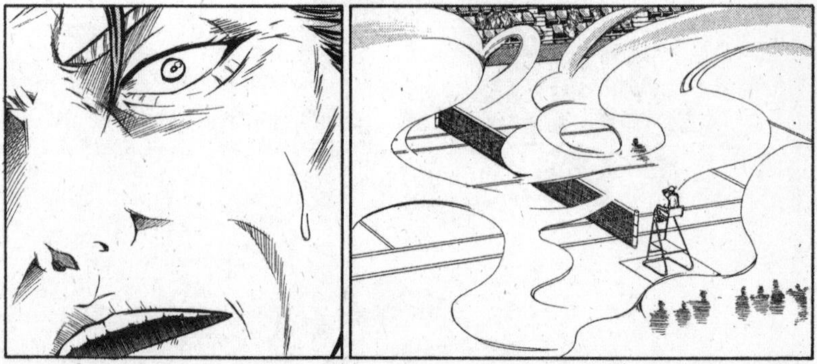

READ THIS WAY

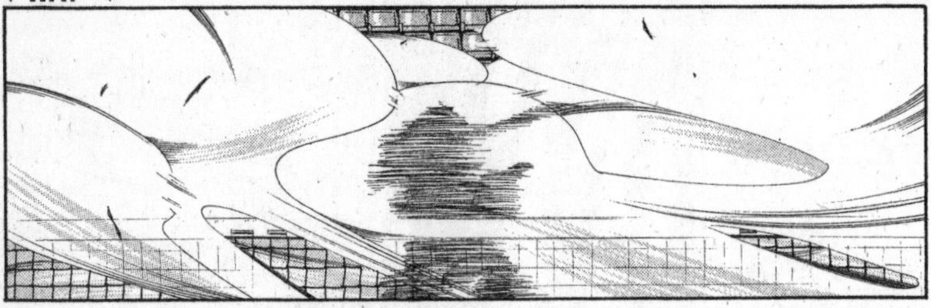

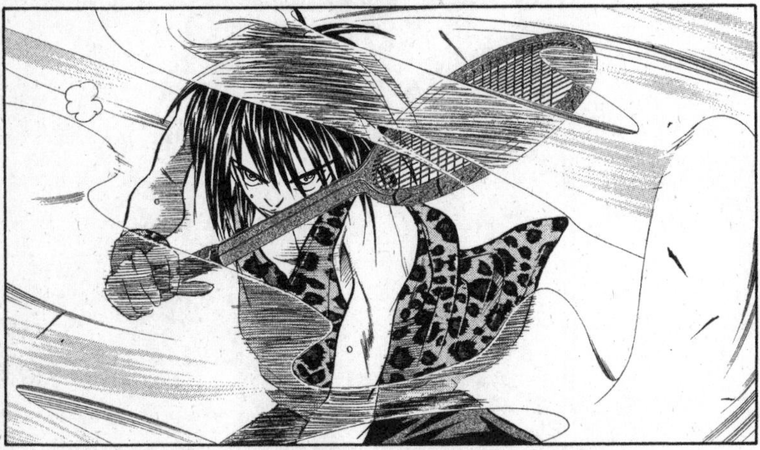

GENIUS 340: TO THE PRINCES OF TENNIS

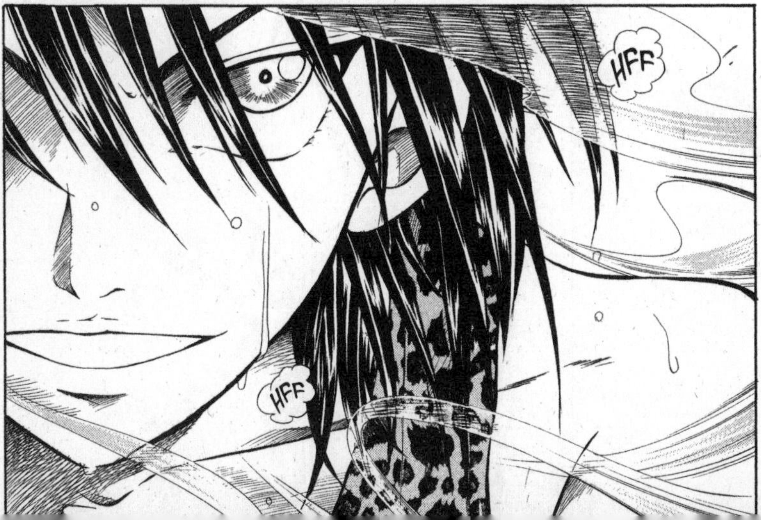
HFF
HFF

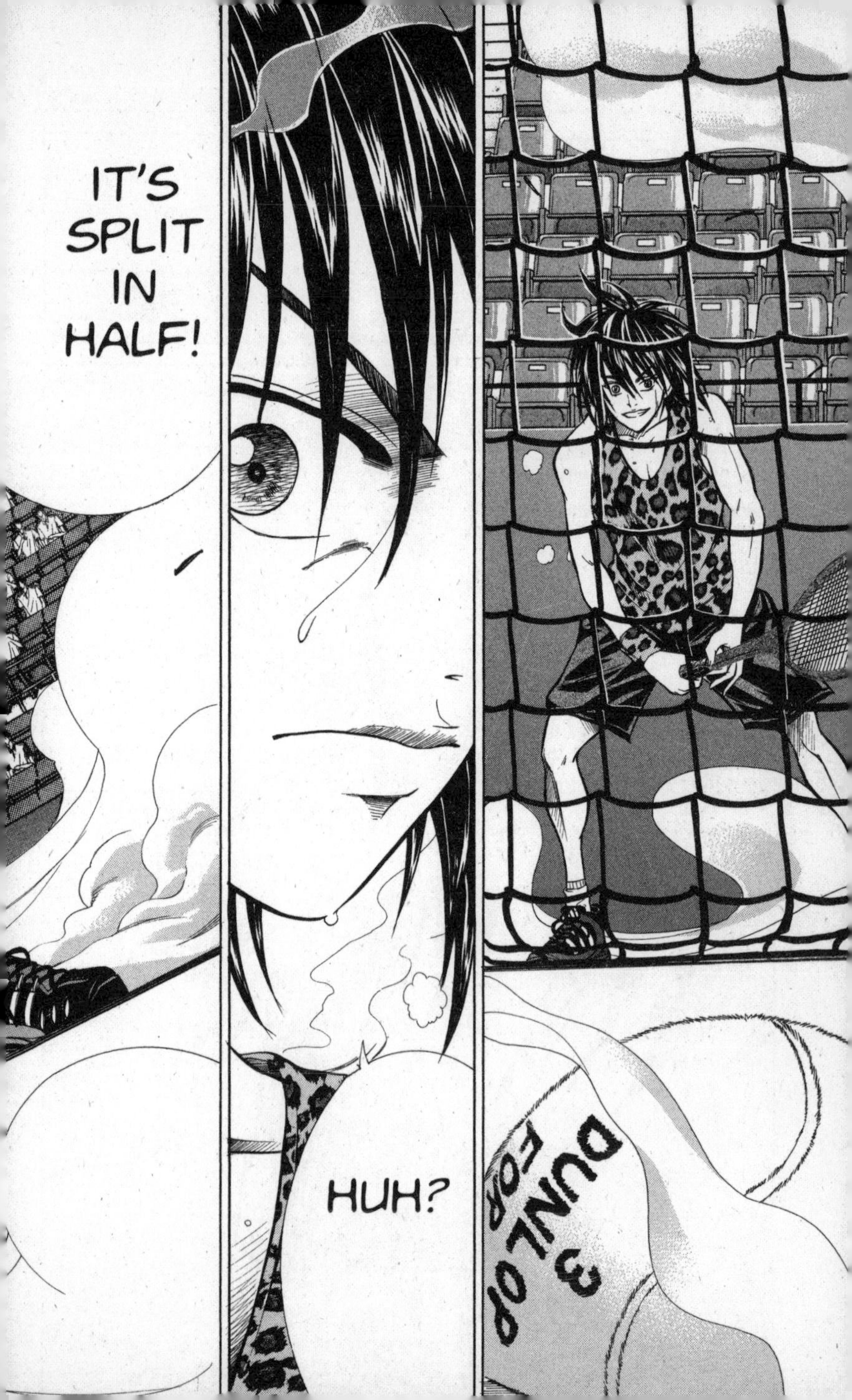
DUNLOP
HUH?
IT'S SPLIT IN HALF!

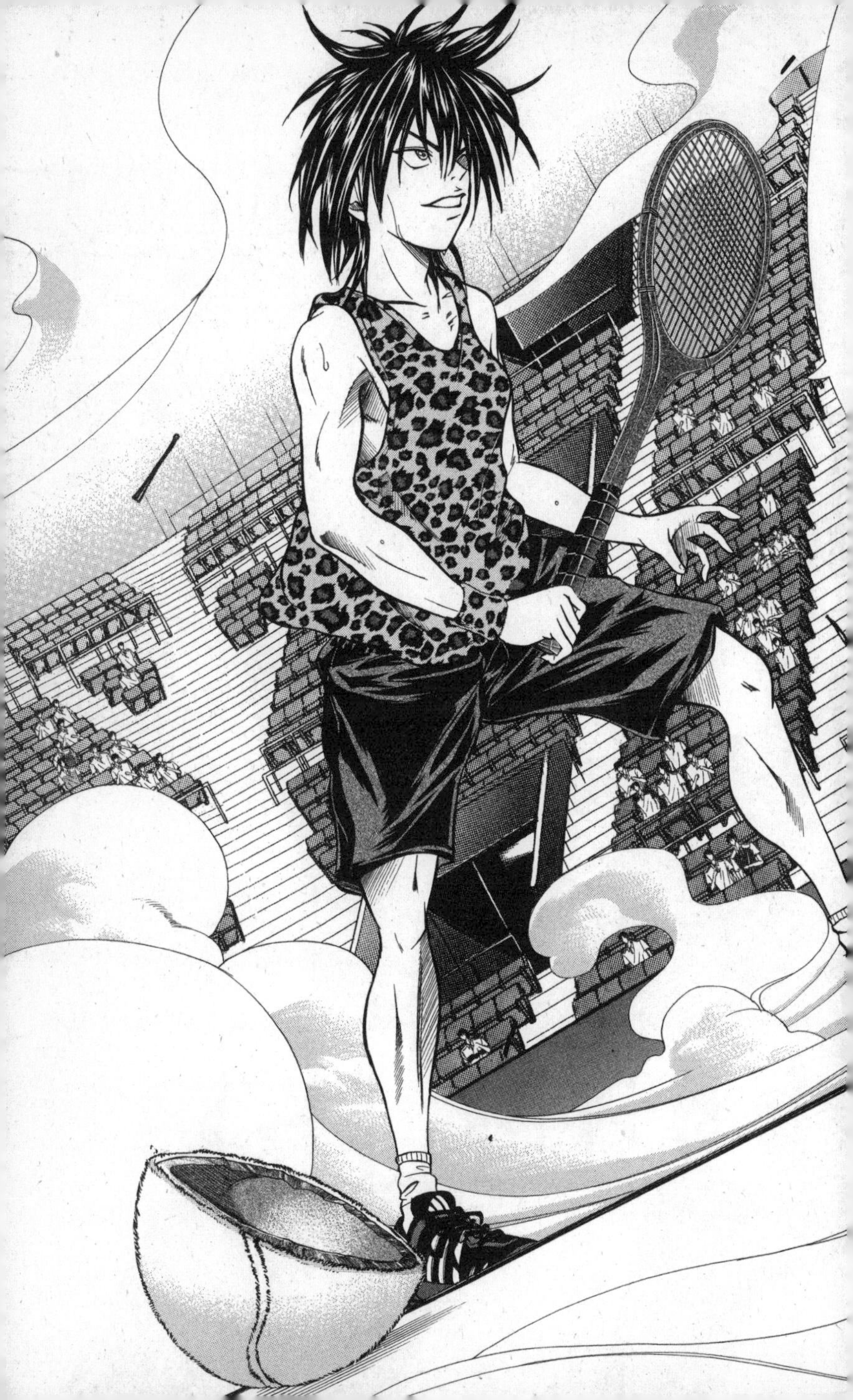

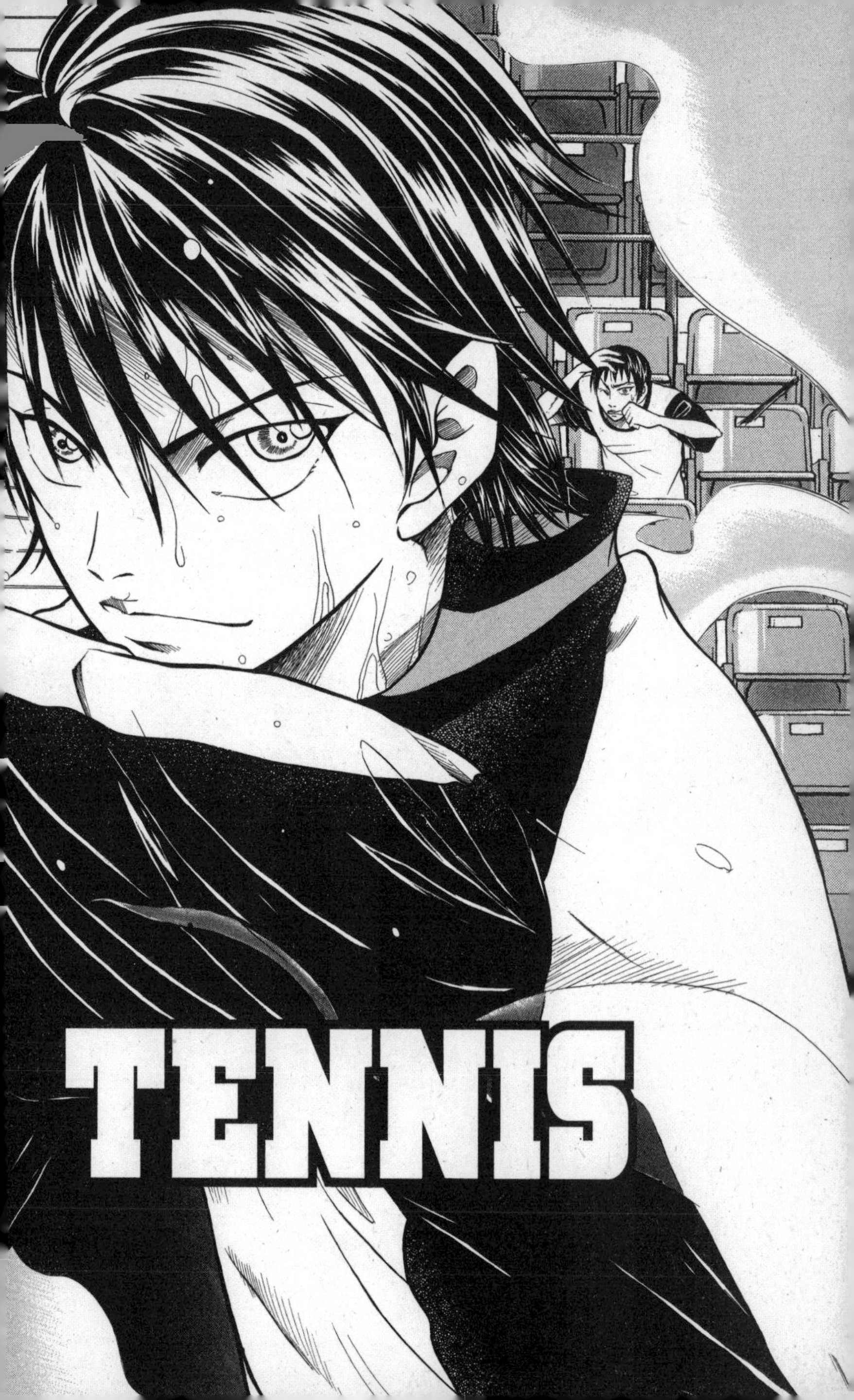
TENNIS

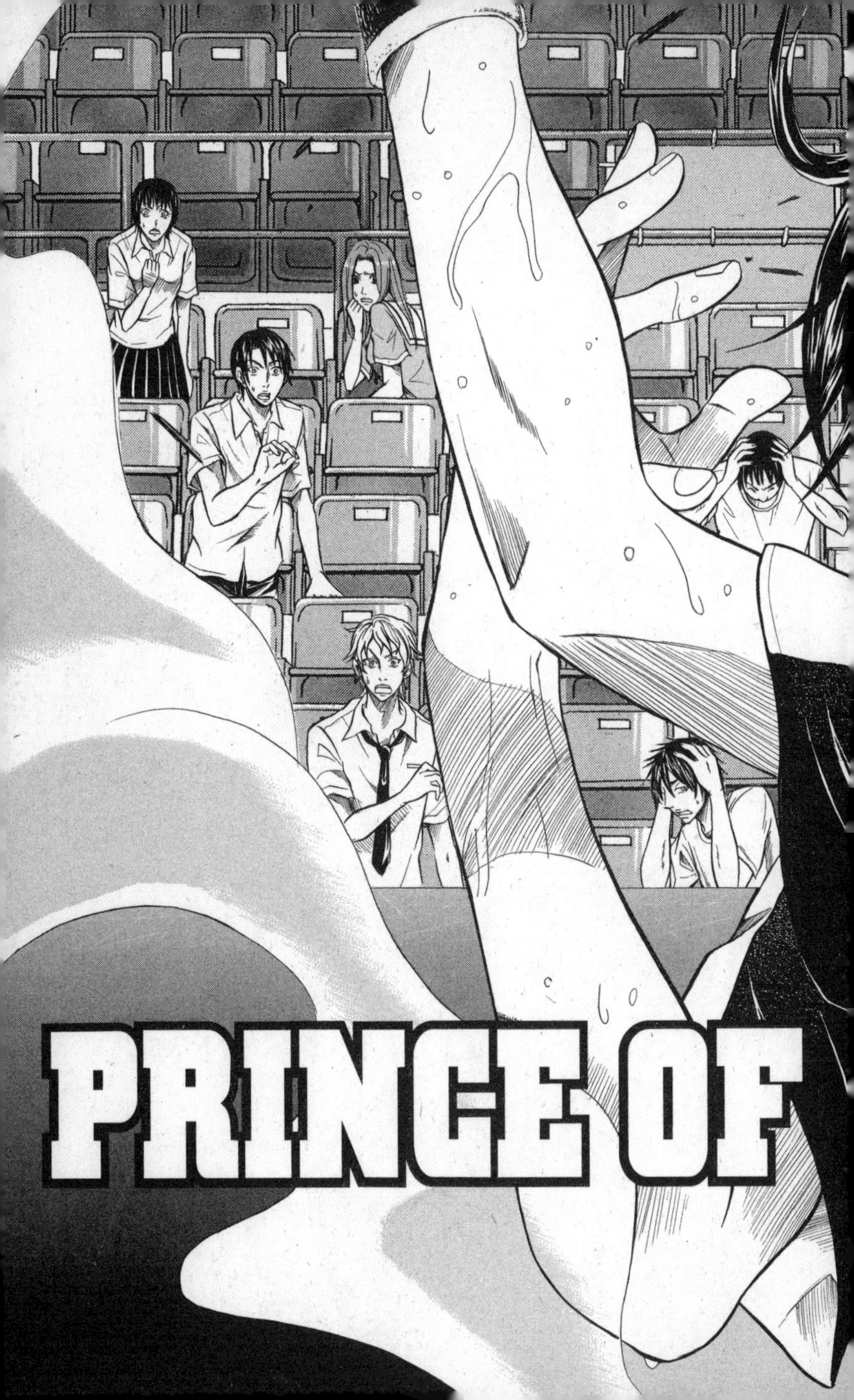
PRINCE OF

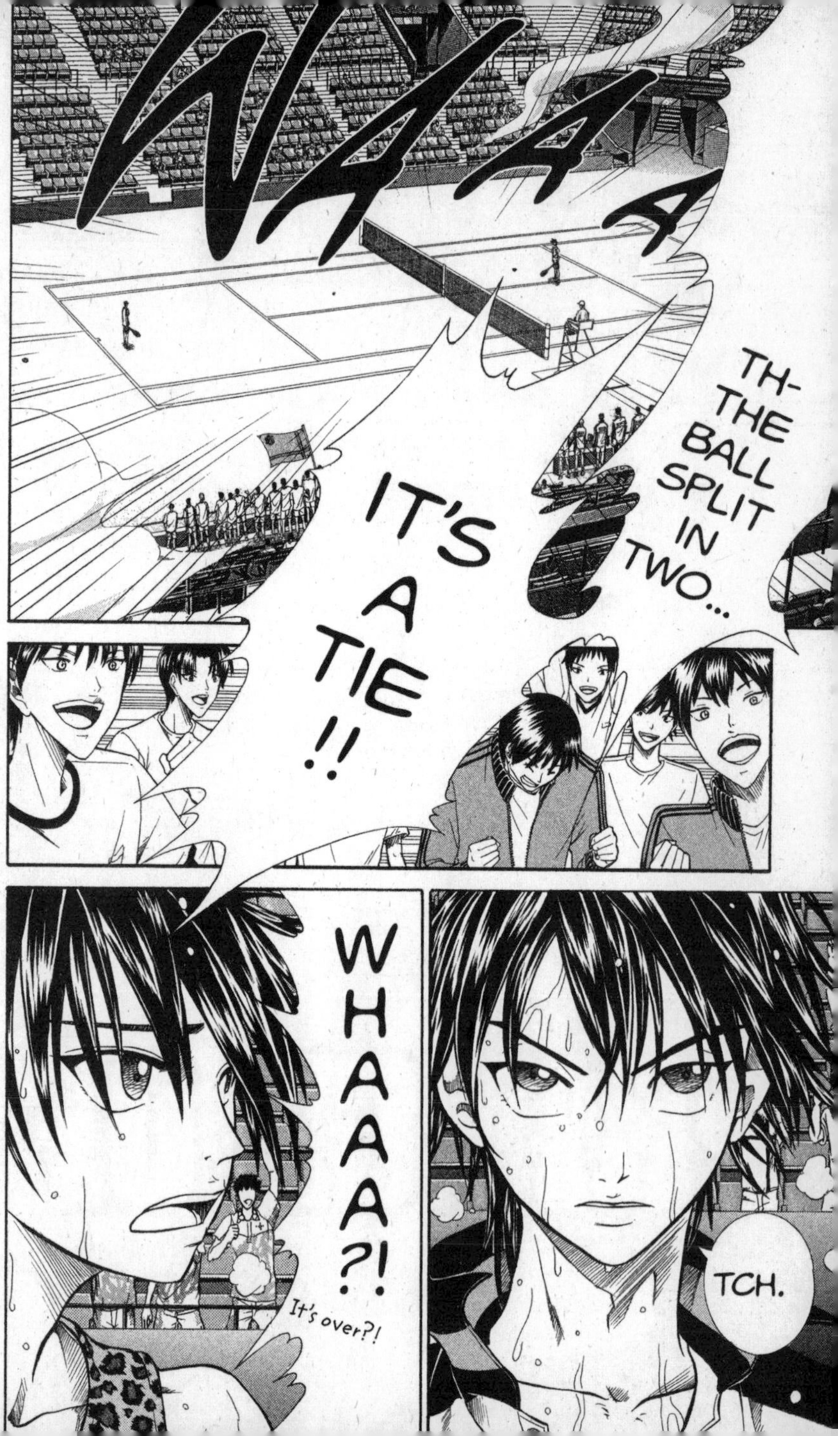
WAAAA
TH-THE BALL SPLIT IN TWO...
IT'S A TIE!!
TCH.
WHAAA?!
It's over?!

READ THIS WAY

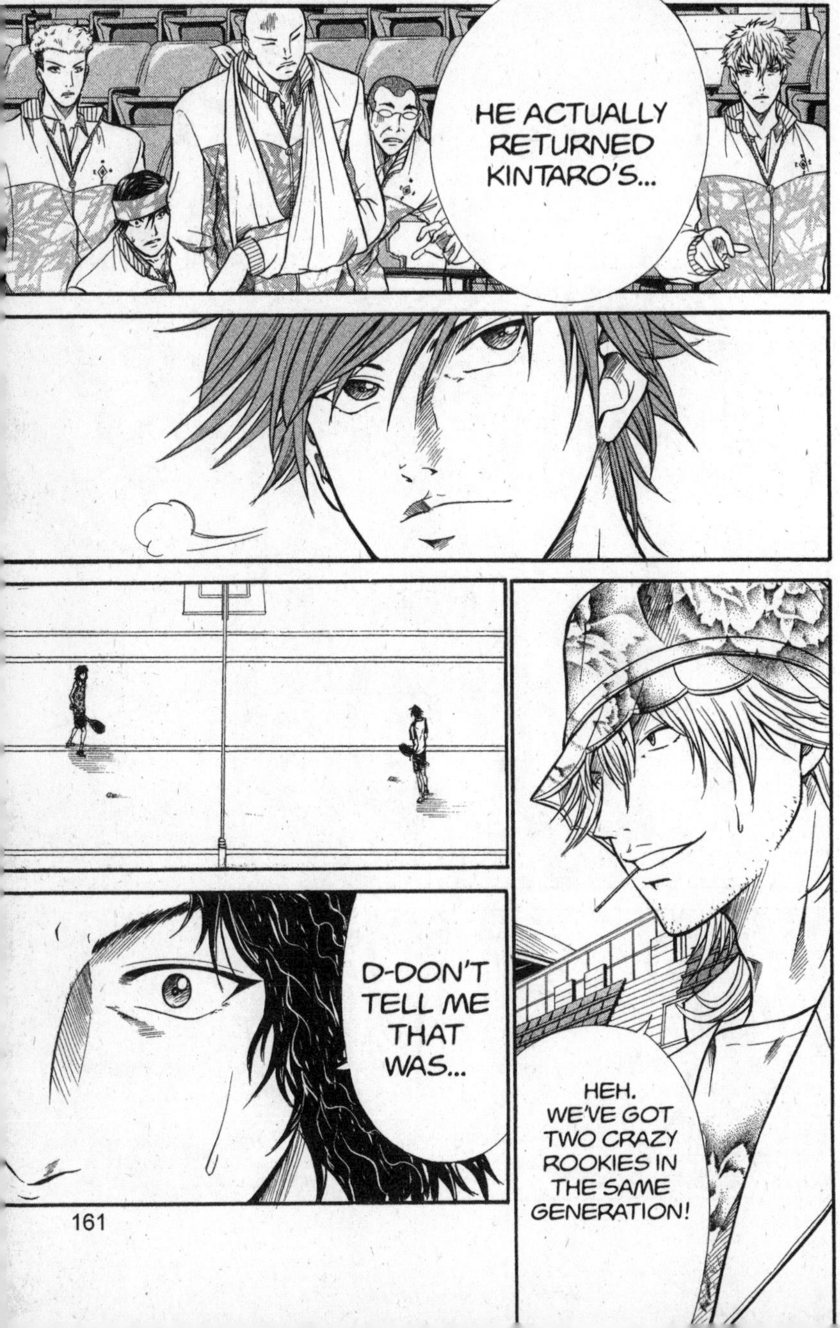
HE ACTUALLY RETURNED KINTARO'S...
D-DON'T TELL ME THAT WAS...
HEH. WE'VE GOT TWO CRAZY ROOKIES IN THE SAME GENERATION!

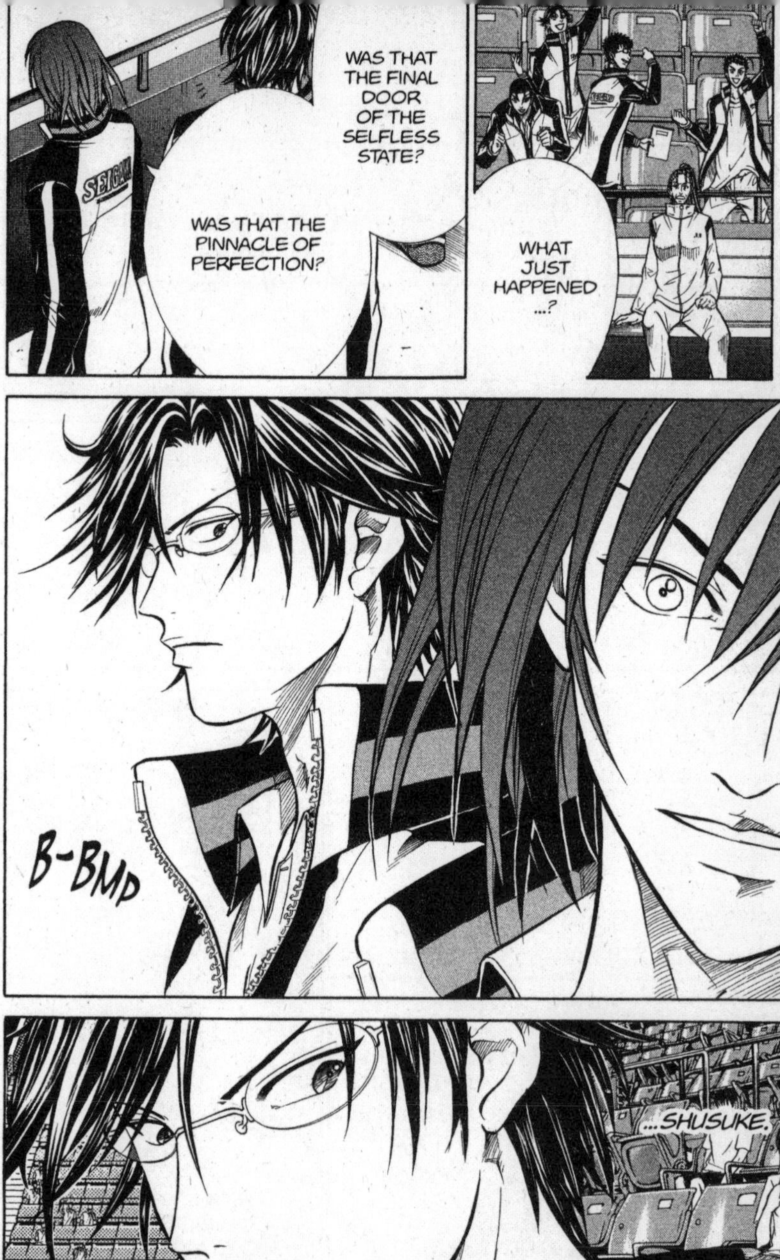
WHAT JUST HAPPENED ...?
WAS THAT THE FINAL DOOR OF THE SELFLESS STATE?
WAS THAT THE PINNACLE OF PERFECTION?
B-BMP
...SHUSUKE.

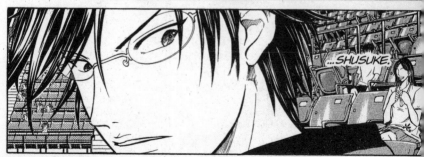

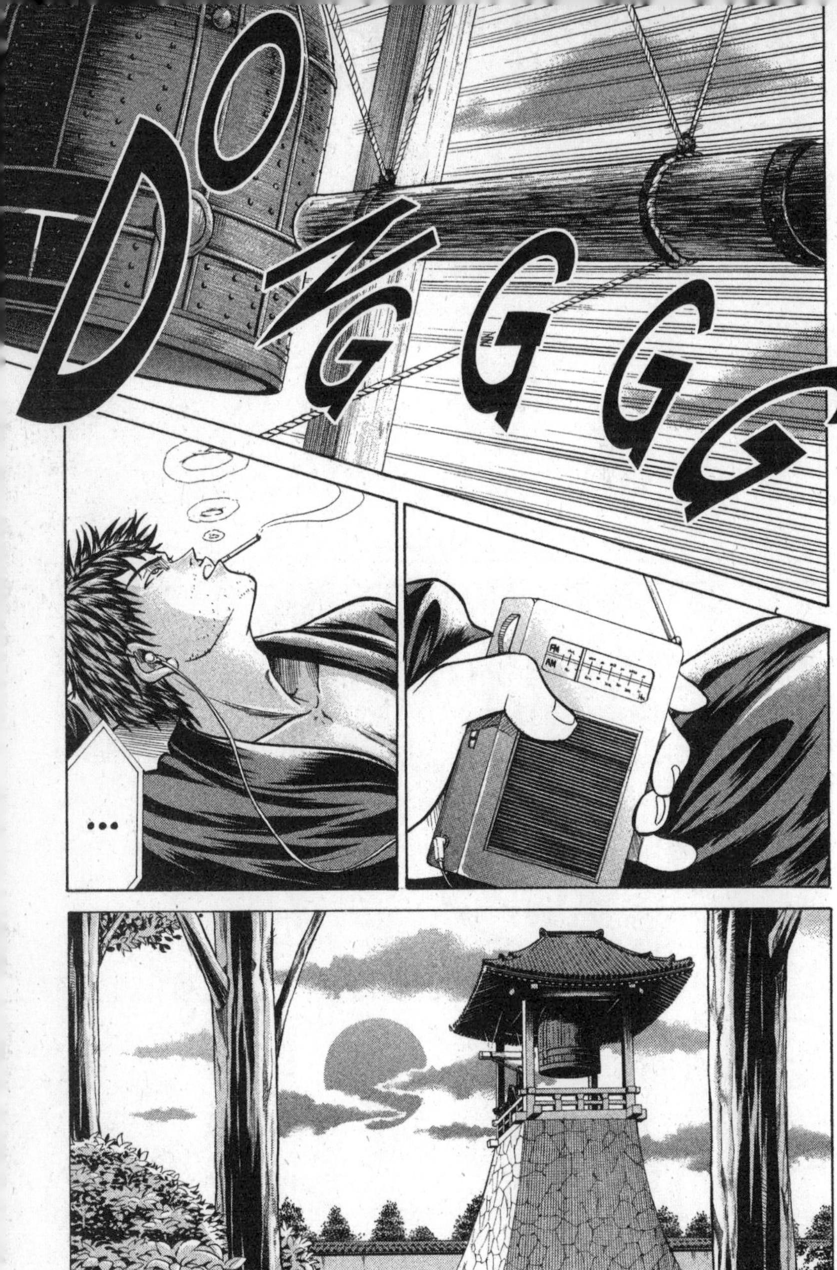
DONGGGG
...

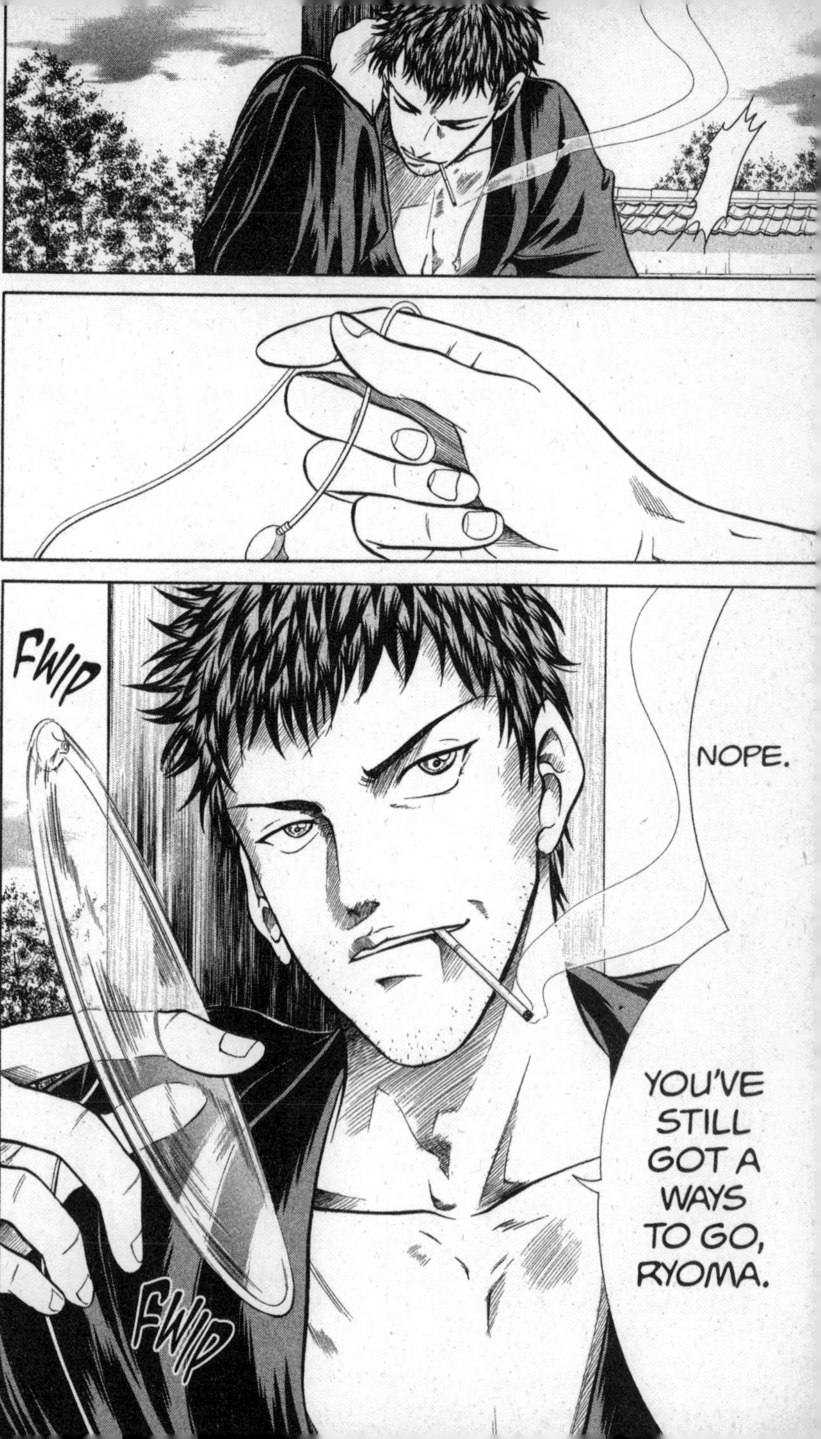
NOPE.
YOU'VE STILL GOT A WAYS TO GO, RYOMA.
FWIP
FWIP

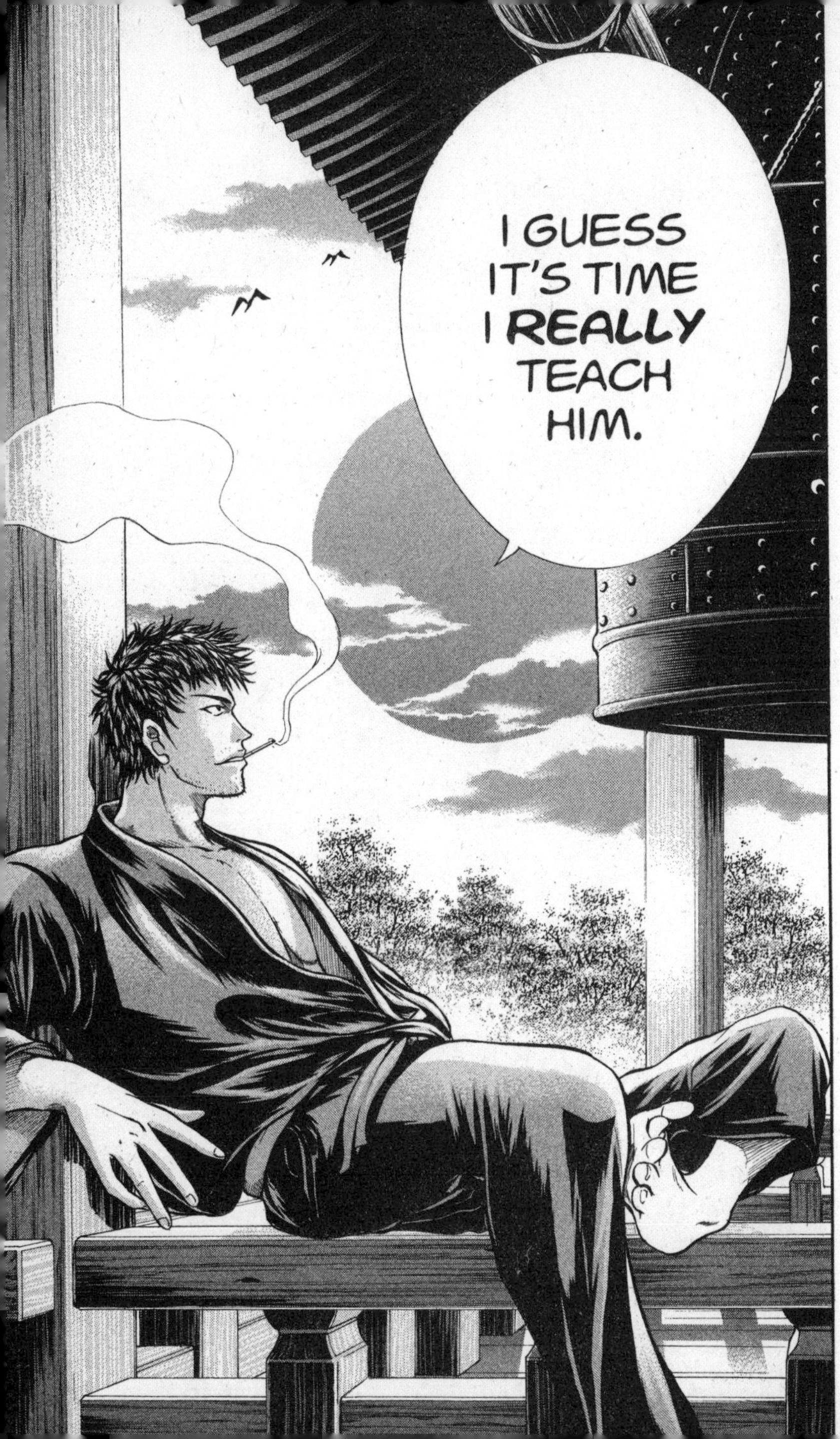
I GUESS IT'S TIME I **REALLY** TEACH HIM.

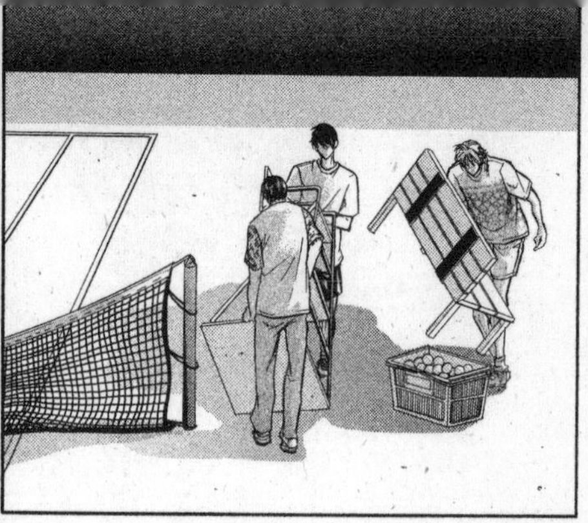

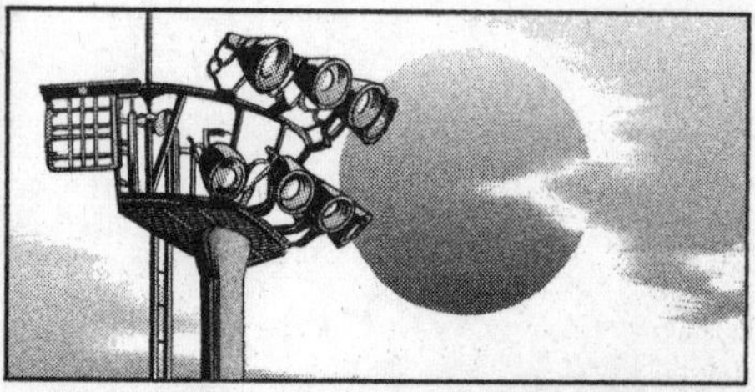

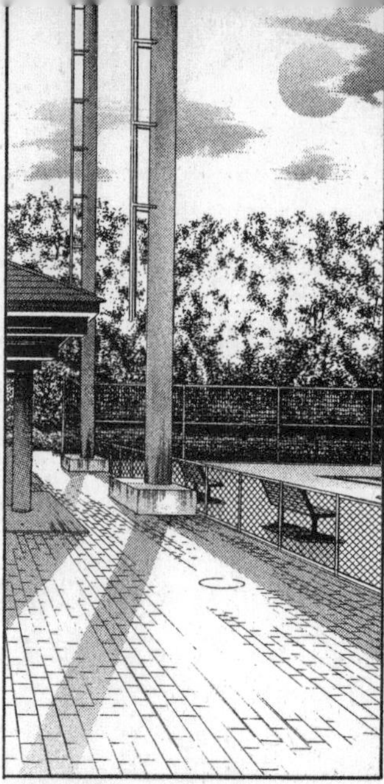

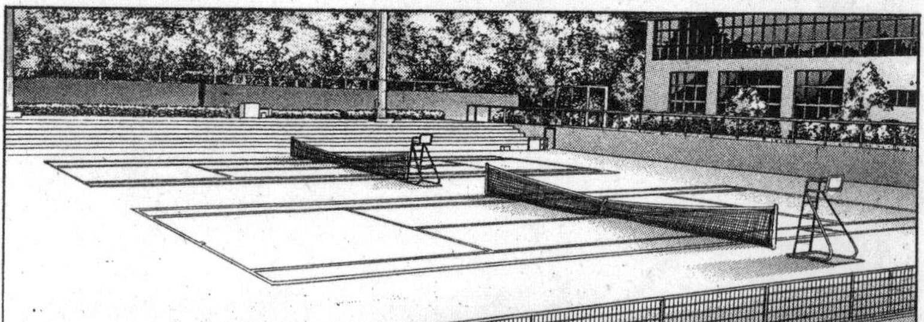

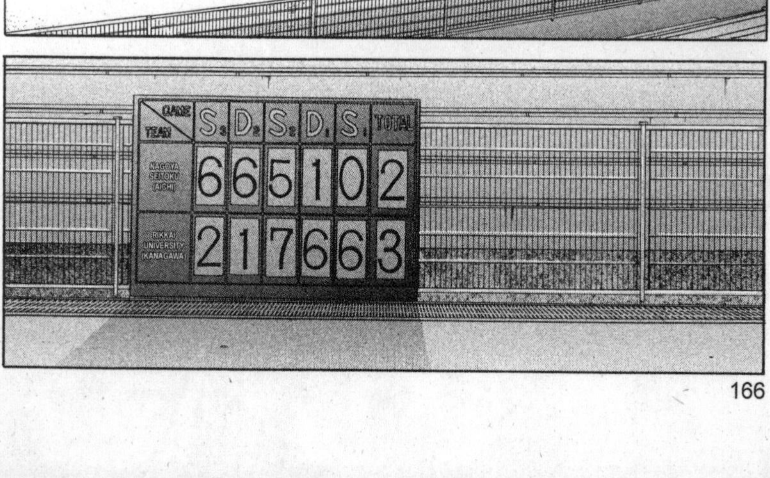
GAME
TEAM
S3 D2 S2 D1 S1 TOTAL
NAGOYA SEITOKU (AICHI)
6 6 5 1 0 2
RIKKAI UNIVERSITY (KANAGAWA)
2 1 7 6 6 3

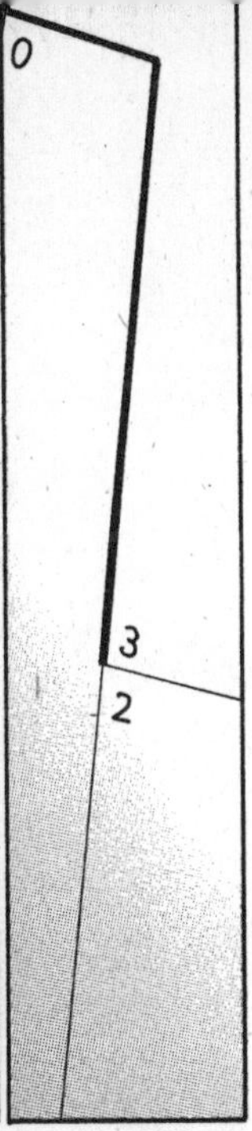
0
3
2

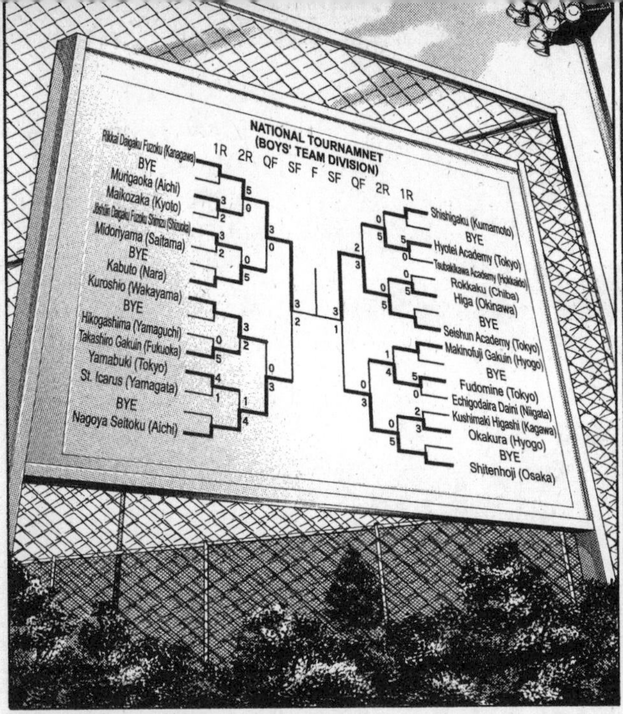
NATIONAL TOURNAMNET
(BOYS' TEAM DIVISION)
1R 2R QF SF F SF QF 2R 1R
Rikkai Daigaku Fuzoku (Kanagawa)
BYE
Murigaoka (Aichi)
Maikozaka (Kyoto)
Joshiin Daigaku Fuzoku Shimizu (Shizuoka)
Midoriyama (Saitama)
BYE
Kabuto (Nara)
Kuroshio (Wakayama)
BYE
Hikogashima (Yamaguchi)
Takashiro Gakuin (Fukuoka)
Yamabuki (Tokyo)
St. Icarus (Yamagata)
BYE
Nagoya Seitoku (Aichi)
Shishigaku (Kumamoto)
BYE
Hyotei Academy (Tokyo)
Tsubakikawa Academy (Hokkaido)
Rokkaku (Chiba)
Higa (Okinawa)
BYE
Seishun Academy (Tokyo)
Makinofuji Gakuin (Hyogo)
BYE
Fudomine (Tokyo)
Echigodaira Daini (Niigata)
Kushimaki Higashi (Kagawa)
Okakura (Hyogo)
BYE
Shitenhoji (Osaka)

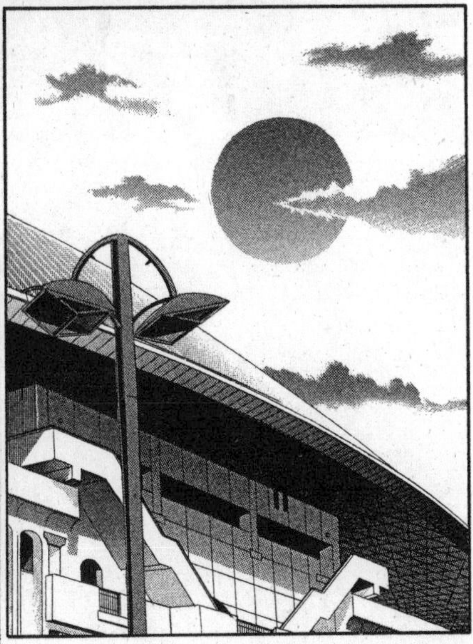

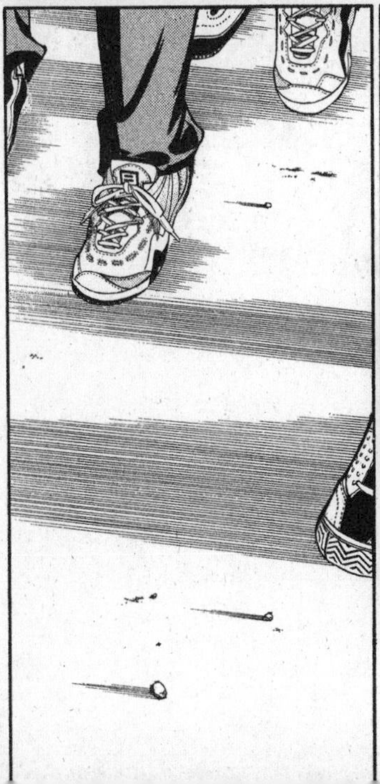

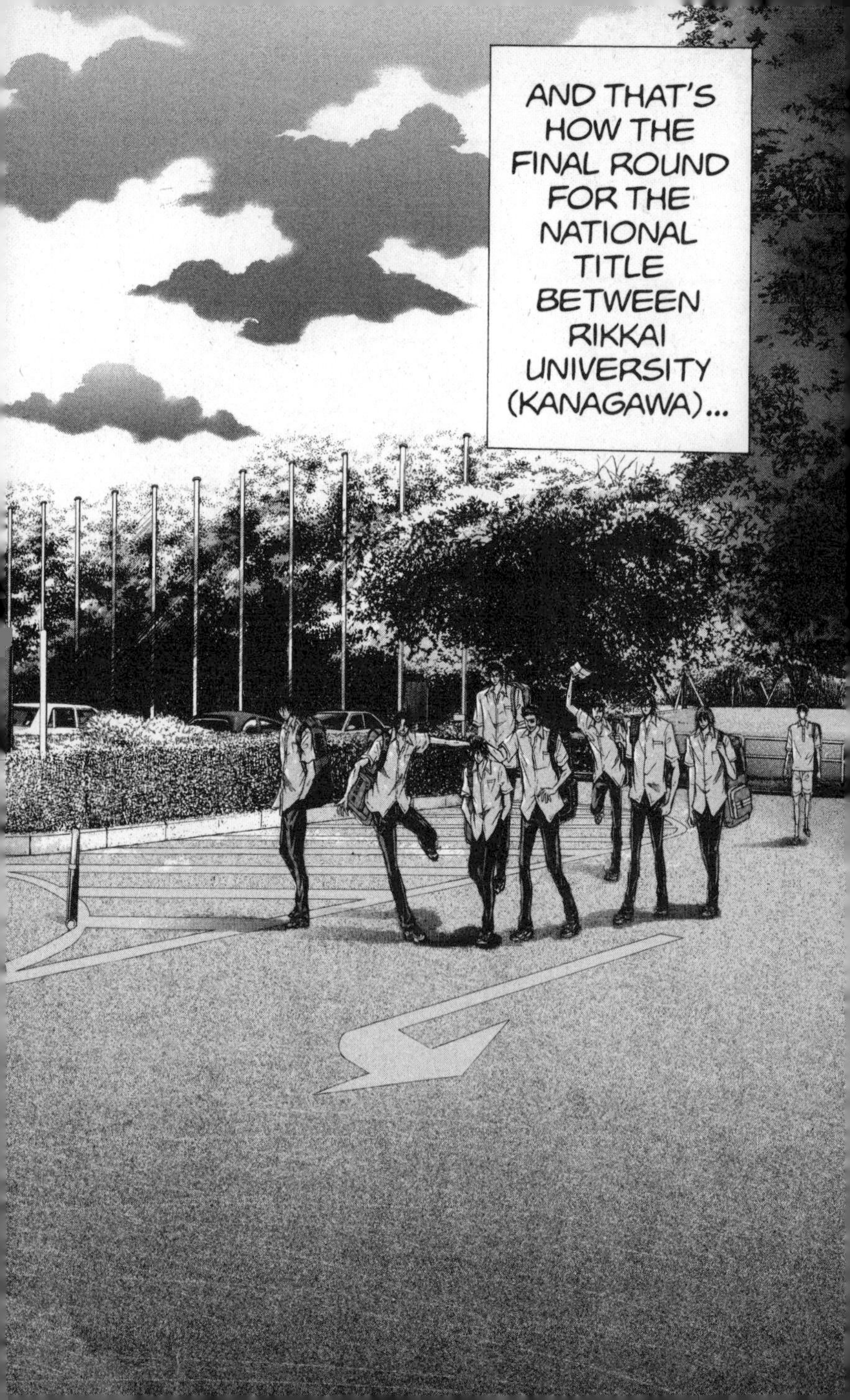
AND THAT'S HOW THE FINAL ROUND FOR THE NATIONAL TITLE BETWEEN RIKKAI UNIVERSITY (KANAGAWA)...

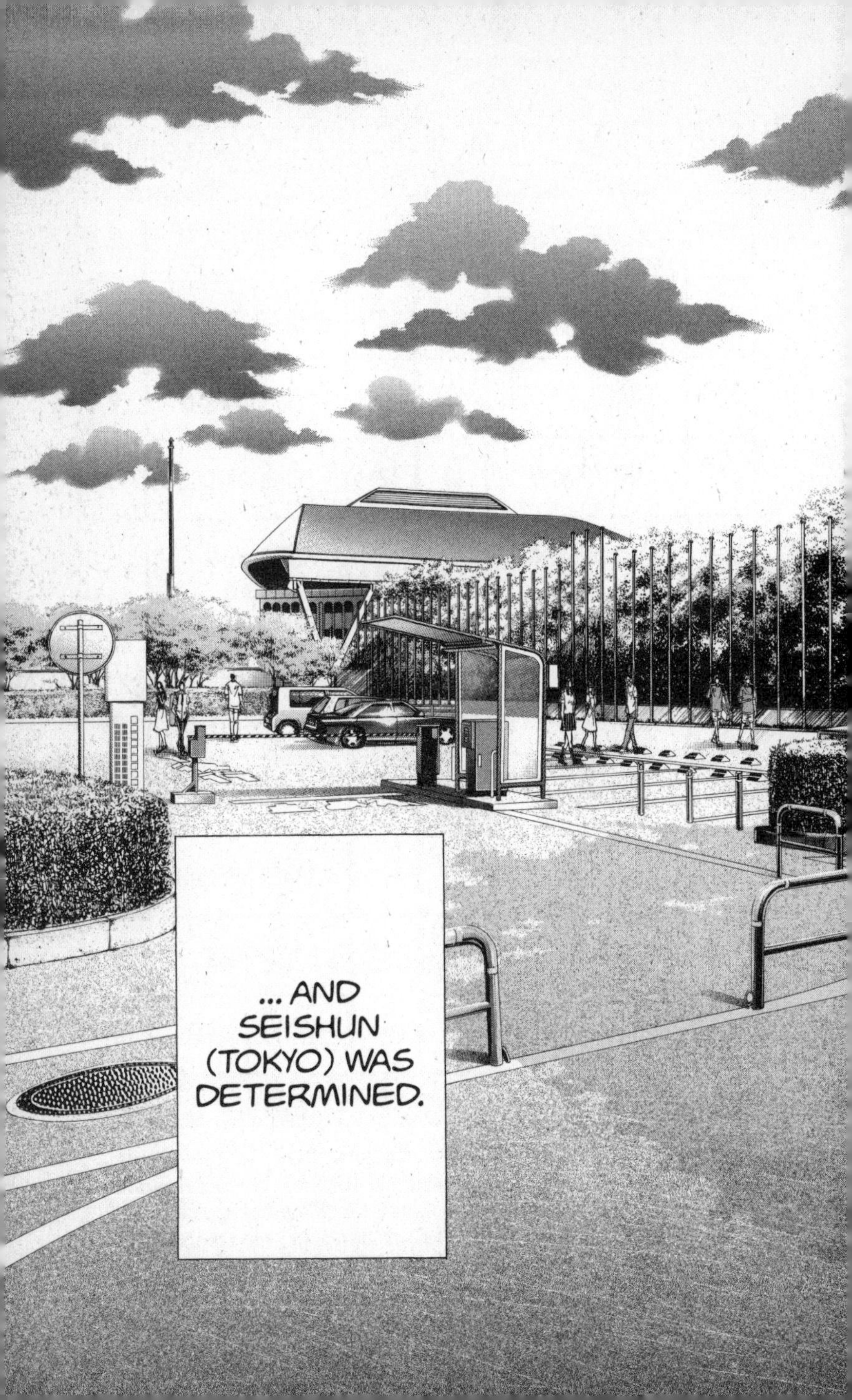
... AND SEISHUN (TOKYO) WAS DETERMINED.

VALENTINE'S DAY CHOCOLATE RANKING 4

31ST	HAJIME MIZUKI	17	42ND	RYOGA ECHIZEN	6
32ND	KENYA OSHITARI	16	42ND	ATSUSHI KISARAZU	6
33RD	JACKAL KUWAHARA	15	42ND	YUDAI YAMATO	6
34TH	AKIRA KAMIO	13	42ND	SENRI CHITOSE	6
34TH	KURANOSUKE SHIRAISHI	13	46TH	JIN AKUTSU	5
36TH	KOJIRO SAEKI	11	46TH	HIKARU AMANE	5
37TH	SHINJI IBU	10	46TH	TAKESUE	5
37TH	KEI TANISHI	10	49TH	KENTARO AOI	4
39TH	HIROSHI CHINEN	9	49TH	TSUBASA NISHIKIORI	4
40TH	KIPPEI TACHIBANA	9	49TH	YUTA FUJI	4
40TH	KINTARO TOYAMA	8	49TH	KENTARO MINAMI	4

(REMAINDER OF THE RESULTS OMITTED)

The results for 2007's Valentine's Day Chocolate Ranking (2,708 total) are listed above. At first glance, it appears that Keigo won by a landslide, but one person actually sent 586 chocolates for him! Considering that, it was a pretty close race at the top. What will the results be like next year? To all those who sent chocolates, thank you very much!

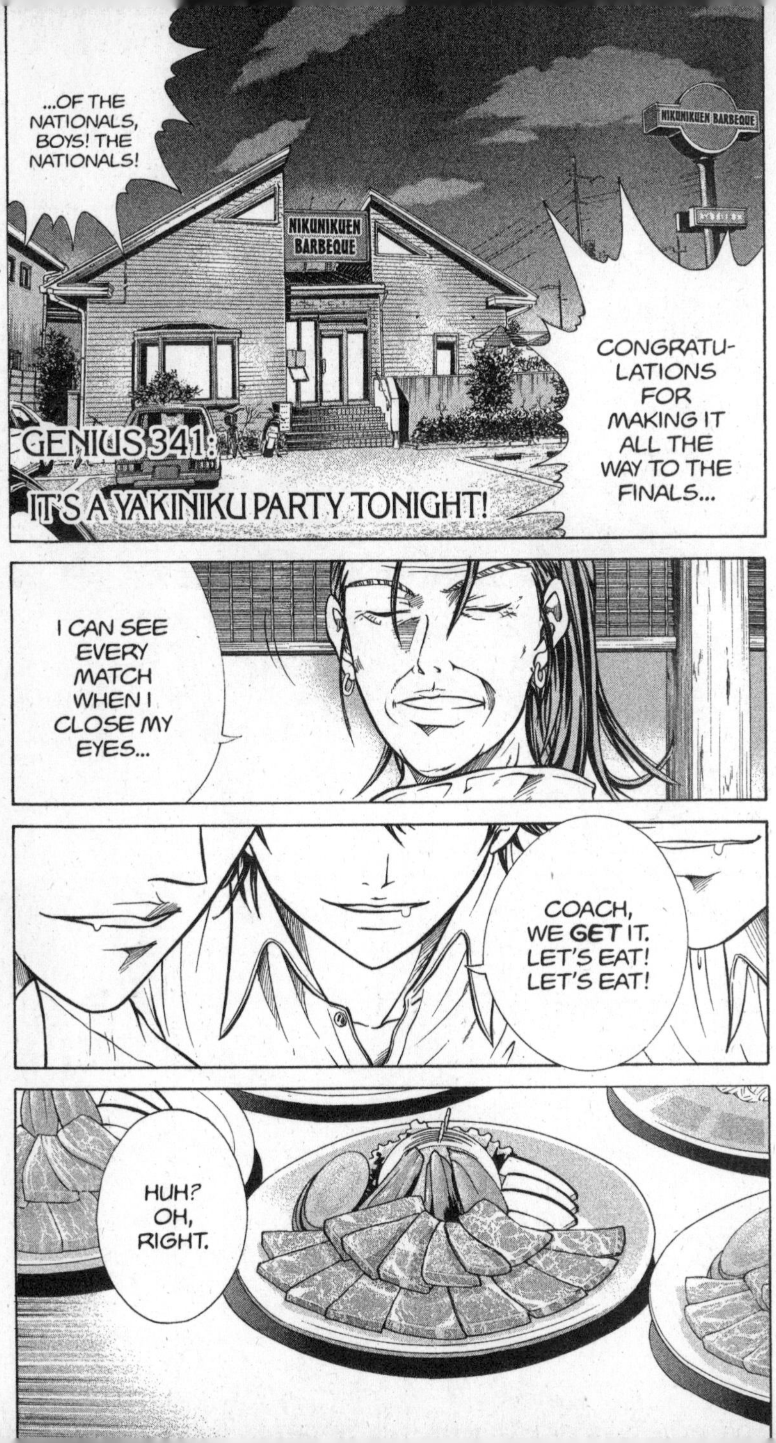
NIKUNIKUEN BARBEQUE
CONGRATULATIONS FOR MAKING IT ALL THE WAY TO THE FINALS...
...OF THE NATIONALS, BOYS! THE NATIONALS!
NIKUNIKUEN BARBEQUE
GENIUS 341: IT'S A YAKINIKU PARTY TONIGHT!
I CAN SEE EVERY MATCH WHEN I CLOSE MY EYES...
COACH, WE GET IT. LET'S EAT! LET'S EAT!
HUH? OH, RIGHT.

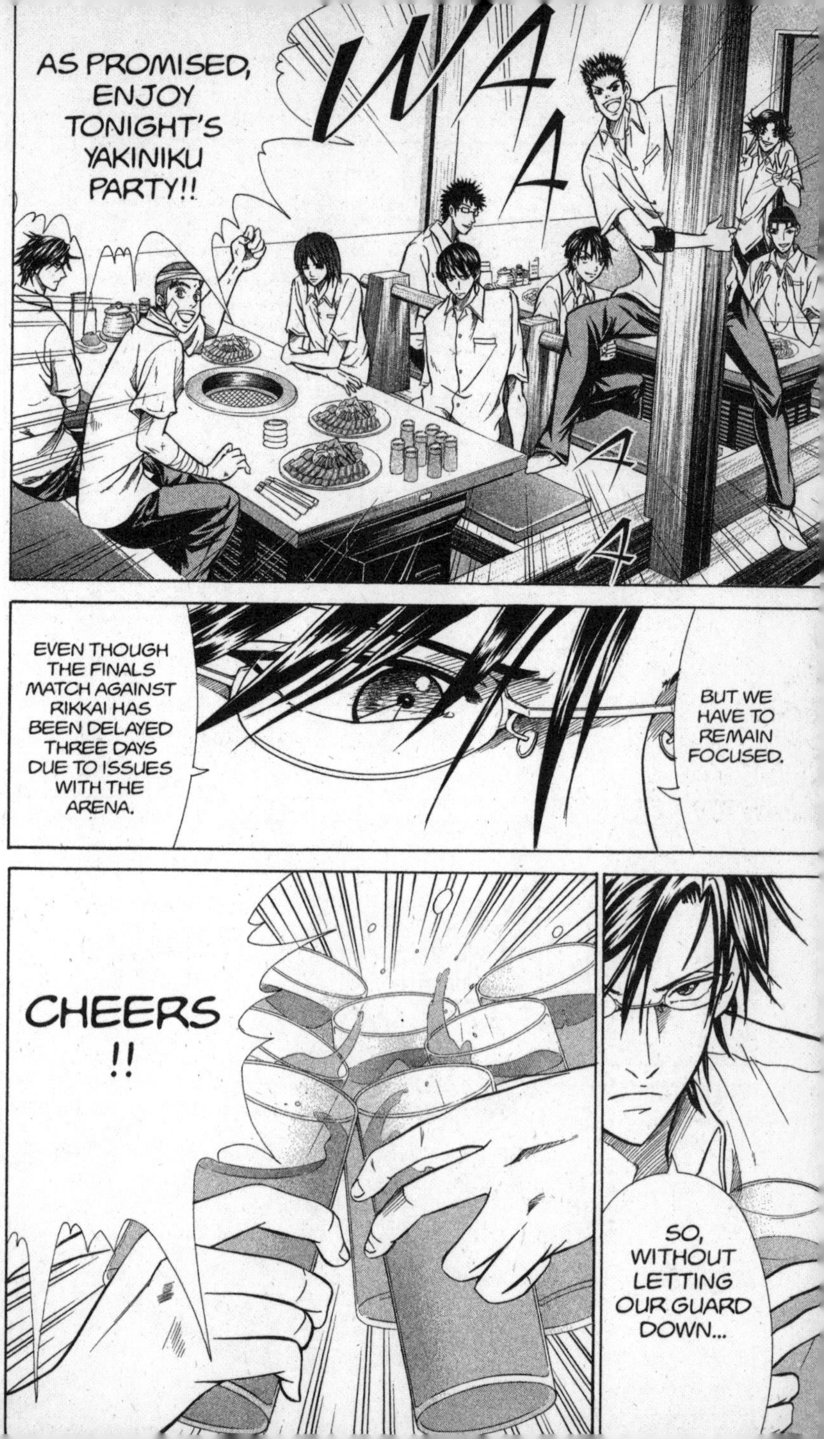
AS PROMISED, ENJOY TONIGHT'S YAKINIKU PARTY!!
WAAAA
EVEN THOUGH THE FINALS MATCH AGAINST RIKKAI HAS BEEN DELAYED THREE DAYS DUE TO ISSUES WITH THE ARENA.
BUT WE HAVE TO REMAIN FOCUSED.
SO, WITHOUT LETTING OUR GUARD DOWN...
CHEERS!!

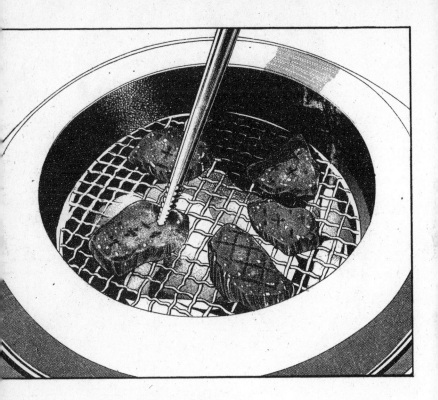

GENIUS 341:

IT'S A YAKINIKU PARTY TONIGHT!

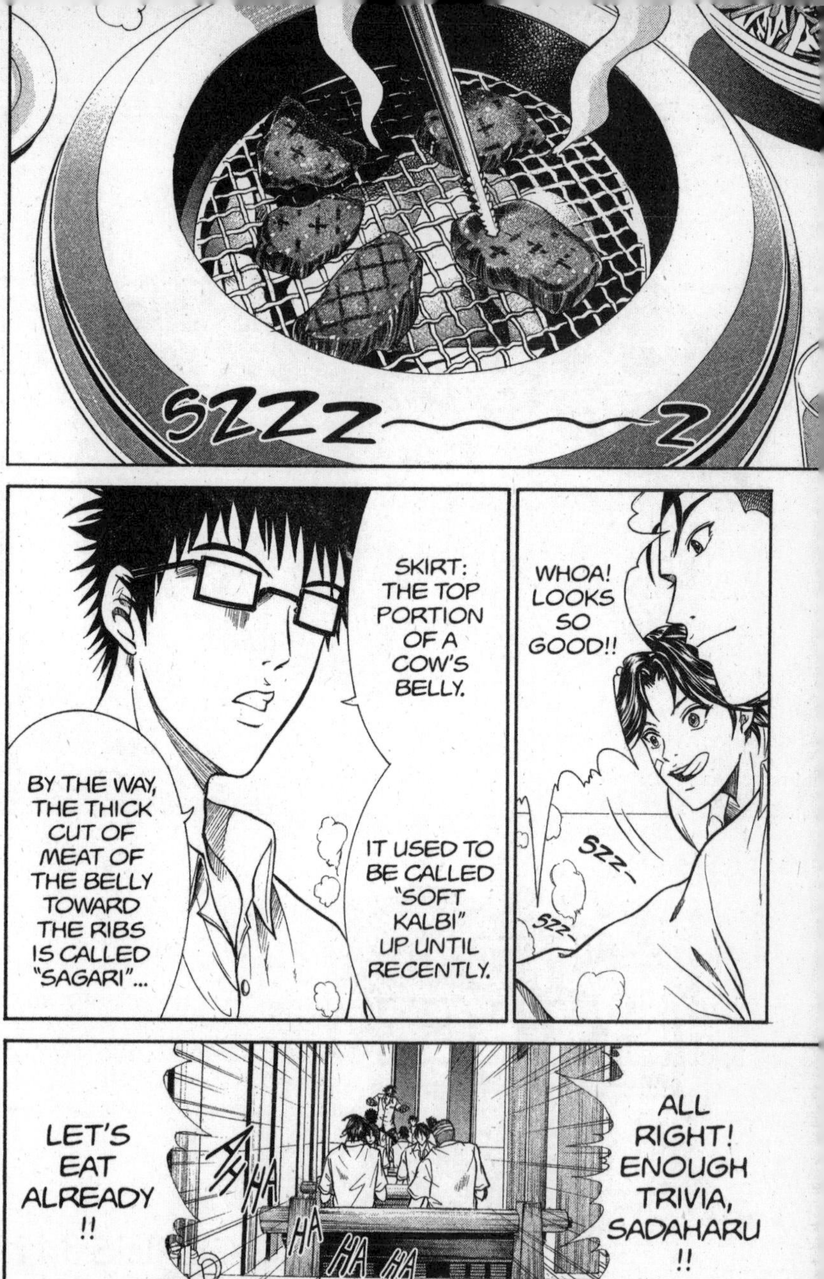
SZZZ—Z
WHOA! LOOKS SO GOOD!!
SZZ-
SZZ-
SKIRT: THE TOP PORTION OF A COW'S BELLY.
IT USED TO BE CALLED "SOFT KALBI" UP UNTIL RECENTLY.
BY THE WAY, THE THICK CUT OF MEAT OF THE BELLY TOWARD THE RIBS IS CALLED "SAGARI"...
ALL RIGHT! ENOUGH TRIVIA, SADAHARU!!
AHHA HA HA HA HA
LET'S EAT ALREADY!!

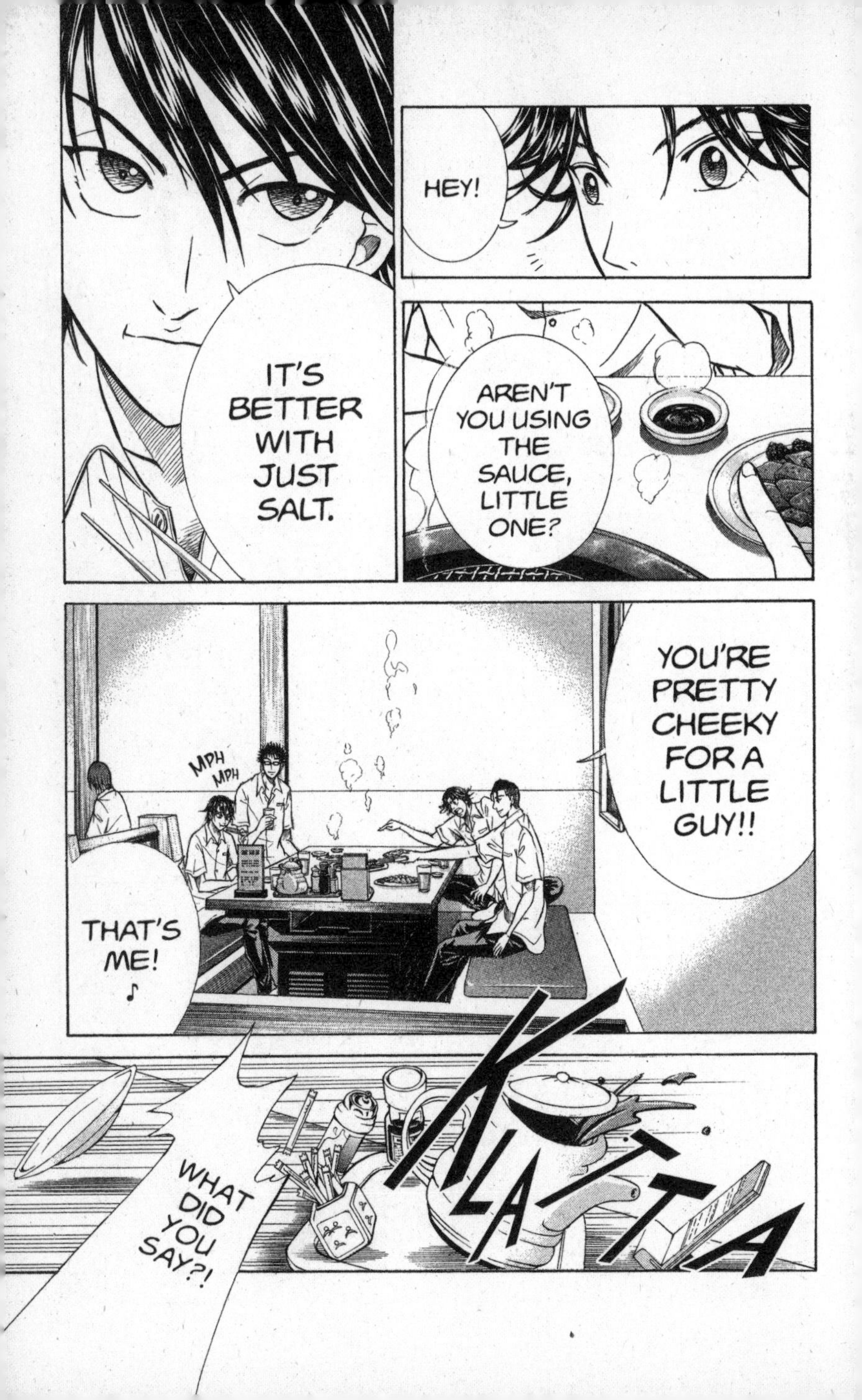
HEY!
AREN'T YOU USING THE SAUCE, LITTLE ONE?
IT'S BETTER WITH JUST SALT.
YOU'RE PRETTY CHEEKY FOR A LITTLE GUY!!
MPH MPH
THAT'S ME! ♪
KLATTA
WHAT DID YOU SAY?!

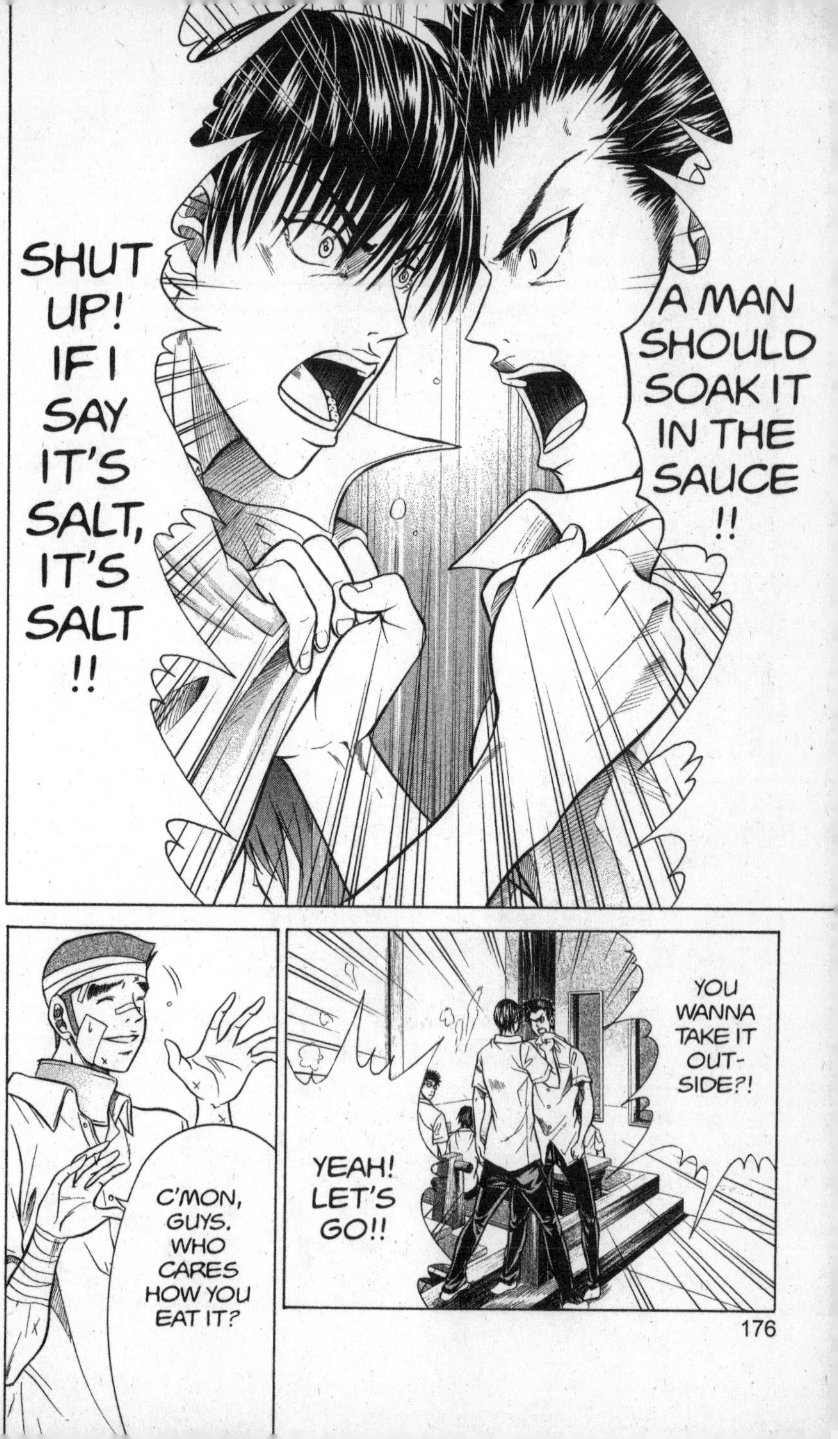
A MAN SHOULD SOAK IT IN THE SAUCE!!
SHUT UP! IF I SAY IT'S SALT, IT'S SALT!!
YOU WANNA TAKE IT OUT-SIDE?!
YEAH! LET'S GO!!
C'MON, GUYS. WHO CARES HOW YOU EAT IT?

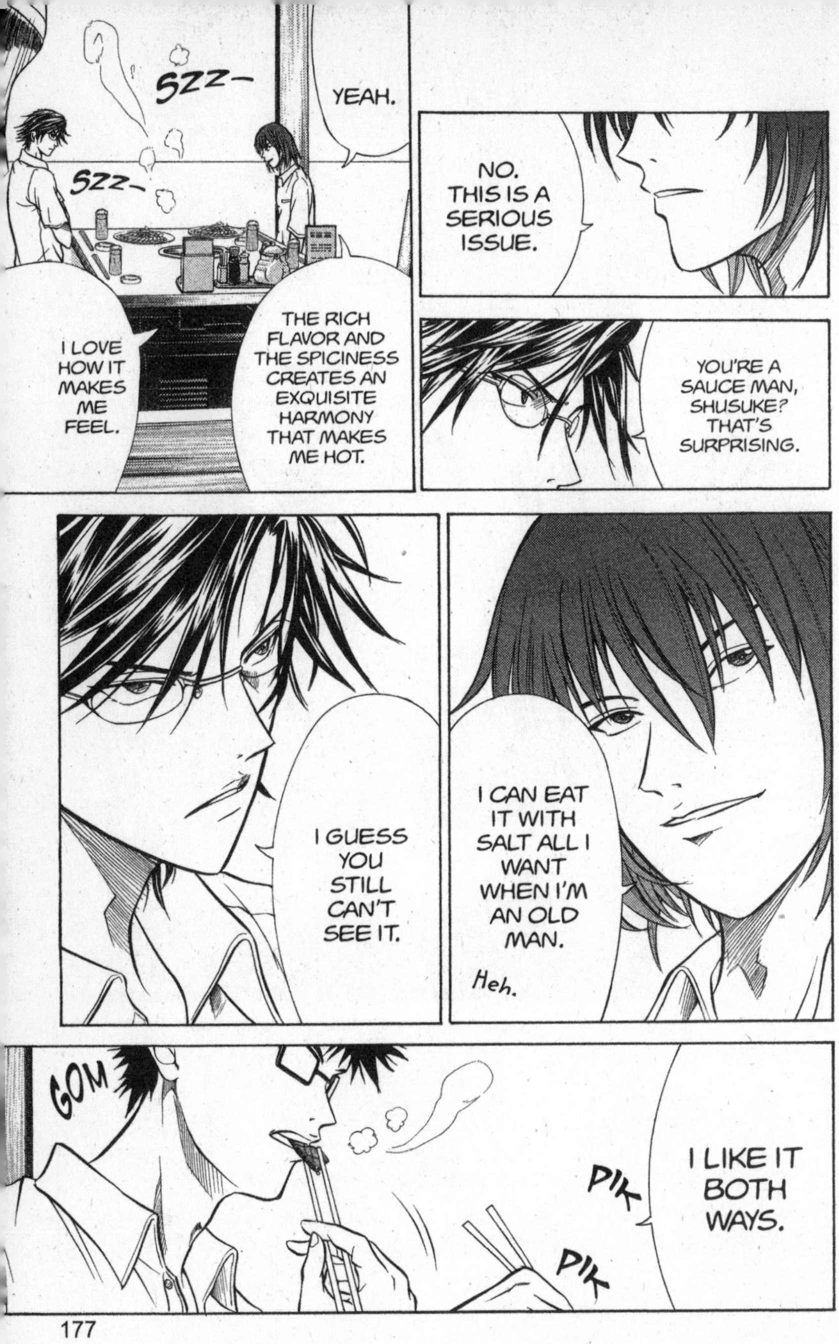
SZZ—
SZZ—
YEAH.
THE RICH FLAVOR AND THE SPICINESS CREATES AN EXQUISITE HARMONY THAT MAKES ME HOT.
I LOVE HOW IT MAKES ME FEEL.
NO. THIS IS A SERIOUS ISSUE.
YOU'RE A SAUCE MAN, SHUSUKE? THAT'S SURPRISING.
I CAN EAT IT WITH SALT ALL I WANT WHEN I'M AN OLD MAN.
Heh.
I GUESS YOU STILL CAN'T SEE IT.
I LIKE IT BOTH WAYS.
PIK
PIK
GOM

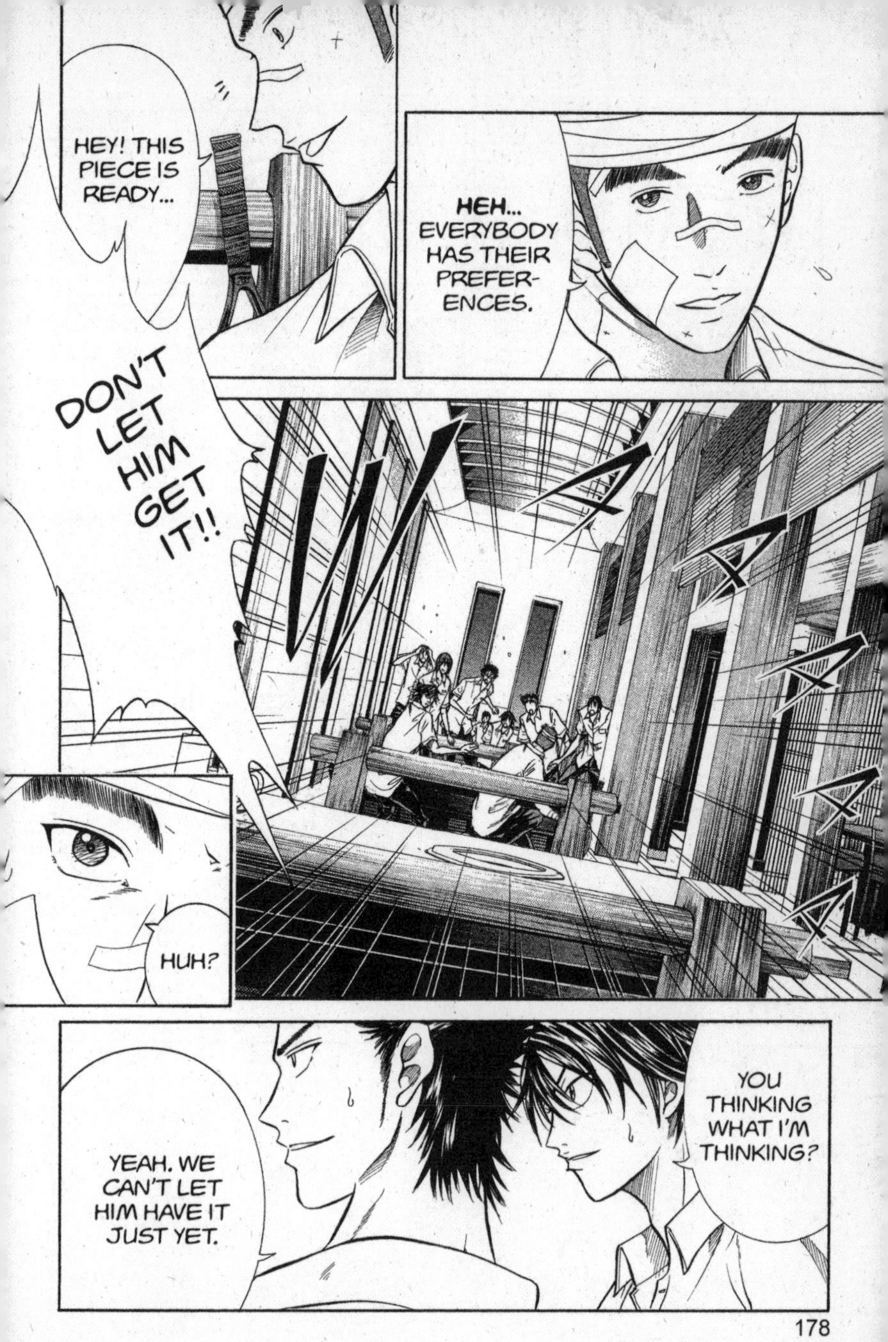
HEH... EVERYBODY HAS THEIR PREFER-ENCES.
HEY! THIS PIECE IS READY...
DON'T LET HIM GET IT!!
WAAAAA
HUH?
YOU THINKING WHAT I'M THINKING?
YEAH. WE CAN'T LET HIM HAVE IT JUST YET.

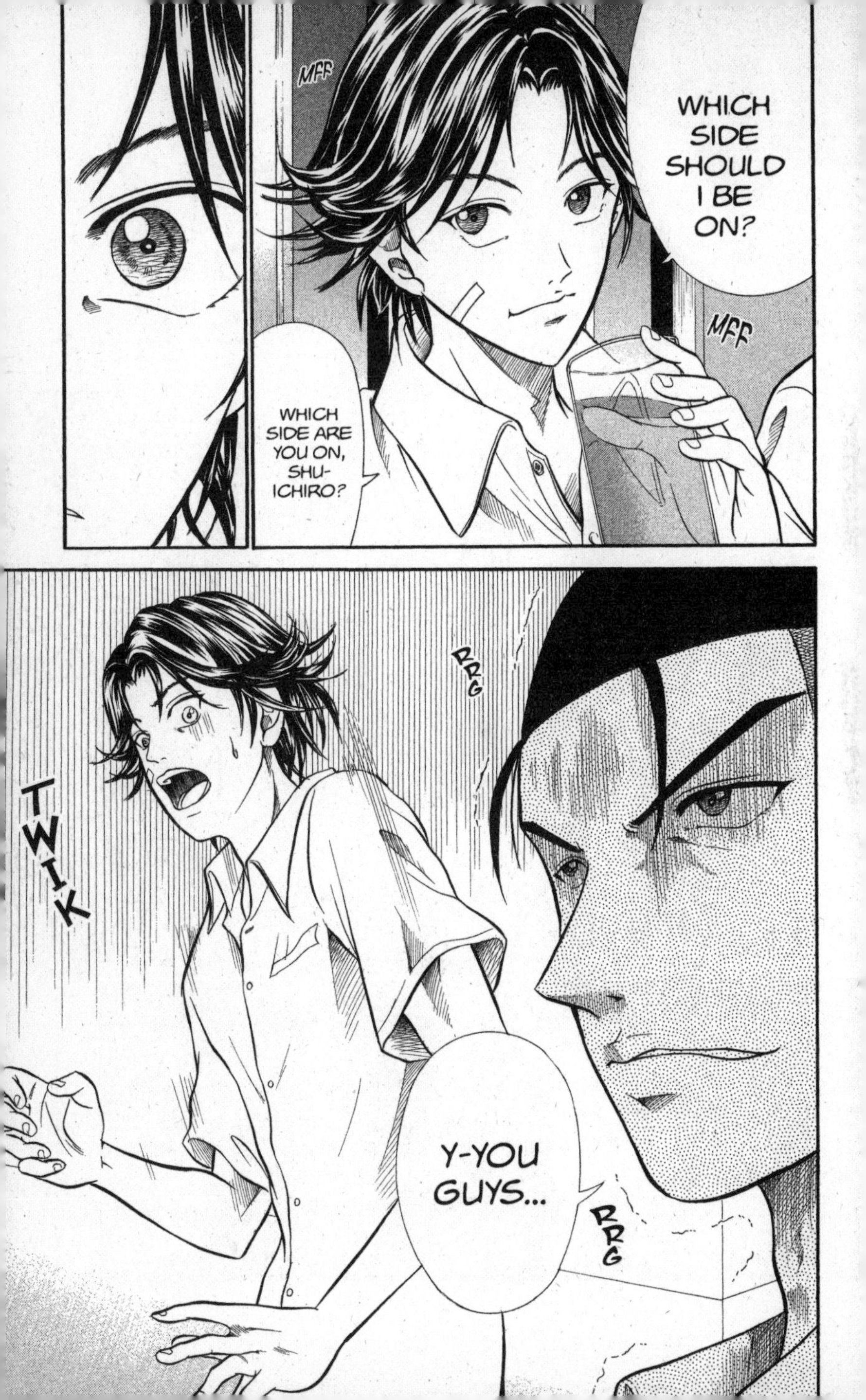
MFF
WHICH SIDE SHOULD I BE ON?
MFF
WHICH SIDE ARE YOU ON, SHU-ICHIRO?
RRG
TWIK
Y-YOU GUYS...
RRG

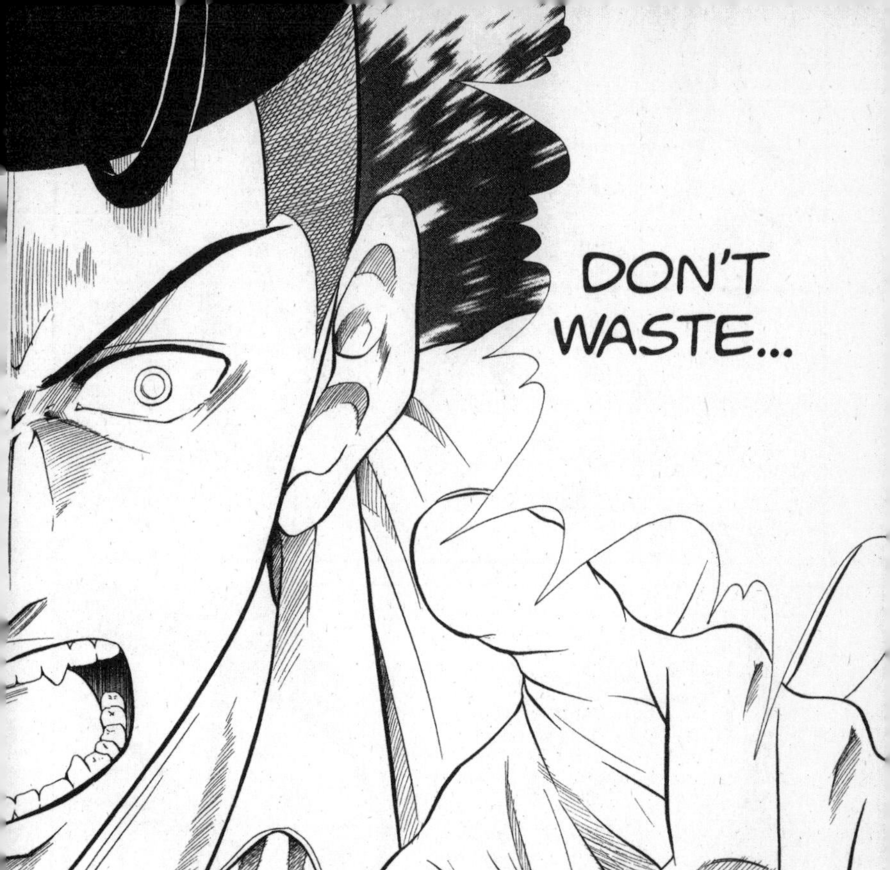
DON'T WASTE...
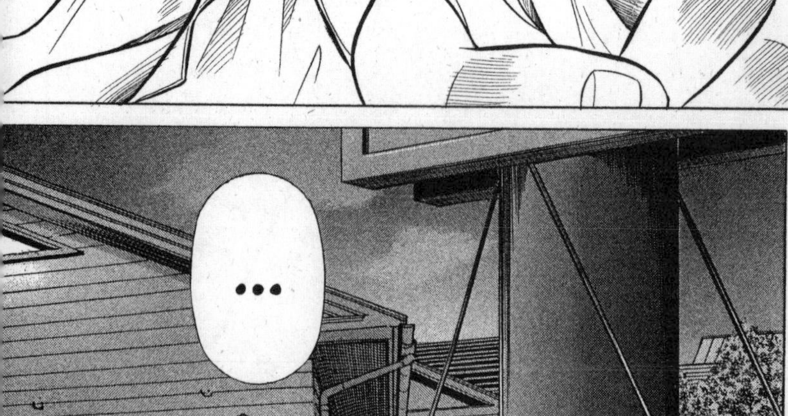
...

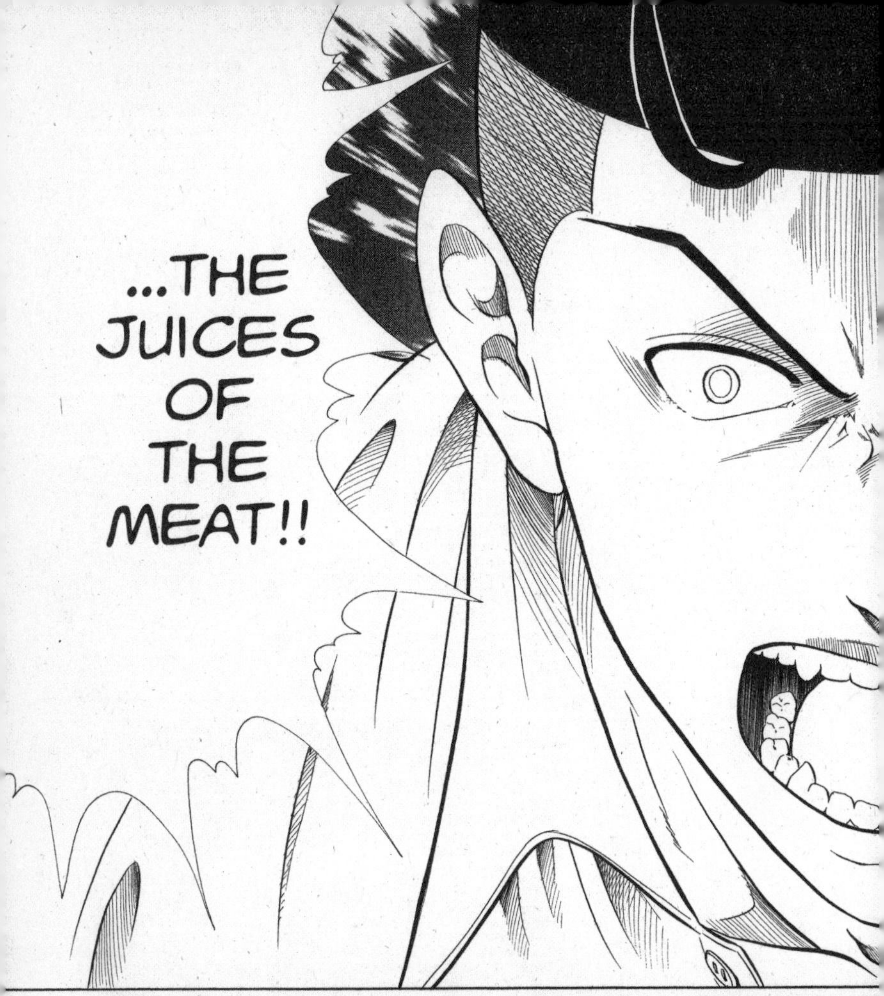
...THE JUICES OF THE MEAT!!
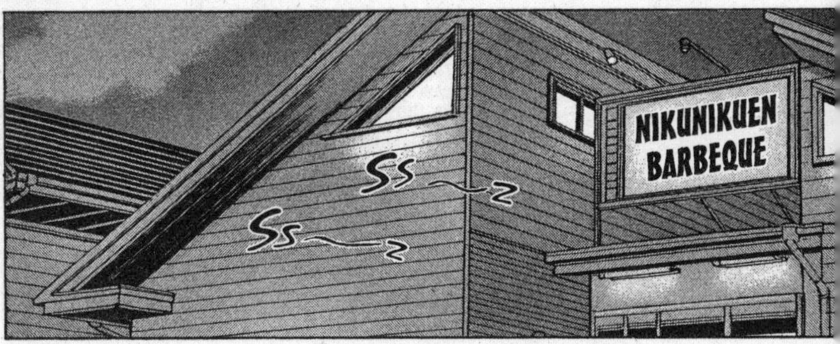
NIKUNIKUEN BARBEQUE
SS~Z
SS~Z

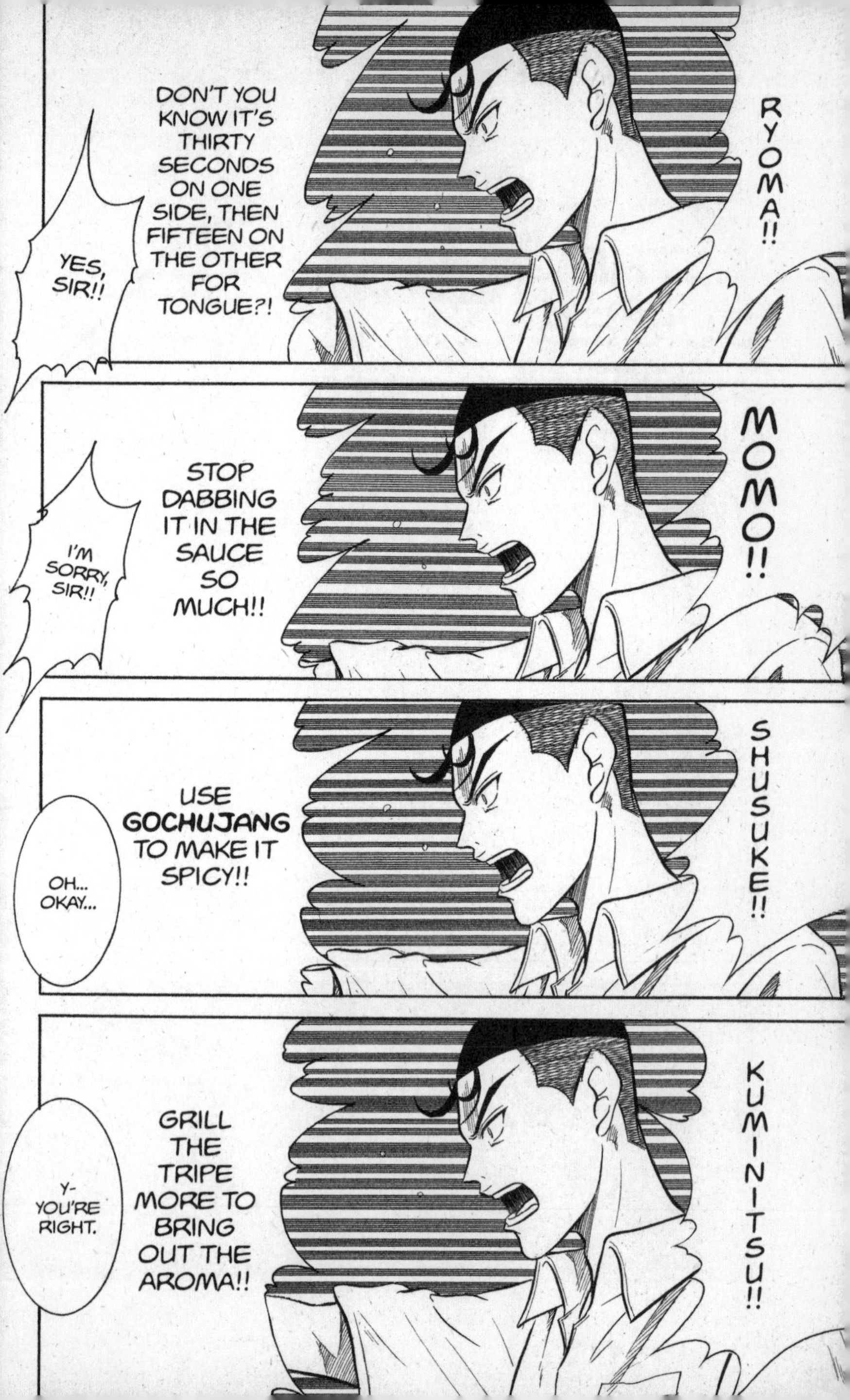
RYOMA!!
DON'T YOU KNOW IT'S THIRTY SECONDS ON ONE SIDE, THEN FIFTEEN ON THE OTHER FOR TONGUE?!
YES, SIR!!
MOMO!!
STOP DABBING IT IN THE SAUCE SO MUCH!!
I'M SORRY, SIR!!
SHUSUKE!!
USE **GOCHUJANG** TO MAKE IT SPICY!!
OH... OKAY...
KUMINITSU!!
GRILL THE TRIPE MORE TO BRING OUT THE AROMA!!
Y-YOU'RE RIGHT.

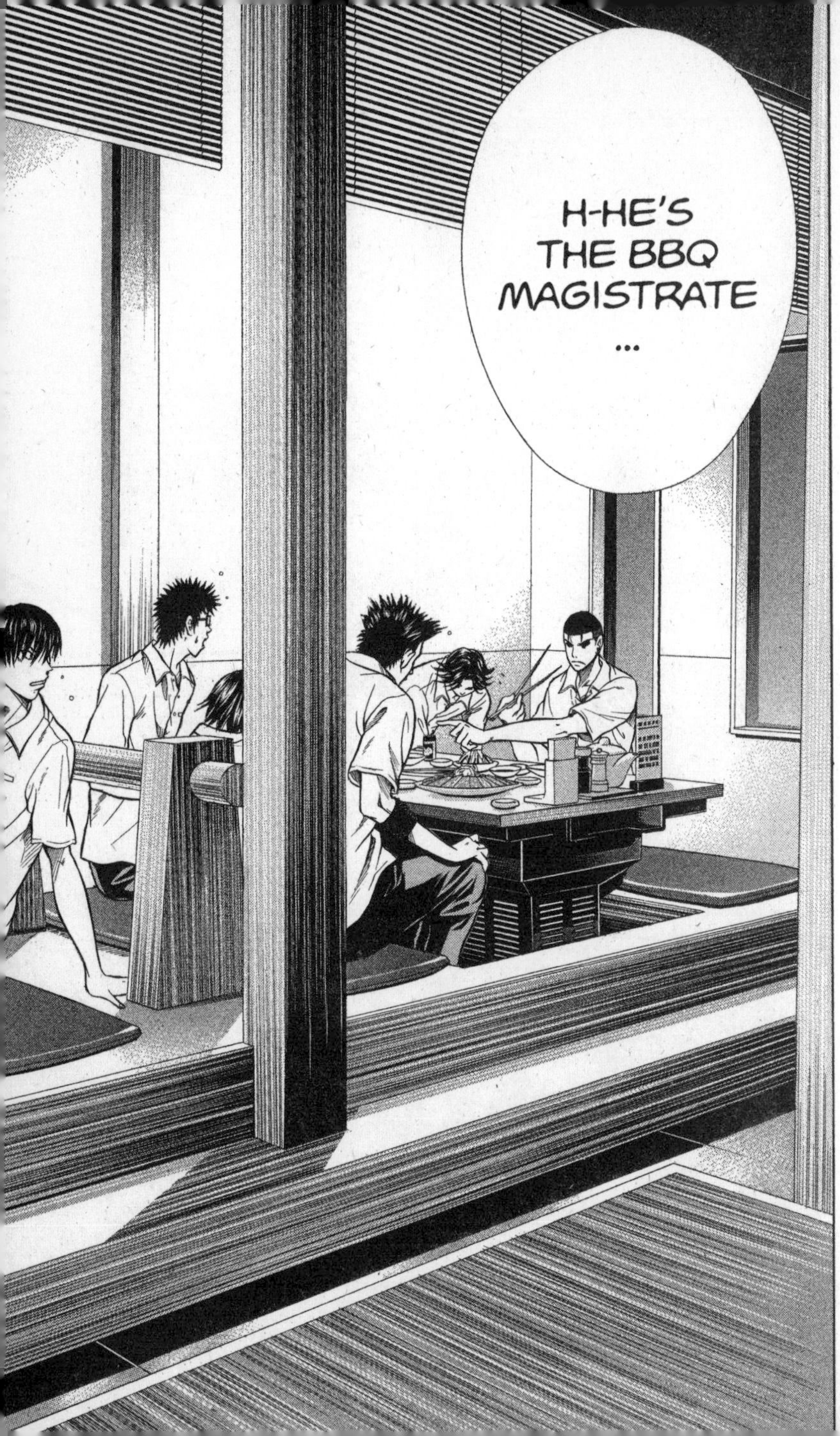
H-HE'S THE BBQ MAGISTRATE ...

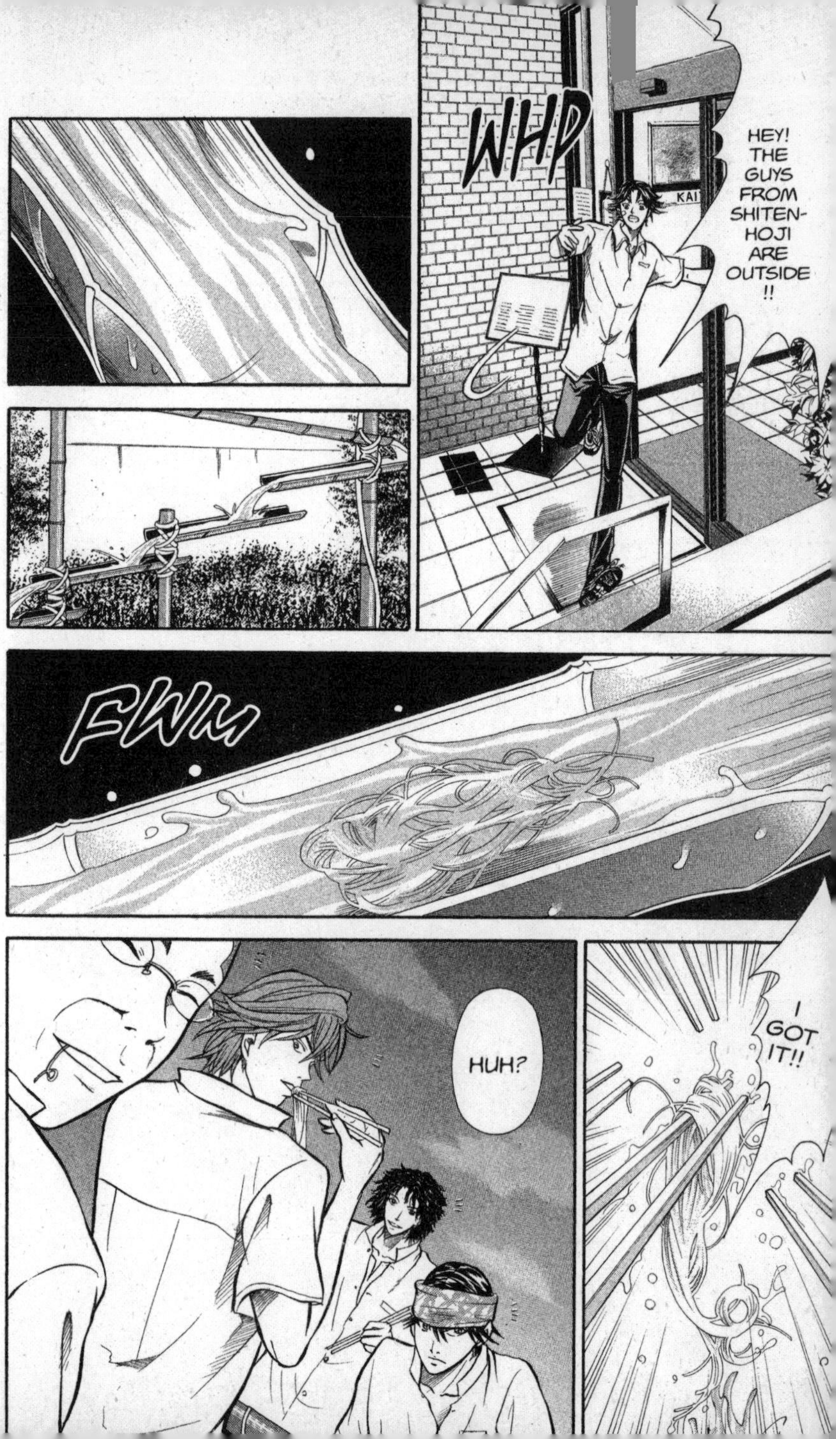
WHP
HEY! THE GUYS FROM SHITEN-HOJI ARE OUTSIDE !!
KAI
FWM
I GOT IT!!
HUH?

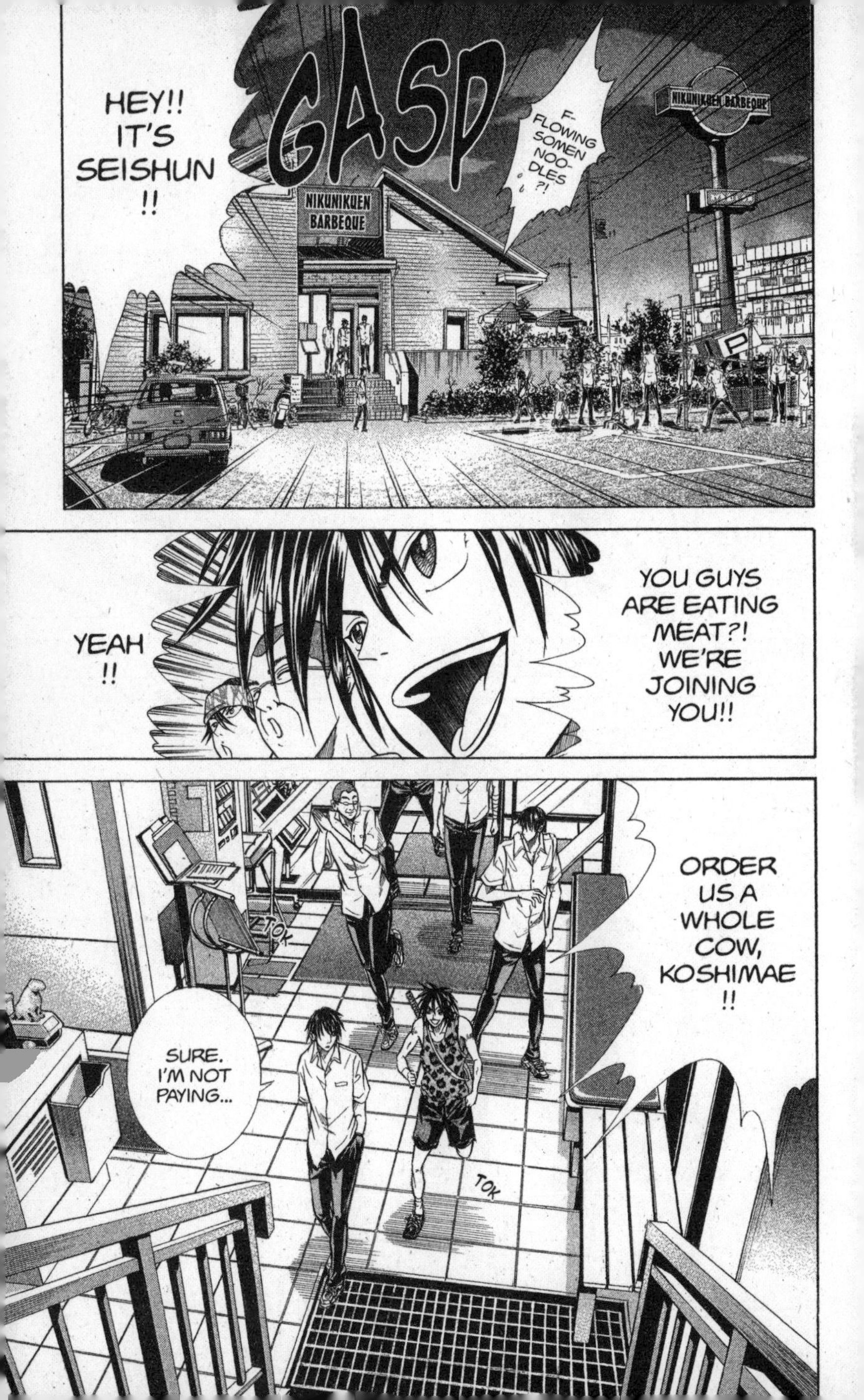
NIKUNIKUEN BARBEQUE
F-FLOWING SOMEN NOODLES?!
GASP
NIKUNIKUEN BARBEQUE
HEY!! IT'S SEISHUN!!
YOU GUYS ARE EATING MEAT?! WE'RE JOINING YOU!!
YEAH!!
ORDER US A WHOLE COW, KOSHIMAE!!
TOK
SURE. I'M NOT PAYING...
TOK

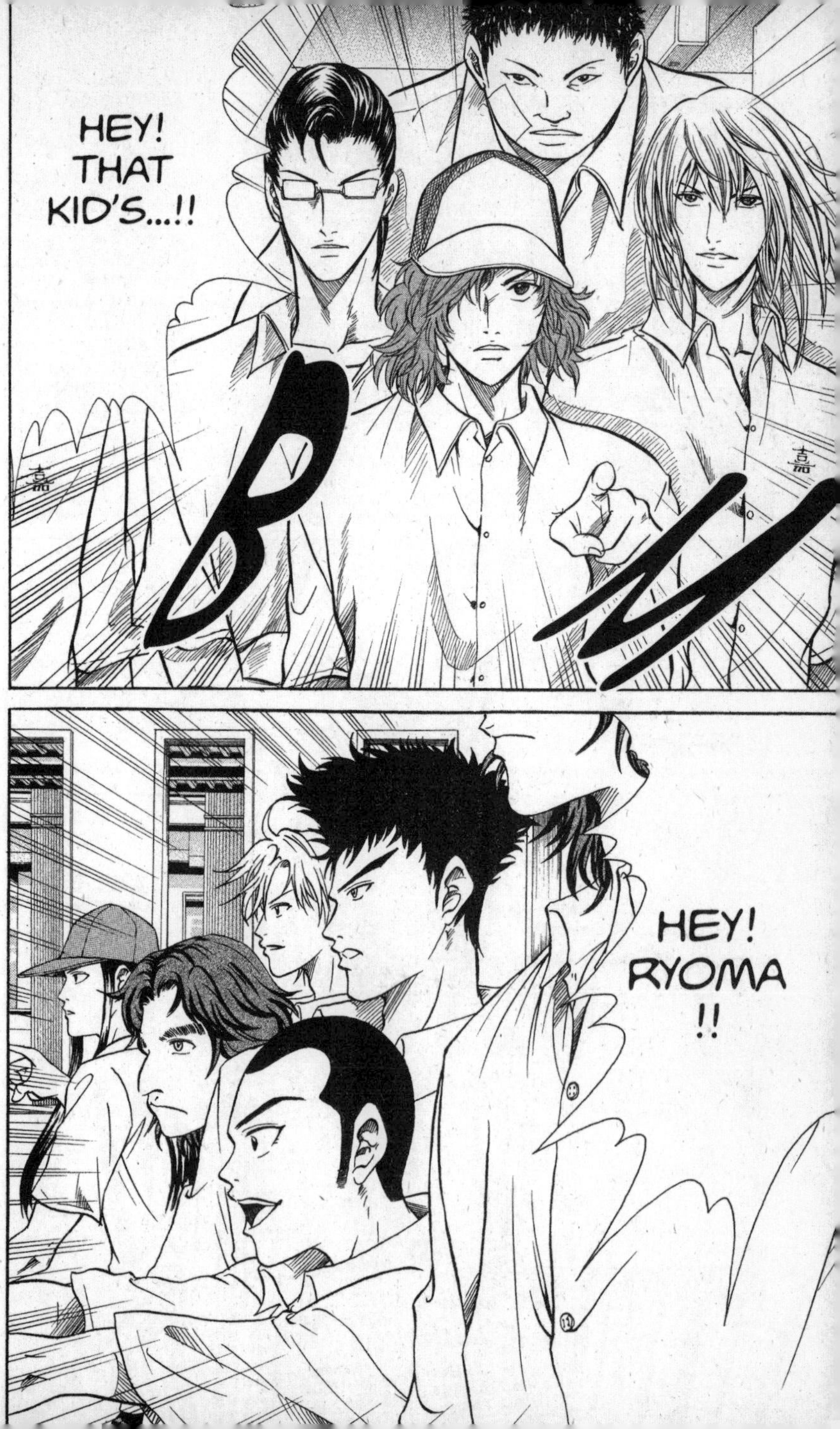
HEY! THAT KID'S...!!
BM
HEY! RYOMA !!

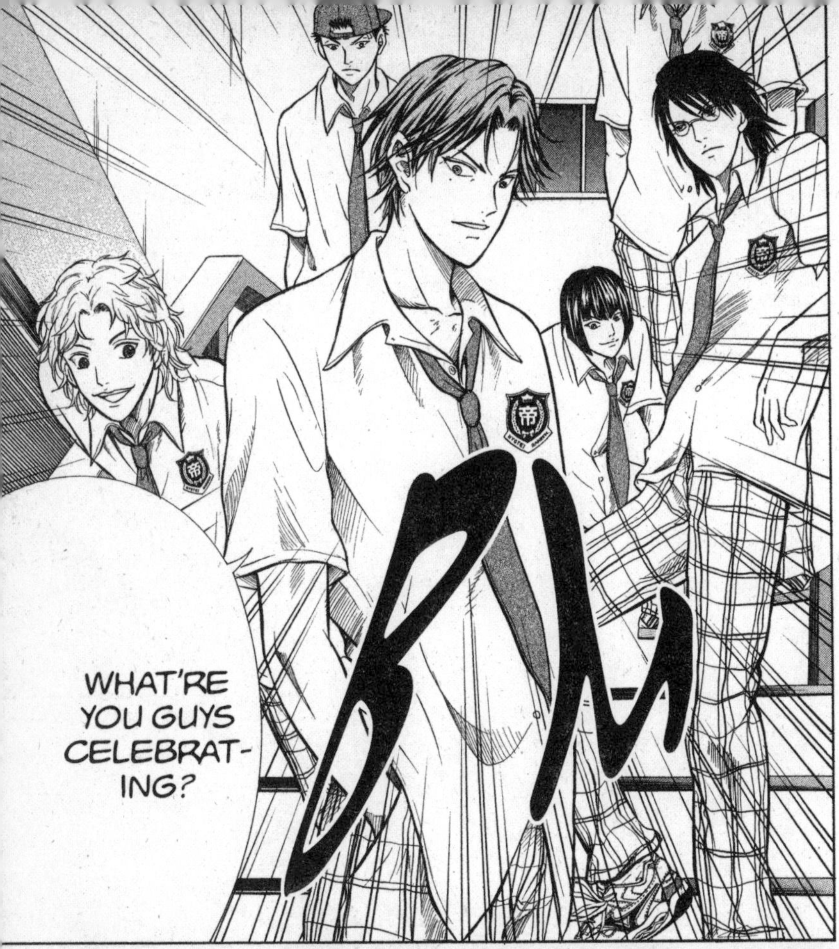
WHAT'RE YOU GUYS CELEBRAT-ING?

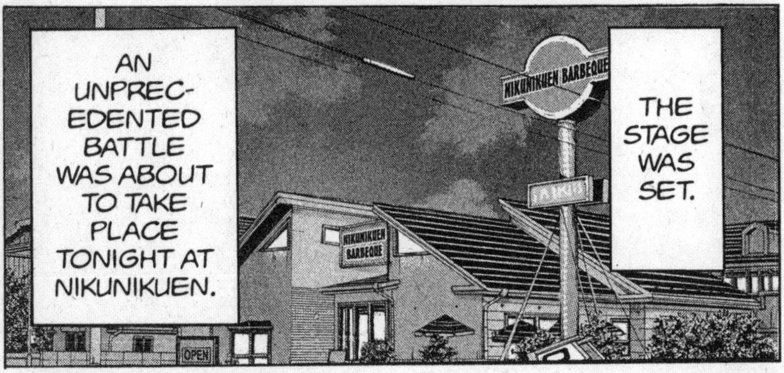
THE STAGE WAS SET.
AN UNPREC-EDENTED BATTLE WAS ABOUT TO TAKE PLACE TONIGHT AT NIKUNIKUEN.
NIKUNIKUEN BARBEQUE
NIKUNIKUEN BARBEQUE
OPEN

TO BE CONTINUED IN VOL. 39!

In the Next Volume...

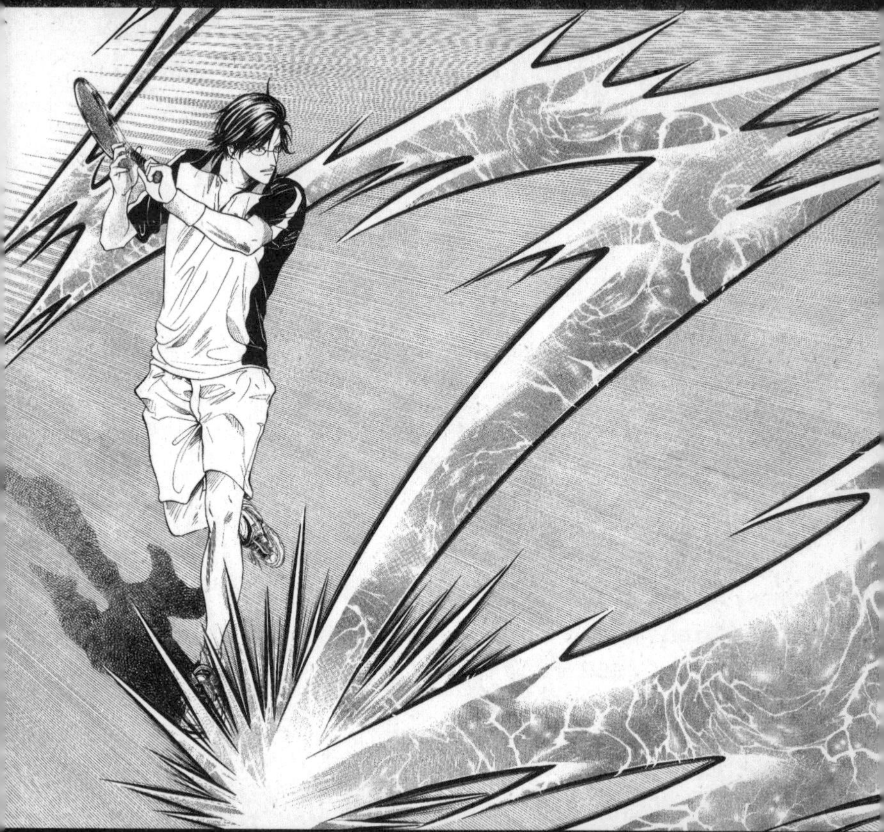

Flare-up! Barbecue Battle!!

Before the Seishun boys hit the courts for the final round of Nationals, they hit the yakiniku table for an all-out barbecue blitz! When the time comes for Seishun to take on Rikkai at the tournament, Ryoma is stuck in Karuizawa! Help comes from an unexpected quarter to get Ryoma to the stadium. The first game is the long-awaited match that will ignite the perfect storm: Seishun captain Kunimitsu vs. Rikkai's Sanada!

Available October 2010!

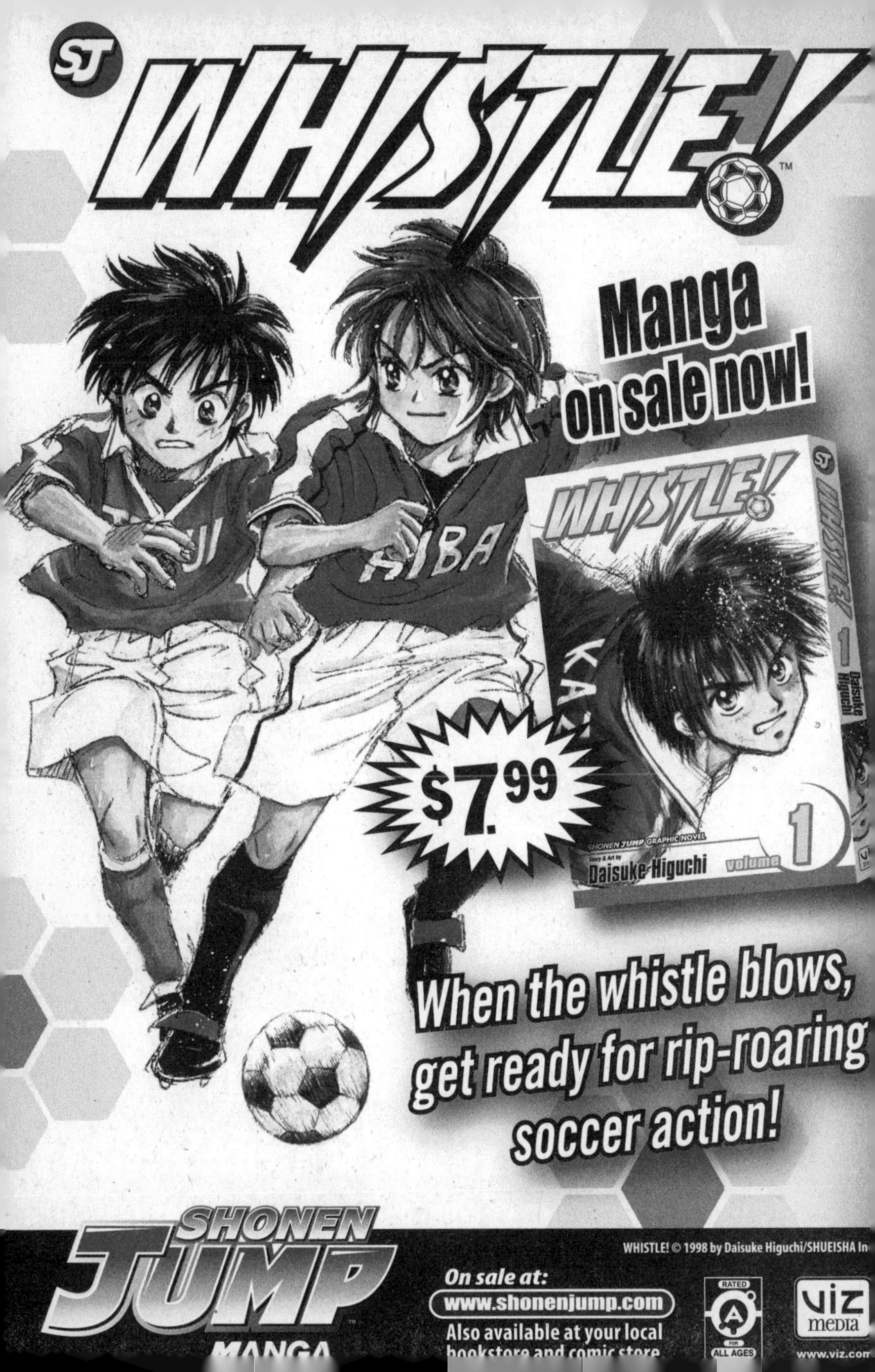
SJ
WHISTLE!™
Manga on sale now!
WHISTLE!
WHISTLE! 1 Daisuke Higuchi
SHONEN JUMP GRAPHIC NOVEL
Story & Art by
Daisuke Higuchi
volume 1
$7.99
When the whistle blows, get ready for rip-roaring soccer action!
SHONEN JUMP MANGA
WHISTLE! © 1998 by Daisuke Higuchi/SHUEISHA In
On sale at:
www.shonenjump.com
Also available at your local bookstore and comic store.
RATED A FOR ALL AGES
VIZ media
www.viz.com

SHONEN JUMP

THE WORLD'S MOST POPULAR MANGA

BLEACH

STORY AND ART BY
TITE KUBO

ONE PIECE

STORY AND ART BY
EIICHIRO ODA

Tegami Bachi
LETTER BEE

STORY AND ART BY
HIROYUKI ASADA

JUMP INTO THE ACTION BY TELLING US WHAT YOU LOVE (AND WHAT YOU DON'T)

LET YOUR VOICE BE HEARD!

SHONENJUMP.VIZ.COM/MANGASURVEY

HELP US MAKE MORE OF THE WORLD'S MOST POPULAR MANGA!

 RATED T FOR TEEN ratings.viz.com

 VIZ media www.viz.com